THE

PRACTICAL GARDENING ENCYCLOPEDIA

THE PRACTICAL GARDENING ENCYCLOPEDIA

SWEET WATER PRESS

4900 Practical Gardening Encyclopedia
This edition published in 1999
by Sweetwater Books

Printed and bound in Singapore

ISBN 1-58173-181-7

Credits
Edited, designed & typeset: Ideas into Print
Photographs: Neil Sutherland
Additional layouts: Jill Coote
Decorative borders: Ian Mitchell
Illustrations: Mainline Design, Stuart Watkinson
Production Director: Gerald Hughes
Production: Ruth Arthur, Neil Randles, Paul Randles, Janine Seddon, Karen Staff

Compiler
After leaving school, Sue Phillips worked for a year on a general nursery before studying horticulture at Hadlow College of Agriculture and Horticulture, Kent for three years. For the next five years, she was co-owner and manager of a nursery in Cambridgeshire before joining a leading garden products company as Garden Adviser. This involved answering gardening queries, handling complaints, writing articles and press releases, speaking at gardening events and broadcasting for local radio. In 1984, Sue turned freelance and since then has written several books, contributed widely to various gardening and general interest magazines and appeared often on radio and TV.

Contributors
The principal contributors for each section are credited on the contents pages.
Other contributors: Carol Gubler, Nicholas Hall, Ann James and John Mattock.

Photographer
Neil Sutherland has more than 25 years experience in a wide range of photographic fields, including still-life, portraiture, reportage, natural history, cookery, landscape and travel. His work has been published in countless books and magazines throughout the world.

Half-title page: Pelargoniums and marigolds are ideal for hanging baskets.
Title page: *Zinnia* 'Chippendale' and *Sedum spectabile* 'Meteor' in a border.
Copyright page: *Hibiscus syriacus* 'Red Heart' thrives outdoors in a sheltered spot.
Contents 1: A selection of annuals, including antirrhinum, sunflower, rudbeckia and aster, suitable for indoor display.
Contents 2: Yellow *Osteospermum* and purple *Brachyscome* are set off superbly in this painted terracotta trough.

INTRODUCTION

The Magic of Gardening

I 'discovered' gardening when I was four, and several decades later still find it as fascinating as ever. The great thing about it is the way something new is always happening. It's like living in the middle of a horticultural soap opera, with an ever-changing cast and unlimited sub-plots. The set and its attendant characters alter visibly from week to week - just see what I mean when you come back from a short holiday. Each year there are new varieties to discover in the annual crop of seed catalogs, new trends to dabble with and new planting schemes to explore. And apart from the dazzling variety of the plants themselves, there are the imponderables of pests, problems and weather that combine to make each season a new gardening adventure. But some things never change - the basic skills of sowing, planting and cultivation. In this book I have brought together some of the best basic techniques, bright ideas and designer magic to create a practical guide to gardening that really works. Your garden will certainly appreciate the difference.

Sue Phillips

CONTENTS

PART ONE

BASIC SKILLS

Basic gardening skills are not complicated and once mastered, even a complete beginner can achieve good results, using a small range of equipment and for little expense. New skills, specialist gadgets and more expensive plants can come later, making gardening a hobby that you can go on learning for life.

Above: Results in the garden will only be good if the ground is in 'good heart': well supplied with plant foods and organic matter and cultivated deep enough to allow good penetration by roots.

BASIC CULTIVATION

Digging is the basic cultivation of the gardener. You must dig any ground that is being cultivated for the first time or that has just been cleared of an old crop. A spade is the normal tool used for digging, but on heavy ground, a strong fork is much easier to use and just as effective. The choice depends on how well the soil holds together. If it falls through the prongs of a fork, use a spade instead. There are several reasons for digging. The main one is to break up the soil so that excess water can drain away and roots can penetrate in their search for water and nutrients. As the ground is broken up, air is able to reach down into it so that the roots can 'breathe'. Digging creates a suitable tilth for sowing or planting. When you dig cultivated ground, you bury any existing weeds and weed seeds, thus reducing the competition that faces new young plants in the vital first weeks. Digging is also the most thorough and reliable way of burying bulky organic matter, such as garden compost, that is vital if the soil is to 'live' and support good crops. Under average garden conditions, add both bulky organic matter and plant foods to the soil at least once a year.

Single digging

1 When single digging a plot, use a line to mark out the position of the first trench, which should be 9-10in(23-25cm) wide.

2 Using a spade, methodically scrape the surface rubbish and weeds off the marked area to produce a clean surface.

3 Dig out the soil to a spade's depth and barrow it away to the far end of the plot, where it will be used to fill in the final trench.

4 Clean out the loose earth in the bottom of the trench. It is now ready to receive the soil from the second trench.

5 If there is not much debris on the surface, turn the soil from the second trench over and forward into the first one without doing any scraping. Keep working backwards down the plot, turning the soil over and forwards into the previous trench as before.

6 Keep the trench open and clear so that there is room to accommodate the next 'row' of soil excavated from the previous trench. Fill the final trench with the earth dug out from the first one. If you are digging a vegetable plot in the fall, leave it to weather until spring.

7 A fork is one of the most useful tools for breaking down previously dug soil into a tilth that is suitable for sowing or planting. Do not dig the soil; instead, knock the clods apart with the back of the fork.

8 After breaking down the clods, make the tilth even finer in preparation for sowing by raking the surface of the soil backwards and forwards. Remove any stones or hard lumps that collect in the teeth of the rake.

Hoeing the ground

Once your plants are growing, they will inevitably be challenged by weeds. The cheapest way of dealing with these is to hoe them out, using either a Dutch or a draw hoe. Never try to cultivate the ground when it is wet enough to stick to the tools. Clean the tools after use.

Above: *The Dutch hoe is useful for removing weeds in borders and ideal between rows of vegetables. Use it shallowly when the soil is dry and weeds are tiny.*

Above: *The same principles apply to the draw hoe. Catch the weeds early, otherwise they will soon be competing with the crop for water, nutrients and space.*

Using a hand trowel and fork

All garden tools can be made of either ordinary or stainless steel. Stainless steel costs more, but does not go rusty. It is also strong and less likely to bend if given hard use. As a general rule, always buy the best tools you can afford; the better they are, the longer they will last.

Left: *The easiest way to dig out individual weeds or those growing amongst other plants is with a small weeding fork. Try digging out the entire plant complete with roots. Remove weeds before they can shed seed.*

Left: *Use a hand trowel for planting, applying mulches in confined spaces and removing big weeds around shallow-rooted plants such as rhododendrons, where careless hoeing may damage the roots.*

SOILS AND MULCHES

Good garden soil takes several years of regular cultivation to create, and soil improvement should be part of every gardener's regular routine. This happens in several stages. First, whenever you make a new bed or border, dig in plenty of well-rotted organic matter, such as garden compost or composted manure, into the whole area, burying it to the full depth of the spade. Use about a barrowload per square yard; you will need more on light sandy or chalky soils. Then each time you add a new plant, dig a bucketful of organic matter into the bottom of the planting hole. Finally, spread a mulch over the soil surface to trap moisture in the soil and smother out weed seedlings. Reapply mulches each spring (or spring and fall on very dry sandy or chalky soils). If low maintenance is your aim, spread a decorative layer of a long-lasting surface mulch of gravel or bark chips over a carpet of landscape fabric, which totally prevents weeds.

IMPROVING THE SOIL

Due to the special characteristics of organic matter, the same materials can be used to open up heavy soils and improve their aeration and drainage, and improve moisture retention in dry sandy or chalky soils. Dig in organic soil improvers, such as well-rotted garden compost or horse manure, coir or moss peat, before planting, fork them in between established plants or use them as a surface mulch.

Types of soil

These are the main types of soil found in gardens; each one can be improved with soil conditioners and by feeding and mulching to make good conditions for growing a wide range of plants.

Clay soil forms hard clods in summer, when cracks often appear in the soil. When wet, the soil is sticky and a handful forms a ball that holds its shape.

Chalky soil is very alkaline, fast-draining and low in nutrients, which are locked up chemically. It looks pale, with a whitish cast if chalk rock is present. Particles of pure chalk may be visible. Pale soil may cover a layer of chalk rock lower down.

Water runs quickly through sandy soil; puddles vanish immediately after rain and a handful of damp soil will not hold together in a ball.

Good garden soil holds moisture, but is never boggy. Its dark color is due to the organic matter added over several years of regular cultivation.

Woodland soils contain large amounts of leaf mold. They are usually slightly acid, rich, fertile and free-draining.

Soil improvers

Moss peat is naturally acidic. Use it to acidify neutral or slightly acid soil before planting acid-loving plants.

Well-rotted garden compost made up of kitchen and disease-free garden waste (no perennial weeds, weed seeds or woody material).

Sedge peat or old growing bag mixes lighten clay soils and increase the moisture-holding capacity of light soils.

Gritty sand contains a mix of particle sizes. Dig it in to 'cure' clay.

Composted horse manure. Stack it in a heap until soil-like in consistency or layer it between waste to help compost heaps rot down faster.

Coir. Use it alone as a soil improver or in the form of ready-made sowing and potting mixtures.

TESTING THE SOIL

One of the first tasks to do in a new garden is to test the soil to discover whether it is alkaline, neutral or acid. This in turn determines the types of plants that will grow best in it, and whether any remedial treatment is necessary. Before testing the soil, ensure that you take a representative sample by gathering several specimens from all round the garden. Take the samples 4in(10cm) below the soil surface, and avoid obvious abnormalities, such as areas that have been used for bonfires, compost heaps or mixing cement, etc. This investigation can save expense and disappointment later on.

Soil testing kits

1 With this type of kit, put a little dry soil into the tube, up to the level indicated. Add water to the next mark on the side of the tube, replace the cap and shake well.

2 When the water changes color, compare it to the chart provided to see if your soil is acid, neutral or alkaline. Now you can tell which kinds of plants will suit it.

Conditioning the soil

Once you know whether your soil is acid, neutral or alkaline, you can use the appropriate soil additives and improvers to condition it. The aim is to turn a soil that may only have supported rather specialized plants into one in which a much wider range of normal garden plants will thrive.

Calcified seaweed breaks down clay soils and neutralizes acid ones. A source of magnesium, calcium and trace elements.

General purpose fertilizers restore the soil's major nutrients.

Sulfur chips acidify a neutral or slightly alkaline soil.

Mulches

A mulch is a layer of material spread over the soil surface to 'seal' moisture into the soil, smother out annual weeds, and give a decorative finish. Garden centers stock a range of suitable mulches.

Cocoa shell chips are slightly acid and break down quickly. Apply to damp soil in early spring.

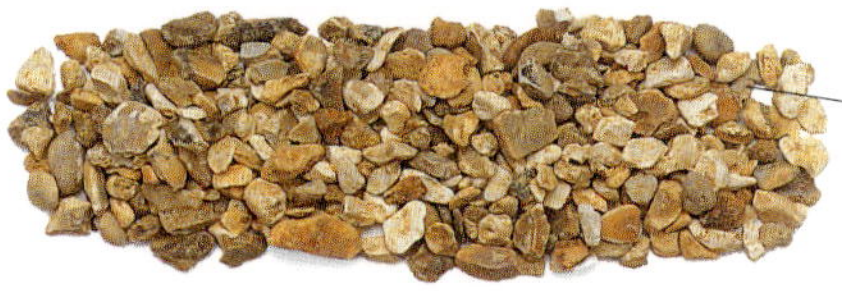

Use gravel on dry gardens or over landscape fabric for low-maintenance gardens.

Chipped bark, a long-lasting mulch, is ideal for shrub borders. Top it up every few years.

Right: *To help retain moisture, mulch heather and conifer beds in spring with 1-2in(2.5-5cm) of well-rotted organic matter, such as garden compost. Alternatively, apply bark or wood chippings, or cocoa shell chips (as here).*

Above: *Coarse bark chippings applied while the soil is still wet retain moisture in the soil and help to suppress weed growth.*

Left: *Unlike organic mulches that slowly rot, gravel lasts forever. Push it right up close to the neck of the plant for maximum effect.*

MAKING GARDEN COMPOST

Garden compost is one of the most common and effective forms of bulky organic matter to add to the ground. It is made from plant remains, including weeds, spent vegetables, lawn mowings, hedge clippings, leaves and soft prunings. You can add sawdust, straw, hay, pet litter and bulky animal manures, but never add anything of a meaty nature. The secret of good garden compost is to use a good mixture of raw materials: plenty of soft vegetation plus a high proportion of shredded woodier things. The choice between a compost heap or composting bin rests largely on the amount of raw material available. If there is plenty, a heap is better, but where raw material is limited, use a bin. Small heaps never make good compost. Fill up bins in one operation; they quickly heat up and make the best compost.

1 With a new heap or bin, try to make the first batch of material a coarse and woody layer, such as these rose prunings. It ensures that the heap will have good drainage and aeration.

2 Keep adding more coarse material until you build up a foundation layer of vegetation about 6in(15cm) deep in the bottom of the bin or heap, once you have firmed it down.

5 Continue adding more raw material. These potato tops are soft and full of water so, ideally, you should follow them with rougher material to keep the heap open. Shred or chop woody prunings first.

6 Add more shredded prunings to assist the decomposition process by aerating the heap. This, in turn, leads to heating up. Woody flower stalks, thorny prunings, cabbage and other brassica stalks are all suitable.

7 With this bin you add slats as the heap rises. The gaps are for ventilation. Add more activator for every 10in(25cm) of vegetation. The activator contains an agent to reduce acidity; the microorganisms prefer an alkaline environment.

3 Now you can start to add soft materials as well, such as these grass mowings. It is vital to build up alternate layers of fine and coarse material to allow the rotting process to work properly.

4 When the heap is about 10in (25cm) deep, sprinkle on an activator to help microorganisms break down the material. You can use a granular or liquid activator, or layers of fresh manure or soil.

8 An important part of good composting is to stop the generated heat escaping. Any substantial covering, such as a thick layer of black plastic, will do this and it will also stop rain from cooling the heap.

9 The result is humus-rich, fibrous garden compost that will improve your soil physically and chemically, either as a mulch or when dug in.

Shredding woody and thorny waste

Some of the best raw materials are woody or thorny and cannot go directly onto the compost heap. By shredding these prunings you can make sure that none of this valuable vegetation is wasted. Where it is allowed, you could burn prunings and put the ashes on the heap.

Fall flower stalks, woody prunings, cabbage and other brassica stalks are first rate, but chop or shred them first.

Thorny prunings after they have been put through an electric shredder.

Comfrey as compost

Left: *To make a rich compost for the garden, layer comfrey leaves with other plant material. Include vegetable waste, but avoid adding perennial weeds and roots. Use compost from an existing heap as a 'starter'.*

Liquid manure

A few comfrey plants are worth growing in a corner of the garden simply for the purpose of making a powerful and nutritious liquid manure. Infuse an armful of fresh comfrey leaves in a barrel or bin of rainwater for about four weeks and then use the liquid as a plant food. Use the decomposed leaves to enrich the compost heap or fertilize your tomatoes.

Left: When spraying, make sure that your applicator can reach under the foliage. This is just as important as covering the top surface. Always read the manufacturer's instructions and follow them carefully.

ROUTINE TASKS

Little and often is the key to gardening success. This explains why the gardener who spends an hour or so every evening apparently wandering about enjoying their borders usually has a much better-kept garden than the person who only appears on fine weekends, and then spends all their time in a sunlounger. For, or course, the wanderer is not merely wandering, but also observing and, where necessary, doing something. If you attend regularly and promptly to the weeding, watering, feeding, tying up, trimming and deadheading, it is much quicker and easier to take care of a garden. But if things get out of control, then instead of a few light chores, gardening becomes hard work, involving serious undergrowth clearance and resuscitating half-dead plants. There is more than one way of doing most key jobs. Plants in containers, for example, can be fed using slow-release products that last a whole season, as an alternative to weekly liquid feeding. If time is tight, simplify frequent jobs, such as watering, by using irrigation systems that ensure that plants stay well cared-for when you cannot be there. A huge range of products and equipment is available to help take care of routine chores. The trick is to find out which suits you best; if a job is enjoyable, you will feel more inclined to do it. And the results of a little light gardening regularly will be a garden that looks and feels loved and responds accordingly - without creating problems.

Below: Nip out the soft terminal bud on a green shoot rather than wait until it has grown and then have to shorten an overlong shoot.

Above: Never tie a young shoot to a wire too tightly. The shoot will expand, but not the string. Leave a little slack for this swelling. String is available in a range of strengths and thicknesses.

Watering

In very dry weather, give newly planted flowers and annuals a good soaking every few days, rather than light waterings more often. Water in the evenings, especially in hot weather, to give plants time to take up water before the following morning's sun causes it to evaporate.

Left: Irrigation systems that use porous water pipes do not waste water, as only the area under the piping gets wet. This also ensures that weeds are not watered.

Right: Irrigation systems that deliver water to individual plants via drip nozzles are ideal for plants in containers. Systems like this can be connected to an outdoor tap via a preset water computer.

Left: Having planted a new shrub such as this rose, water it in well, concentrating the water near the stem and around the edge of the rootball. Continue watering through the first season when the soil is dry.

Feeding plants

1 Feed flowering plants regularly from spring to midsummer. Sprinkle a good general-purpose fertilizer between the plants.

2 Water thoroughly after feeding to dissolve the feed and make it available to plants. In prolonged dry spells, give liquid feeds instead.

Right: Keep all powdered feeds in a closed container, as they take up moisture from the air. Keep the feeding program simple - your plants will be the better for it.

Below: Liquid feeds are very popular. Follow the maker's directions carefully; do not be tempted to make the feed too strong. It is better to feed your plants at half-strength twice a week than to overdo it.

Deadheading

Deadheading is specially worthwhile for plants with a potentially long flowering season, such as hybrid tea roses and bedding plants. But even when the flowering season is short, deadheading keeps plants looking tidy and removes dead petals.on which gray mold may form. Do not deadhead plants from which you expect fruit or hips later on.

Left: *Deadheading roses. Cut the heads back to a bud or to a shoot that has yet to flower. Then cut back the other half to a bud. This will usually grow into another flower head.*

Below: *Once a heather bed is established, wait until flowering is over, then clip back the old blooms with shears and tidy up the plants. This will encourage strong growth next season.*

Right: *As camellia flowers start to fade, gently nip off the dead heads between thumb and fingernail. This improves the shrub's appearance and lets new shoots emerge from behind the old flowers. Avoid damaging the new shoots when deadheading.*

SOWING A LAWN

The most important part of starting a new lawn, whether it be from seed or turf, is the soil preparation. The area should be dug far enough in advance of sowing or turfing for it to settle naturally, so that no hills or holes appear after the lawn is growing. This will mean digging at least a month ahead of putting down a lawn. Once dug, the ground should be raked and trodden over as often as you can. The raking will continue to break down the surface into a fine tilth and, at the same time, it will bring any stones to the surface, which you should remove. It is seldom necessary to use a roller in the preparations. It can sometimes be justified straight after digging as the first stage of breaking down the clods. However, it is used purely for that; it is not an aid to firming. Treading down the surface frequently is the best way of firming it. Raking between treadings will remove rises and fill in hollows. The final job before sowing or turfing is to apply and rake in a suitable pre-sowing or turfing fertilizer. This will give the new lawn a good start in life by supplying it with the specific nutrients that it will require during its first few all-important weeks of life.

When buying lawn seed, choose a mixture that will suit the kind of lawn you want. If it is to be trampled over by hordes of children, it must contain ryegrass. If it is solely for decoration, ryegrass can be omitted. If you are in doubt, ask a knowledgeable shop assistant. When sowing by hand, cover the area twice, the second time at right angles to the first. Use half the full sowing rate each time.

CREATING A WILDFLOWER LAWN

The best time to sow a wildflower lawn is in spring or fall. You can either mix your own grass and flower seed or buy it ready-mixed.

1 To create a wildflower lawn, mix suitable species into grass seed. Stir them together well, as flower seed, being smaller, will sink to the bottom.

2 Sprinkle the seed mix over the previously dug, raked and leveled soil, but do not use fertilizer; it encourages grass, but discourages the wildflowers.

3 Sow 1-2oz of seed per square yard (28-56gm per square meter). Rake it in lightly so most is covered. Water well and keep watered in dry spells.

Above: Once a stand of wild flowers is established, it will self-seed every year. Cut wildflower lawns in late summer, when seed has been shed.

Sowing lawn seed

1 Treading down the surface systematically and often - but only when the soil is dry - is an important part of preparing the ground. It not only firms the surface and breaks up lumps, but also shows up hills and holes that you can rake level.

2 Apply a pre-sowing or turfing fertilizer. Alternatively, a fall lawn feed is fine, but it must not contain a weedkiller or mosskiller.

3 Rake the fertilizer evenly into the soil surface. Sowing seed directly onto a layer of fertilizer could damage the young roots.

4 When sowing by hand, first mark out the area to be sown into yard or meter squares. Allowing about 1.5oz/sq.yd(50gm/sq.m) of seed, sow each square with the appropriate amount.

5 A spreader makes it unnecessary to mark out the area and also ensures even sowing. As with hand sowing, two half-rate applications at right angles gives the most even coverage. It is vital to set the correct rate of application.

6 Rake the seed in lightly to cover most of it; do not worry that some of it shows; the sowing rate takes this into account.

7 Water well with a sprinkler or watering can to settle the soil surface. Germination usually takes 10-14 days. Do not use a roller.

Weeds in the lawn

No matter how high the quality of the grass, weeds can ruin the whole effect of a lawn. They smother the grass and give the lawn a neglected appearance. Some, such as dandelions, have deep tap roots that are difficult to dig out; a lawn weedkiller is the only certain treatment.

***Above:** Dandelions are difficult to dig out successfully; kill them with a lawn weedkiller. Pick off the flowers before they set seed.*

***Above:** You can rake patches of clover before mowing to weaken it, but lawn weedkiller is the only complete and lasting treatment.*

***Above:** Plantain seeds readily from brown flower heads and dies back in winter, leaving a bald patch. Treat with lawn weedkiller.*

***Above:** Daisies are not easy to kill with a lawn weedkiller. Apply a second dose four weeks after the first. Raking helps reduce them.*

Lawn weedkillers

You can dig out a few individual weeds, but apply a selective weedkiller if there are rather a lot. Weedkillers are perfectly safe when used as directed, so always follow the manufacturer's instructions carefully.

***Above:** To treat the whole lawn, fit a dribble bar to a watering can. On a dull day, the area stays wet, so weedkiller has longer to work.*

***Above:** A handsprayer is effective and economical for 'spot' treating weeds. You can buy them filled and ready-to-use.*

LAYING TURF

The quickest way to get a 'usable' lawn is unquestionably by laying turf. In essence, you are transplanting grass to your garden. However, and this is where any difficulties might arise, you have to remember that you are dealing with living plants. This means that, from the moment the turf is laid, you must on no account allow it to become dry. If it does, the individual turves will shrink, gaps will appear between them and they will dry out even quicker. Shrinking involves movement and movement will prevent new roots forming and growing into the underlying ground.

Soil preparation is just the same - and just as important - as for sowing seed and, like seed mixtures, there are different grades of turf available for the quality of lawn you require. This will be reflected in the price of the turf. In turn, the price will reflect the quality of the turf. There is no such thing as a bargain when buying turf. Cheap turf will be of poor quality. It may be broken, thin, full of weeds or just poor-quality grass. Beware.

You can lay turf at any time of the year, but the fall and spring are best. The weather is usually mild and the soil damp. Winter is also acceptable, but do not lay turves during prolonged cold spells. Avoid the summer; the newly laid turves will dry out if not watered constantly, the grass will grow and need mowing and the turf will deteriorate if it is not laid within a day or so of lifting. Discuss the delivery of the turf with your supplier. It is no use having it at the beginning of the week if it cannot be laid until the weekend.

1 To avoid gaps, leave a hump at the end of each turf as you place it against the previous one. This will be pushed flat later. Do not create a 'squared-up' lawn by having the ends of adjoining turves level. Stagger them slightly as you work.

2 This is the first row of turf, so the plank from which you should work is on bare ground. When laying subsequent rows, the plank is on the last row you laid.

3 After laying each turf, push down the hump you left at the end to make a tight fit against the neighboring turf. This will go a long way towards preventing drying out.

4 To make sure that the turf is hard against its neighbor lengthways, tap it into place with a fork. No great force is needed; use just enough to get rid of the gap.

5 Press or pat down each turf, so that it makes good contact with the ground. This removes any air pockets and ensures that the severed roots are touching the soil.

6 This is how the pattern of turf should look. As you complete each row or when the whole lawn is finished, fill in any gaps to prevent the edges drying out.

Sprinkle used potting mix or sifted soil along all the joins, whether there are gaps or not.

7 When you have sprinkled the potting mix or sifted soil along all the joins, brush over the whole lawn, both to work the dressing down into any cracks and to tidy up the area. If you find wider gaps, sprinkle seed on top of them.

8 Just as when sowing a new lawn, water the newly turfed area thoroughly when you have finished. This not only washes any remaining soil into the cracks, but also ensures that the turves have adequate moisture.

Below: In many ways, the lawn is the centerpiece of the ornamental garden. A good lawn improves the appearance of the most ordinary flower beds, while a poor one diminishes everything around it.

Lawn care

It is one thing to create what you might think of as the ideal lawn, but quite another to keep it in the best condition. This will depend on the quantity and quality of the upkeep you are prepared to lavish on it. All too often the lawn is left to its own devices after the first flush of enthusiasm. Mowing, raking, feeding, watering, spiking, weed and moss control and a host of lesser jobs will all need to be done. Here are some of the more important maintenance tasks.

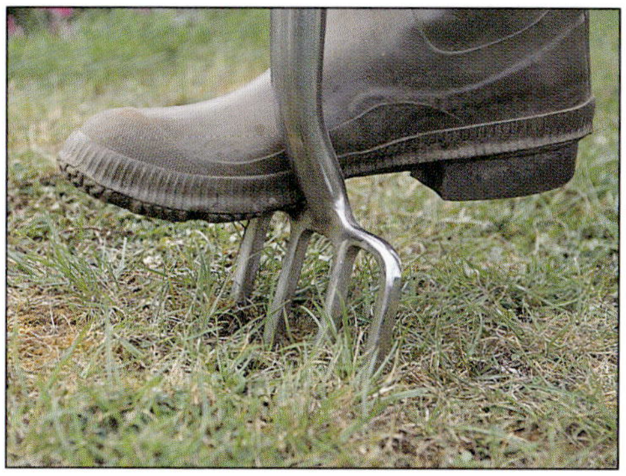

Left: *Compaction of the soil surface leads to poor drainage, waterlogging and weak grass. Spike all or part of the lawn with a garden fork, driving it 4in(10cm) deep and the same distance apart into all the places that need aerating.*

Feeding the lawn

Above: *Grass plants constantly compete for nutrients. You can apply fertilizer by hand, but take care to distribute it evenly.*

Above: *Set correctly, a spreader distributes fertilizer at the ideal rate, leading to an even result and less risk of overdosing.*

Raking the lawn

Right: *In every lawn, dead grass and other plant debris will build up amongst the blades of grass. You must rake out this material regularly if the lawn is to flourish. 'Thatch', as it is called, is a contributory factor to moss and the appearance of yellowing grass.*

PESTS AND DISEASES

Many problems can be avoided by controlling weeds and tidying away garbage. Compost lawn mowings, dead leaves and weeds so that they break down without encouraging pests or disease spores. Remove and burn plants with persistent problems. Wash empty pots, seed trays and boxes after use and store them in a shed. Natural predators will deal with many pests, so plant trees to encourage insect-eating birds, grow clumps of wildflowers to encourage beneficial insects and avoid chemical pesticides so that beneficial creatures are not harmed. However, if a pest or disease problem is serious, use a remedy in order to save a plant. Use environmentally friendly chemical sprays where possible and spray in the evenings when bees are not about.

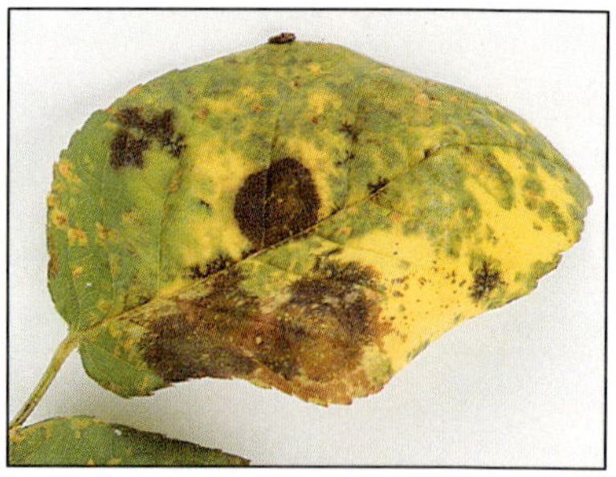

Above: If roses suffer from fungal diseases such as rust, spray them regularly in spring and summer with a proper rose fungicide.

Left: Earwigs are active at night and not only damage flowers (this is a clematis) but can also reduce the leaves to a network of veins.

Above: Powdery mildew on roses. Spray regularly with a fungicide, evenly covering both the upper and undersides of the leaves.

Below: Bluetits and beneficial insects will clear minor outbreaks of aphids, a common pest, or use a chemical that only kills aphids.

Pest control

PART TWO

PLANNING YOUR GARDEN

Good planning is the key to creating a beautiful and successful garden. By following a few practical pointers and adding a little personal flair and imagination good planning can transform a raw new plot, untamed jungle or cramped and gloomy backyard into your dream garden in just a single season.

BOUNDARIES

The boundaries of the garden plot should be your first consideration when planning the total look and style of your hoped-for scheme. What goes around the perimeter can have a considerable influence on the final effect and should be designed in conjunction with other major features. Most likely, you will have inherited some kind of wall, fence or trellis, which may or may not be suitable. Replacement can be expensive, so you might have to compromise by redesigning certain areas at first, say around key spaces such as the patio. If you find the effect totally unacceptable, resort to some kind of disguise or cover-up, such as inexpensive trellis, climbing plants or decorative screens. First decide whether the structure is doing the job for which it is intended; a lightweight post-and-rail fence is fine where you want to appreciate a fine view beyond the garden, but for privacy or shelter you need something more substantial. Before constructing or changing any permanent structure, check exactly which boundaries you or your neighbor are responsible for and make sure there are no local planning restrictions on size and style. Traditional choices for boundaries include fences, walls, and hedges, but consider other options such as screens of living plants, or trellis supporting fast-growing climbers - the latter is specially useful for providing quick cover without exceeding a predetermined height.

Left: Timber fence posts and panels are available in various styles. Allow the timber to weather, or stain or paint it to suit your scheme. If you grow climbers on the fences, be aware of the need for occasional timber treatment/painting.

Left: A hedge takes longer to establish, but makes an attractive, natural background for other features. Choose hedging plants of suitable vigor for the planned height; for example, strong-growing conifers, will soon outgrow a small garden.

Above: Wattle fencing has a nice natural look for rural gardens, but a short life - about five years. It is useful as a temporary fence while hedging gets established.

Right: Painted picket fences look most attractive in country gardens and make a good background for flower borders. Leave room behind shrubs for repainting the fence.

Above: Forsythia makes a good hedge, but it must be clipped in winter, just before it flowers, to keep it tidy. This form is created by first training suitably placed branches into the desired shape.

Below: Here, a length of ornamental trellis breaks up the rather regular effect created by a boundary fence bordering three sides of this square garden plot.

Below: With the fence and screen in place, the effect of mixing and matching styles is clear to see.

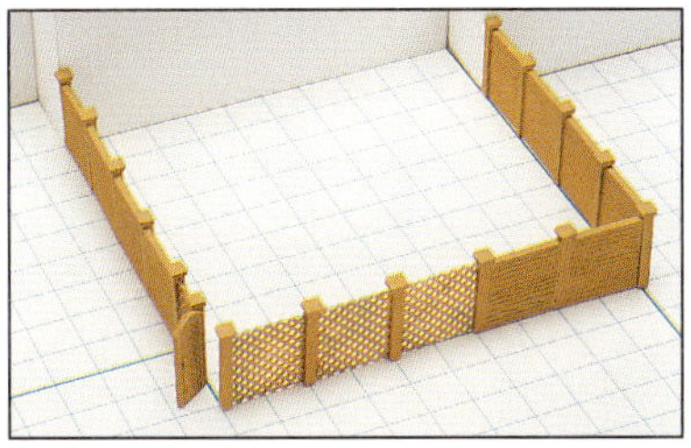

Boundary types

Fences: *These take up the least room of any boundary, but need good foundations or metal posts to secure them, and regular timber preservative treatment. They have a relatively short life, but do provide an instant effect. Solid fences, such as close-boarded or panel, are animal-proof and best where privacy is needed. Open fences, such as picket or post-and-rail, are best where you want to enjoy the surrounding views.*

Walls: *Walls are the most expensive but permanent boundary. They reflect heat, so you can train tender shrubs against them. Walls can be solid (brick, dry stone, rendered aggregate or concrete block) or open (decorative wall blocks).*

Hedges: *Hedges are the cheapest way of establishing a boundary and look the most natural, but can take several years to reach the height required and then need regular trimming. Being wider, they take up more space than walls and fences (allow for 3ft/90cm width) and their roots will dry out surrounding borders. Formal clipped hedges (beech, privet, yew and hornbeam) are traditional favorites but the most work to maintain. More relaxed, informal, flowering hedges (roses or forsythia) take up even more width - allow for 6ft(1.8m).*

Above: *The ends of a picket fence can have quite elaborate profiles. Cut these with a jigsaw.*

Shrub border: *In this case, a border becomes a boundary. Evergreens or prickly berberis are good used this way.*
Screen: *A row of identical plants such as bamboos or cordon-trained apples grown on post and wire fencing.*
Fencing with climbers: *Chain-link fencing or trellis with climbing plants make a pleasant screen. These alternative boundaries let you dictate the ultimate height and choose plants or supports accordingly. This avoids the need for regular clipping or plants growing too tall, as can happen with normal hedges or rows of conifers, e.g. Leyland's cypress.*

Below: *A clipped yew hedge forms the classic background to a traditional mixed border.*

Below: A free-standing patio is an interesting option providing it can be well sheltered. A round patio can liven up a regular square plot.

Above: Sometimes it is better to site the patio at the further end of the garden, if this is where it will receive most sunshine.

Left: Introducing a curve and a slight change of level is instantly softer and changes the whole look of the garden. Use your imagination at the early planning stages; visit other gardens and look at magazines for ideas.

PATIO STYLE

The patio is essentially an outdoor living area, a firm, dry level surface where you can relax in the sunshine or enjoy an alfresco meal. Although the most convenient place for a patio is close to the house, try to site it where it will receive maximum sunshine. This may mean a spot at the opposite end of the garden, in which case provide some form of permanent dry access from the house, such as a path or stepping stones. The size and shape of your patio can be an important element in the overall impact and success of your garden. If the traditional square or rectangle looks too formal or does little for a small, regular plot, experiment with curves and circles. Decide which facilities you want to include - seating, cooking (a barbecue), an ornamental pool or built-in planting beds. Choose the flooring first; paving slabs, a pattern of warm brick, friendly wooden decking or a clever combination of different materials. Next, consider the 'walls'. Do you want climbing plants smothering a trellis or pergola? Or decorative screens and a background of evergreens? Finish off with a few carefully chosen 'ornaments', such as pots for your patio plants, a statue, sundial or maybe a small moving water feature. Try to keep everything in style and the final effect will be stunning.

Above: Use the same materials for flooring, raised beds and features such as built-in barbecues for continuity. Different materials look 'bitty' in a small space.

Left: To keep work to a minimum, you do not need a lot of plants to decorate a patio; furnishings that match containers establish a sense of style and supply color.

Above: Wooden decking with a brick surround creates a warm, friendly atmosphere on the patio. Conifers and perennials provide easy-care planting.

Above: Town center patios (as here) need screening to provide privacy from surrounding gardens and passers-by, as well as for shade or shelter. Screens can also be used as supports for climbing plants.

Above: In the garden design shown above, the main patio is situated immediately behind the house, as this is the area that receives maximum sunshine right through the day.

Below: A smaller paved seating area at the opposite end of the garden makes an excellent additional feature visually and is designed to catch the last rays of the afternoon sun.

Patios

Here are a few points to consider when planning and siting a patio.

Sun: *Site a patio so that it is in the sun when you use it, perhaps facing the evening sun, or in full sun for all-day use as a suntrap.*

Shade: *Shady seating areas can be a cool, restful alternative; use pergola poles planted with climbers, trees or decorative screens to provide shade.*

Shelter, privacy and security: *Pale walls reflect heat and light into a patio. Protection is vital; patios are traditionally at the rear, enclosed by walls, decorative screening or tall plants. Pots, barbecues and furniture are easily removed so keep them out of sight from the road.*

Sound: *Surrounding walls and screens help to deaden road noise. Tinkling fountains, wind chimes and bees buzzing in the flowers help to give the area a sense of tranquility.*

Changing levels: *Add interest to a flat site by lowering or raising a patio and using steps to link it to the main garden.*

Water: *A pond is a restful addition; build a raised formal round or square pond with wide edges that double as seating, or make a less formal sunken pond.*

Above: *Avoid siting the patio immediately beyond the back door if the house shades the area for most of the day.*

Above: *An adjoining or nearby building may cast unwelcome shadows on some parts of the garden at certain times of day.*

Above: *In this situation, the whole garden enjoys the benefits of full sunshine and only the front of the building is in shade.*

Right: *Outdoor eating is an essential feature of many patios, so outdoor tables and chairs can become part of the 'fixtures and fittings'. Use hardwood or cast aluminum if they are to be left outside, and add detachable cushions to bring indoors after use.*

LAWNS

Grassy areas are not simply there to fill in the gaps between other features. A well-planned lawn can be an excellent design feature, even a focal point, if its shape and size are thoughtfully integrated into your general garden plan. Although a lawn requires a certain level of commitment in terms of maintenance, with trimming, watering, feeding and aerating during the growing season, grass is quick and easy to establish - whether from seed or turves - and can be adapted to any size or shape. However formal, it can offer a wonderfully soft, very natural effect that you could never achieve with an expanse of paving or hard landscaping and is complementary to all other features and materials. A lawn, especially where it has been planted in a definitive geometric shape, such as a circle, rectangle or square, makes an excellent setting or surround for other features, such as a pond, a statue, flower beds or a sundial.

Below: Grassing over one corner distracts attention from the true limits of a small plot. Once other features are in place, the original square will have 'disappeared'.

Right: A large circle of grass has been edged in brick and partially screened by dense planting to make a focal point of the circular pool and fountain at the far end.

Right: A circular lawn immediately softens the hard-edged boundaries of a square plot and creates a more informal feel to the garden. It is also a very easy shape to mow and edge.

Right: Instead of positioning a square lawn dead center of a square site, try placing it on the diagonal, which produces a far more interesting effect. Or use two overlapping square lawns of different sizes.

Above: Grass can add fluidity and movement to an informal garden, as it flows like a wide green stream between trees and foliage plants.

Right: A thyme lawn made of several randomly planted varieties flowers in patches all summer and makes a colorful, scented feature.

Below: Experiment with lawn shapes and sizes in conjunction with other features until you find one that works from every angle.

Lawn options

Grass: *The traditional choice for garden 'carpeting'. Select a hard-wearing mixture that contains ryegrass for a drought-resistant, easy-care lawn that will get tough wear and tear.*
'Fine' lawns are traditionally seen in front gardens or where a 'bowling green' finish is wanted. They need regular care and watering in dry weather.
Special mixtures are available premixed for shady areas, dry soil and other problem spots.

Wildflower lawns: *These are grown from seed and available as ready-made mixtures of wildflower seed and grasses, or, blend your own to create natural meadow-style features. Low-maintenance wildflower lawns are suitable for wild or rough areas or wild gardens. Cut them twice yearly in early spring and again after the seedheads dry, so that the seed is scattered first, but be sure to eradicate perennial weeds before sowing.*

Alternative lawns: *Clover lawns are very drought resistant and remain green in summer when the grass browns. You need not mow them; cutting removes the flowerheads (thus deterring bees) and can create a striped effect. Clover can be mixed with grass seed to give an eco-friendly lawn that 'grows' its own fertilizer, since clover fixes nitrogen from the air in its roots.*

Hard surfaces: *In small areas gravel or paving, etc., may be more convenient, as they need no upkeep or special equipment, such as a mower, to maintain them. Unlike grass, they do not wear out if the same small area is heavily used. Where children and dogs play, an alternative soft surface such as bark chippings is a better choice and can be redeveloped into a lawn later on.*

Above: *A chamomile lawn has a 'shaggy carpet' texture. The non-flowering form 'Treneague' stays fairly short without any mowing.*

Herb lawns: *Since these are decorative but not hard wearing, add 'stepping stones' or a paved path to walk on if they are to be subject to regular use. Plant a mixture of creeping thymes or non-flowering chamomile through a shallow layer of gravel. A sunny site and good drainage are vital.*

Flower lawns: *Choose low, hummock-shaped and creeping rock plants with paving or gravel paths for a decorative flowering lawn. It needs a sunny spot with good drainage and is intended as a decorative feature rather than as an alternative to grass.*

Below: *Do not mow a grass lawn naturalized with colorful spring crocuses until six to eight weeks after the flowers are over.*

BEDS AND BORDERS

Plants are vital for softening the edges of harder landscaping materials and for breathing life and color into your design. Plan for them at the earliest stages by incorporating suitable beds and borders into the main scheme. Beds with geometric shapes, perhaps raised and edged in matching materials, are an obvious choice for patio areas and might incorporate seating areas or even a pool, but they can work equally well as part of a more formal layout. The gentle curve of a less formal border is attractive, but do not make it too elaborate. Mark out the shape when experimenting with an idea on site. Herbaceous borders and ornamental beds with annual color can be very time-consuming unless you plan them carefully. First ensure that all parts of the bed or border are easily accessible by not making them too wide or too deep. Then design a good backbone of evergreens, shrubs and reliable perennials and use a few annuals only for seasonal color and interest in selected areas, depending on how much time you have. You might also be selective with the varieties you choose; some of the newer types have been deliberately bred so that they are shorter than traditional ones, so that you can still grow your favorites without the need for staking. Also look out for plants that are recommended as free-flowering, which means that they keep on producing blooms for several months.

Above: Disguise the boundaries of a regular plot with informal plant borders. Make them unequal in size and length for a natural effect.

Above: Patio beds can be quite imaginative; interlocking shapes can be more interesting than squares and rectangles.

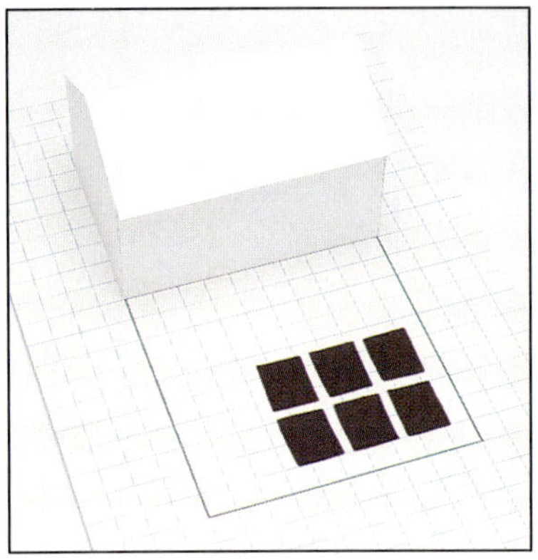

Above: The regular layout of a classic vegetable plot or formal herb garden means beds are easy to maintain, while presenting a certain well-ordered charm.

Below: Bay, rosemary, thyme, chives and marigolds are perfect for creating a formal patchwork effect of subtle colors and textures.

Left: In a cottage-style garden, a profusion of different plants is allowed to create an informal mass of shapes and colors that conceals a formal planting arrangement.

Above: The trick of creating a superb, traditional herbaceous border is to fill it generously with a wide variety of contrasting flower shapes, sizes and colors.

PLANTS IN BORDERS

Consider the plants you will be incorporating into the beds and borders, as this may influence their style and position. For example, bright annuals and scented plants are ideal for raised beds around the patio; herbs and vegetables need a good, sunny site; a pool, sculpture or seating area may require a backdrop of greenery.

Above: An island bed positioned on the diagonal creates a diamond shape. It avoids the effect of a grassy formal border that a square cut out of the lawn would create.

Below: Hebes, heathers, dwarf rhododendrons and small conifers create an undulating 'mini-landscape' with room for seasonal interest, such as spring bulbs.

Below: Raised beds incorporated into the patio design successfully make the link between the paved area and the rest of the garden. Fill them with colorful plants.

How to achieve an all-year-round effect

Above: A stylish arrangement of conifers suits a large island bed, blending greens and golds in varying heights and shapes.

Evergreens: *Make these the backbone of your design; for a real year-round garden allow two thirds evergreens to one third deciduous shrubs and flowers. Choose plants with contrasting foliage shapes, and plenty with variegated or colored foliage.*

Bark and stems: *Colored or contorted stems and distinctive bark provide winter interest. Contorted hazel, birches and dogwoods are specially useful.*

Fruit and berries: *These provide seasonal interest when few flowers are out; many kinds are held well into winter. They also attract birds to the garden.*

Bulbs: *Spring and fall bulbs provide carpets of color when little else is out in flower, yet do not take up much space. They die down for much of the year and can be planted underneath shrubs, specimen trees and in the lawn, as well as in borders.*

Seasonal features: *Instead of dotting plants with seasonal interest throughout the garden, concentrate them in specific areas to create spring, winter or fall 'cameos', which will make far more impact.*

Containers: *Use colorful containers as portable gardens to provide an instant splash of color and interest wherever it is needed, and - suitably planted - at any time of year.*

Above: Using containers in the border enables you to introduce new colors and shapes to the planting as the seasons change.

WATER FEATURES

The light-reflecting properties of water in a pond or pool in the garden or on a patio immediately add a new dimension to your design. A pool is a natural focal point and makes a stunning, easy-care feature once installed. It also gives you the opportunity to install a moving water feature, such as a fountain, spout or cascade, to add sound and sparkle to the scheme. Position a pool carefully. Water and water plants need plenty of light and sunshine. For an informal, natural pool, sketch out a rough kidney shape. Alternatively, choose a more formal square, rectangle or circle. You might even consider two or more pools linked by a cascade. The materials you choose to edge your pool will significantly influence its final look. Formal pools tend to be edged in brick, stone or paving to match other features in the garden. Grass, pebbles and other natural materials combined with suitable pool-edge plants are more in keeping with informal ponds. Water plants are lush and glossy, often dramatic, and a well-planned display can include a marvellous variety of shapes, sizes and forms.

An informal lagoon shape offers plenty of scope for a large pool. Do not make it too complicated; the narrow areas will restrict water flow and cause stagnation.

A formal square is ideal for pools on different levels and with interlocking effects.

A circular pool can be formal without looking hard-edged, and makes an attractive raised feature, complete with fountain.

A simple kidney shape is perfect for most informal settings. It is often semi-concealed beneath a display of moisture-loving plants.

A rectangle is a popular choice for large formal pools on the patio and in the garden, and can include a wide range of features.

Below: A beach of cobblestones contrasts with the upright linear stems of iris and grasses growing in and around this informal pond.

Above: An informal kidney shape makes an excellent starting point for a natural pond or pool. It is quite straightforward to construct.

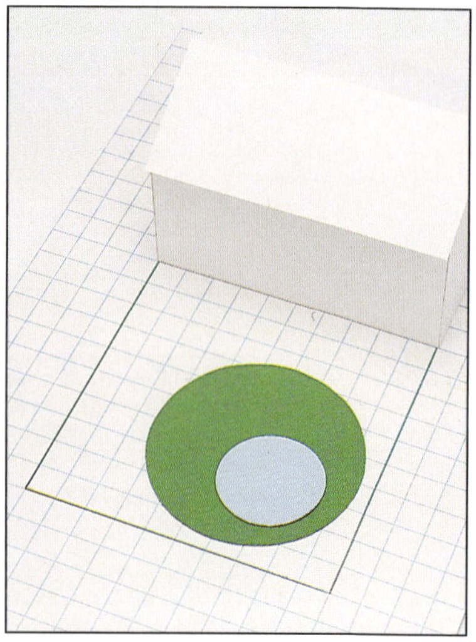

Above: Here, a round pool takes its lead from a circular grassed area and transforms the lawn into an important focal point.

Above: A raised water feature such as this introduces a classic cottage garden style into a patio setting. Here, foxglove, iris, ferns and ivy cluster at the water's edge.

Below: Whether simple or intricate, always plan and construct a garden pool with care. Once established, a well-planned water feature will be easier to maintain.

Pond design options

In shade: *Use fountains for reflected light and sparkle with shade-loving plants such as hostas, but avoid water plants, as most need more light to thrive.*

Water features: *Where there are small children, avoid standing water, however shallow. Instead, choose fountains or water gushing up through a millstone or from a jar into gravel, then recycled via a concealed pump.*

Above: *Small water features are safe and add interest in the smallest corner of the garden.*

Formal ponds: *In a formal garden, choose geometrical shapes for a pond, such as squares, rectangles or circles. They could have raised edges or be sunken within a paved area. Traditionally, they were used for growing a range of water lilies.*

Informal ponds: *Irregular, kidney or teardrop shapes suit dramatic water's edge planting, with varied heights and foliage shapes and sizes, often with natural rock features, cascades, or an adjacent bog garden. Design the pond with at least one shelving edge, so that any wildlife can get out, and plenty of planting shelves to support pots of marginal plants. Position the shelves so that 1in(2.5cm) of water covers the tops of the pots.*

Wildlife ponds: *Very informal ponds with shelving edges to allow pondlife to emerge and birds to bathe. Surround them with waterside wildflowers.*

Stream features: *These natural-looking features are lined with butyl, as for ponds, on level or sloping sites, with water recirculated by a concealed pump. Use them as an isolated feature or to link two or more ponds. Landscape them with clumps of upright plants (such as irises) and cobblestones, or surround them with waterside plants or a bog garden.*

Below: *In this formal complex, limited planting helps the pool to retain its sharp outline edged in brick and blue-stained decking.*

PATHS AND WALKWAYS

An essential item in the garden is some form of access that remains reasonably dry and safe underfoot in all weathers and allows you to move from one feature to another. Without it, you will create unsightly tracks. But walkways, paths and stepping stones have important design possibilities, too. They can look strictly formal, carving the plot into distinct geometric shapes, or they can meander between features, creating a more relaxed feel. Because the eye naturally follows the shape and line of any pathway into the distance and beyond, the path can influence the appearance and shape of the site visually. Take it straight from A to B and the plot seems shorter, but describe a more circuitous route and the garden instantly appears bigger and more interesting, especially if you cannot see right to the end. If a solid path seems too dominant, use stepping stones or a staggered wooden walkway. The materials you use will influence the look and feel of your garden; stone slabs and pavers can be adapted to both formal and informal schemes. For a cottage garden style, lay brick in ornamental herringbone patterns, or for a woodland feel, lay a path of wood chips with log slices as stepping stones. To soften the effect of paths and walkways, encourage them to blend into the general garden scheme. Let plants spill over the edge; low-growing, carpet-forming prostrate plants, such as creeping thyme, are also useful for growing between the pavers or bricks of a path. Or position tubs or pots of plants along the route to soften the edges and corners.

Below: An informal 'path' of flagstones with grass in between them, helps prevent lawns wearing out in places where people regularly walk.

Above: A staggered wooden walkway running from a patio or wooden-decked area is stylish and simple to install. It is also deals with the problem of a sloping site.

Above: A strict framework of concrete or paving slab paths divides the garden into a formal arrangement of planting beds with a pleasing symmetry.

Above: Small squares, scaled to the size of standard pavers, can be used to chart a path of stepping stones, and saves a lot of trial and error when it comes to laying down the real thing.

Above: 'Stepping stones' set into a lawn reduce hard wear in narrow passages between borders. Set them deep enough so that the mower can run over the top.

Left: Use plants to soften path edges. Here, helianthemum and silver foliage spill onto the cobbles.

Below: Here, stepping stones are laid to skirt the lawn and link the main patio to the smaller paved area at the bottom of the garden.

Designer tips for paths

Left: *Paths do not have to be straight-sided; use them as a design feature, filling the space between distinctly shaped flower beds.*

Everyday use: *Paths that take you where you need to go - to the garage, a gate or a washing line - should go as straight as possible, otherwise people will cut corners and walk over the flower beds.*

Heavy use: *Paths that carry heavy weights, such as vehicles, need to be wide enough and have deeper foundations than those that will only be walked on.*

Scenic routes: *Paths intended to encourage meandering round the garden should twist and curve to slow you down and open up new vistas at each turn. They can be narrow, decorated by containers, or lead to seats, arbors or dead ends. They need little or no foundations as they will not have to carry weight.*

Levels: *Use paths and walkways to create the appearance of changing levels. Make 'bridges' over beds of plants, a pond, bog garden or even plain gravel. Or set railway sleepers into the ground at an angle with gravel between them to 'suggest' steps.*

Textures: *Use paths and paving to create changes of texture and to contrast with plant material. Make full use of flat pavers, chunky setts, smooth rounded cobblestones and crisp gravel.*

Permanent or temporary: *Permanent paths need proper foundations such as a hardcore base to avoid them breaking up. Temporary paths made of gravel or paving laid straight onto soil are often useful in a garden where the layout is likely to change, for example in cottage gardens or vegetable plots.*

Below: *An informal path of gravel shovelled over the soil makes an ideal base from which to explore a flower bed at close quarters.*

TRELLIS AND PERGOLAS

Trellis, screens, pergolas and arches give shelter, they hide, and they provide support for climbing plants. But they can work magic, too: clever illusions that will transform gardens both large and small into places of interest and intrigue. Use them to disguise features you would rather not see, or to divide the plot into more interesting 'garden rooms'. If you are going to smother the structure in plants, something basic is fine, providing it is strong enough to take the weight of the plants. Along a boundary, where the trellis might have to withstand strong winds, go for stronger panels and erect them in the same way as you would a fence. An archway or pergola not only provides a support for climbing plants, it also adds height and a new dimension to the garden and an ornamental entrance. A pergola might lead from one part of the garden to another or show off a particular group of climbing plants, such as a wisteria walk. It can be erected as an attractive form of shelter or shade over the patio. Ideally, link the feature to a related structure: a wooden archway making a break in a fence, or an ornamental brick or wrought-iron arch adding interest to a high wall. A pergola might link the house to the garden, or be positioned over an existing path to create a covered walkway. If you are using an arch to frame a view, site it in exactly the right place to make that view a good one. Check that people can walk through it without stooping, remembering that later it will be festooned with climbing plants. It is this sort of attention to detail that makes a good design successful.

Right: On a trellis, a quick-flowering annual, such as this *Ipomoea purpurea* (morning glory), creates a temporary effect while you are waiting for perennial climbers to mature.

Above: These plastic-covered metal frames create a light and airy walkway and provide an ideal support for clematis and other climbing plants.

Left: Experiment with positioning your pergola structure in different directions. It might run parallel or at right angles to the house wall with equal effect.

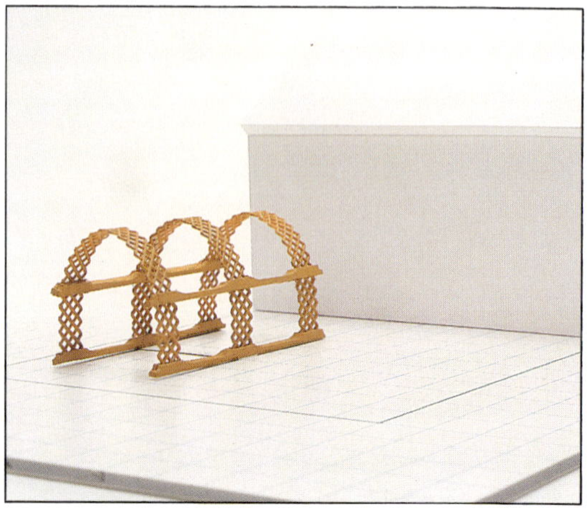

Right: A series of arches makes a delightful feature and a wonderful flowery walk when the framework is covered in a profusion of plants.

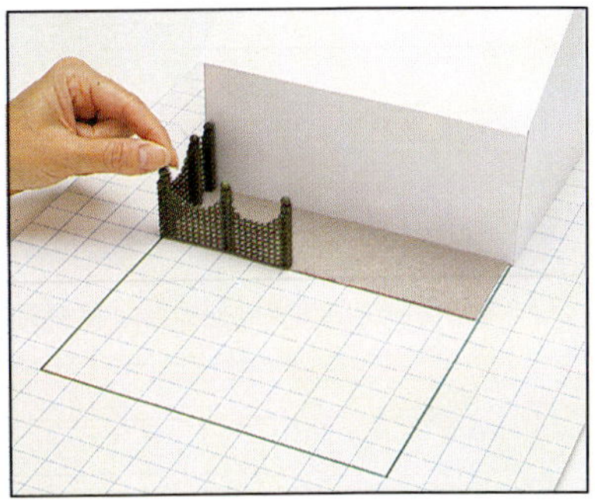

Above: Sturdy or ornamental trellis panels might shelter a patio from drafts or create a private area where you can relax in seclusion.

Above: Simple plant supports can add height and interest anywhere in the garden. These wired posts are ideal for cordon fruit trees.

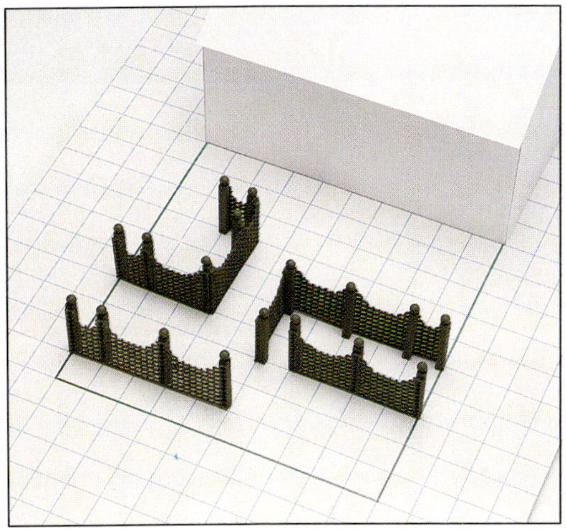

Left: By breaking up the plot into individual sections, you make it more interesting, limiting both what can be seen and the pace and route you use to walk around it.

Below: As part of the main garden design, an ornamental wooden archway makes a decorative entrance to the small paved area at the end of the plot and frames a view.

Climbing plants

Climbers: *All climbers need tying up to their supports to start with. After a year, self-clinging plants will hold themselves up, but many climbers need tying up regularly. As the soil at the base of walls is dry and often filled with rubble, plant climbers a short distance - 18in(45cm) - from the support and 'lead' stems to it via canes or rustic poles. Beware of any climbers growing into crevices, e.g. under roof tiles, as they expand as they grow and can lift tiles or enlarge gaps.*

Clingers: *Self supporters, such as climbing hydrangeas and ivies, hang onto bare walls using aerial roots that grow into crevices and then expand to jam themselves in place. They do not harm sound walls, but can make crumbly mortar or bricks worse. Clematis cling using angled leaf stems to hook onto supports - they need netting or trellis to grip onto.*

Above: *Here, a pergola has been embellished with trellis, on which to display a specimen of* Clematis *'Ville de Lyon', a very fine, free-flowering summer hybrid.*

Right: *This arbor is almost completely hidden by the golden hop,* Humulus lupulus *'Aureus', and forms a frame around a white chair - itself a focal point at the end of a brick path.*

Twiners: *Self-supporting plants, such as honeysuckle, wisteria and Russian vine, cling on using twining stems. They grow quickly and need keeping in check; if allowed to grow round drainpipes and guttering, they expand and can pull them away.*

Wall shrubs: *Many tall or tender, normally free-standing plants, such as* Fremontodendron *and* Ceanothus*, are often trained against walls. Their stems need to be supported; tie them loosely to horizontal wires or trellis secured to the wall.*

TREES AND SHRUBS

Trees and shrubs are essential to your background planting scheme, providing height and a sense of maturity even to the most modest garden. If space is limited, plant a small single specimen tree in a strategic position - preferably one that can offer spring blossom, fine summer foliage, fall color and interesting berries or fruits. Alternatively, miniaturize the look with a pair of clipped evergreens in pots on either side of a flight of steps or a seat. Dwarf conifers provide winter interest in containers around the patio or in the rockery. Larger gardens can enjoy larger-scale effects. Team trees with shrubs, such as birches with rhododendrons. On a bank or steep slope, a scrambling plant, such as the glossy evergreen bramble *Rubus tricolor,* will help to bind and stabilize the soil. Under big trees with a dense canopy of foliage, such as the horse chestnut, the rain cannot penetrate and the soil is too dry for most plants. Here, an area of pebbles or bark chips may be the best option. Elsewhere, look for quick-growing, creeping and ground cover plants that thrive in dappled shade. In spring, the area below trees is perfect for a bright show of spring bulbs among the grass.

Below: A mixture of deciduous and evergreen trees and shrubs, here including *Malus, Physocarpus* and *Taxus*, creates a good year-round framework to the garden.

Above: Where you are planning a group of trees, odd numbers often create a better effect than even ones. Try for a range of heights and canopy shapes within the group.

TREES AND WATER

Above: Do not site trees near a pond, where shade and falling leaves can cause green scum and pollution.

Above: Keep water features clear of the tree's shadow. Plants and water need light if they are to function properly.

Choosing a tree for foliage

Acer grosseri hersii. Bright green leaves turn red in the fall.

Acer platanoides 'Crimson King'. Deep purple foliage turns orange in the fall.

Acer platanoides 'Drummondii' has creamy white-edged leaves.

Right: A pair of upright trees such as these fastigiate yews, *Taxus baccata* 'Standishii', help to create a spectacular entrance.

Below: In this small, semi-formal garden the trees are restricted to a pair of clipped bay trees in tubs. These add height and style to the small paved seating area.

Using trees and shrubs in the garden

Height: *Check the ultimate height of a tree before planting it in the garden. Avoid planting over drains or where trees may cause problems of shade and access as they get bigger.*

Fallout: *Consider the possible nuisance value of fallen leaves and blossom, the sticky sap shed by limes and the excess seed shed by some acers.*

Distance: *Small ornamental garden trees can be planted 15ft(4.5m) from the house without problems, but as a general rule, a safe planting distance is the same as the ultimate height of the tree. To be absolutely safe, do not plant large forest or woodland trees, such as beech, closer to the house than one and a half times their ultimate height.*

Left: *Do not plant a tree any closer to a building than its ultimate spread. It should not be cramped by other features, nor likely to create a hazard to them. Cutting branches will spoil its shape and produce a lopsided effect.*

Walls: *Plant wall-trained trees at least 12-18in(30-45cm) from the wall and keep them well watered, as soil at the base of a wall is often poor and dry.*

Pots: *Trees and shrubs restricted in pots will stay much smaller than those planted in open ground, but they will need frequent watering, particularly in warm weather. Semi-bonsai training can make large kinds suitable for small spaces.*

Underplanting: *Trees and shrubs underplanted with ground cover make a low-maintenance garden, especially if planted through porous landscape fabric or slitted plastic, which prevents weed growth. Conceal the fabric or plastic with a layer of decorative bark or gravel.*

Below: Erythronium revolutum *is a spring-flowering perennial that thrives in the partial shade provided by deciduous trees.*

Left: This rockery fulfils several roles: it provides a useful focal point at the end of the pool, creates an interesting planting area within the small formal patio at the end of the garden and livens up a boundary corner.

Left: Adding the finishing touches to your garden can be fun. Try to keep the style of decorative pots, tubs and furniture in keeping with the general theme or atmosphere you have tried to create.

MAKING A GARDEN SPECIAL

With the plan finished and all the major hard landscaping features in place, you now have a good idea of how your garden is going to look and work. What comes next are the finishing touches that add character to your scheme. A sundial, sculpture or birdbath adds interest to a dull corner or creates a focal point on the patio, in the center of the lawn, in a 'garden room' or at the end of a path. Garden ornaments and accessories can be used to reinforce a theme or to create one. Use ornaments such as forcing pots to contrast with carpets of plants; an old garden roller leaning up against the trunk of a gnarled apple tree suggests the timeless quality of a cottage garden. A careful choice of containers can conjure up a certain atmosphere: terracotta for a Mediterranean feel, old wooden barrels for a rustic look, painted Versailles planters or traditional stone urns to decorate a formal scheme. Add to these the appropriate outdoor furniture and accessories and, later, a suitable selection of plants, and the setting is complete. Garden furniture is available in a wide range of styles, from rustic wooden benches to decorative Lutyens-inspired seats. The opportunities and the looks you can create are endless, but make sure yours are in tune with the rest of your garden design. Positioning these final features is equally important. Containers of different heights and sizes tend to look best arranged in odd numbers, such as threes or fives. For a more formal look, position tubs or pots geometrically - on either side of an entrance or flanking a seat.

Left: A collection of terracotta pots planted with spring flowers has brought this dull brick wall to life early in the season. Replace the bulbs with bright annual flowers for the summer.

Right: A pair of matching trimmed topiary trees on either side of a doorway looks stunning in a formal setting. These are box; clip them about four times a year for a neat appearance.

Above: A quiet corner of the border can become a place for relaxation if you add a simple seat, such as this stone bench, among the flowers.

Right: Assess the finished plan to see if the features fit together and work on a practical level. Now is the time to change any details you are not happy with before the real construction work begins.

Below: The garden that started life as a dull, rather limited square plot will be smart and stylish, with a range of easy-to-maintain features in a surprisingly small area.

Adding character

Water and rocks: *Potted ponds make ideal features in small gardens, as do rockery beds and scree and sink gardens.*

Below: *A large group of shallow, terracotta containers planted with a collection of saxifrages makes a striking feature arranged on a gravel path in a sunny spot. Rearrange them for a fresh look.*

Scented plants: *Grouped in containers by doorways or seats, or threaded throughout a sheltered garden, scented plants release delicious wafts of perfume as you walk around.*

Collections: *Try groups of bonsai plants in oriental pots attractively placed on raised staging, or herbs in a traditional geometric herb garden surrounded by dwarf box hedges.*

Furniture: *Themed garden furniture, for example, rustic in cottage gardens, modern in contemporary gardens, classic in traditional gardens.*

Period features: *Given a new look, features such as potted topiary, a fruit arch, carpet bedding, herb lawns or seats add character to any garden.*

Comfort: *Why not create a comfortable outdoor living area, complete with upholstered recliners, outdoor dining table and chairs, trolley, outdoor lighting, built-in barbecue, insect-repellent lamps and candles, plus, perhaps, a hot tub, swimming or plunge pool?*

Right: *A classical statue on an imposing pedestal not only adds height to this traditional setting, but also looks great against the dark green background. The statue is essential to the whole impact of the formal vista edged with clipped box and yew.*

Focal points: *Use architectural features, such as a seat, sundial or statue in a niche in a wall, to draw the eye; use them at the end of a path, in the center of a formal geometric-shaped garden or under an arbor. Use arches to frame a beautiful view.*

OTHER GARDEN SCHEMES

In many ways, a large garden is more difficult to design than a small one. There is all that space to fill. The way to tackle it is to divide the plot into new, more manageable areas and then to deal with each one in turn. The areas should interconnect to form a logical whole. The same principle applies to long, narrow gardens; first, break up the length of the plot and get rid of that tunnel effect. Divide the garden into outdoor 'rooms', using screens or trellis covered in climbing plants, so that part of the garden is hidden from view. Or provide a special feature at the far end of the plot, which not only shortens the focal length of the overall view, but also gives an impression of width. Avoid straight lines, especially down the length of the site, which only emphasize the boundaries. Trees are always useful for making a tall, natural screen to disguise the true length of the garden.

Gardening on a grand scale

The general scheme for this large country house is simple but sophisticated. A large water feature provides spectacular views and reflections from the house, and an extensive decked leisure area overlooks the water.

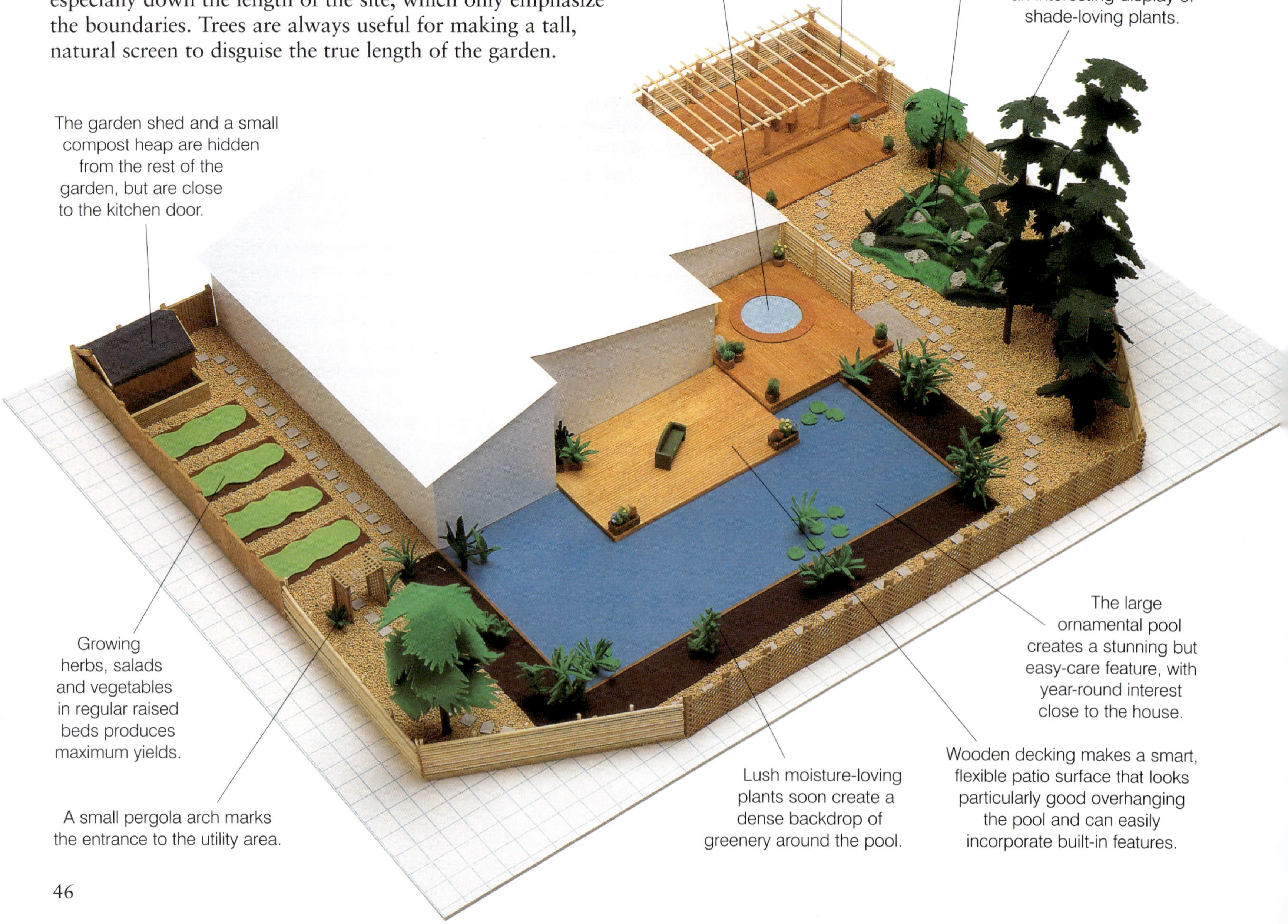

Coping with a narrow garden

The aim is to distract from the long straight lines of the plot. Curvaceous flower borders are broken on one side by an informal pool and stepping stones follow a random course across the grass to a semi-circular patio with a gazebo.

A paved area provides a clean, dry approach to the house and somewhere to sit in all seasons.

A low wall makes a boundary between patio and garden without obscuring the view.

Stepping stones in a pleasant grassy area have a far less formal appearance than a path.

An informal, kidney-shaped pond includes lush water plants with dramatic foliage shapes.

A small specimen tree creates a focal point, as well as height and seasonal interest.

An ornamental gazebo on the second patio adds interest where most gardens have run out of inspiration.

Designer tips

Perspective tricks: *Make a short garden look longer by making the lawn wider close to the house than at the far end, or by using bright colors close to the house and blue, purple and misty mauves in the distance. Perspective trellis uses a series of receding shapes to make the center seem to diminish into the distance. Use this strategy for adding detail to flat walls, or to 'frame' statuary or a mirror.*

Mirrors: *These make a small garden seem larger or reflect light into dark areas to 'open them up' visually. Make sure that they are securely fixed and framed for safety. Position them in such a way that it will quickly be obvious that they are mirrors, or where overhanging shrubs or beds or seats in front of them prevent visitors accidentally walking into them.*

Below: *This brick arch, flanked by trimmed box trees, is reflected in a mirror that creates a superb impression of light and space.*

Above: *A rock garden and pool feature work well together. Here, tiny plants have been tucked into soil pockets between the rocks.*

'Borrowed' landscape: *Make a small garden look bigger by cutting a gap in the boundary hedge to 'frame' a view over the surrounding countryside.*

Garden rooms: *Divide L-shaped or even more eccentric-shaped plots into a series of garden rooms to make them easier to manage. Such shapes are much easier to divide up in this way, as their natural shape lends itself to division much more easily than a normal rectangular plot.*

Levels: *Suggest changing levels in a flat garden with evergreen hedges or borders at varying heights to create a more rolling landscape, plus visual tricks such as 'steps' inclined at an angle into flat ground.*

Contour planting: *Use irregular-shaped island beds cut into natural hollows to landscape a 'difficult', unevenly sloping site to best advantage.*

Sloping sites: *Terrace a steeply sloping site and develop each 'layer' as a separate garden with its own character. As you go up, each layer will provide less shelter and faster drainage, so will suit different plants.*

MAKING A ROCK GARDEN

Rock gardens are raised beds created to provide extremely well-drained conditions for plants from a mountainous native habitat. A thick layer of gravel and broken rocks on the surface of the bed allows fleshy plants to rest on a fast-drying surface to avoid rotting, and a high proportion of gravel in the soil beneath means that surface water runs away fast. However, a well-planned rock garden should not become bone dry in summer. The ideal rock garden soil is well drained but moisture retentive. This is easily achieved by mixing topsoil, gritty sand and gravel, and a low-nutrient form of organic matter (such as peat or coir) in roughly equal quantities. Planting rock plants in early spring gives them some time to establish before summer sun dries out the top of the bed too much. However, plants can be put in even when in flower, provided you water them for the first few months. Relatively few rock plants tolerate searing hot sun all day - most prefer a situation that gives them a few hours of shade cast by nearby rocks or bigger plants.

1 Before adding a new plant to a bed, scrape away the gritty topdressing from the planting site using a narrow-bladed trowel.

2 Dig a hole slightly larger than the pot in which the new plant is growing. Put the excess soil in a bucket to keep the area clean.

3 Knock the plant out of its pot and plant it. Break up the soil at the base of the hole so that new roots can grow into the ground.

4 Replace the gritty topdressing around the plant. Leave an area of clear gravel around distinct groups of plants to show them off.

PART THREE

GARDEN PROJECTS

There is more to creating a garden than simply planting things. Boundary walls, steps and hard surfaces are all major elements that have both a functional and a decorative purpose. Seating and simpler features, such as a bird table or wooden planter, add the finishing touches that give a garden its own character.

MAKING A PATIO

The quickest way to lay a garden path or patio surface is to bed paving slabs on a sand bed. Most slabs are made in shades of buff, red and gray; the surface texture may be smooth, textured, riven to resemble natural split stone, or embossed in imitation of stone setts or paving bricks. Some paving ranges also offer interlocking hexagonal slabs with two types of half hexagon for finishing off the edges of the paved area, and slabs with a quadrant cutout in one corner; four of these placed together create a circular opening to fit round a tree or other feature. Start by marking out the site with pegs and string lines so that you can take accurate measurements and draw up a simple scale plan. This will be invaluable for estimating materials and is a useful guide if you intend to create a pattern using slabs of different colors. Then clear and excavate the site, provide an edge restraint to stop sand from leaching out and start laying the slabs.

1 Unless your subsoil is firm, you will need to spread and compact a layer of solid material over the site. Gravel or crushed rock is ideal. The material used here is 'scrapings', taken from the surfaces of roads under repair.

2 Excavate the site to the required depth, level the subsoil and spread a 3in(75mm)-thick layer of the filling. Compact it with a length of fence post. It is vital to ensure that the foundation is firm and stable before you start.

Use wooden pegs to support the edge restraint.

5 The paving should have a slight fall (away from the house if this is adjacent) to help rainwater to run off it. Use a batten and spirit level to check the direction of fall.

6 Start by laying just four slabs in one corner of the site, setting small wooden spacers between adjacent slabs to ensure an even gap for the pointing later on.

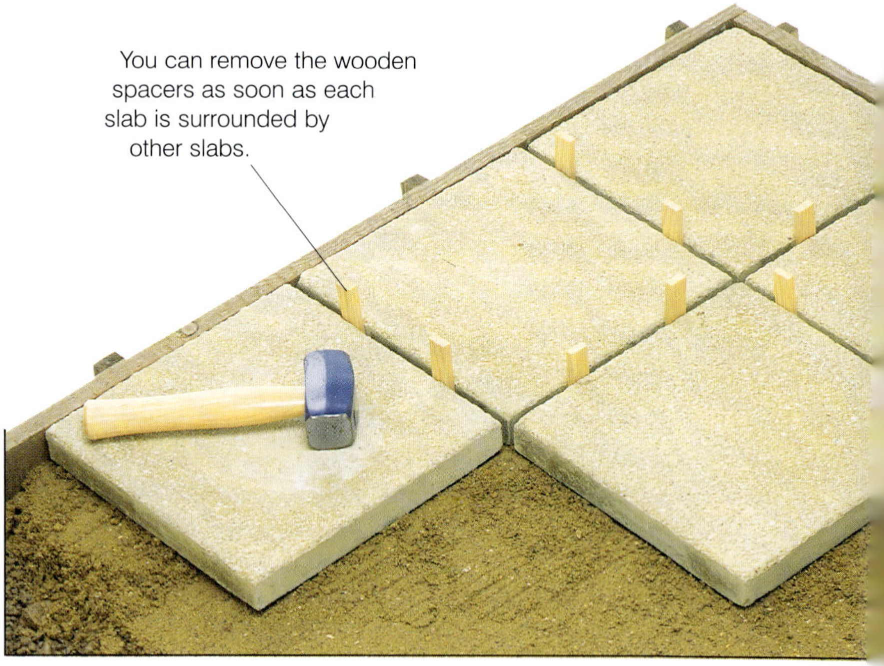

You can remove the wooden spacers as soon as each slab is surrounded by other slabs.

7 Continue laying slabs across the site, kneeling on a board on the sand bed if you cannot reach right across the area from the edge. Use the handle of a club hammer to tap each slab into place before laying the next one. Check the fall regularly as you work with a spirit level and straightedge.

PEBBLES AND COBBLES

Pebbles and cobbles introduce shape and texture to paving. Bed them in mortar if people are to walk on them or if they are to line a water course. In decorative areas in flower beds they can be loose laid.

3 Shovel out the bedding sand on top of the compacted filling and rake it out evenly to a depth of 1-2in(25-50mm) across the site. If you are laying slabs over a large area, arrange for a bulk delivery of sand to the site.

4 If you have edge restraints, use a notched batten to level the sand so its surface is just less than the slab thickness below the top of the edging. Most slabs are about 1in(25mm) thick, although some terracotta tiles are thinner.

8 Remove the last spacers and spread some fine sand across the surface. Brush it well into all the joints with a soft-bristled broom, then sweep off the excess. Kiln-dried sand is ideal for this purpose.

Laying brick pavers on sand

Above: *Fix the edge restraints, place the border pavers and then build up the pattern - here a herringbone one - using a string line as a guide as you work.*

Right: *A square arrangement of slabs and pavers has a pleasing symmetry. Experiment with other patterns on paper first.*

Laying slabs on mortar

Left: *To give the slabs adequate support, place the mortar on a concrete base in a square beneath the edges of the slab and add more mortar beneath the center. Use a fairly sloppy mortar mixture so that it is easy to spread beneath the slabs.*

Laying crazy paving on mortar

1 Set the first corner stone in place and then complete one edge of the area, including the next corner stone. Then start building up the jigsaw effect with large and smaller stones.

2 Allow the mortar bed to harden overnight. Fill and point the joints. Draw the trowel point along the joint to leave a ridge and two sloping bevels. This will help it shed rainwater.

WOODEN DECKING

Wooden decking is a natural alternative to hard paving in both formal and informal gardens. The raw material is widely available and costs broadly the same as paving (unless you choose an exotic hardwood instead of softwood). It is much easier to cut to size than paving slabs or blocks, quickly blends in with its surroundings as it weathers and is more forgiving to walk or sit down on than hard paving. The only disadvantages of wooden decking are that it will need some occasional maintenance work and that it can be slippery in wet weather. Make sure that all the sawn joists and planed planks for the decking have been pretreated with preservative and apply a preservative stain to the completed structure, paying special attention to any cut ends you have sawn during construction. To keep the decking clear of damp ground and reduce the incidence of rot, set the joists on bricks, ideally with a pad of damp-proof membrane or roofing felt between bricks and joists. Clear the ground beneath the decking and apply a long-term weedkiller before you begin. Since wood is easy to cut to size and shape, you can create any number of decorative designs. Carefully work out the design on paper first, adjusting the spacing between the planks to ensure that a whole number will fit the area you want to cover. You can create chevron and diamond patterns by reversing the direction of the planking on adjacent areas of the decking.

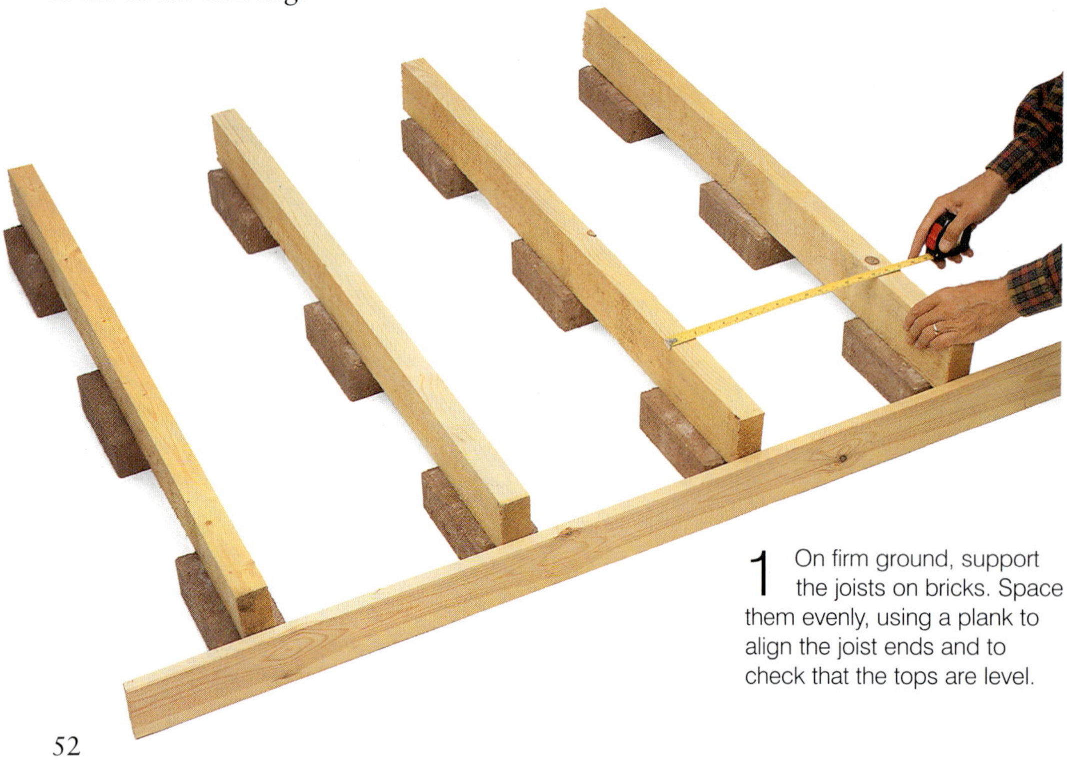

1 On firm ground, support the joists on bricks. Space them evenly, using a plank to align the joist ends and to check that the tops are level.

2 Cut a fascia board to match the width of the decking and secure it to the joist ends with galvanized nails. Fix a batten across the tops of the joists at the other end of the decking.

3 Cut the first plank to length, position it across the joists so that its front edge projects over the fascia board and forms a projecting nosing. Secure it to each joist with two nails.

4 Leave a slight gap between adjacent planks so that rainwater can drain freely. Set a slim batten against the first plank, then position the second plank against the batten.

5 Secure the plank to each joist with two galvanized nails. You can use a string line as a guide to help you align the nail heads across the decking. Punch the nail heads just below the wood surface.

Hide the supports with pebbles or low-level planting.

6 The completed decking is an attractive feature in its own right. There is no limit to the size and shape of wooden decking you can create.

Finishing touches

Above: *Treat the decking with a clear or colored preservative stain or wood dye to improve its resistance to rot and insect attack.*

Above: *Butt-join planks as necessary over the center line of a joist. Sand the cut ends first to prevent injury from splinters.*

Decking tiles

You can buy small, preassembled wooden decking tiles made from preservative-treated softwood. Simply lay these on supporting joists to create whatever area of decking you require.

1 The tiles have closely spaced slats held together by two support battens. Make up a framework of preservative treated joists to support the tiles.

2 Space the joists to allow the tiles to meet along the center line of each joist and lay in the individual tiles in the desired pattern.

3 Nail through the slats into the joists. For invisible fixings, drive screws between the slats through the support battens.

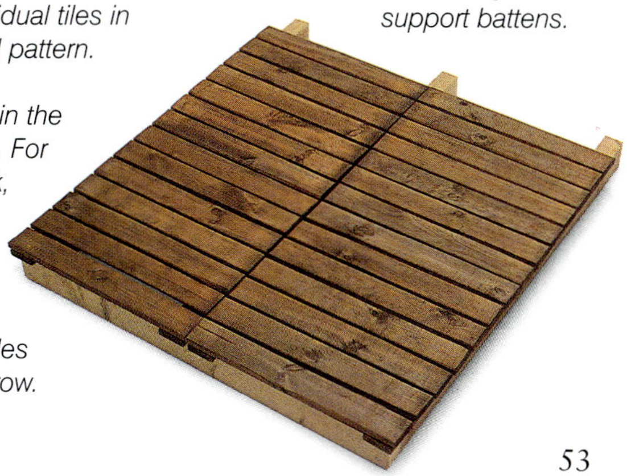

4 These tiles run in the same direction. For a checkerboard look, rotate alternate tiles through 90°. Or lay adjacent rows of tiles with the slats in one row at right angles to those in the next row.

GRAVEL IN THE GARDEN

A path or other area of gravel can be an attractive feature in any garden. True gravel is available in a range of mixed natural-earth shades that look particularly good when wet. You can also buy crushed stone, which is rough-edged rather than smooth, in a range of colors. Both are relatively inexpensive to lay, but do have several practical drawbacks. They need some form of edge restraint to prevent the stones straying onto lawns or into flower beds. They need regular raking and weeding to keep them looking good. They can attract dogs and cats, who find them ideal as an earth closet. And lastly, pushing a laden wheelbarrow along a gravel path is very hard work! If you do choose gravel, work out carefully how much material to order. Decorative aggregates are sold in small carry-home bags, weighing from 55 to 110lbs(25 to 50kg), and by volume in large canvas slings or in loose loads that are delivered to your door. You will need a bulk delivery for all but the smallest areas. A cubic yard of gravel weighs well over a ton, and will cover an area of about 12sq yds to a depth of about 3in(75mm); in metric terms a cubic metre weighs about 1.7 tonnes and will cover just over 13sq m to the same depth.

1 Excavate the area until you reach solid subsoil. Set out preservative-treated boards around the perimeter of the excavated area and drive in stout corner pegs.

2 Secure the boards to the pegs with galvanized nails. Add more pegs at 3ft(1m) intervals all round the area to prevent the boards from bowing out later on.

4 To form a firm base for the gravel, cover the membrane with a layer of crushed rock or fine hardcore. You will need at least 2in(50mm) of rock on firm subsoil, more if it is soft.

5 Compact the base layer by running a heavy garden roller over it. Fill in any hollows and roll it again until you no longer leave any footprints in the surface. Thorough preparation prevents sinking in the future.

6 Taking care not to disturb the compacted base layer, spread out the gravel or decorative stone. Fill the area up to the level of the perimeter boards.

3 The best way of discouraging weeds from growing up through a gravel path is to put down a porous membrane (normally used to line plant containers) over the subsoil.

7 Level the gravel with a rake. Draw a wooden straightedge along the tops of the perimeter boards to identify high spots or hollows. Rake again.

Below: This gravel path meanders its way between neat miniature hedges and summer plants such as purple-leaved *Heuchera*.

A gravel walkway with brick patterns

You can mix smooth paving materials, such as slabs or block pavers, with gravel to create interesting and attractive patterns and contrasts. The blocks also help to keep the gravel off lawns and flower beds. This simple but effective path is cheap and easy to make. Rake the ground to remove any debris, level it and tread it down. Cover the compacted earth with a good layer of moistened sand and flatten it

1 Lay a line of bricks from side to side, level with the side edges. Pavers set on edge are neater for the sides, but make them firm and level.

2 Fill the triangular spaces with shingle and tread it down gently so as not to push the edging bricks out of line before it has settled.

***Below:** Edge this simple but effective formal path with suitable plants. The path is cheap and easy to make and there is no need to cut the bricks.*

BRICK WALLS

Bricks are a good choice for outdoor building projects, being relatively inexpensive, widely available and supplied in standard sizes and in a wide range of colors and textures. Apart from choosing a brick for its looks, there are two other important factors to consider: its quality and its type. Bricks used in the garden must obviously be weatherproof, so check that you buy at least ordinary quality bricks or, better still, special quality. The former are durable enough for most jobs but will not withstand severe exposure to the weather. As far as brick type is concerned, the choice lies between *commons* and *facing* bricks. You can use so-called commons wherever the appearance of the brickwork does not matter, but facings are the better choice for projects where looks are as important as performance. Brickwork gets its strength from the way the bricks in each course interlock, a process known as bonding. The simplest brick-laying bond, stretcher bond, is used in walls 4in(100mm) thick, and is created by offsetting the bricks in each course by half their length. Such a wall is not very strong, however, and should not be more than about 21in(530mm) or seven bricks high unless reinforcing piers are incorporated to strengthen the structure. For walls higher than this you should use brickwork 8½in(215mm) thick, and there are several established alternative methods of arranging the bonding in walls built in this way. Lay some of the bricks end-on as headers so that they pass right through the wall and bond the whole structure together. You can build a free-standing wall in this way to a height of 4ft 9in(1.45m) or 19 bricks without piers, and to 6ft(1.8m) or 24 bricks if the wall has piers at roughly 10ft(3m) centers. The result is a strong, stable and attractive wall.

1 Most garden brickwork will involve turning corners. Draw the building line on the foundation strip in chalk and use a square to mark a right angle at each corner.

2 Use a mortar mix of 1 part cement, 1 part lime or liquid plasticizer and 5 parts building sand. Spread a generous bed of mortar on the foundation strip.

4 Butter a generous wedge of mortar onto the end of the next and each subsequent brick before positioning it. This will abut the brick that is already in place.

5 To turn a corner in stretcher-bond brickwork, place the next brick at right angles to the first one and tamp it down so it is level with and square to its neighbor.

8 As you place each brick and tamp it down into its mortar bed, use the edge of your trowel to trim off excess mortar from the joint on both faces of the wall. Hold the trowel with its blade flat to the wall as you trim off the mortar. Scoop up the mortar droppings to keep the site tidy.

3 Set the first brick on the mortar bed. Tamp it down with the handle of a club hammer and check that the brick is level in both directions. A spirit level is an invaluable aid to ensure that each course of bricks is truly level and the face of the wall is truly vertical.

6 Complete the first course by adding bricks end to end. Start the second course with a corner brick vertically above the corner brick in the course below.

7 Complete the second course. Repeat the layout in the first two courses to build up the wall. Check levels with a spirit level and straightedge laid across the wall.

9 After completing between four and six courses, point the joints, including the one at the bottom, before the mortar can harden off. Use a pointing trowel to form a sloping weathered joint.

BRICK PIERS

Free-standing walls must be strong enough to withstand strong winds and accidental impacts. You can do this up to a point by increasing the wall's thickness, but if this is not practical, incorporate brick piers at intervals to provide reinforcement. These are generally twice the wall thickness and are used at the ends of the wall, at corners and at intervals of 10ft(3m) along the length of the wall. Piers may be visible from one side of the wall; substantial ones from both sides.

Double thickness walls

ENGLISH WALL BOND

For added strength and stability, this walling bond has alternate courses laid in running (stretcher) bond and header bond; in other words, one course is laid with the bricks arranged face out, followed by a course laid with the brick ends exposed.

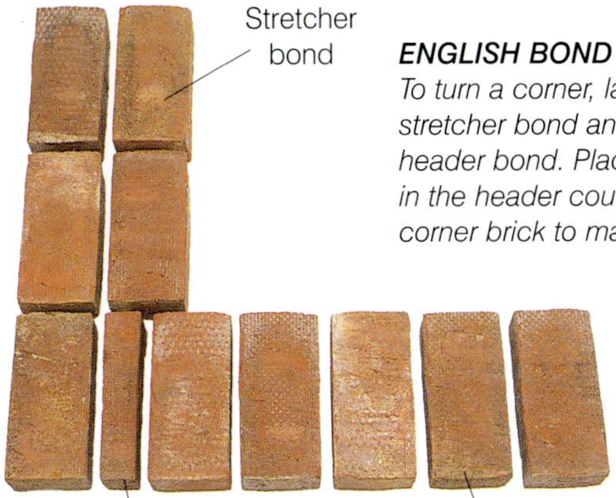

ENGLISH BOND - LAYER A

To turn a corner, lay one section in stretcher bond and the return one in header bond. Place a queen closer in the header course next to the corner brick to maintain the pattern.

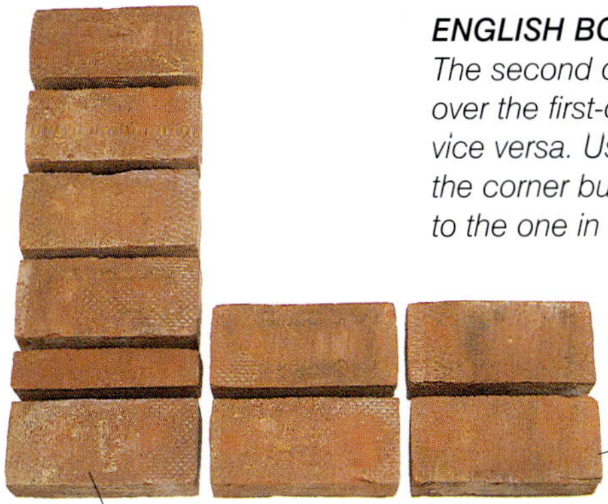

ENGLISH BOND - LAYER B

The second course has stretchers over the first-course headers and vice versa. Use a queen closer at the corner but lay it at right angles to the one in the course below.

Below: *As the wall builds up, the design of the alternating stretchers and headers becomes clear.*

BUILDING A SCREEN WALL

Brick and stone provide a solid structure that is ideal for boundary walls, but there may be situations where you would prefer an open screen, perhaps to surround a patio without cutting out too much sunlight or to conceal an eyesore. Pierced screen walling blocks are one option. These square blocks are easy to build up into a see-through screen that you can either leave to weather naturally or decorate with masonry paint. The blocks are a standard 11⅜in (290mm) square, so they build up into a regular 11¾in (300mm) grid with a ⅜in(10mm) thick mortar joint and are usually 3⅝in(90mm) thick. Since you cannot cut them down, any wall you build with them must be an exact multiple of 11¾in(300mm) in length and height. You can use the blocks on their own to create a complete screen, building up end, corner and intermediate piers with specially shaped pilaster blocks that are sized so that three match the height of two walling blocks. As an alternative, you can build areas of blockwork into solid brick or stone walls as decorative infill panels. As the blocks are simply stack-bonded in vertical columns instead of having an interlocking bond like brickwork, a wall more than about two courses high is inherently very weak and could be toppled by high winds.

1 Set the first pilaster block in place on a mortar bed. This one has one recessed face. Set a spirit level on the block to check that it is level in both directions. Tamp it down gently if necessary.

2 Butter mortar onto one edge of the first block, rest it on the mortar bed and lower it into the recess in the pilaster block. Mortar the edge of the next block and position it against the first one.

4 Add the third pilaster block to build up the end pier to 24in (610mm). This is the maximum height you can achieve without internal reinforcement rods. Fill the central cavity with mortar.

5 Add the second course of blocks on top of the first, checking that the blocks align and that the mortar courses are of even thickness. Trim off excess mortar and point the joints neatly.

6 If the wall is rising no higher than two courses, it needs no additional reinforcement. Simply spread a layer of mortar on top of the wall and pier blocks, ready for the pier caps and coping stones.

3 Build up the end pier by adding the next pilaster block. Use a spirit level to check that the block is level in both directions and also truly vertical. Trim off the excess mortar between the blocks.

As screen walling blocks are relatively fragile, tamp them down close to the corner so that the force of the blow is transmitted downwards through solid material.

7 Set the pier cap in place first, checking that it is centered on the pier blocks. Then position the first length of coping, butting it up to the pier cap. Tamp it down gently so that it is perfectly level.

Expanding upwards and outwards

You can buy special pilaster blocks for building up corners, intermediate piers and three-way piers where one wall meets another at right angles. All these blocks are 8in(200mm) high. Two wall blocks exactly match the height of three pier blocks, so a wall with pier blocks must therefore have an even number of courses.

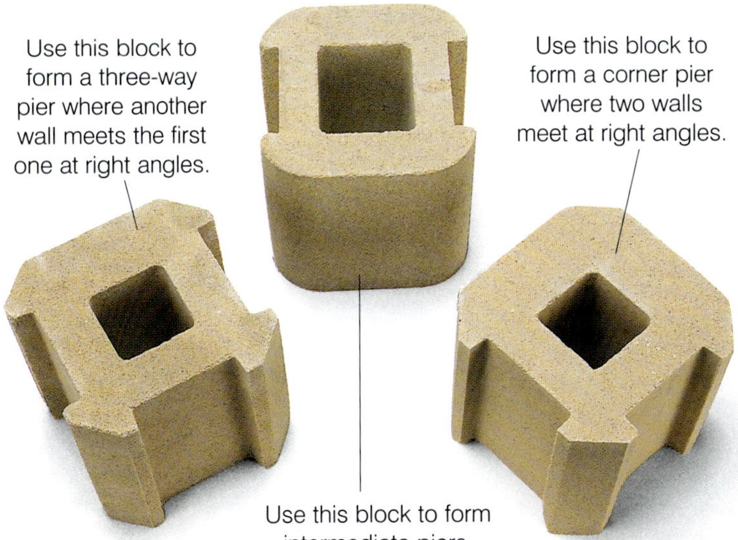

Use this block to form a three-way pier where another wall meets the first one at right angles.

Use this block to form a corner pier where two walls meet at right angles.

Use this block to form intermediate piers.

Building higher

1 Bond every other course of blocks to the piers with a strip of expanded metal mesh. Hook the strip over the reinforcing rod, press it down into the mortar bed and add more mortar on top before positioning the next course.

2 Add two more courses of walling blocks and two more pier blocks. If the wall is to be more than four courses high, allow the mortar to harden overnight before continuing as before.

Fixing in a fence post

To secure a bolt-down fence support, drill out each fixing hole to the required depth. Separate the bolt and washer from the anchor sleeve and push the sleeve into the fixing hole with the expanding plug at the bottom. Check that the support is level. Stand the fence support over the fixing holes and drop in the four bolts. Tighten each bolt firmly to expand the anchor fully.

1 Push the spike into the ground at the required post position. Place the striking block in the socket and start to hammer in the spike.

2 Regularly check that the spike is being driven in precisely vertically, by holding a spirit level against two adjacent faces of the socket in turn.

3 Drive the spike in with repeated hammer blows until the base of the socket is at ground level. Then hammer the post into the socket.

4 Use your spirit level again to check that the post is vertical. If it is not, try tapping the socket sideways to correct the post's tendency to lean.

FENCE PANELS

Whatever type of fencing you erect, you must ensure that the supporting posts are secure. Traditionally, part of the post was buried in the ground and anchored with a collar of concrete, but because the base of the post was below ground level, it eventually rotted, even if the wood was treated with preservative. On the other hand, a steel fence spike (and its close relative, the bolt-down fence support designed for use on hard-surfaced areas) keeps the vulnerable post completely above ground level. Both types have a square socket into which you fit the post end and come in sizes to accept 2in(50mm), 3in(75mm) and 4in(100mm) posts. Some have a socket with steel teeth that lock the post permanently in place as it is hammered in. Others have a bolt-operated clamping action reinforced by screws or nails. This system allows you to remove the post without disturbing the socket. Fence spikes are hammered into the ground, using a wood or resin striking block for protection. It is vital that the spike remains vertical as it is driven in; underground stones can deflect it, making this type of fixing unsuitable for rocky soils. In this situation, use a shorter spike designed for concreting in. To secure fence supports to concrete or other solid masonry bases, use expanding metal anchors, which allow the support to be removed if necessary in the future.

1 On low panels, nail or screw U-shaped metal fixing clips to the inner face of the post near the top and bottom. Add a third clip halfway up for full-height panels.

2 Support the fence panel on bricks or wood to hold it clear of the ground. Slide the edge of the panel into place against the post. The clips will hold it upright.

3 Site the next fence post close to the first panel, allowing clearance for the clips. Make sure that the fence spike is vertical and on line as you drive it in.

4 Attach the fence clips to the second post, level with the first. Stand the post in its socket and hammer or clamp it into place. Nail through the fixing clips.

Secure the clip to the panel with galvanized or other rustproof nails. If you have access to the other face of the fence, drive in another nail through the clip from that side, too.

Below: Remove the support blocks after fixing each panel in place. Keep soil away from the base of the panels to prevent them from rotting.

Building a picket fence

Picket, or paling, fences are made up as separate panels by nailing precut pickets to two or three horizontal rails, which are then fixed to their supporting posts so that the lower ends of the pickets are held clear of the ground. They are usually about 3ft(900mm) high and commonly used to fence front gardens, where appearance is a more important consideration than high security.

1 Use a spacer to set the distance between pickets. Leave a gap between the first picket and the post; check that the picket is square to the rails.

2 Leave the spacer in place as you drive in the nails to ensure that each picket is parallel with the previous one. A base-board keeps the pickets level.

3 Support the completed panel on blocks between the posts. Nail the rails to the posts. Their ends should align with the center of the post. For stronger panels, use screws.

Below: *Always be sure to use wood that has been pretreated with preservative, since the exposed endgrain is vulnerable to rot. Microporous paint or stain allows the wood to breathe.*

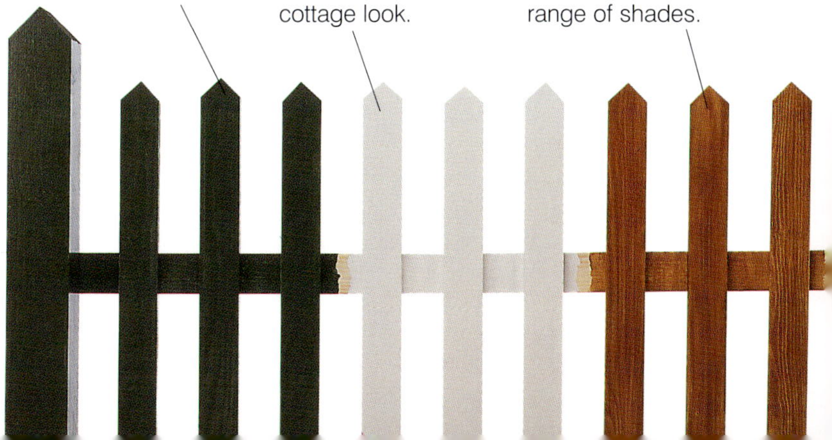

A colored stain can match your garden design.

White paint has a traditional cottage look.

Solvent- and water-based stains are available in a wide range of shades.

BUILDING BRICK STEPS

If your garden slopes steeply and is terraced, you will need to construct steps for access from one level to the next. These are more than simply functional; a well-designed flight of steps can be an important visual element in the overall landscaping plan. Construct them from materials that complement those used elsewhere in the garden for walls and paved surfaces. Bricks have a neat, formal look; decorative stone walling blocks give a softer appearance. Paving slabs are ideal for forming the treads. Where you are linking two terraced areas, you can design the steps in a number of ways. The flight can descend at right angles to the wall or be built parallel with it - often a better solution where one level is higher than the other or where space is restricted on the lower level. A rectangular flight is the simplest to build, but you could create a series of semicircular steps instead. If the structure is more than two or three steps high, tie the structure to the wall against which it is being built to prevent the two from parting company if there is any movement of the subsoil. Use a process called toothing in, which involves removing a brick from alternate courses of the terrace wall so that one end of the corresponding whole brick in the side walls of the steps can be mortared into the structure.

1 The first step is made up of two courses of bricks laid on a suitable foundation. Start the second course with a half-brick to maintain the stretcher bond and complete it with whole bricks. Check all levels.

2 Build up internal supporting walls to carry the rest of the structure. You can use old bricks for this, and leave the vertical joints unpointed.

3 Using a spirit level at every stage, build up the brickwork for the second tread on top of the side and supporting walls. Add two more courses of internal brickwork to support the edges of the treads on the second step.

Ideally, risers should be no more than 7in (180mm) high - two bricks plus a paving slab is ideal.

CUTTING BRICKS

If you need to cut a brick to size, start by marking the cutting line on the brick and score it all round with the tip of a brick bolster (bricklayer's chisel). Place the brick on a bed of sand and drive the chisel with blows from a club hammer to break the brick at the marked cutting position. The sand helps to spread the impact along the cutting line.

4 Place the treads on the first step. Trowel on a generous mortar bed, lower the slabs into place and tamp them down so that they have a slight fall towards the front edge to help drainage and prevent puddles that could freeze.

5 Repeat the process for the second step. Then fill and point the joints between the pairs of slabs, and also the gaps at the rear of each tread. This two-step flight will use the face of the terrace wall as the final riser.

6 Complete the flight by bedding two slabs in place at the top of the flight, with their edges just projecting beyond the face of the terrace wall.

For a good grip in wet or wintry weather, choose slabs with a textured surface for steps.

Rustic steps

1 Mark out the site with pegs, string lines and one of the riser logs as a width guide. Cut away the turf from the bank between the two string lines.

2 Lay the bottom riser across the slope and secure it with two stout pegs driven vertically into the ground at each side.

3 Position the next log riser and part-drive one fixing peg. Use a batten and spirit level to position the riser accurately.

4 Nail edging planks of sawn softwood to the sides of the tread. Make sure these are also treated with preservative.

5 Peg and nail the other risers. With edging planks in position on the first tread, fill in the space with gravel or bark.

Each log is positioned so that its underside is level with the top edge of the log below it.

6 Complete the flight by adding edging planks to the sides of the other treads. Then fill and compact with gravel or bark.

SEATING IN THE GARDEN

No garden should be without some sort of seating, be it formal or informal. One inexpensive, permanent and thief-proof solution is to build your own, using bricks, mortar and preservative-treated wood. This simple bench consists of two piers of brickwork and a slatted seat, screwed to the masonry to create a sturdy, good-looking, surprisingly comfortable garden structure. The seat can be left with a natural finish (protected by clear preservative), or can be stained or painted if you prefer a colored finish. You can build it directly on any existing paved or concrete surface or set it on two paving slabs on some well-rammed subsoil to provide a stable base.

1 Decide on the width of the bench and build up the two piers in the same way. Use a spirit level on a timber straightedge to check that the two piers are level with each other.

Build up the piers, positioning two bricks side by side and a third at right angles to them in each course. Check that each face is truly vertical.

2 Cut two seat support blocks from 2in(50mm) square softwood, slightly longer than the depth of the piers. Fix one to the outside face of each pier with screws and wallplugs.

3 Cut two seat edge slats to length and attach them to the ends of the support blocks. The overlap at each end helps to conceal the support blocks when the bench is completed.

4 Screw on the first seat slat so that it rests on top of the front edge slat and forms a neat angle. Use a spacer slat on edge to position the next slat. Countersink all the screw heads.

Choose bricks that match those used to build your house if you plant to site the seat close by - say on a patio.

5 Continue fixing the slats to the seat support blocks, using your spacer slat to ensure even gaps. Use one predrilled slat as a pattern for drilling the screw holes in the others.

6 With the final slats screwed in place, the seat is ready for use. Apply two coats of clear preservative or use paint or stain if you prefer a colored finish to the natural look.

Round off the edges of the slats with sandpaper to prevent splinters.

If you are using slabs as supports, compact the subsoil well and bed them onto some sand so that you can level them easily.

A seat around a tree

1 Buying a prefabricated softwood tree seat avoids the need for some fairly complex carpentry. Before you assemble it, treat the seat with preservative wood stain that will not fade and is water-repellent.

2 Cut away the turf, compact the subsoil and lay a bed of sand in the excavation. Put each stone in position and tamp it down to get it level.

3 Stand the first prefabricated seat section in place on its stones, then offer up the second section. Raise or lower the stones slightly as necessary.

4 Thread the bolts, each with a washer on, through the predrilled holes. Add another washer before fitting the nut so that it does not bite into the wood. Tighten up well.

5 The assembled seat turns a bare tree trunk into an attractive garden feature. Seats are available in various sizes to enable you to match a range of tree diameters.

A WOODEN PLANTER

Planting in above-ground containers has many advantages. For a start, you can work from a standing rather than a kneeling position. Whatever you decide to plant is self-contained and weeds are easy to keep under control. You can move the container around if you wish, placing it in sunshine or shelter as necessary. Groups of containers can also be an ideal way of breaking up the featureless expanse of a large patio. You can use all kinds of containers, but wooden planters are some of the most versatile. You can make them in virtually any shape and size, from a slimline windowbox to a large ornamental square or rectangular display centerpiece, using the technique shown here. Tongued-and-grooved cladding is an ideal material for the planter's sides; you simply use as many planks as are necessary to give the height of container you want, and you can easily remove the tongue from the topmost planks to leave a neat square edge. Internal posts form the corners of the container, and the removable base panel sits on battens fixed to the inner face of the side walls. A series of drainage holes bored in the base panel allows the planter to drain freely in wet weather or after watering.

1 Decide on the dimensions of the planter you want to make and cut enough lengths of cladding to form the four sides. Sand the cut ends smooth to remove splinters.

2 Interlock and glue the planks to form each side. Use a hammer and an offcut to knock them tightly together. If glue oozes out, wipe it off with a damp cloth.

3 Make up the short ends of the planter first. Cut two corner posts for each end, then glue and nail the assembled side panels to the posts with the tongued edge uppermost.

4 The base of the planter will rest on slim battens glued and pinned to the inner faces of the side and end walls, flush with their bottom edges. Cut and fix the two battens to the assembled end walls of the planter first.

Cut and fix the support battens to the inner faces of the two long side panels, in the same way as described in step 4.

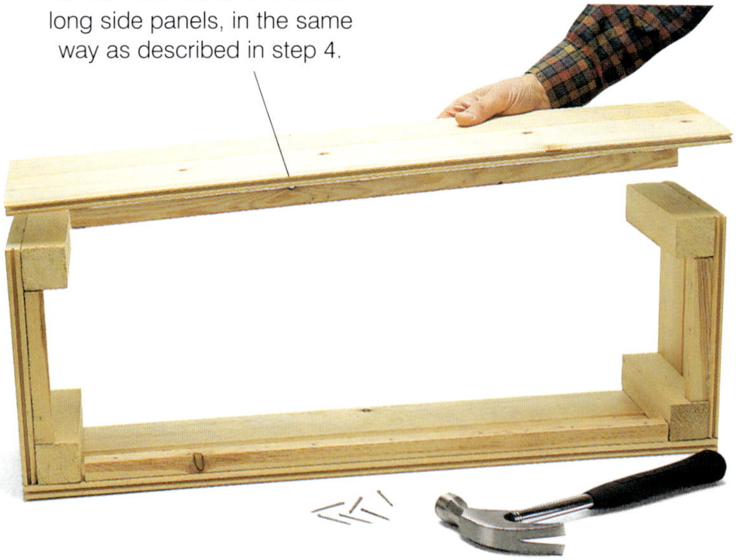

5 Place one long side wall on a flat surface and the two completed ends next to it. Measure the distance between the corner posts. Glue the side walls to the two end sections. Using just adhesive at this stage allows you to align the corner joints and check that the whole assembly is square.

6 When the glue has set, nail the side walls to the corner posts. Stand the planter upside down on a plywood sheet and draw round the internal profile of the planter walls to mark the outline of the base.

7 Drill a series of equally spaced holes in the base using a flat wood bit. Drill into scrap wood so that the edges of the holes do not splinter as the bit bursts through.

8 Drop in the base so that it rests on the support battens on the inner faces of the walls. Pin and glue it in place if you like.

9 To finish the top edges, cut down some narrow strips of cladding and glue the grooved edges to the exposed tongues.

10 If it was made from treated wood, you can leave the planter as it is. Otherwise, finish it with two coats of microporous paint or wood stain in the color of your choice.

A windowbox for spring

You can paint a basic wooden planter in a variety of ways, using preservative stains available in a wide range of colors. Stencil motifs and decorative wood moldings also add unusual, individual touches.

Left: *This smart red windowbox is made from tongue-and-grooved cladding, topcoated with high gloss burgundy red paint. The mainly red and yellow planting scheme brightens up dull winter days.*

A seaside windowbox

Left: *This wooden box has a strong seaside flavor. The wood was painted with blue emulsion, diluted down so that it just colored the wood like a stain, rather than masking it completely.*

The finished windowbox has been planted up with a selection of primroses, pansies, ivy and *Skimmia japonica* 'Rubella'.

BUILDING A COLD FRAME

A cold frame is a useful addition to any garden. It is basically a bottomless box with a glazed lid and is used like a miniature greenhouse to grow seeds and cuttings and to acclimatize tender plants that have been raised under cover before they are finally planted out in the garden. It can stand on a hard surface, such as a patio or path - the best idea if you intend to fill it with seed trays and plant pots - or can be placed directly on the soil so that you can plant things in it. You can buy ready-made cold frames, but making your own is a simple and satisfying project that allows you to tailor-make the frame to just the size you want. You can make the cold frame entirely from softwood, or build up the base in brickwork and add a wooden-framed lid. The lid can be glazed with glass, but plastic glazing materials are safer and easier to work with. Hinge it to the base so that you can open it during the day for ventilation and fit a simple catch to the front edge to keep it closed at night; strong winds could lift and damage it otherwise. If you want a larger planting and growing area than a single frame provides, simply add further bays to the basic structure as the need arises. Site the completed frame in a sunny position, ideally sheltered from the prevailing winds, and keep the lid clean to allow the maximum amount of sunlight to reach the plants inside. Cover it on cold nights.

1 Cut the planks that will form the front, back and sides of the frame to the desired length. Mark angled cutting lines on the two top side boards and cut carefully along them. Keep the saw vertical as you cut.

2 Cut front legs to the height of two full boards, plus the thinner end of the top side board. Drill holes in the boards. Screw the bottom two boards to one leg.

3 Interlock the grooved edge of the second full board over the tongue on the first board. Tap it down to close up the joint. Screw the board to the leg as before.

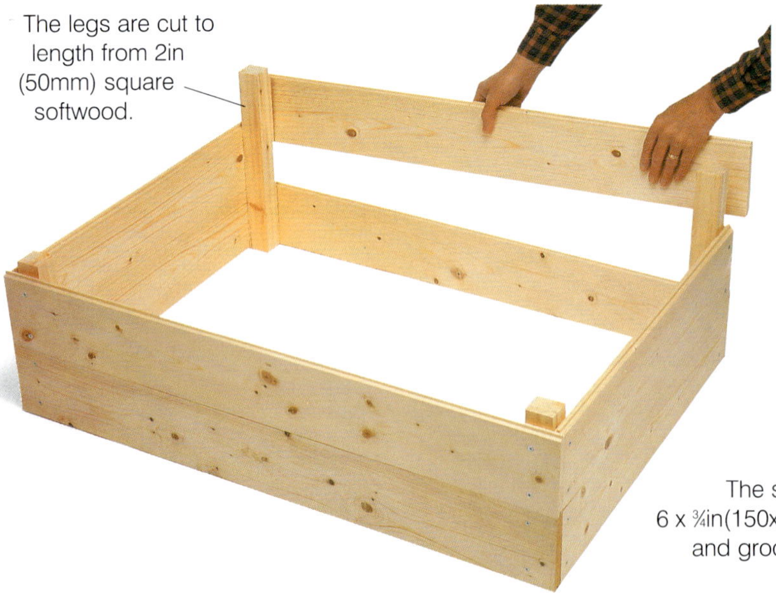

4 Cut the back legs to match the height of two full boards plus the thicker end of the top side board. Continue to build up the box; attach the second set of boards all round with screws.

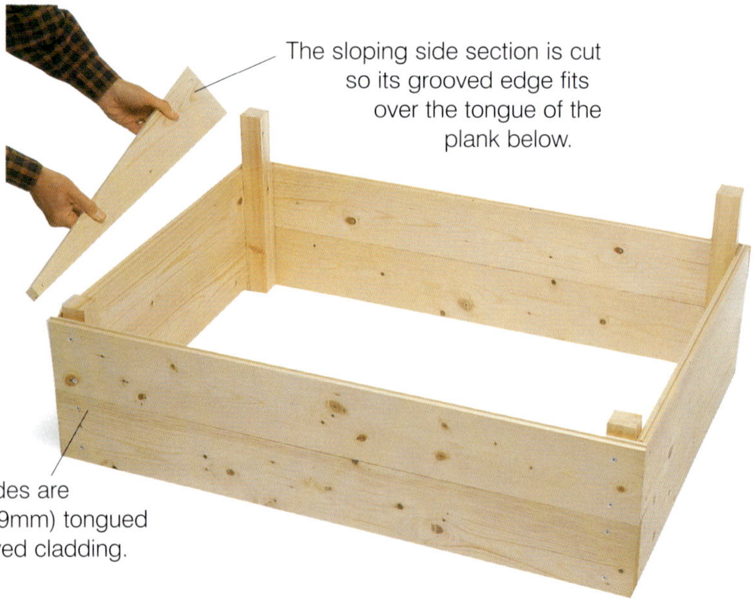

5 Offer up the two tapered top side boards, interlocking the tongued and grooved edges as before. Attach them to the legs with two screws at the back and one screw at the front.

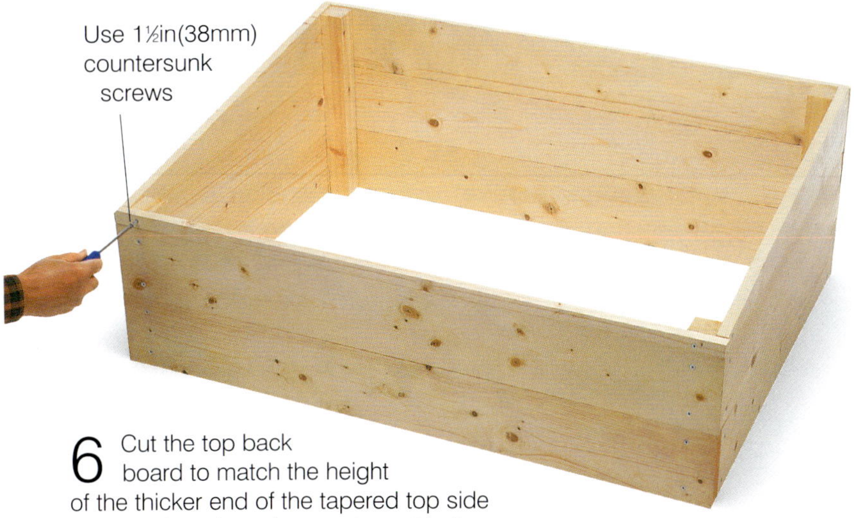

6 Cut the top back board to match the height of the thicker end of the tapered top side boards. Cut a board to create a strip the same height as the thinner end of the top side boards. Screw to the front legs to complete the base.

7 Treat the frame and lid with two coats of preservative stain and leave it to dry with the lid propped open. Check that the brand of wood stain you buy is not harmful to plants.

8 Complete the screw fixings all round and check that all the screw caps are snapped in place. Prop the lid open for ventilation.

Making the cold frame lid

1 Cut the components to size. The two side pieces overlap the cut ends of the front and back pieces. Drill and counterbore holes for fixing screws; glue and screw the frame together.

2 Lay the assembled frame over the glazing material - this is twin-wall polycarbonate, a tough and rigid translucent plastic sheet. Use a felt pen.

3 Glue and screw strips of 1x2in(25x50mm) wood to the sides of the lid to protect the edges of the glazing sheet and cover the corner fixing screws.

4 Position the hinges about 9in(230mm) in from the corners, and attach using ¾in (19mm) screws.

5 When the stain is dry, place the glazing sheet on the lid and drill and screw. Use plastic screw cups with snap-on covers.

NEST BOX AND BIRD TABLE

If you want to persuade birds to stay in your garden a little longer, try offering them some secure accommodation. All they require is a simple box that provides shelter from the elements and protection from predators. It needs a simple sloping roof to help shed rainwater and a hole in the front to let the parents in and the offspring out. The diameter of the hole will help to determine which species use the box, so select it to favor those that visit your garden most regularly. Fix it securely where it gives the birds a degree of privacy. It is best not to put it too near the house or close to where you feed birds in the garden. Once it is occupied, do not disturb it until the fledglings have flown. Then remove the lid and take out the old nest, which can harbor pests and will discourage future occupants.

For much of the year, birds visiting your garden will find their own food. However, a bird table will make it much easier for you to observe their feeding habits, and in winter it will provide a welcome boost to their food supply. It does not need to be an elaborate structure, just a simple platform with a raised lipping all round to stop food blowing off the surface. Ideally, set the post into a socket in the ground.

1 Using a plank of softwood 6in(150mm) wide, cut the four sides and the base of the nest box to length with a panel or tenon saw. Support the offcut as you complete each cut to prevent the wood from splintering.

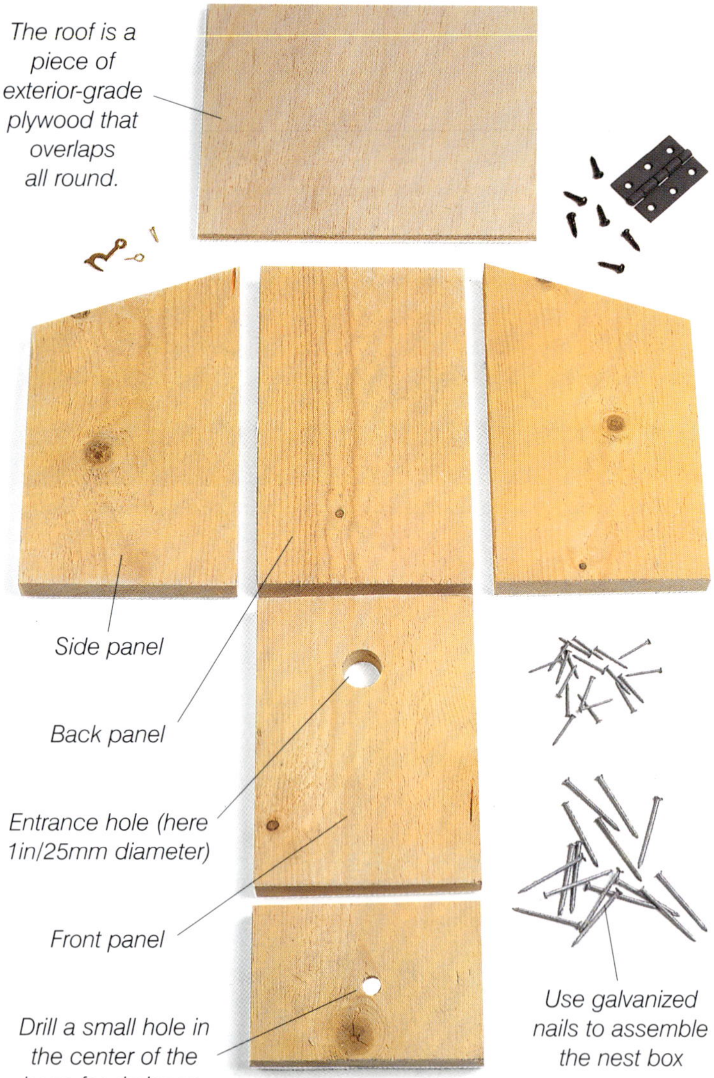

The roof is a piece of exterior-grade plywood that overlaps all round.

Side panel

Back panel

Entrance hole (here 1in/25mm diameter)

Front panel

Drill a small hole in the center of the base for drainage.

Use galvanized nails to assemble the nest box

2 Lay out the pieces before assembly. The box will be 8in(200mm) high at the front and 10in (250mm) at the back. Drill the entrance hole in the front panel about 2in(50mm) below the top edge.

3 Start by nailing the back wall to the edge of the base. Raise the underside of the base just above the bottom edge of the wall to protect its endgrain from rot.

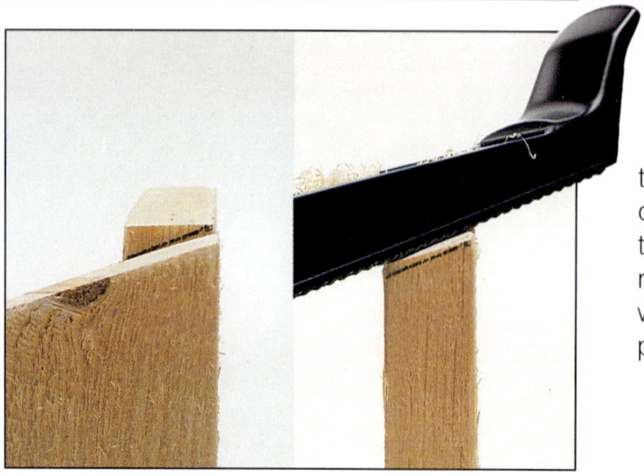

4 Chamfer off the top edge of the back wall to match the slope of the side walls. Use one of these to mark the angle, then remove the waste wood with a plane or planer file (as here).

5 Check the alignment of the tops of the side walls with the chamfered edge of the back wall. Nail on the sides; punch the nail heads in slightly to create a smooth finish.

6 Slide the front wall into place. Drive nails through the side walls into the front wall. Then nail it to the front edge of the base.

7 Screw an offcut to the rear wall of the box. You can then drive nails or screws through this support to fix the box in position.

8 Attach the roof to the support, using a rustproof hinge and screws. Check that these do not pierce the inside of the roof.

9 Use a hook-and-eye catch to keep the roof closed. Fit the eye to the underside of the roof and the hook to the side of the box.

10 Treat the outside with a water-based wood stain. Allow it to dry thoroughly before securing it in its chosen location.

Making a bird table

1 Cut the softwood lipping to length and fix it in place by pinning the plywood base to each length in turn. Leave the final length of lipping shorter than the other pieces.

2 Mark and drill holes in the base for the supporting blocks. Apply waterproof adhesive to one edge of each block and press it into place, aligning it with the pencil lines.

The table is made from exterior-grade plywood and 1x2in(25x50mm) softwood.

3 Turn the table base over and drive screws through each of the four clearance holes into the supporting blocks beneath.

4 Position the post between the two blocks and use a try square to check that the top and post are at right angles to each other. Drive two screws through each block into the post.

Put out a range of food. Clear debris by brushing it through the gap.

5 Give the table two coats of water-based preservative wood stain to protect it and make it easier to clean. Allow this to dry thoroughly before setting the table up in your garden.

HELPFUL HINTS

Tasks such as laying patios, mixing concrete, building brick walls and putting up fences can present quite a challenge. These tips make the job easier and improve the final result.

CUTTING STONES AND PAVING SLABS

Below: Score a deep cutting line across the slab. With the slab on a sand bed, cut it with a chisel and hammer. Move the chisel along until the slab splits.

Above: When laying crazy paving, you may need to break up a stone or improve the fit. Sandwich it between two stones and crack it cleanly with a firm hammer blow.

Concrete mixes

Use only ordinary Portland cement to make concrete. You can buy coarse sand and aggregate separately or ready-mixed as combined aggregate. The maximum aggregate size should not exceed ¾in (20mm).

Left: If you are using combined aggregates, mix one part of cement to five parts aggregate, measured by volume. Keep all materials dry before mixing them together.

Left: With separate sand and gravel, use 2½ parts of sand and 3½ parts of gravel to 1 of cement. Mix the ingredients and add water until the mix just holds its shape.

A pointing guide

If the pointing mortar stains the slab surface as you work, reduce the problem by using a guide - a plywood offcut with a slot cut in it to match the joint width. Fill the joints through the slot. Using a fairly dry mortar mix will help to prevent it spilling onto the slabs.

How many bricks will I need?

When it comes to estimating the number of bricks you will need to build a wall, use these figures as a guide: 50 bricks per sq yd (60 per sq m) of wall built in stretcher bond; 100 per sq yd (120 per sq m) for bonds such as English and Flemish where the finished wall is one brick thick. Add an extra five per cent to your quantities for breakages. The coloration of bricks can vary from batch to batch, so buy as many as you need in one go.

SIMPLE GUIDES FOR ACCURACY

Right: A builder's square helps to set out right angled corners accurately. Cut a triangle off the corner of a plywood offcut. The bigger the square the more accurate it will be, but keep it manageable for ease of handling.

Left: A simple gauge rod is a big help in ensuring even joints. Set out a row of bricks on their faces, ⅜in(10mm) apart. Hold a length of planed wood on top of the bricks and mark all the joint positions. Extend the pencil marks across the face of the gauge and onto one edge. Allow for a mortar joint at ground level.

Right: If you find it difficult to align nail heads by eye, pin a length of string between adjacent fence posts and use this as a nailing guide. This also ensures that the nails go into the center of the arris rail.

PART FOUR

SHRUBS AND TREES

Shrubs and trees are the heart of any garden and there are suitable plants for every type of soil, site and season. They represent superb value for money, since they live, grow and flower for many years, either in a border of their own or as a backdrop for a mixed planting of other shrubs and flowers, underplanted with bulbs.

SPRING-FLOWERING SHRUBS

Along with snowdrops and daffodils, early-flowering shrubs are one of the first signs of spring. Since there is little color in the garden so early, plant them together to form spring 'cameos' that stand out better in a landscape that is still looking winter-bleak. Later shrubs, such as forsythia, star magnolia *(Magnolia stellata)* and bridal wreath *(Spiraea* x *arguta)*, flower shortly after the new foliage emerges, giving a fresh green halo to the blooms. As spring proceeds, a succession of new shrubs opens in turn, giving the garden a new look from week to week. Make the most of this feature by including as many different types as possible. Spring shrubs are very versatile - most can be used in several different ways. Spectacular compact shrubs, such as star magnolia, make brilliant specimen plants; a single plant makes a great centerpiece for a small front garden, surrounded by grass. It can also be grown in a large tub in a courtyard or patio - magnolia needs shelter or the flowers do not last. Bridal wreath makes billowing white clouds that are useful for filling out the back of a border and invaluable for cutting to use in flower arrangements.

Above: Depending on the variety, shrubby cherries can either run randomly, spreading pink blossom through a border, like this *Prunus tenella* 'Fire Hill', or form specimen shrubs or small trees - like the Mount Fuji cherry *(Prunus incisa)*.

Right: *Chaenomeles japonica* can be grown either as a free-standing shrub or trained against a wall.

Viburnum

Viburnum bodnantense 'Dawn' has very fragrant, pale pink clusters of flowers that appear on the bare stems throughout winter.

Viburnum tinus is a popular, medium-sized evergreen shrub that produces white, perfumed flowers from late fall to early spring. It tolerates light shade.

Viburnum bodnantense 'Deben' has deeper pink flowers than 'Dawn'.

Viburnum tinus 'Eve Price' has pink buds that open to faintest pink-tinged, well-scented flowers.

PRUNING EARLY-FLOWERING SHRUBS

Early-flowering shrubs produce their best flowers on shoots that grew during the previous year. Prune them straight after flowering to give the plants the longest possible time in which to produce long, vigorous shoots for flowering in the following year. Cut back or remove the oldest branch systems and weak or dying shoots.

Below: Young viburnum plants may be naturally a bit straggly. A light trim before planting will encourage the plant to develop a dense, bushy shape. Cut off unwanted branches close to the base.

Above: Removing the old flowering wood of *Forsythia* opens up the shrub and encourages strong new shoots to grow. It keeps plants young and strong.

Magnolia

Magnolia hypoleuca 'Jane' is a relatively new hybrid with elegant dark buds that open to medium-sized mauve flowers.

Magnolia x *soulangeana* 'Burgundy' is a pink and mauve variety of this popular species, which normally has the palest pink-tinged, off-white flowers.

Magnolia x *soulangeana* 'Pickard's Sundew' has large, waterlily-like flowers.

Magnolia x *loebneri* 'Leonard Messel', a compact hybrid, is happy on slightly chalky soils.

Magnolia stellata remains compact and bushy; tolerates slightly chalky soils.

Magnolia stellata 'Rosea' is a good pink form of the star magnolia. Tolerates slightly chalky soils.

Above: *Ribes sanguineum* 'White Icicle' (left) is a new variety, with white flowers. Gold-leaved *R. sanguineum* 'Brocklebankii' (middle) is rather slow growing. *R. sanguineum* 'Porky's Pink' (right), also a new variety, has bright pink flowers.

Training chaenomeles against a wall

Start by spreading out the main stems and tie them to horizontal wires secured to wall nails. Wall-trained chaenomeles need regular tying in to keep them growing flat against their support. This will encourage side shoots that, with luck, will grow flush with the wall and can be trained in. Horizontal branches flower better than upright ones.

Right: *Tie in any shoots that are growing out over the wall. They will increase the branch structure and create extra flowering space. The aim is to create a well-shaped plant, full of flower.*

Left: *Immediately after flowering, shorten outward-growing shoots back to a few inches from the wall. Use sharp secateurs.*

Below: *Chaenomeles produces suckers from the base. Remove these from a wall-trained shrub because they spoil the shape.*

Choosing a good plant

A long, leggy plant will branch, if at all, from the ends of the shoots, giving a rather open sort of bush.

This specimen of *Chaenomeles* x *superba* 'Geisha Girl' is compact and branching freely from the base.

SUMMER SHRUBS

As the season progresses, the white, pink and yellow flowers of spring give way to the more varied and richer tones of summer. Summer shrubs range in size from huge dominant buddleia and lavatera - ideal for the back of a border - to medium-sized weigela and small mounds of potentilla that are ideal for the front row. Many summer shrubs look good planted with old-fashioned roses, such as the purple-leaved *Weigela florida* 'Foliis Purpureis' and hardy fuchsias; the latter flower until the end of summer and tolerate light shade under bigger shrubs. Or team mass-flowered summer shrubs, such as spiraea and beauty bush *(Kolkwitzia amabilis)*, with foliage shrubs, particularly those with colored leaves. Use big evergreen, summer-flowering shrubs, such as escallonia, for the backs of borders, as flowering hedges or 'garden dividers' since their year-round foliage helps give the garden structure, even out of season. Buying summer-flowering shrubs growing in pots from garden centers makes it possible to add plants in full flower to a border and see the effect immediately. By buying in flower, you can also check that the plant is a good flowering form and matches the description or photograph on the label. However, when planting in summer, remember that good soil preparation and frequent watering are vital, as new shrubs dry out quickly in hot weather.

Buddleia

1 In mid-spring, use a pruning saw to cut down the long, thick, woody, old stems to about 2ft(60cm) from the ground.

2 The best flowers appear at the tips of the young stems. Hard pruning brings them down to a height where you can see them.

Buddleia lindleyana 'Lochinch' grows 6ft(1.8m) high and 4ft(1.2m) across.

B. davidii 'Black Knight' is very tough and tolerant of most soils.

B. officinalis 'Pink Delight' has a good bright color.

B. d. 'Nanho Blue'. All the Nanho varieties grow to about 6ft(1.8m) in a single season.

Tree peonies

Right: *Paeonia suffruticosa.* The tree peonies have huge fragile flowers like crumpled tissue paper. They make striking large shrubs, useful in big borders, or as specimen plants in a sheltered spot. In exposed areas, they can be grown in large tubs in a conservatory to prevent the wind ruining the flowers.

Spiraea

Spiraea 'Shirobana' makes an open spreading shrub, growing to about 4ft(1.2m), with flat heads of pink-and-white flowers.

Cut *S. japonica* 'Candlelight' down almost to ground level each spring to maintain the large golden leaves.

S. japonica 'Magic Carpet' grows 18in(45cm) high and 24in(60cm) across. Prune it to 4in(10cm) in early spring.

Potentilla

These bushy, free-flowering plants grow in quite poor soils as long as they are well drained. Most do best in sun, although some red shades fade fast and prefer light shade.

Right: As soon as all the flowers are finished each year, clip the plants over with shears, but do not cut into old, dark-colored wood.

P. fruticosa 'Abbotswood' has a dwarf compact shape with dark foliage that offsets white flowers.

P. fruticosa 'Tangerine' forms a low, mound-shaped spreading plant.

P. fruticosa 'Goldfinger' can reach 3ft(90cm) high with deep golden flowers.

P. fruticosa 'Primrose Beauty' has pale yellow flowers.

PRUNING LAVATERA

During the winter, old stems become woody and dark colored. They protect the plant in cold conditions, but if not removed in mid-spring, they soon make the plant look leggy and untidy.

1 Lavatera usually dies back to ground level in winter, but by mid-spring, new growth appears near the base. Cut off old stems close to ground level.

2 All that remains will be a small rosettelike cluster of young leaves virtually sitting on the ground. Strong new shoots will quickly grow from these.

Exotic shrubs on the patio

A warm sheltered patio is the ideal place to grow exotic shrubs in summer. Citrus trees (orange, lemon, etc.) bear fruit and strongly perfumed flowers at the same time. For spectacular flowers on bushy shrubs, go for bottlebrush, plumbago and grevillea. One of the best exotic trees is Albizia julibrissin, *the silk tree, which has ferny foliage and pink fluffy flowers. Grow all these non-hardy plants in tubs or large pots and move them into a frost-free greenhouse or conservatory for the winter. Repot them every two or three years into fresh soil-based potting mix in spring and feed regularly all summer.*

Above: Caesalpinia pulcherrima *has mimosa-like foliage and large bunches of flowers with long stamens. Bring it inside in winter.*

Given a rich potting mix, *Hibiscus syriacus* 'Meehanii', a variegated variety, does well in pots.

When bruised, the leaves of *Salvia grahamii* smell of blackcurrants. It flowers from early summer to late fall.

Zauschneria californica 'Dublin' (Californian fuchsia) flowers in mid- to late summer.

Convolvulus cneorum has pale pink, circular flowers from late spring to late summer.

LATE-SEASON SHADES

Although most trees and shrubs flower in spring or summer, some kinds look their best 'out of season' and these are specially valuable for extending the year-round appeal of a garden. Fruit and berries are at their best in the fall, and encourage birds to visit and feed, but if you want crops that will last well into winter, choose pyracantha, hawthorns, and crab apple 'Golden Hornet', which the birds leave till last. In winter, trees and shrubs with strikingly colored bark such as birches, *Cornus alba* cultivars (such as 'Westonbirt') and *Acer griseum*, are at their most noticeable. After the leaves have fallen, they contrast well with evergreen foliage backgrounds. (Prune out the old, dull stems of cornus each spring to encourage more highly colored young growth.) Winter-flowering shrubs are few, but worth looking out for. Most reliable is winter jasmine, which flowers in mild spells throughout winter and early spring. Witch hazel does nearly as well, given a mild sheltered spot to protect the flowers. Less common winter and early spring shrubs, such as wintersweet and the shrubby, scented *Lonicera fragrantissima*, are well worth hunting for. Choose a few plants from each group and team them with evergreen ground cover, such as bergenia, ivies or periwinkle, for the most striking display.

Berries and catkins

Above: Cotoneaster berries ripen in late summer. This is *C. conspicuus*.

Right: In most skimmias, male and female flowers grow on separate plants, so you need both for the female to set berries; *S. j. reevesiana* (front), a hermaphrodite form, berries even if grown alone.

Below: Given a crisp fall, *Liquidambar styraciflua* produces a fiery display of foliage color in small spaces. Birches and *Acer palmatum* are also good choices.

Above: *Jasminum nudiflorum* is a sprawling shrub, best trained up a wall. It flowers in mild spells during winter and early spring. Unscented.

Above: In late fall, as the previous year's fruit ripens, *Arbutus unedo* produces white bell-like flowers. The round, red fruits taste insipid, so are not normally eaten.

Right: The evergreen foliage of *Garrya elliptica* is distinguished by long greenish catkins throughout the winter. In cold regions, it can be trained against a shady wall.

Right: *Hamamelis,* such as this 'Orange Beauty', enjoy neutral to acid soil. In a sheltered spot, the spidery flowers appear in the fall, in mild spells in winter and in spring. A dark background helps to show them off well.

Bark

Trees and shrubs with colorful bark team well with evergreen foliage and shrubs with late berries. Give them light and fresh air. Do not plant them with climbers such as ivy, which cover the bark, and do not let nearby shrubs swamp them, or green algae may spoil the tree trunks.

Right: *The bark of* Acer griseum *'peels' away from the trunk, giving a shaggy look that is specially noticeable in winter.*

Above: Betula utilis jacquemontii *has dazzling silver-white bark that peels away naturally. Do not tear it away as it protects the trunk.*

Right: Acer capillipes *has striated snakeskin-like bark, coral red young shoots, and brilliant fall tints. It needs a sheltered spot.*

Stems

Right: Cornus alba *'Sibirica' is one of the colored-stemmed dogwoods. To see it at its best, cut the old stems down hard every spring and grow it in front of a blue or green evergreen background. For gold stems, grow* Salix alba vitellina. *Cut the old dull stems close to ground level each spring to encourage new shoots, which have the best color.*

GROUND COVER SHRUBS

Ground cover plants are low and spreading and naturally form a weed-smothering carpet of foliage. They may run along the ground rooting as they go, such as periwinkle and ivies, or sprawl like as *Cotoneaster horizontalis* to build up layer upon layer of foliage. But they can also be squat bushy plants, such as santolina, which are simply planted closely enough that the stems knit together to carpet the ground. The big common factor is that ground cover shrubs are cheap, fast-growing and easy to propagate. They are ideal for a new garden that needs a 'lived in' look or for a large garden that needs a low-cost planting scheme. But one of the main reasons for using ground cover plants is that because they shade the soil with a heavy mantle of foliage, they prevent weed seeds from germinating, and thus weeding is greatly reduced. Use ground cover shrubs under taller trees and shrubs, where their flowers and foliage add a welcome bottom layer of color; use them as an alternative to grass for steep banks, in woodland gardens, or on wasteland to deter littering. Between them, there are ground cover plants to suit every site and situation from wet shade to hot, dry, sunny soil. Choose plants that suit the conditions, and ground cover plants will establish quickly.

Above: The distinctive semi-evergreen branches of *Cotoneaster horizontalis* grow into shapes like overlapping fishbones; use it to cover the ground or low walls.

Below: *Vinca major,* the greater periwinkle, grows on 'problem' banks, in shade under trees or beneath shrubs in a border, where it scrambles up into low branches.

Shrubs providing ground cover

Right: In acid soil, *Gaultheria procumbens* makes good ground cover in woodland and under border shrubs. Its winter berries show up well above the foliage.

Below: *Prunus laurocerasus* 'Otto Luyken' makes low, spreading bushes with glossy evergreen leaves and candlelike clusters of white flowers in late spring.

Below: *Hypericum olympicum* is a pretty ground cover plant for hot, sunny, dry spots, such as a large rock garden or well-drained border. A slow spreader with big golden flowers in summer.

Tidying up vinca

If you want to keep vinca contained within a smaller space, just cut back long stems in spring and pull out those that have rooted where you do not want them. Where the plant has spread unchecked, you will need to clear through the many layers of stems that have built up.

Vinca produces leafy upright stems that carry flowers and wiry horizontal runners that root virtually anywhere they touch the soil. From each set of roots new shoots appear that start a new plant.

1 Separate the wiry horizontal runners from the more upright leafy shoots that carry the flowers. Cut out the long runners.

2 Remove the old dead stems and debris that have built up in the base of the plants until you expose relatively clear soil.

3 Spread a mulch of 1-2in (2.5-5cm) of any well-rotted organic matter (such as garden compost) around the plants.

4 This helps to restore the soil, which usually becomes impoverished where a neglected carpet of vinca has run riot.

FRAGRANT SHRUBS

Scented plants add an extra dimension of enjoyment to the garden. Plant them beside seats or along paths or borders where you can get close to plants and appreciate their full fragrance. Use them next to doorways and near windows that are left open in summer, so the fragrance can waft inside. On sheltered patios or in courtyards the perfume proliferates in the warmth and is 'trapped' by enclosing walls. Shrubs with scented leaves, such as rosemary or santolina, are useful edging plants - lightly bruising their leaves releases their fragrance, so put them where people will brush past them. Avoid growing too many strongly scented shrubs in close proximity to each other; instead, place them at intervals so that you become aware of the changing scents as you walk round the garden. Choose shrubs that flower at different times of year. In spring, some of the strongest scents are those of *Daphne, Viburnum fragrans* and *V. carlesii*. In early summer, lilacs and philadelphus are outstanding, and from midsummer to fall, roses are the dominant flower fragrance. In winter, enjoy the subtle but clear scents of the winter-flowering shrubby honeysuckles *(Lonicera* x *purpusii* and *Lonicera fragrantissima)* and wintersweet *(Chimonanthus praecox)*.

Above: *Syringa vulgaris* 'Congo' is one of the many hybrid French lilacs. The beautifully scented flowers fade slightly as they age.

Above: *Philadelphus* 'Belle Etoile' is one of the best mock oranges for perfume. Prune it after flowering in late spring to keep a tidy shape.

Left: The herbal aroma of the foliage of *Rosmarinus officinalis* 'McConnell's Blue' blends well with that of other evergreen herbs.

Itea ilicifolia has spectacular long trailing 'ropes' of greenish white sweet-scented flowers in late midsummer.

Korean lilac *(Syringa vulgaris)* is a compact plant with fragrant, lilac-pink flowers.

Both the flowers and foliage of the gold-leaved *Choisya ternata* 'Sundance' are delicately scented.

Daphne burkwoodii 'Astrid' has variegated semi-evergreen leaves, a perfect frame for the pale pink, scented flowers.

Daphne tangutica is a small evergreen shrub with purple-stained, scented white flowers in spring.

Right: Daphnes need well-drained, humus-rich soil. The easiest to grow is *D. mezereum, a* small deciduous shrub with fragrant purplish flowers in early spring.

Below: Large plants, such as pineapple-scented broom (*Cytisus battandieri*), are most effective grown on walls next to paving so that the perfume is reflected back on warm air.

Planting a lavender hedge

A row of identical lavender plants makes a good, low flowering hedge or edging to a path or formal bed. Lavender likes a warm, sheltered, sunny situation, with not too rich but well-drained soil. Avoid winter wet.

1 When young plants fill their pots, cut back the tops to tidy them and encourage bushy growth. By this time, the young plants will be ready for planting.

2 To make a dwarf hedge, set out a straight row of lavenders about 6in(15cm) apart. Plant them into well-prepared soil, without breaking up the rootballs.

3 Water in the new plants and continue watering them whenever the soil is dry for the first few months until the plants are established.

Right: *A dwarf hedge of lavender makes a neat path edging and is ideal for outlining a formal feature such as a herb garden. This deep purple-flowered cultivar is 'Hidcote'. Clip plants after flowering to keep them in shape.*

DIVERSITY OF ROSES

As well as the thousands of different named rose varieties, there are also several basic groups of roses, each with a separate 'personality'. Best known are the modern roses, once known as hybrid tea (with a single flower at the end of each stem) and floribundas (with a cluster of flowers). The great characteristic of this group is that they keep flowering continuously from early summer through to the fall. Old-fashioned roses are cottage garden plants - the parents of modern roses - often rather untidy plants, with more cabbagey flowers. Most flower only for about six weeks at the start of summer. Shrub roses are the species; big strong plants with small, often single flowers followed by striking hips. Good for natural and wildlife gardens, many species roses also make superb, thorny hedges. Both shrub and old-fashioned roses are often grown in mixed borders, treated as flowering shrubs. Ground cover roses are low spreading plants that flower all summer, good for banks or the front of borders. However, weeding between the prickly stems is painful. Ground cover roses grafted onto upright stems make very attractive small weeping standard trees, ideal for a patio. Smaller in scale are the true patio roses, which are like small bushy plants flowering all summer; they are good in tubs or small beds and borders. Miniature roses are the smallest of the lot, not indoor pot plants but real small-scale roses. They need a mild spot and good growing conditions if they are to thrive.

Above: Most rugosa roses are known for enduring tough conditions, and for their big single flowers and large hips. This specie rose is *Rosa rugosa* 'Complicata'.

Below: 'Just Joey', a hybrid tea, has attractively ruffled, coppery colored petals. It is perfumed, good for cutting, weatherproof and fairly disease-resistant.

Right: The gaily striped *Rosa Mundi,* also known as *Rosa gallica* 'Versicolor', is probably one of the oldest garden roses, bred in about the fourteenth century. Unscented.

ENCOURAGING HIPS

Shrub roses generally need little pruning. Many, such as *Rosa rugosa* and *R. moyesii*, produce large single flowers and hips. Do not deadhead them or the hips will not form. This is *Rosa rugosa* 'Frau Dagmar Hastrup'.

Below: 'English Miss' is a very fragrant, weatherproof, disease-resistant floribunda rose, with the classic pointed rosebuds opening out to fully double flowers.

Below: The arched stems of 'Pink Bells' cover the soil with a low mound of foliage. Slightly scented flowers from mid- to late summer.

DEADHEADING

The reason for removing the dead flowers from roses is that if they are left to form seed, the bush virtually stops flowering. Once the seed has formed, the plant's job is to build and ripen it, not produce flowers. To enjoy the beautiful hips produced by some shrub roses, just prune the plants lightly in spring.

Above: Many roses make good standard plants to add height to a border or to turn an otherwise prostrate or lax variety, such as this 'Crimson Shower' (a rambler), into a small weeping tree.

Above: 'Nevada', a hugely popular, cream-colored, modern shrub rose, has enormous, slightly fragrant, single flowers on large arching plants in midsummer and early fall.

Right: Miniature roses are really only happy grown outdoors, where they need shelter and good growing conditions. This 'Orange Sunblaze' is at home in a patio pot.

Rose grower's checklist

Mid-spring: *Prune hybrid teas and floribunda roses. Mulch all roses and feed them with a specially formulated rose fertilizer. This contains potash for strong flowering and magnesium for good flower color.*

Below: *Do not let any fertilizer fall on the base of the plant, as this could cause scorching.*

Early summer: *Unless you are growing disease-resistant roses (find which these are in rose growers' catalogs), start spraying regularly against blackspot and other rose diseases. Special rose fungicides are available that tackle all the main rose diseases. Continue spraying regularly until fall. Hoe shallowly every week to avoid weeds taking hold.*

Midsummer: *Give a second application of rose fertilizer and water it well in if the soil is dry. Keep new roses well watered for their first summer. Remove dead flower heads weekly to ensure a constant succession of new flowers from hybrid teas and floribundas, but do not deadhead species grown for hips. Shorten the long stems of old-fashioned roses after flowering is finished.*

Late midsummer: *Prune climbing and rambler roses when flowering is finished - some cultivars have only one flush of flowers, others two and a few flower for most of the summer.*

Fall: *Collect up fallen leaves and other debris and burn it all to help prevent disease spores reinfecting plants. Plant new roses; if blackspot and other disease is a severe problem or you want to avoid spraying, consider replacing susceptible cultivars with disease-free kinds. Avoid replanting in exactly the same spot as before - move a few feet away if possible. Do not replant old rose beds where several bushes have failed - start a new rose bed in this instance.*

Below: *When spraying, make sure that the applicator can reach under the foliage. Follow the maker's directions.*

Planting and staking a tree

1 Remove the tree from its container. Plants lift out easily from rigid plastic pots. In the case of plastic bag-type pots, first slit the sides carefully with a knife.

2 If there are any suckers arising from the base, do not snip them off. Scrape back the soil to expose their junction with a root and cut them out from there.

3 Dig a planting hole larger than the tree's rootball, hammer in a short stake to one side of it, then plant so that the top of the rootball is roughly flush with the soil surface.

4 Firm the soil down well to make sure that there are no air pockets left in it. These would leave roots hanging in space, where they tend to dry out and die.

5 Water well in after planting, even if the soil is moist. This helps to wash the soil down around the roots. If the soil sinks, add more to bring it to the right level.

6 While the soil is wet, scatter about 2in(5cm) of good mulching material over it to retain moisture in the soil and suppress weeds. These are bark chippings.

7 Secure the trunk to the stake with a tree tie, positioned just below the lowest branches. Place the 'buffer' between the stake and the trunk to prevent chafing.

FLOWERING TREES FOR SMALL GARDENS

In a small garden, the wrong trees can very quickly outgrow their welcome. By growing too large they can overshadow much of the garden and preventing sunloving plants from thriving, as well as smothering the garden with a blanket of leaves at fall. To avoid trees becoming a nuisance, choose kinds that stay small and either have a light canopy of branches or make neat upright shapes so that they cast little shadow. But because even small trees must justify their space, look out for those that offer several attractions - perhaps a good show of flowers plus fruit or berries, architectural shapes, or fall leaf colors. Crab apples and tree forms of cotoneaster, such as *Cotoneaster salicifolius* 'Pendulus', offer good displays of flowers and fruit. Some large shrubs can be trained as small trees; this keeps them looking neater and takes up less room, and other plants can then be grown underneath them. Good shrubs for this treatment include *Buddleia alternifolia* and *B. globosa, Rosa* 'Canary Bird' and *Clerodendrum trichotomum* var *fargesii.*

Some of the best small flowering trees for gardens include cherries, such as the upright *Prunus* 'Amanogawa', which is studded with pale pink double flowers in late spring, and Cheal's weeping cherry, with slightly deeper pink flowers on a short, bushy, weeping tree. In mild regions, the Judas tree *(Cercis siliquastrum)* is fascinating, as the purple pealike flowers grow straight out of branches or even the trunk; if they are damaged, new stems grow from the remains of the old trunk. The heart-shaped leaves are also a feature.

Above: *Amelanchier lamarckii* has off-white blossom In spring, followed by summer berries and then a superb display of fall tints.

8 Keep new trees watered, especially if they are planted during spring or summer when the weather is dry. This form of stake is suitable for long-term support.

Alternative staking

A short stake prevents roots rocking, but lets the trunk flex and develop tough fibers so that it can stand without support after a year or two.

Crab apple trees and prunus

Crab apples are reliable and prolific. Look for Malus *'Profusion' (wine red blossom and deep red fruit), 'Golden Hornet' (off-white blossom and golden fruit) and 'John Downie' (white blossom and peach-flushed yellow fruit). When sold on dwarfing fruit tree rootstocks, crab apple trees grow to full size within a few years and then get no bigger.*

Left: Malus *x* lemoinei *is a fairly upright hybrid with a modest crop of large wine-red flowers that team well with the purplish foliage. This makes a good back-ground for other flowers throughout the summer months.*

Right: Crataegus laevigata *'Paul's Scarlet' is a superb small flowering tree for a windy garden. It produces a mass of frothy, double, deep pink blossom in early summer, but no fruit.*

Below: *Check the label before buying prunus as some kinds make huge trees. Those shown here are fine.*

Left: *Acer palmatum atropurpureum* has purple-bronze foliage all summer and looks great in woodland or sheltered gardens. It also makes a superb specimen plant in a container. Plant it in a mixture of soil-based and ericaceous potting mix.

DISPLAYS OF FOLIAGE

Foliage forms the backbone of the garden. Evergreens are the first choice. To give a real year-round effect, evergreens should ideally make up two-thirds of the total plants in a mixed border. Alternatively, create a totally evergreen border using shrubs such as variegated elaeagnus and gold *Choisya ternata* 'Sundance' with gold-berried pyracantha - ideal to blot out a distant eyesore or provide some privacy in an otherwise open garden. Some deciduous shrubs also provide outstanding foliage displays. Use them in borders as foils for flowering shrubs; some have striking shapes that make them specially useful as specimen plants. Several berberis have purple leaves, but the pink-splashed purple leaves of 'Harlequin' are particularly attractive. However, some of the most spectacular deciduous foliage belongs to acers. *Acer negundo* 'Flamingo' makes a small tree or large bush, its green young stems clad in flaglike cream-and-green variegated foliage, flushed shrimp-pink at the tips. *Acer japonicum* 'Aureum' has pleated, gold, fanlike leaves all summer. Japanese maples are smaller and bushier, and need light shade, shelter and acid soils to thrive; they have mini-maple foliage in purple or fresh grassy green.

Right: *Choisya ternata* 'Sundance' has glossy, bright gold, evergreen foliage; to avoid leaves browning or bleaching, grow it in a sheltered spot, out of the strong midday sun.

Foliage shrubs

Striking foliage

Above: Striking evergreens, such as *Fatsia japonica,* make good architectural plants for a prominent place and are valued for floral art.

Above: *Cotinus coggygria* (smoke bush) makes a showy specimen for a big border or for planting alone in a lawn. The green-leaved form takes on good fall color.

Right: Planted in drifts, bamboos make unusual living screens. They do best in a sheltered, sunny spot, in rich, well-drained soil that never dries out badly.

Formation pruning of a young tree

Nurseries often sell 'feathered' young trees, meaning that all the side shoots have been left on the plant so that the customer can choose whether to grow it as a multistemmed tree, a bush or as a normal standard tree on a single trunk. It is cheaper than buying a trained tree, as you do the training yourself. This is Liquidamber styraciflua.

1 For a standard, choose a strong young tree with one upright stem and vigorous side shoots at the top of the stem.

2 Working up from the base, using sharp secateurs, cut away all unwanted 'feathers' (side shoots) flush with the stem.

3 Leave five or seven strong side shoots round the top of the tree. Remove the tip of each one to encourage branching out.

4 Cut out the tip of the main upright shoot growing from the top of the tree to divert all the tree's energy into the branches.

SHRUBS FOR SUN

Most shrubs do best in situations that provide direct sun for half the day or more, but a site with strong direct sun all day which also has hot, dry, impoverished soil is difficult to colonize. Few shrubs are happy in such conditions. But by choosing carefully from amongst the more drought-proof shrubs, and taking some trouble to get new plants established, it is possible to garden in even the most difficult spot. If the soil is not too impoverished, buddleia, *Lavatera olbia* 'Rosea' and hardy hibiscus will fare well, adding extra color later in the season. And in poor dry soil in front of a wall, ceanothus or *Fremontodendron californicum* make good drought-proof shrubs suitable for wall-training. Low spreading shrubs, such as cistus, senecio, santolina, *Genista lydia* and hebe, are ideal for covering dry banks or for the front of a border. Larger shrubs, including olearia, tamarix, *Romneya coulteri* with its huge white poppy-flowers, Japanese bitter orange *(Poncirus trifoliata)* and brooms, including the Spanish broom *Spartium junceum*, make a taller back row for a border. It is always worth improving 'problem' soil as much as possible (see panel), since this makes it possible to grow a much wider range of plants. By adding plenty of organic matter and nutrients, plants such as hardy hibiscus, buddleia, clerodendron, helianthemum and others will all thrive in previously 'difficult' places.

Above: *Fremontodendron californicum* is a large evergreen shrub for a mild region on dry neutral to chalky soil; it does well trained against a sunny wall. The bristly leaves may cause irritation.

Right: The green, rushlike stems of *Spartium junceum* (Spanish broom) do the job of foliage in this virtually leafless plant, so the large yellow pea-flowers show up well against nearly bare stems.

Above: All the Californian lilacs *(Ceanothus)* thrive in a hot, sunny, sheltered spot. Most make large bushy plants, but 'Blue Cushion', shown here, makes a low mound.

Shrubs for hot sun

Above: *Hibiscus syriacus* 'Woodbridge'. Hardy hibiscus thrives in a warm, sunny, sheltered spot with well-drained soil. Wind can damage buds and blooms.

Right: *Helianthemum* (rock rose), such as this 'Rosa Königin', makes good summer-flowering ground cover for a hot sunny spot. It pays to improve the soil before planting.

Below: Tamarix is an exceptionally wind-tolerant large shrub, suitable for seaside situations and exposed hot dry beds. *Tamarix tetrandra* (seen here) flowers in mid-spring.

Coping with poor soil

First improve the soil by digging in as much well-rotted organic matter (such as garden compost or animal manure) as possible. On sandy or gravelly soils this quickly breaks down and disappears, but it will last long enough to help hold water while new plants get established. You can assist poor dry soils further by digging in water-retaining gel crystals, which last virtually forever. A 1-2in(2.5-5cm) layer of gravel, granite chippings or even cobblestones works as a good mulch on these soils (water condenses underneath the stones overnight, thus helping plants survive), and only needs topping up every few years. The secret of planting in these conditions is to plant in the fall, when the soil is moist and winter rains will help new plants to become established. Water plants in dry spells the following summer. If planting in spring is inevitable, you must water new plants regularly throughout their first season. Avoid planting in summer entirely.

Right: Genista lydia, *a small ground-hugging broom, flowers in mid- to late spring. Its slightly cascading habit makes it ideal for a raised bed or bank.*

Versatile hebes

Hebes are small, bushy, summer-flowering evergreen shrubs with characteristic bottlebrush-like flowers. They thrive in a sunny, sheltered spot in light, free-draining soil, flowering from early to late summer.

SHRUBS FOR SHADE

For planting in shade, the right choice of shrubs is vital - if 'normal' kinds are planted in insufficient light they become weak and leggy, with pale foliage and few if any flowers. In reasonable soil, spotted laurel *(Aucuba)* is a good choice for shade, as are *Euonymus fortunei* and *E. radicans* varieties, *Symphoricarpos* (snowberry), *Pachysandra terminalis* and *Hypericum calycinum.* Variegated forms are specially useful for brightening up shady spots. Variegated *Pachysandra* makes particularly striking ground cover. In rich, leafy, shaded soil, hydrangeas are particularly successful. As well as the familiar domed flowers, lacecap varieties are available - these have a ring of open blooms surrounding a circle of sterile florets that look as if they have not opened properly. Species hydrangeas make a pleasant variation on the theme; *H. quercifolia* has oak-shaped leaves and large, tousled, greeny-white flower heads, while *Hydrangea paniculata* has white flowers shaped like inverted ice-cream cones, and *H. sargentiana* has huge velvety leaves and light purple lacecap flowers. Hydrangeas are one of the very few really colorful flowers that enjoys shade; plant them in huge drifts for the most spectacular displays.

Left: Evergreen berberis make good plants for shady spots, even where the soil is dry. The only situation they do not enjoy is one with bad drainage. This is *Berberis* x *lologensis* 'Stapehill'.

Above: *Skimmia japonica reevesiana* likes acid soil and light shade. This hermaphrodite form produces its long-lasting winter berries even when grown alone. A good plant for tubs.

Hydrangea flowers

CHANGING THE COLOR OF HYDRANGEA

1 Grow pink varieties of hortensia hydrangea on chalky soil and blue ones on acid soil. If you grow blue types on chalky soil, use a hydrangea colorant or they will turn pink.

2 Mix the product (which is based on aluminum sulfate) with water and apply it as directed by the manufacturer. Repeat the treatment regularly during the growing season.

Below: *Mahonia* x *media* bears long racemes of lily-of-the-valley scented blooms in any well-drained soil in dappled shade.

Above: Variegated cultivars of *Aucuba japonica* are good plants for introducing sunny-looking splashes of light to a shaded area.

Right: *Symphoricarpos albus* (snowberry) makes a loose, twiggy, suckering shrub, covered in winter with large, white opaque berries.

Euonymus japonicus 'Aureopictus'. Many euonymus varieties are useful for brightening up shady corners.

Mahonia aquifolium 'Atropurpurea' is an evergreen shrub with purple-tinged leaves that thrives in partial shade.

Shade under big trees

The most difficult type of shade to colonize satisfactorily is that commonly found under big trees, where the soil is also poor and dry. Where it is very dark indeed, nothing much except perhaps butcher's broom (Ruscus aculeatus, *a low spiny evergreen with red berries) and plain green ivies, such as* Hedera hibernica, *will grow. Plain green plants are best for deep shade, as variegated plants need a little more light. Variegated plants certainly brighten up a slightly shady spot, but cannot cope with deep shade. In this situation, a better plan may be to create a landscape based on things other than plants - perhaps a seat fitted round the trunk of a large tree and a carpet of pine cones and needles overlooking a gnarled sculptural chunk of 'driftwood'. Where shade is less severe, tough plants, such as evergreen berberis,* Lonicera pileata *(an evergreen, ground-covering shrub), hollies,* Mahonia aquifolium *and* Prunus laurocerasus, *can usually be relied on, but improve the soil well before planting. If planting is difficult because the soil is full of tree roots (a common problem in this situation), spread a mulch of well-rotted organic matter, leafmold, etc., at least 6in(15cm) deep over the area and plant into that. Keep new plants well watered for the first year to help them become established in dry shade.*

Right: Ruscus aculeatus *will grow in deep shade. Plant several close together for good ground cover and to ensure plenty of the large red berries.*

Below: *Planted in deep shade, ivies, such as this* Hedera colchica *'Dentata', spread their stems out towards the light, rooting as they run.*

TREES AND SHRUBS FOR ACID SOIL

The majority of popular trees and shrubs are happy on any reasonable garden soil, ranging from slightly acid to slightly chalky. However, some shrubs must have acid soil. These are the lime-haters, which include rhododendrons, pieris and camellias, summer-flowering heathers, witch hazels, Japanese maples *(Acer palmatum)* and most magnolias, except *M. stellata*. When grown on soil containing lime, essential nutrients are chemically locked up by the chalk, resulting in yellow leaves - a condition known as chlorosis. You can usually tell if a garden is on acid soil if plants such as rhododendrons grow freely in the neighborhood. If you are unsure, do a soil test to check the pH before buying plants (see page 17) and check plant care labels in garden centers - they should tell you which plants need acid soil.

Left: *Rhododendron* 'Christmas Cheer' flowers in early to mid-spring, which is several months earlier than most other cultivars.

Right: A woodland setting suits *Pieris japonica* 'Purity', with its unusually large, white, waxy-looking flowers. These are well set off by the glossy, coppery-colored young leaves in spring.

CHLOROSIS

The foliage of this pieris is turning yellow due to chlorosis, but it will quickly recover when it is repotted into fresh ericaceous potting mixture, which is suitable for lime-hating plants. To prevent chlorosis, feed these plants with a product containing sequestered iron each spring.

CAMELLIAS

Unlike rhododendrons, camellias will tolerate neutral - but not chalky - soil. They also grow in sun, providing the soil is moist and summer conditions are not baking hot. Pink and red camellias are generally the most reliable; white flowers turn brown around the edge in cold or windy weather and also when they go over.

Above: In mild winters, cultivars of *Camellia* x *williamsii*, such as this one called 'Debbie', often flower sporadically from late fall onwards, given a well-sheltered spot.

Above: Nurseries in acid-soil areas usually stock a good range of ericaceous plants. *Kalmia latifolia* 'Nipmuck' is the sort of lucky 'find' you might make.

Left: *Gaultheria mucronata* 'Mulberry Wine' is a fabulous plant, covered in mid- to late summer with large magenta berries that ripen to a deep purplish color. It is evergreen and very hardy.

Modifying the soil

Lime haters can be grown in gardens without naturally suitable soil given a little extra effort. If the soil is roughly neutral, it can be modified slightly by using acidic forms of organic matter as a soil improver (such as moss peat, rotted pine needles or cocoa shell) or treated with sulfur chips (which acidify the soil for about two years before retreatment is necessary). Using an ericaceous feed and watering with sequestered iron each spring are also beneficial. However, even when used all together, these methods are not enough to make chalky soil suitable for lime-hating plants. On chalky soil, grow plants needing acid soil in tubs of ericaceous mix. Keep plants well watered in summer, and feed with ericaceous feed to counteract any lime in the tapwater. Ideally, use rainwater, which is naturally more acidic. Repot in early spring every two or three years. Alternatively, make an isolated bed by excavating 3ft(90cm) deep and lining the area with plastic, or make a raised bed, similarly lined. Refill the bed with an equal mixture of good-quality topsoil and acidic peat or leaf mold. This ensures that the roots of lime-hating plants cannot penetrate into limy soil.

Watering and feeding acid-loving plants

1 Water rhododendrons in well after planting. As their roots remain close to the surface, water them generously during dry spells, even when established.

2 Special feeds for acid-loving plants, such as these rhododendrons, are ideal for pots or plants in the ground. Apply in spring as new growth starts.

3 Add a dose of liquid tomato feed to the water during midsummer. This is high in potash and will encourage bud formation at the shoot tips.

4 After watering well in spring, apply a 1in(2.5cm)-deep mulch of chipped bark, moss peat or, as here, cocoa shell, all of which are slightly acidic.

CHOOSING PLANTS

Some trees and shrubs deserve special mention as they have features that makes them invaluable for filling problem spots round the garden, or providing special interest. Listed here are some particularly useful kinds.

E = Evergreen
SP = Good for seaside planting

Trees and shrubs tolerant of heavy clay and/or badly drained soils

Betula
Cornus alba cultivars
Corylus avellana cultivars
Cotoneaster
Kerria japonica
Rosa rugosa
Salix alba cultivars
Sambucus nigra cultivars
Sorbus aucuparia
Symphoricarpos
Viburnum lantana and
V. opulus

Trees and shrubs for exposed gardens

(These plants are good for hedging, windbreaks or outer boundary borders)
Acer campestre
Arundinaria (E)
Betula
Buddleia cultivars
Crataegus
Elaeagnus x *ebbingei* (E)
Ilex aquifolium & cultivars (E)
Rhododendron ponticum (E)
Rosa rugosa and
R. pimpinellifolia cultivars
Sambucus nigra cultivars
Sorbus aucuparia cultivars
Viburnum lantana, *V. opulus*

Shrubs for shade, moist shade and/or light woodland

Acer palmatum cultivars
Aucuba japonica (E)
Camellia (E)
Gaultheria (E)
Hydrangea
Rhododendron (E)
Symphoricarpos

Shrubs for hot dry sunny situations in poor soil

Atriplex halimus (SP)
Buddleia
Cytisus
Escallonia macrophylla (SP)
Genista
Hebe
Hippophae rhamnoides (SP)
Hypericum calycinum
Olearia
Perovskia
Spartium junceum
Tamarix (SP)
Ulex europaeus 'Flora pleno'

Decorative compact and trouble-free trees for small gardens

Acer griseum,
A. negundo 'Flamingo'
Acer palmatum cultivars,
e.g. 'Senkaki'
Amelanchier lamarckii
Betula pendula 'Youngii'
B. utilis, *B.u.* var. *jacquemontii*,
Gleditsia triacanthos 'Rubylace' and 'Sunburst'
Malus, e.g. 'Profusion', 'John Downie', 'Golden Hornet'
Mespilus germanica
Prunus 'Amanogawa', *P. incisa*

Hypericum x *moserianum* 'Tricolor'

Shrubs with aromatic foliage when crushed

Caryopteris x *clandonensis*
Choisya ternata (E)
Myrtus communis (E)
Perovskia 'Blue Spire'
Rosa rubiginosa
Rosemary (E)
Lavender (E)
Santolina (E)

Shrubs with scented flowers

Choisya ternata (E)
Cytisus battandieri
Daphne mezereum
Elaeagnus x *ebbingei* (E)
Hamamelis
Lavender
Mahonia japonica and 'Charity' (E)
Malus 'Profusion'
Myrtus communis (E)
Perovskia 'Blue Spire'
Ribes odoratum
Roses - many but not all
Spartium junceum
Syringa hybrids
Viburnum bodnantense 'Dawn',
V. b. 'Deben', *V. carlesii*,
V. farreri, *V.* x *juddii*

Camellia japonica 'Ballet Dancer'
C. j. 'Bill Stewart'
C. j. 'R.L. Wheeler'
C. j. 'Devonia'

Flowering shrubs to attract wildlife

Berries for birds

Amelanchier lamarckii
Cotoneaster
Malus (all)
Prunus avium, *P. padus*
Rosa rugosa
Sambucus nigra cultivars
Sorbus aucuparia
Viburnum opulus 'Compactum'

Flowers for butterflies and/or bees:

Buddleia
Heathers(E)
Hebe

Buddleia davidii 'Harlequin'
B. d. 'Nanho Blue'

Trees and shrubs for dry shade and/or under large trees, close to buildings

Euonymus japonicus and
E. fortunei (E)
Berberis (evergreen kinds) (E)
Buxus sempervirens (E)
Cotoneaster (low and ground- covering types)
Rubus tricolor
Vinca (E)

PART FIVE

CONIFERS AND HEATHERS

Conifers and heathers are naturally successful partners. Combining the ground-covering habit of heathers with the variety of conifer shapes, plus the seasonal interest of grasses, evergreens and certain herbaceous plants, you can create an easy-to-maintain garden that changes through the seasons but looks good the whole year.

PLANTING A CONIFER

Once well-established, conifers are generally trouble-free and easy to look after, but it is worth taking trouble over their planting and initial care. Newly planted conifers often fail simply because the soil around them dries out too much or the foliage is desiccated by harsh drying winds. Both conditions can cause the foliage to turn brown; at best, young plants will be left with spoiled foliage that may never be replaced with fresh green growth, and at worst they die. The soil should be moisture-retentive, but not waterlogged.

Early fall and late spring are the best times to plant conifers, along with other evergreens, but plants grown in pots can be planted out during the rest of the year, too, as long as the soil is in reasonable condition and neither too hot and dry nor too cold and wet. Although conifers are often recommended for growing as windbreaks, they must become well established before being subjected to drying winds, so it is good practice to surround them with a temporary windbreak. Feeding is not the main priority after planting; once plants have made it through the first winter, sprinkle a light dose of general-purpose feed or a special formulation for conifers around the plants and water it in well.

Below: A varied selection of conifers, both tall and low-growing, add color and year-round interest to this rock garden feature. Always keep the eventual sizes in mind.

Planting technique

1 Dig a hole that is slightly bigger than the plant rootball. Make sure that it is free of weeds, roots and debris. Good preparation means that conifers get off to a good start.

Fork well-rotted organic matter, such as garden compost or manure, into the soil over the entire bed.

PREPARING THE ROOTBALL

1 Moss or liverwort around the plant can be a sign that it has been in the same pot for some time and is short of feed.

2 Scrape the moss away carefully and remove any weeds. If the soil surface seems compressed, loosen it slightly.

3 Carefully loosen any dense-packed roots out from the mass. The bottom of the rootball will be loosest.

4 Tease a few of the biggest roots out slightly before planting; this allows roots to start growing out into the soil.

2 Remove the conifer from its pot and lower it into the hole. Check that the plant is upright and that its best side, if any, faces front.

3 Fill in round the roots with the surrounding topsoil. Do not to put the plant in too deep; the top of the rootball should be barely covered by soil.

4 After planting, water in very thoroughly. If the rootball is bone dry before planting, stand the plant in a bucket of water for an hour or until bubbles stop rising.

5 Apply a deep mulch of bark chippings or similar material to retain moisture in the soil. If they dry out, newly planted conifers turn brown and are unlikely to recover.

Protecting your conifer

As an added precaution - vital in exposed areas - surround newly planted conifers with a windbreak to protect them from strong winds, which can turn the foliage brown and may kill the plants. Conifers planted in the fall are most at risk, since the weather is windiest then.

1 A windbreak protects newly planted conifers. It can be made of perforated plastic sheet, as here, or hessian, interwoven fabric or sheep hurdles.

2 The windbreak must be securely fixed, but need only be left in place for the first winter. This plastic windbreak is being wired to a sturdy cedar stake.

Coping with dog damage

1 Dogs repeatedly lifting their legs over a conifer can cause it to turn brown near the base on one side. Wash it down with plain water immediately.

2 Use an animal repellent in the form of granules, gels, powders and tie-on capsules. Renew them frequently, especially after rain, for the best effect.

CONDITIONING THE SOIL

Improve the soil with plenty of organic matter, and if the soil is not naturally acid, add an acidic soil improver such as sphagnum moss.

1 After digging, fertilizing and raking the bed level, spread a layer of moss peat or other organic matter over it to improve the soil. This helps it to hold both water and air, thus aiding root development.

2 Fork the peat into the top of the soil. As conifers and heathers are relatively shallow rooted, improving the surface helps to retain moisture around the roots and 'backs up' the effect of mulching later.

MAKING A CONIFER AND HEATHER BED

Heathers and conifers naturally associate well together and need the same conditions - an open, sunny site with plenty of fresh air, and neutral or acid soil that neither dries out nor becomes waterlogged. An acidic soil improver is beneficial, but not enough to turn chalky soil into one suitable for most heathers. You can grow heathers and conifers in traditional beds and borders, but one way to plant them is in island beds - informal shapes such as 'teardrops' cut out of the lawn. Being open on all sides, such beds are easy to weed, and because more light and air can reach the plants, they tend to be healthier and relatively pest-free. The secret of an attractive heather and conifer bed lies in teaming plants with highly contrasting shapes, colors and textures. Upright, flame- and dome-shaped conifers contrast with bushy or open branching shapes, and all are set off by a continuous carpet of heather underneath. Choose heathers from all the main groups, so that you can have something in flower virtually all year round and use a few conifers with colored foliage, or with colored tips to young foliage in spring, or that take on bronzey hues in winter for seasonal variation.

1 Space the conifers, allowing for the size they will reach in ten years; see the plant label. Surround them with heathers spaced 12-18in(30-45cm) apart; these should make a complete carpet within two years.

2 Water all the plants very thoroughly. If the pots are dry when you buy them, soak the roots for a few hours before planting so that the rootball gets wet right through. The best way is to submerge the pots in water.

3 Finish with a decorative mulch to help retain moisture. This cocoa shell looks very good with this type of planting. Cocoa shell is slightly acidic, and the chocolate smell deters cats.

Below: A colorful patchwork of heathers provides the ideal foil for a wide range of conifers planted in this low-maintenance garden border.

Feeding ericaceous plants

Different kinds of feed are available for ericaceous plants. Use soluble crystals to feed plants and to help acidify the soil. Use solid ericaceous fertilizer to improve the soil before planting or around established plants. Sequestered iron is a 'tonic' for ericaceous plants. There is also a liquid version that needs diluting before use; this is best for pots.

Soluble feed for acid-loving plants. Dissolve the crystals in water and use regularly during the growing season.

Solid ericaceous fertilizer. Scatter it on the soil and water in well. Use each year in spring and to improve soil before planting.

Granular sequestered iron supplies iron in a fast-acting, easily assimilated form. Ericaceous plants need iron, which is chemically locked up by any lime in the soil. If lime is present, plant leaves turn yellow due to iron deficiency.

1 After spring weeding, sprinkle fertilizer on moist soil around individual plants, or thinly between plants in an ericaceous bed. This will feed the plants through the summer months.

2 Gently work the fertilizer into the top 1-2in(2.5-5cm) of soil with a small hand cultivator. Avoid going too deep or you may damage the shallow roots of heathers and other ericaceous plants.

A pot of winter heathers

1 Cover the drainage hole with a 'crock' to contain the potting mix or use small gauge wire gauze, which also keeps out worms.

2 Fill one third of the container with potting mix. Ericaceous mix is not necessary, as winter heathers do not mind a little lime.

3 A dwarf conifer will form the centerpiece. Position it so that the top of the rootball is about 0.5in (1.25cm) below the rim of the pot.

4 Firm the conifer down gently. Space the heathers evenly around it, squeezing the rootballs slightly to make them fit in.

5 Fill the spaces between the heathers with extra potting mix until the pot is loosely filled. This prevents the roots from drying out.

Erica x *darleyensis* 'Darley Dale'

Chamaecyparis thyoides 'Purple Heather'

Erica carnea 'Rosalie'

Erica carnea 'March Seedling'

6 Water thoroughly and sit the pot on a matching saucer in its final position.

WINTER HEATHERS

Winter-flowering heathers provide a carpet of evergreen, naturally compact, trouble-free ground cover that is full of flower throughout the winter. Unlike other heathers, they do not even need acid soil. Any reasonably well-drained garden soil in an open situation and full sun suits them, but add plenty of well-rotted organic matter before planting. The best-known winter heather is *Erica carnea,* which has a large range of readily available cultivars. Some have colored foliage, but other members of the heather family are better in this respect. Also available, but with a far smaller choice of cultivars, are *Erica mediterranea* and *E.* x *darleyensis.* Winter-flowering heathers associate superbly with conifers and the winter stems of birches, dogwoods, pollarded willows and *Rubus cockburnianus.* Evergreen shrubs team well with heathers, too; try architectural kinds, such as *Viburnum rhytidophyllum* and *V. davidii,* those with berries or fruit, such as *Skimmia japonica reevesiana* and *Arbutus unedo,* or ones with colored foliage, such as *Choisya ternata* 'Sundance'. Also choose plants with strong complementary shapes, such as brooms, and herbaceous plants with distinctive forms, such as bergenia and grasses.

Erica carnea 'Springwood White'

Erica carnea 'Rosalie'

Erica carnea 'White Perfection'

Above: *Erica carnea* 'Pink Spangles', 'Springwood White' and 'Vivellii' make good ground cover. Plant them 10in(25cm) apart and they will provide cover in one year.

Above: As soon as the flowers start to turn brown, around mid-spring, clip winter heathers over lightly with hedging clippers or sheep shears. This tidies and reshapes the plants by removing the dead flower heads.

Erica carnea 'Myretoun Ruby'

Erica carnea 'Pink Mist'

Planting up a heather basket

With their compact shape and free-flowering habit, winter-flowering heathers are ideal for hanging baskets. Buy evenly shaped plants just coming into flower at the start of the season and fill up the basket, as plants cannot be expected to grow and hide gaps at that time of year.

1 Half-fill the basket loosely with a good-quality potting mix. Do not fill the reservoir of a self-watering basket until you have finished the planting up.

2 Knock the ivy out of its pot and plant it - with its stake - so that the top of the rootball is about 0.5in(1.25cm) below the rim of the pot. Firm it in gently.

3 Fill the sides of the basket with flowering heathers so that the shoots cascade over the edges without swamping the gold-leaved heathers.

4 Arrange the ivy trails around the edge of the basket and in the heather. This looks best where the inside of a low hanging basket will be easily visible.

SUMMER HEATHERS

Cultivars of *Calluna* (ling) and *Erica cinerea* provide continuity of color in a heather bed, as they flower mainly from mid- to late summer into the fall. Mix them with winter-flowering heathers and those with colored foliage to ensure a good year-round display in beds and borders with conifers. The plant labels will tell you exactly when different cultivars can be expected to flower. Cultivars that flower well into fall look specially good under birches, where they make a dramatic contrast with the stark white bark of the trunks, and team well with deciduous plants displaying fall foliage tints. Use cultivars with a long flowering season to provide summer and fall color in a border of camellias and rhododendrons, which are spring-flowering. Acid-loving plants that flower at other times are specially valuable for out-of-season interest. Unlike winter heathers, the summer-flowering kind must grow in lime-free soil. If the soil is not naturally acid but merely neutral, you can improve it by adding moss peat, which is acidic. Sulfur chips are also available to acidify the soil - these last two years before another treatment is needed. Before applying sulfur chips, use a soil test kit to identify precisely what the acid-alkaline balance is so that you can assess the correct dosage. All heathers do best in well-drained soil in an open, sunny situation, although a few individual varieties will tolerate some slight shade for part of the day.

TREE HEATHERS

Tree heathers provide useful height and loose spire shapes in a heather bed. They prefer full sun, although they tolerate slight shade for part of the day.

Above: The summer flowers of *E. arborea* 'Alpina' are white and bell-shaped, held at the tips of the shoots and honey scented.

DABOECIA

These plants are a type of summer-flowering heath, but grow larger than heathers, to about 18in(45cm) tall and 36in(90cm) or more in spread. Provide them with sunny, well-drained, lime-free or acid conditions. Clip back the old foliage lightly in spring.

Above: A close up of *Daboecia cantabrica* 'Hookstone Pink'. Daboecia flowers are larger than those of heathers, but there are fewer of them on each spike.

Left: *Daboecia cantabrica* 'William Buchanan' provides a contrast to a yellow-foliaged heather.

Taking heather cuttings

Propagate heathers in late midsummer. If you clip winter heathers after flowering, the new growth will be ready for propagating by then; with summer-flowering varieties look for non-flowering shoots. Use a 50:50 blend of ericaceous mixture and silver sand to root the cuttings.

1 Take 1.5in(3.75cm)-long tip cuttings from the current season's growth. Strip the tiny leaves from the lower half, taking care not to damage the stems.

2 Dip the shoots into enough hormone rooting powder to cover the wounds where leaves have been removed. Tap off any excess and dibble in the cuttings.

3 Water the cuttings in gently and allow to drain. Cover the top of the pot with plastic film or a large plastic bag fixed around the sides of the pot. Leave this on for six to eight weeks.

Calluna vulgaris 'Oxshott Common'

Calluna vulgaris 'Blazeaway'

Erica cinerea 'Contrast'

Calluna vulgaris 'Tib'

Calluna vulgaris 'Velvet Fascination'

DWARF CONIFERS

The miniatures of the conifer world include countless delightful little treasures; choice, fluffy, curly, shaggy or spiky, craggy specimens, many are also rare and collectable. Most were not deliberately bred, but occurred naturally as chance 'finds' - the result of witches'-brooms (very compact bunches of unusual foliage that occasionally appear high up in the branches of large conifers) that are removed and propagated. Use dwarf conifers in pots raised up on staging to decorate a patio or walled alcove in a sheltered part of the garden, or group them with alpines on a raised bed or rocky scree. They are useful for creating miniature gardens, since the shapes available duplicate those of full-sized conifers; indeed, model railway enthusiasts hunt out dwarf conifers to make perfect small-scale replicas of mountain landscapes for their tracks to run through. Check carefully before you buy dwarf conifers; not all plants sold under that name stay small for long. Use the plant label, a text book or nursery catalog to check the height after ten years. And since genuinely dwarf conifers are very slow-growing, avoid planting them with fast-growing or sprawling plants that would smother them and cause the foliage to turn brown.

Spruces

The fascinating shapes and textures of small spruces perfectly complement any small heather and conifer feature or rock garden.

Above: *Picea mariana* 'Nana', a dense, blue-gray, globular plant, is blue tinged in summer. It reaches just 12in(30cm) when fully grown.

Picea glauca albertiana 'Conica' grows into a neat, pyramid with bright green new growth in spring.

Below: *Pinus mugo* 'Winter Gold' grows slowly to make a dense bushy plant. Its bright gold-tipped shoots show up well in winter.

Pines

Dwarf pines remain compact for many years. Provide well-drained (but not too dry) soil and plenty of sun and fresh air.

Pinus pumila 'Globe', a dwarf bushy plant, has blue-gray needles and cones from an early age. It grows just 2ft(60cm) in ten years.

Pinus mugo 'Humpy', is another very dwarf form suitable for rock gardens. It grows to 30in(75cm) in ten years.

Pinus densiflora 'Jane Kluis', is a new, very dense-needled, compact pine reaching 2ft(60cm) in 10 years.

Junipers

Juniperus communis 'Compressa' tolerates poor, hot dry soil, and grows very slowly to make a perfect conical shape roughly 18in (45cm) high after ten years.

Picea glauca albertiana 'Alberta Globe' is a rounded form with bright green spring foliage. It reaches 2ft(60cm) high in ten years.

Picea abies 'Nidiformis' makes a wide, spreading,plant that reaches 1ft(30cm) high and 2ft(60cm) across in ten years.

Chamaecyparis

Compact chamaecyparis are prized for their tight lacy foliage, slow growth and delightful shapes. Provide good-quality, free-draining soil that never dries out completely.

Above: *C. lawsoniana* 'Minima Aurea' is slow growing, with tightly packed, rather curly looking gold foliage that contrasts well with the deep green center of the bush. It remains a good gold color all year round.

C. obtusa 'Nana Lutea' has bright gold foliage that holds its color well in winter.

C. pisifera 'Nana' has soft, almost permed foliage and develops a perfect cushion shape.

Creating a 'bonsai' conifer

With a little trimming, you can accentuate the natural characteristics of virtually any conifer. Start with a plant that is already growing into an interesting shape. Pot-grown specimens are easier to work on.

1 Plan what you want to alter before cutting and trim a little at a time Use sharp scissors, secateurs or bonsai shears.

2 Clip away small sections of foliage to accentuate that part of the shape you want to exaggerate. Gauge the effect.

3 To help you decide whether to remove a section of foliage or not, try 'blanking' it out with a piece of white card.

4 Take your time; meditation is all part of the art. The shape of this plant looks like a peacock - it could easily end up as one.

Most conifers put on growth in one big spurt in late spring. Retrim them every year at this time to keep the shape neat.

5 The finished plant retains the attractive lacy texture and billowing shape of the original, but now it is more clearly visible.

MEDIUM CONIFERS

Medium-sized conifers that reach about 6ft(1.8m) tall after ten years are the most generally useful type for most purposes in most small to medium-sized gardens. They include a good range of shapes, from upright spires, rounded domes and more open bushy shapes, to flattened ground-covering types. Colors include the full range of reds, golds, blues and various shades of green. Although some conifers will stand some light shade, do not grow any of the colored foliage kinds in anything but full sun or their color fades to a very unhealthy looking, washed-out pallor and they will not grow well. Use a mixture of medium conifers in all shapes and colors to create contrasts in a heather bed. Flame-shaped conifers look good grown in pairs, one on either side of a doorway, to create a formal entrance. Very narrow types can even be trained over a frame to form a feathery foliage archway. A collection of dome-shaped conifers in different sizes can make a stunning 'architectural-looking' feature in an area of gravel, doubling as a minimalist living sculpture on a modern patio (you can improve their shape by clipping them), or lining the edge of a drive. And low, spreading conifers make good ground cover, useful for linking more strikingly shaped plants together in a low-maintenance planting scheme. Between them, the different types offer plenty of scope without any risk of outgrowing their welcome.

Thujas

The smallest thujas reach 2 or 3ft (60 or 90cm) after ten years and have interesting shapes, colors and foliage textures.

Right: *T. orientalis* 'Aurea Nana' consists of rows of overlapping 'fans' of foliage and makes a neat bush. Must have good drainage.

Thuja occidentalis 'Sunkist' is a newer variety with gold-touched ends to the green foliage.

Left: The flare-topped flame shape and rich green lacy foliage of *C. lawsoniana* 'Ellwoodii' team specially well with modern buildings, heather beds and stonework. It is a plant with real character.

Chamaecyparis

Medium-sized *Chamaecyparis,* range in shape from globular and bushy to upright, splay-topped or weeping.

C. pisifera 'Filifera Nana' has green foliage and grows very slowly to make a small to medium-sized dome-shaped bush with a flat top.

Chamaecyparis lawsoniana 'Ellwood's Gold' has unique, lacy, gold-edged foliage.

Junipers

Junipers that reach 4-6ft(1.2-1.8m) tall in ten years are very useful in a spot where a bigger plant is needed that will not outgrow its welcome.

Right: Where it is happy, *Juniperus scopulorum* 'Skyrocket' can grow to 12ft(3.7m) or more in ten years.

Juniperus chinensis 'Kuriwao Gold' makes an irregular bushy shape, boldly splashed with gold.

Juniperus x *media* 'Sulphur Spray'

C. pisifera 'Boulevard' has soft, tufted, blue-green foliage with turquoise highlights and a conical cumulus cloud shape.

Above: The gold filigree foliage of *C. pisifera* 'Filifera Sungold' creates an eye-catching centerpiece in a garden of conifers, evergreens and fall foliage color. Needs sun.

Plants that go well with conifers

Right: *Plants with tall or spiky shapes or large rounded leaves make good contrasts with both heathers and conifers, and look good grown together in groups among them. It does not take many such groups to soften the effect and to add touches of seasonal variation.*

Yucca filamentosa 'Bright Edge'

Liatris spicata

Bergenia cordifolia

Below: *Choose plants with linear shapes, strong colors and robust stems. Mix evergreens with plants such as* Molinia, *which bring in seasonal highlights to make the most of a bold display.*

Miscanthus sinensis 'Zebrinus' (tiger grass)

Phormium tenax 'Rainbow Maiden'

Molinia caerulea 'Variegata'

SPECIMEN CONIFERS

Because of their naturally imposing shapes, conifers are often chosen to stand alone in a special part of the garden, perhaps surrounded by lawns or as focal points in a low bed of ground cover plants or heathers. Specimen trees need to be superb examples of their type, symmetrically shaped, free from blemishes or brown patches, and with a full suit of foliage from bottom to top. Some types of conifer make naturally more outstanding specimen plants than others. In the grand parkland-style gardens of the past, giant trees, such as redwoods or Cedar of Lebanon, were the natural choice. In today's smaller spaces, it is important to choose specimen trees in scale with their surroundings. Here, spectacular shapes are often more important than sheer size. Blue spruces, *Cedrus deodara* and weeping cedars trained on supports all stand out well from their backgrounds. Tall, upright trees, such as fastigiate yews, also stand out well from a low background. Or consider making a specimen group of trees - perhaps three or five of the same kind (pines look specially good when grown in this way) as the group takes on a unique shape that is more than the sum of its parts.

BEAUTIFUL PINE CONES

Very young plants of *Abies koreana,* the Korean fir, produce striking violet cones that stand up from the branch (unlike many conifers where they are lost in the foliage).

Above: *Picea pungens* 'Koster' is symmetrical in shape, with a clear silvery-blue color that lasts all year. Although tall eventually, it takes ten years to reach 6-9ft(2-2.8m).

Abies koreana 'Silberlocke', has silvery backs to the leaves that curl upwards, giving them a two-tone effect. It reaches about 5ft(1.5m) in ten years.

Pinus x *schwerinii* is a rare variety grown for its long, elegant drooping needles. It grows to 15ft(4.5m) in ten years.

Sciadopitys verticillata (Japanese umbrella pine) has long needles radiating outwards. This slow starter stays dwarf for ten years but eventually makes a big tree.

Picea pungens 'Erich Frahm' is a slow-growing, compact, broadly conical-shaped blue spruce that makes a good specimen plant in a small border.

Above: Mature specimens of *Cedrus atlantica* 'Glauca' produce a profusion of upright, medium-sized cones that provide good seasonal interest.

Right: The young spring growth of *C. deodara* brings fresh green highlights into the foliage. For medium-sized gardens, try the smaller and slower golden form, 'Aurea'.

There are many named cultivars of the Austrian pine, one of the most rugged species suitable for windy coastal situations and limy soils. This one is *Pinus nigra* 'Bright Eyes'.

Cedrus deodara 'Aurea' is an exceptionally striking conifer with a nodding tip and gold-tinged foliage, especially conspicuous in spring. Reaches about 8ft(2.4m) in ten years.

Specimen yews

Right: Taxus baccata *'Standishii' makes a pillar shape that looks equally good out in the open or growing parallel to a doorway.*

T. b. 'Fastigiata Robusta' reaches about 6ft(2m) in ten years. Tolerates some shade.

Taxus baccata 'Fastigiata Aureomarginata'. Dark green leaves edged in yellow.

Taxus baccata 'Standishii' is ideal for containers or small gardens.

Pruning and shaping a yew tree

1 Create a more pronounced pillar shape by spiralling green, plastic-coated flexible wire loosely around main branches.

2 Maintain a clean outline by clipping to encourage side shoots. These thicken up the plant and produce upright stems.

USING CONIFERS IN THE GARDEN

Conifers are invaluable for all sorts of special uses in gardens, besides their more usual decorative role. Many kinds make superb hedges: the more dense, slow-growing kinds, such as yew or thuja, are more satisfactory than fast-growing types, such as Leyland cypress, which quickly becomes a nuisance. Some conifers, notably yew, can be clipped to form topiary shapes; hedges with ornamental, castellated or undulating tops are also possible. And many kinds of medium-sized conifers can be clipped into cloud formations like living sculptures for front gardens and patios. Conifers make useful screens and windbreaks, hiding eyesores and sheltering exposed gardens. On a small scale, conifers can be planted or trained to screen utility areas within a garden, or act as internal screens, dividing up a large area into garden rooms. Use a tall, narrow, upright conifer to mask a distant telegraph pole or pylon by planting it close to the house in line with the object. Or block out an unattractive view with a tall spreading conifer planted at the garden boundary. Conversely, a conifer hedge or group of plants can be trained to frame a pleasant view, either by cutting 'peepholes' or by training the stems round a preformed metal shape or over rustic poles.

Left: *Picea pungens* 'Procumbens', a dwarf blue spruce with low, spreading branches, makes a striking contrast in a heather bed.

Right: Spreading junipers make a good, low-maintenance ground cover 'link' between garden features, such as paths and a lawn, supplying contrasting foliage colors and textures. This is *J. squamata* 'Blue Carpet'; use it for any 'difficult' spot in dry sun.

Below: Junipers are famed for their ability to put up with inhospitable, hot, dry conditions in the garden. This makes spreading kinds, such as this *Juniperus horizontalis*, ideal for a heather bed bordered by a gravel path.

Juniperus communis 'Effusa' is less common than the conical species and grown for its exceptionally neat, low, spreading habit.The foliage is silvery beneath.

Juniperus horizontalis 'Andorra Compacta'. Once they cover the ground, horizontal junipers create a dense layer that smothers out weeds. Fallen foliage under the plants contributes to the weed supressant effect, while mulching the plants.

Juniperus davurica expansa 'Variegata', a dwarf plant with thick horizontal branches, eventually makes a low, ground-hugging mound.

Juniperus horizontalis, the popular creeping juniper, and its cultivars are all good, tolerant plants that put up with extremes of heat, drought and cold without browning.

Thuja occidentalis 'Smaragd'

Thuja plicata 'Zebrina'

Thuja occidentalis 'Holmstrupii'

Above: Although more expensive than plain thuja hedging, named varieties will give a hedge with more interesting foliage. By choosing relatively small varieties, you can control their ultimate size.

Left: A traditional country garden with herbaceous borders backed by yew hedges. Try to leave a bare strip of ground between the back of the border and the hedge for easy access when clipping.

Christmas trees

Choose conifers with pyramidal shapes and well-spaced branches that leave room for attaching pendant decorations. Blue spruces have good color.

Above: Picea pungens *'Hoopsii' has a silver-frosted effect on the foliage. Broader at the base than 'Koster', it makes the perfect 'designer' Christmas tree.*

Left: *The traditional Christmas tree, Norway spruce, is sold with cut roots. Reduce its tendency to shed needles by spraying it with an anti-transpirant spray.*

The neat, pyramidal habit of *Picea glauca albertiana* 'Conica' makes it an ideal 3ft(90cm)-high Christmas tree.

Being a live plant growing with all its roots, *Picea orientalis* 'Gracilis' is unlikely to shed its needles unless it dries out badly.

PROBLEM SOLVING

The biggest single cause of problems in conifers is drying out, which can happen at almost any stage, although young plants are most at risk. Newly planted conifers that turn completely brown within a few weeks or months of planting have usually died from wind 'scorching' the foliage. Another cause of early loss is drying out at the roots, usually caused if plants are dry when first planted. To avoid these problems, soak dry plants and tease open a potbound rootball slightly, plant into improved soil and shelter new plants with a windbreak for the first winter. Older plants can also be affected by browning. Dry soil is the usual cause; in this case, only the lower parts of the plant are usually affected and, although disfigured, it does not die. Watering and improving the soil by mulching each spring with organic matter or bark chippings would prevent the problem, but once it has occurred, the brown foliage will never revert to green. The best solution is disguise. Either plant climbing ivies or euonymus over the brown foliage or plant evergreen shrubs in front of the affected plant. Some conifers are less tolerant of exposure than others, so make sure that any susceptible plants are given a sheltered site, otherwise this, too, can be a cause of browning in future.

PEST PROBLEMS

Conifers are fairly pest-free, but watch for two particular problems. Spider mites are very tiny insects that mainly affect dwarf conifers with dense leaves. They cause the foliage to go yellow or bronze towards the shoot tips; in severe cases, minute webs can be seen and needles drop. Spruce aphids are long lean 'greenfly' tucked in among the needles, especially of blue spruces. Check plants regularly for both problems in spring and summer; spray with a systemic garden pesticide (shown below) to eradicate them.

1 Dry soil is the commonest cause of basal browning in conifers. In the case of aging horizontal junipers, as shown here, entire branches sometimes die off due to a root disease, leaving the remaining plant looking normal.

2 In either case, you can improve the plant by removing the brown branches entirely; cut back to a junction with a healthy green stem. Replacing the affected plant is probably the best long-term solution.

3 The exposed soil will be full of old needles and rather impoverished. Clear the debris, fork in plenty of well-rotted organic matter and a dressing of fertilizer. Replant the area with conifers or shrubs.

PART SIX

CLIMBING PLANTS

Climbers are superbly versatile garden plants. Not only do they provide a wide variety of flowers and foliage textures - and in many cases, the extra bonus of fragrance - but they also introduce the elements of height and disguise, an especially useful combination when they are used to shroud a garden boundary or building.

DIVERSITY OF CLIMBERS

There are thousands of climbing plants and their role in nature is to use other plants to clamber skywards, using twining stems, suckers or tendrils. There is even a strangler fig in the rainforest that, having germinated in the canopy, kills the tree it climbs down. Many climbers are woody and capable of enormous growth and it is this characteristic that we use to encourage them to cover walls and arches. Sadly, many of the very colorful climbers are frost-sensitive and will not grow outdoors in temperate areas. Rainforest climbers may be spectacular, but are only suitable for tropical or Mediterranean climates. However, there is also a world of opportunist climbers that can be grown as annuals or biennials and they will grow quickly and produce plenty of interesting foliage and vivid color. Among the most popular and easy-to-grow climbers are clematis, roses and wisteria. Gardeners enjoy these and other hardy climbers as species or improved varieties.

Above: This is 'Pompon de Paris', a miniature climbing rose that bears charming pink flowers early in the season - one of the many climbing and rambling roses.

Right: *Jasminum polyanthum* needs full sun to thrive. It is an evergreen woody climber that thrives on being pruned back every year. The dainty flowers are borne in fragrant profusion through summer to late fall.

Above: Honeysuckles are superb climbing plants, providing elegant flowers, many scented, and a harvest of berries in the fall. This is *Lonicera* x *americana*, a medium-sized honeysuckle.

Left: Climbers with decorative foliage can make a stunning impact in the garden. This ornamental vine is *Vitis coignetiae.* Temperatures during the night and degree of exposure to sun and shade during the day make the difference between ordinary fall colors and dazzling ones.

Right: Clematis are superb climbing plants that offer a huge variety of flower colors and sizes. The compact 'Lady Northcliffe' is one of the best blue varieties.

Below: Virginia creepers are great climbers and ideal for covering walls and fences. Many take on wonderful fall tints, but the large leaves are lost in winter.

Below: The massed flowers of Chinese wisteria, *Wisteria sinensis*, Deciduous wisterias are very hardy and vigorous climbers that bring color and elegance to the garden.

Below: *Hedera helix* 'Goldchild' is slow, slender, neat and easy. Its short flexible shoots are ideal for twining through a trellis.

How do climbers climb?

Climbing plants use a wide range of techniques to cling onto surfaces and other plants. These include twisting and twining stems, tendrils and sticky discs, and tiny roots that arise from the climbing stems.

Right: *In this clematis, several stems and leaf tendrils have formed a knot of vegetation, enabling other stems to climb further up their support.*

Above: *The woody stems of the mile-a-minute, or Russian vine* (Fallopia baldschuanica) *twine around each other to form a strong framework. Give it room.*

Right: *The coiled tendrils of a passion flower cling onto any nearby support - usually the stems of the same plant.*

Above: *The tendrils and sticky discs of Virginia creeper secure the plant to the surface. These also provide some cushioning and protection from wind.*

Right: *The ivy's tiny adventitious roots grow directly from the main stem and grip the surface tightly. They provide secure anchor points, allowing the stems to grow further on.*

CLEMATIS

Clematis is a widely distributed genus spread over many parts of the world, from the subtropical and tropical reaches of South America, the West Indies and West Africa to the temperate Northern Hemisphere, the Himalayas, China, Japan, New Zealand and North America. Because of this wide natural distribution, there are species and varieties suited to almost any growing conditions in the garden or greenhouse. The variation in the flowers is amazing, from the small, starlike flowers of *Clematis vitalba* rambling over hedges and banks to the exotic Japanese floridas. It is not just the shapes of the flowers that are so varied, but the range of colors spans the entire spectrum. From the pure blue European alpinas to the fiery red American texensis, they have all at some time been put into the garden melting pot to produce the large range of varieties and types available today. With reasonable growing conditions, a little extra care after planting and a firm support, clematis will flourish with hardly any maintenance. Much has been written about clematis wilt and complicated pruning strategies, but if well-grown, clematis are relatively disease-free and simple to cultivate. It is no surprise that given such a range of shapes and colors and with so many uses in the garden, clematis are highly popular garden plants.

Above: *Clematis orientalis* 'Bill McKenzie' has the largest flowers of this species. They are followed by wonderful seedheads, much appreciated by birds in winter. Species clematis repay extra feeding and watering with a wealth of flowers.

Above: *C. cirrhosa* 'Freckles' is an evergreen variety. In a sheltered position, with a substantial amount of sun and winter warmth, this distinctive, vigorous plant is one of the earliest clematis to flower.

Above: *Clematis montana* originates from the Himalayas. This vigorous grower flowers early in the season and soon covers walls, fences or trees. Some forms have a wonderful fragrance.

Right: 'Gravetye Beauty', a texensis hybrid, has upright, red, tulip-shaped flowers. Grow it so you can look down into the blooms.

Below: Both the flowers and seeds are visible on this summer-flowering *C. integrifolia* 'Rubra'. This herbaceous species grows to about 3ft(90cm).

Above: The viticellas flower prolifically in late summer and early fall, in sun or partial shade. This is 'Etoile Violette', which has larger flowers than most viticellas.

Right: 'Hagley Hybrid' is an old and reliable summer hybrid with dusky pink flowers that does well in shade. Light pruning in spring encourages earlier flowering.

Above: *Clematis alpina* has a number of lovely hybrids, including 'Francis Rivis', shown here. It blooms in spring, producing the largest flowers in the group.

Right: 'Lasurstern', an early, large-flowered clematis, bears lavender-blue flowers through the summer. This group includes many popular clematis, such as 'Nelly Moser'.

Planting a clematis

It is important to position clematis plants at least 3in(7.5cm) deeper than the soil level in the original container. This ensures that if wilt strikes, or you run a hoe too close to the stems when weeding, the plant will regenerate from the base and grow on strongly.

1 Dig a hole twice the size of the plant and half as deep again. Break up the sides of the planting hole to allow the roots access into the surrounding soil.

2 Remove the plant from its pot and lower the rootball into position. Make sure that the surface of the rootball is at least 3in(7.5cm) below soil level.

3 Fill the space around the rootball with the soil and potting mixture. Ideally, add some organic material to the soil at the base of the planting hole.

4 Once the plant is in place, firm the soil down around the base to ensure that the rootball makes close contact with the soil in the hole.

5 As well as adding organic material to the planting hole, you can also sprinkle fertilizer around the base of the plant, keeping it away from the stem.

6 Give the plant another good watering to ensure that the soil is settled and there are no air pockets. If the soil level sinks, add more soil as necessary.

HONEYSUCKLES

Honeysuckles make important statements in the garden. They fill up vertical spaces, ramble over unsightly structures and can be trained up pillars and posts. But perhaps the greatest virtue of honeysuckles lies in their ability to fill spaces and produce flowers that are not only usually scented, but also have unique shapes, typical only of honeysuckles. As climbing vines, they may need some support and assistance to reach their goal, but their effectiveness as bowers and scent producers is invaluable. Not that all honeysuckles have scent; some have sacrificed their scent for stunning good looks. There has been much hybridization of honeysuckles to increase the range of colors and forms. When making a choice, you should consider not only the early- and late-flowering varieties, but also those with beautiful fruits in the fall, including *Lonicera periclymenum* (the wild woodbine), with its red globular berries. In the newer hybrids there is a tendency for even larger flowers, and their colors may be quite striking or, in contrast, quite subtle. *Lonicera* x *tellmanniana,* for example, has gorgeous yellow blooms, but these are unscented. Honeysuckles grow in most soils, as long as they do not become waterlogged. They can reach up to 30ft(9m) in height if given sufficient support. As native honeysuckles prosper in the dappled light of the understory of woods, it is not surprising to find that they make good subjects for shady gardens, but they can thrive in direct sun as well.

Above: *Lonicera* x *italica* 'Harlequin'. The flowers of this hybrid are set off by superbly variegated foliage in green, cream and pink.

Left: The two-tone flowers of *Lonicera x heckrottii* have orange throats. Notice how the upper leaves are fused together. These flowers are borne in summer and pervade the air with their fragrance.

Left: *Lonicera sempervirens* has typical honeysuckle flowers: long, thin and tubular and borne in pairs close together.

Right: The coral, or trumpet vine, honeysuckle, *Lonicera sempervirens,* has attractive red-orange flowers with yellow throats; unfortunately they are scentless.

Right: The beautiful apricot yellow flowers of *Lonicera* x *tellmanniana* make a good color match with the marjoram and poppies as they grow together on a dry stone wall.

Above: These are the stalkless flowers of *Lonicera periclymenum* 'Belgica'. They appear on bushy plants in early summer and are followed by fine clusters of berries.

Below: The beautiful red-and-cream flowers of *L. periclymenum* 'Serotina' are wonderfully scented. It is one of the so-called late-flowering Dutch honeysuckles.

Planting a honeysuckle in a tub

Honeysuckles are universal favorites and there are many different species and cultivars to choose from. They can be grown in many different ways: in hedgerows, up trees, as pillars or as specimens in a tub with a trellis support, as shown here.

1 Fill the tub with potting mixture and make a hole for the rootball, allowing about 2in(5cm) of soil below the roots.

2 Place the plant - with its cane - into the planting hole, without losing too much of the soil adhering to the roots.

3 Gently firm in the soil to eliminate air spaces. Add more potting mix if necessary, but leave space for watering.

4 Use soft string to tie the individual climbing stems carefully to the trellis. Tie the knots loosely. Also use string to attach the cane to the trellis.

5 Give the honeysuckle a generous watering and then water it every day for ten days so that it becomes established. Do not allow it to dry out after that.

CHOOSING A GOOD PLANT

Even if pruned, the top growth must have substantial, disease-free wood and the strength to bear healthy growth and flower.

Above: Pot-grown climbing or rambler roses should have a healthy root system and strong shoots. Plant out in spring.

Above: Bare-rooted climbers are best planted out in the fall. This is a good, sturdy example, with three strong shoots.

CLIMBING AND RAMBLER ROSES

Both ramblers and climbers make quality contributions to the garden, not only because they have large and abundant flowers, superb colors and, in some cases, scent and a habit of repeat-flowering, but because they add both a vertical and a horizontal dimension. Climbers tend to be extremely vigorous, reaching well up into the trees or over the house. They have sturdier stems, are more resistant to mildew and bear larger flowers and smaller flower trusses than ramblers. Some are repeat-flowering, whereas most ramblers flower only once. As ramblers are derived from hybrids, their spirit of adventure is generally diminished, but they can be encouraged to decorate walls, pillars, old tree stumps and trellis. They also perform well as weeping standards. The differences in plant growth have an effect on how you prune climbers and ramblers. Climbers flower from old wood, which makes them easier to manage. They usually need no pruning. Ramblers flower from new growth and all old wood must be cut back to a suitable bud in winter. Encouraging a newly planted rose to cover a wall or trellis will occupy the mind while you consider which stems to cut out (or not). However, clearing out dead wood and any stems that cross each other will help to keep these decisions to a minimum.

Left: *Rosa banksiae* 'Lutea' adorning a sunny wall. This is a large growing species that needs a mild climate to thrive. Avoid pruning, as the flowers are produced on older stems.

Above: The climbing floribunda 'Dublin Bay' being trained onto a rope support. This is a decorative way of growing climbing roses.

Left: The vigorous climber *Rosa filipes* 'Kiftsgate' can grow through trees and cover huge areas. The creamy scented flowers, borne in late summer, are followed by a profusion of small bright red hips.

Above: 'American Pillar' growing with *Dipsacus* and *Hebe*. This variety of rambler rose is very vigorous and has a good crop of midsummer flowers, but it is very prone to mildew.

CLIMBERS AND RAMBLERS

Generally speaking, rambler roses have pliable stems and will do better when trained against a firm support. Climbing roses have stouter, woody stems and need less support. 'Zéphirine Drouhin', a climber (below left), has the advantage of being thornless as well as fragrant. 'Blush Rambler' (below right) is well proportioned, but needs to be pruned back to maintain this shape the following year.

Planting a climbing rose

Choose a moderate climber for walls or restricted spaces. A more vigorous variety is needed on a fence. Most climbers or ramblers will grow on a pergola. Choose a fast-growing variety to grow into a tree.

1 Dig a hole about 12in(30cm) across and deep. Make sure the hole is at the center of the trellis and not to one side.

2 Dig over the base of the hole to aerate the soil and improve drainage. Add rotted manure or other organic matter.

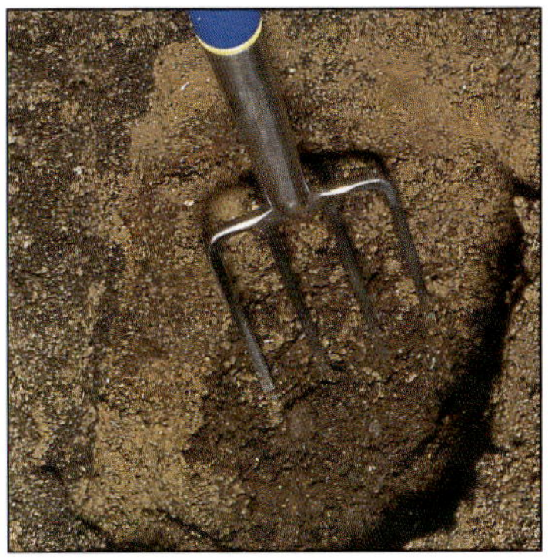

3 Fork the organic matter into the hole so that it will not reach the roots. Too much or too fresh manure can 'burn' roots.

4 Plant the rose, using a cane to check the depth. Fill in with soil plus peat substitute and some slow-release fertilizer.

5 Firm in the soil to eliminate any air pockets, which can interfere with root development and cause waterlogging.

6 Spread out the branches; even though they are short, and tie in the shoots to the trellis with soft string and a simple knot.

THE VERSATILE IVIES

Ivies contribute more to gardening with their leaves than their flowers. Being evergreen, they are good at covering walls or the sides of buildings, but keep an eye on them in case their adventitious roots make a mess of the masonry. As ivies grow neatly and tightly, they can also be clipped to various shapes, which is an advantage in Italianate-style gardens. Trimming removes the flowers, which most people are happy to forfeit, but in some varieties the flowers are very small and add character to the plant. They are also very attractive to insects, which hibernate in the shelter of the evergreen leaves. There are many ways in which you can take advantage of the various colors and leaf shapes of ivy. They can be employed with great success to hide any unsightly garden structures. Use them informally in wilder types of garden or clip them regularly in more formal plantings to keep them within prescribed limits. Specimens in pots can be encouraged to climb a small pyramid of trellis. Another feature of ivies is that they can be used for topiary, providing you have a framework over which they can grow and you trim the plants regularly to shape. This means that ivy can be used with great effect in small spaces and, if grown in pots, can be moved around to create different moods. Because ivies are comparatively vigorous, it does not take long for the topiary subjects to take shape.

Left: The yellow edges and irregular yellow patches on the attractive leaves distinguish *Hedera helix* 'Marginata Major' from other varieties. Its flower buds are just waiting to burst open.

DIVIDING IVY

A pot of ivy from the garden center is made up of several rooted cuttings that are easy to split and replant where you want them.

1 Knock the ivy out of its pot and pull the plantlets apart, taking care not to damage the roots too much in the process. Replant them without delay.

2 You can divide the original plant into ten or more separate rooted cuttings that you can plant in small groups to fill particular spaces.

A selection of ivies

Below: There are so many ivies to choose from that it is easy to plan a bold foliage feature with them alone or combine them with other plants.

'Buttercup' is prized for its radiant unvariegated color. It shines out from half shade but will stand direct sun without scorching if not too dry.

'Glacier' is a true classic. Bright young growth dulls to a soft gray-green, excellent where a change from green and yellow is needed.

The elegantly waved and beautifully colored leaves of 'Clotted Cream' are best displayed climbing through a tall shrub. Its slender habit will not inhibit its host's growth.

Keep 'Luzii' small and neat, as the muddled variegation is not attractive in large amounts. An accommodating, compact, small-leaved ivy.

'Midas Touch' has strong green-and-gold marbling on polished leaves and unique copper-pink stems. Beware of overusing it.

'Goldchild' is slow, slender, neat and easy. Its short flexible shoots are ideal for twining through a trellis.

Above: *Hedera helix* 'Atropurpurea' has purple-tinged leaves that are particularly conspicuous in winter.

Above: *Hedera hibernica* (Irish ivy) is very useful for ground cover in deep shade. The variegated form needs better light to thrive.

'Erecta' has an attractive 'architectural' appearance, good for associating with rocks or statuary. It is an extremely slow-growing variety.

'Ivalace' does not cling but can be bound on a post and clipped. Quite slow in dry ground.

Where not too dry, 'Manda's Crested' eventually makes a strong, carpet of foliage.

The running shoots of 'Sagittifolia' will race away as soon as the plant is settled. Pinch out the tips to encourage it to thicken up.

'Green Ripple' is an unobtrusive background ivy, capable of clothing a sizeable area of ground or wall. Easy to control where necessary.

Ivies for particular places

There are several hundred varieties of ivy available, with a wide range of leaf forms, sizes and colors. Ivies are versatile and attractive evergreen foliage plants with a host of uses all round the garden.

Ground cover: *Trailing ivies are particularly useful in shady places or beneath dense shrubs in a border, where few other ground cover plants will grow. Once well established, they will tolerate dry soil under big trees. The best ivy to use in deep shade is Irish ivy,* Hedera helix hibernica, *but any plain green kind, including those with curly edges, such as* Hedera helix *'Parsley Crested', or arrowhead-shaped leaves, such as* Hedera helix *'Sagittifolia', will thrive. These also associate well in damp shade with hardy ferns and euonymus. Variegated ivies need a little more light than plain green kinds.*

Above: *The variegated leaves of* Hedera colchica *'Sulphur Heart' clothe the bare trunk of a tree.*

Covering walls and fences: *Large-leaved ivies, such as* Hedera colchica *'Sulphur Heart', are ideal, as they look the most striking, although brightly colored small-leaved kinds, such as* Hedera helix *'Buttercup' (yellow leaves) or H. h. 'Goldheart', also catch the eye. Ivies climb by means of tiny aerial roots, so they do not need supporting. However, to help new ivies cling to a wall, it is helpful to keep the wall damp by spraying with plain water occasionally until the tendrils have started to grip.*

Ivy in trees: *Contrary to popular belief, ivy is not parasitic and does not directly harm trees. However, if big old trees have a great deal of ivy growing up the trunk and into the crown, this can increase wind resistance and result in trees being brought down in gales. To remove ivy from trees, cut through the stems at the base, and leave them for a few weeks. When they are dead and dry, the stems will peel away from the trunk quite easily.*

Winter hanging baskets and containers: *Small-leaved ivies, particularly variegated or gold-leaved and other fancy kinds, make useful trails for softening the edge of a container, and good foliage backdrops to winter-flowering displays. Ivies do not work so well in summer tubs, as summer bedding continues to grow after planting and quickly smothers the ivy. Ivy also tends to become scorched by hot sun in the situations where summer containers are mainly used.*

Below: *The plinth supporting this figure has disappeared beneath the yellow-leaved ivy, 'Buttercup'.*

Above: In full sun, the evergreen *Jasminum polyanthum* will produce large numbers of scented flowers through summer to late fall. Prune back this woody climber every year.

STUNNING CLIMBERS

Climbers include some of the biggest and most sensational flowers in the garden. Wisteria is the traditional favorite, with its huge 'bunch of grape' shaped early summer flowers in purple or white. Normally grown on a house front, it does need frequent attention - if the vigorous shoots are allowed to grow behind gutters or drainpipes, they expand as they grow, and can eventually force fixtures away from the wall. Proper pruning prevents this problem and also encourages this notoriously slow flowering climber to begin blooming on time, usually about seven years after planting. For a hot sunny spot, even if the soil tends to be a bit dry (a problem close to a wall, since the brickwork deflects rainwater) then passion flower and campsis (trumpet vine) are good choices. Both have spectacular flowers; those of passion flower are like rosettes with centers packed with short 'tendrils', while campsis has huge coral-red trumpet flowers. Though exotic looking, both plants are hardier than they appear. For scent, any of the climbing jasmines such as *Jasminum officinale* (the old cottage garden favorite) or *Jasminum polyanthum* are perfect - the white flowers enable them to team perfectly with other climbers on a pergola or arch. They 'go' specially well with climbing roses, but are also a useful way to add scent to more spectacular but perfume-free flowers. *Trachelospermum* is a particularly useful climber as it twines rather like honeysuckle so will make its own way up rustic poles.

Above: At the end of the season, cut back smaller branches of new wisteria growth to two or three leaves beyond the woody stems.

Left: Chinese wisteria, *Wisteria sinensis,* bears massed ranks of powerfully scented, pale lilac to purple flowers in early summer.

Right: *Passiflora caerulea* has delicate rings of blue or purple in its flowers. It does well growing on trellis or trained against a wall.

Left: Star jasmine, *Trachelospermum asiaticum* is the hardiest kind; the much more tender *T. jasminoides* needs a mild climate and a sheltered sunny spot to thrive.

Below: *Campsis grandiflora* bears these splendid orange-red, trumpet-shaped flowers from midsummer until the fall. Keep it in check by pruning the young shoots back to the old wood. *C.* x *tagliabuana,* a hybrid between *C. radicans* and *C. grandiflora,* is hardier and has shorter trumpets.

Growing wisteria as a standard

Wisterias can be trained as standard 'trees'. Growing them in tubs also encourages wisterias to bloom much sooner. Potted standards take up far less room and are ideal for the patio.

1 *Start with a strong healthy young plant from a garden center, growing up a cane. Begin removing the side shoots from the base, leaving the main stems twisted around the cane.*

2 *Continue removing the side shoots, cutting them flush with the main stems, until about 12in(30cm) from the top of the plant. Shorten long shoots at the top to start forming a head.*

3 *Any long shoots from close to the base of the plant can be trained round the cane to help thicken up the 'trunk' of the plant. Be sure to twist them in the same direction as the other stems.*

FOLIAGE INTEREST

There is nothing quite like employing effective foliage plants to bring nature to your doorstep and if you choose the right climbers, you can soon cover unsightly structures or enclose a small garden to give it a special verdant touch. Luckily, there are a number of good performers, either for climbing up walls or spilling over them. The advantage of gardening with strong leaf effects is that colors and textures can be determined either seasonally or all year round. Climbers that change their leaf color with the seasons add an extra decorative dimension, such as the highly versatile Virginia creepers, *Parthenocissus,* the large-leaved vine, *Vitis coignetiae,* or the exciting pink-leaved kiwi, *Actinidia kolomikta.* Alternatively, choose a golden variety of a climber such as the golden hop, *Humulus lupulus* 'Aureus'. Then there are the curious climbers, which are more leaf than flower, such as the chocolate vine, *Akebia.* However, most of these climbers lose their leaves in winter, so if it is your intention to maintain a permanent green foliage effect, then evergreens, such as the ivies, *Hedera,* or golden honeysuckle, *Lonicera japonica* 'Aureoreticulata', would be suitable for temperate areas. Other climbers with foliage interest include *Celastrus orbiculatus* (bittersweet), with leaves that turn yellow in the fall and bears red berries. *Ampelopsis brevipedunculata* 'Elegans' has striking pink-and-green variegated leaves; in cold regions, it dies down to ground level during the winter and the roots should be protected with a layer of peat or gravel.

Above: Given a good support, evergreen *Lonicera japonica* 'Aureoreticulata', a variegated honeysuckle, will spread quickly.

Above: Trusses of vanilla-scented, spring flowers hang down among the unusual five-lobed leaves that provide the main interest in *Akebia quinata,* the chocolate vine.

Below: The striking fall colors of *Parthenocissus quinquifolia* (Virginia creeper) make an impact in any garden. The blue-black berries add even more interest.

Left: The leaves of the striking *Vitis vinifera* 'Purpurea' turn a deep purple in the fall and often remain on the plant. The foliage is more interesting than the fruits - small purplish 'grapelike' berries.

Above: The blood-red leaves of *Parthenocissus tricuspidata* (Boston ivy) make a stunning show in the fall, but they can all blow away in a single storm. All Virginia creepers are deciduous, so be prepared for bare walls during the winter months.

Below: During the summer, the leaves of *Actinidia kolomikta* take on a variegation of white, pink and green. The curvaceous leaves on a mature bush look as if they have been splashed with paint.

Above: The young leaves of *Actinidia kolomikta* start off green as the woody stems begin to sprout in spring. Actinidias, or kiwis, need support on which to climb.

Pruning hops

Hops burst out of the ground in early spring with an unbelievable enthusiasm and thrust upwards and sideways with long, thin, twining stems. Each plant puts on a prodigious amount of vegetation during spring and summer and all of it must be cut back to ground level in the fall, otherwise you are left with a mass of withered and twisted brown stems that may harbor insects and fungal pests and diseases. Pruning hard back to the base of the plant is essential for these plants, which are both perennial and deciduous.

***Above:** The eye-catching leaves of Humulus lupulus* 'Aureus'*, the golden hop, will smother walls, pillars and unsightly structures.*

1 Towards the end of summer, just before they fall, hop leaves deteriorate. Cut back the plant to ground level, removing all the prolific aerial growth.

2 Cut off one of the main stems 2in(5cm) from the ground. To disengage the stem, cut off the side shoots that wrap themselves around other stems.

3 Cut away all the other stems, leaving short pieces above ground level so that you avoid damaging the plant when working over the beds in winter.

4 Label the plant. Although the cut stems are visible now, the plant remains inactive underground for four months and may become covered with debris.

VIGOROUS CLIMBERS

Certain climbers are so vigorous that they tend to swamp everything they are attached to. Although many plants qualify for this description, a particularly good example is *Fallopia baldschuanica,* the so-called mile-a-minute, or Russian vine. This climber is ideal for temperate climates and is notorious for its prolific growth, hence its common name, but it has the advantage of flowering in the fall after many other climbers have finished. It is a member of the knotweed family, many members of which are weeds. The mass of vegetation produced by such smothering climbers can be left in place if it is not causing a nuisance or you can trim it back roughly to the required shape. The mile-a-minute plant is so fast growing and all-smothering that great care should be taken in positioning it; it is capable of overwhelming a garage within a single season, and unless kept cut back will find its way in through small crevices in a building and can cause considerable damage. Some other plants that qualify as vigorous climbers, however, are less invasive. *Vitis coignetiae* has large textured leaves that take on rich autumn tints at the end of the season; this looks superb growing through large trees, or over a framework of rustic poles mixed with flowering climbers such as clematis. Climbing hydrangea is a good choice for walls and outbuildings as it self-clings; the typical hydrangea flowers last a long time, especially in a shady aspect. Its unusual relative *Schizophragma hydrangeoides* is similar but the variety 'Roseum' has rosy pink flowers.

Right: The leaves of *Vitis coignetiae* are enormous, like dinner plates, and with an unusual texture that makes them a distinctive feature throughout the growing season.

Above: In the fall, the leaves of *Vitis vinifera* 'Brandt' become mottled. They start the summer deep green, but change to yellows and reds, as well as orange, crimson and pink.

Left: When the vine becomes heavy with fruit, loop some string once around the stem and secure it to the support. This prevents the fruit from moving and becoming damaged.

PRUNING VINES

In summer, cut back long shoots that venture over the roof or windows. In winter, cut back the shoots of new green growth to two or three buds on from old, woody growth. Make the cut at the largest bud. Use the same method to train a vine along a wire.

Left: *Hydrangea petiolaris* (climbing hydrangea) will thrive on a shady wall. These plants are slow starters and may take several years to begin flowering. Until then, mulch, feed and water well in summer.

Below: *Fallopia baldschuanica,* mile-a-minute vine, hangs like a waterfall of vegetation from this trellis. The mass of white or pink flowers provides a really effective screen.

Chilean potato vine

At the back of a herbaceous border, Chilean potato vines will scramble up a wall, where they contribute to seasonal foliage and color through the summer and into the fall. They can also be grown in a container, supported on a trellis as shown here, or trained up the side of a house.

1 Plant the potato vine with its cane in soil-based potting mix. Firm in well. Cut off some of the ties and separate the stems.

2 Attach the stems to the trellis with twist ties, which are easy to adjust as the plant grows. Water the plant well.

Varieties of interest

The flowers of Solanum jasminoides *are usually bluish-white; this white-flowered form, 'Album', is a half-hardy evergreen.*

Solanum crispum *'Glasnevin' can climb to 20ft(6m), making a rich display of purple flowers.*

CHOOSING PLANTS

There are climbers for every site and situation. Due to their more exposed growing position, it is vital to choose plants that are right for the conditions, especially when selecting plants for raised open structures such as pergolas and arches.

E = Evergreen

Climbers for decorative fruit and berries

Akebia quinata: sausage-shaped, maroon-chocolate colored fruit
Billadiera longiflora: large blue-purple berries
Celastrus scandens: bittersweet yellow berries ripening to red
Chaenomeles: large green, buff or orange-red fruit
Clematis periclymenum: clusters of red berries
Passiflora caerulea: large, yellow, egg-shaped fruit after a hot summer
Vitis: most ornamental kinds have tiny purplish grapes

Berries of *Lonicera periclymenum* 'Belgica'

Climbers and wall shrubs for walls that do not receive sun at midday

Camellia
Clematis alpina cultivars,
C. montana cultivars, *Clematis* 'Jackmanii', 'Nelly Moser', 'Comtesse de Bouchaud', 'Madame le Coultre'
Cotoneaster horizontalis
Euonymus fortunei and *E. japonicus*
Garrya elliptica
Hedera
Hydrangea petiolaris
Jasminum nudiflorum
Lonicera japonica 'Aureoreticulata'
Pyracantha
Roses: 'Danse du Feu'
'Russelliana'
'Souvenir du Dr. Jamain'

Above: A vigorous montana clematis can grow happily through a tree. It can also be pruned and trained for a more delicate effect.

Scented climbers

Clematis montana
Jasminum officinale affine
Lonicera japonica 'Halliana' (E)
L. periclymenum 'Belgica' and 'Serotina'
Trachelospermum asiaticum (E)
Wisteria sinensis

Shrubs suitable for training against a wall

(A useful means of growing many slightly tender shrubs in cold regions, since the wall gives them some protection)
Camellia
Carpenteria californica
Ceanothus
Chaenomeles
Cotoneaster horizontalis
Cytisus battandieri
Fremontodendron
Garrya elliptica
Hardy fuchsia
Itea ilicifolia
Jasminum nudiflorum
Magnolia grandiflora cultivars
Myrtus communis
Prunus triloba
Pyracantha

Climbers and wall shrubs for exposed/windy situations

Chaenomeles (trained as a wall shrub)
Cotoneaster horizontalis
Euonymus fortunei (when grown against wall makes a good climber without training)
Fallopia baldschuanica (Russian vine)
Garrya elliptica (wall trained)
Hydrangea petiolaris
Jasminum nudiflorum
Lonicera japonica 'Aureoreticulata'
Parthenocissus quinquifolia (Virginia creeper)
Rambler roses
Rubus species - cultivated blackberries and Japanese wineberry

Evergreen climbers that provide all-year-round interest

Camellia (wall-trained)
Carpenteria californica (wall-trained - needs shelter)
Euonymus fortunei cultivars - make good climbers without training when grown against wall
Fremontodendron californicum (wall-trained - needs shelter)
Garrya elliptica (wall-trained)
Hedera (Ivies)
Itea ilicifolia (wall-trained - needs shelter)

Fuchsia 'Cardinal Farges'

Jasminum nudiflorum (wall-trained)
Lonicera japonica 'Aureoreticulata' and 'Halliana'
Magnolia grandifolia cultivars (wall-trained)
Pyracantha (wall-trained)
Trachelospermum asiaticum (needs shelter)

Climbers for winter/very early spring flowers

Abeliophyllum distichum
Camellia (wall-trained)
Clematis cirrhosa var. *balearica* (needs shelter)
C. cirrhosa 'Freckles'
Garrya elliptica (wall-trained. Has green catkins)
Jasminum nudiflorum

Hedera helix 'Luzii'

Hedera helix 'Midas Touch'

PART SEVEN

PERENNIALS

Nowadays, perennials are the fashionable plants to cultivate; they are used in a wide variety of ways, from island beds to containers. Drought-resistant species are the up-and-coming solution to water shortages, while informal meadow-style planting schemes are yet another innovative new style of using perennials.

HOW PERENNIALS GROW

Herbaceous perennials, usually called simply perennials, are hardy plants that die down every winter, leaving dormant roots in the soil, from which new stems grow the following spring. They include all kinds of traditional herbaceous border flowers, such as peony, phlox, delphiniums, lupins, astilbes and hostas. But the term also includes many flowers that do not die down completely in winter, such as *Sedum spectabile*, *Euphorbia wulfenii*, hellebores and red hot pokers, which have evergreen leaves that persist all winter. Although perennials are thought of as summer flowers, since this is when the traditional herbaceous border is at its peak, there are perennials that flower in early spring, such as *Brunnera macrophylla* and *Pulmonaria*, and also in late fall, such as Michaelmas daisies, Japanese anemones and *Schizostylis*. Nowadays it is popular to grow perennials in mixed borders amongst trees and shrubs, or in island beds cut into a lawn. Here, light reaches the plants from every direction, producing more compact growth and giving pests and diseases nowhere to hide. That, combined with modern compact varieties, has made perennials much easier to accommodate in today's gardens. Now they are highly fashionable plants; new varieties are continually being introduced and rare plants are sought after by enthusiasts.

THE PERENNIAL CYCLE

Herbaceous perennials have root systems that survive all year round from which, in spring, fat growth buds appear. These develop into shoots that bear the foliage and flowers that provide such glorious displays of color in the herbaceous perennial border. After the flowers are over, the stems slowly die down, leaving the plants in their winter state. The dead leaves fall and naturally protect the crown of the plant from severe frosts.

Above: A lupin in the summer border at the height of its flowering display.

Left: A lupin after the flowering stems have been cut in the fall. The leaves will die and new shoots will emerge in the spring.

Popular perennials

Euphorbia amygdaloides robbiae. Semi-shade, any soil.

Epimedium sulphureum. Moist but well-drained soil, partial shade.

Brunnera macrophylla. Moist soil, semi shade.

Doronicum caucasicum (leopard's bane). Any moist soil, sun.

Caltha palustris 'Alba' (white marsh marigold). Moist soil, sun.

Pulsatilla vulgaris (pasque flower). Well-drained soil, sun.

Right: Late-flowering perennials, such as *Sedum spectabile, Rudbeckia* 'Goldsturm', *Aster* species and *Solidago* (golden rod) shown here, grow stems and leaves in summer, but do not start flowering till late summer and fall.

Above: Japanese anemone and *Dendranthema*. Both have long-lasting flowers, and given some support, will last well into late fall unless stopped early by frost.

Above: *Meconopsis grandis* (Himalayan blue poppies) thrive best in light woodland. Elsewhere, ensure that they get moist, lime-free, humus-rich but free-draining soil in light dappled shade.

Below: The traditional herbaceous border resembled a corridor with two beds facing one another across a wide path, each backed by its own hedge and leading to a focal point, such as a statue.

Using shapes to make plant associations

Creating winning plant associations is simple when you base them on the wide range of shapes and sizes seen in perennials. Team tall, upright shapes and open, splaying plants with low, ground-covering ones, and rounded, mound shapes with spiky foliage for a traditional look. Use carpets of similarly shaped plants punctuated by occasional dramatic architectural shapes for a more modern, minimalistic effect.

Left: *In moist soil and sun,* Ligularia przewalskii *'The Rocket' makes a large plant with tall, upright, pokerlike flowers that look dramatic shooting up through the back of a large border.*

Below: Hemerocallis *(day lilies) have striking, spiky-looking foliage that is, in fact, quite soft to touch. Plant shapes vary according to the variety; this 'Norton Orange' makes an unusually neat mound in the border.*

Right: Heuchera micrantha *'Palace Purple' has large purple leaves arranged to form neat low clumps. Plant it en masse for ground cover, or in loose rows for the front of a border.*

PLANTING A PERENNIAL

Perennial plants are traditionally planted in fall or early spring, but since they are dormant at that time, you may prefer to delay planting until mid-spring, when some growth is visible. Perennial plants will stay in the same ground for two to four years, so it is vital to spend time on soil preparation before planting. Choose a spot with deep, well-drained soil, free from perennial weeds and in a sheltered, sunny situation. Tackle soil pests with a soil insecticide or dig the ground several times in winter to expose pests to the birds. Incorporate as much well-rotted organic matter as possible, such as garden compost or animal manures. In spring, sprinkle general fertilizer over the area and fork it in. Rake the ground level and remove any stones. After planting, water the plants in and mulch by spreading 1-2in(2.5-5cm) of chipped bark or more well-rotted organic matter over the soil surface, then put in any necessary plant supports or stakes. Keep new plants well watered in dry spells, and hoe carefully around the plants to control weeds.

Planting a perennial

1 Prepare the soil over the entire bed some time in advance of planting. Dig a hole for each plant about twice the size of its rootball. Put the excavated soil next to the hole.

2 Put a spadeful of well-rotted manure or other organic matter in the hole and mix well. Add more manure to the excavated soil, ready for filling in later on.

3 Sprinkle a handful of general-purpose fertilizer into the hole and mix well with the soil. Add half a handful of fertilizer to the soil alongside the hole and mix in well.

4 Tip the plant out gently (knock the base of the pot against something solid if the plant is hard to dislodge). Slide the plant out without breaking up the rootball.

5 Lift the plant by its rootball into the hole. The top of the root-ball should lie level with the soil surface. Rotate the plant until its best side faces the front of the bed.

6 Surround the rootball with the improved soil excavated from the planting hole, and firm it down lightly. Add more soil to bring it up to the level of the surrounding bed.

7 Water the new plants well in, trickling water around the edge of the root-ball. Mulch with 1-2in (2.5-5cm) of rotted organic matter or bark chips and keep plants well watered.

Left: Plant herbaceous peonies so that the top of the rootball is flush with the soil surface. If planting dormant plants as bare roots or moving existing plants, growth buds should be 1in(2.5cm) below ground.

Above: Lift and divide congested clumps of hosta in early spring. Reject old sections from the center and replant the best divisions from round the edge at the same depth as they were before.

Left: Lift and divide large clumps of bearded iris six weeks after flowering ends. Replant young sections of tuber horizontally, with the upper half above ground in a sunny, well-drained spot.

Support mechanisms

Some perennials, such as delphiniums, have naturally frail, slender stems that need support to keep them straight and upright. Others, while more compact, such as gypsophila, make untidy sprawling plants that tend to smother their neighbors unless they are restrained in some way. Various types of plant supports are available to cope with any type of growth; used correctly, they should remain unobtrusive. Put plant supports in place in spring when new growth is visible but before stems are so big that they may be damaged by handling.

Left: *'Grow-through' supports provide a loose cage effect that forces splaying shoots to grow upwards. Place the support over the crown of the plant in spring and adjust the grid to a suitable height; it will soon be lost in the foliage.*

Above: *Delphinium stems are best supported along their entire length by tying them loosely in several places to a tall cane; green canes look least obtrusive.*

Above: *Support bushy mound-like plants by pushing 2ft(60cm)-long twiggy branches in round the crown of the plant in spring; they disappear among the shoots.*

POPULAR PERENNIALS

Even now, when so many new varieties have been introduced, old favorites, such as lupins, delphiniums, red hot poker, campanula and phlox, are the backbone of many perennial planting schemes. For anyone new to perennials, these are the best to start with, as they are generally easy to grow and problem-free. Plant groups of taller kinds towards the back of the bed, and low spreading ones along the front for a graduated effect. Avoid putting clashing colors next to each other; they look fine if separated by foliage or a plant that flowers at a different time. In a small bed, aim for midsummer flowering, when the majority of popular perennials are at their peak. In a larger bed, add plants that give early and later flowers (including spring and fall bulbs) for a longer season of interest. For best effect, mix these all through the border; do not group them together in one spot.

Before buying plants, design a rough plan to give you an idea of how many plants you will need. Choose a good mixture of types in different sizes, taking into account the size each will reach after a couple of years. Many nurseries specializing in perennials can provide a planting plan for a basic bed. Spring is the best time to buy perennials when you are planting an entire bed, since the whole area can be given the same treatment to help plants get established. You can buy and plant perennials in summer, but keep them well watered for the rest of the season. Although they do not really get established until the following year, it is a useful facility that enables you to add 'impulse purchases' to an existing bed or fill odd gaps as necessary.

Above: Red hot pokers (this one is *Kniphofia linearifolia)* make large clumps with sharp-edged, spiky evergreen foliage; they need plenty of sun and a well-drained spot.

Below: Herbaceous peonies are the aristocrats of the border; this is 'Gleam of Light', a stunning variety with scented, chalice-shaped flowers and distinctive foliage.

Above: If regularly deadheaded, penstemons bloom continuously from early midsummer right through to the frost. They also thrive during drought; give them sun and good but well-drained soil.

Left: Use lupins, the classic country garden flowers, in herbaceous borders, cottage gardens or in mixed borders with shrubs and flowers (as here).

Above: In sunny well-drained conditions, the stark shapes of eryngium are softened by the campanula; its flowers pick out the blue tones of the eryngium heads.

Left: *Achillea* is a useful plant in a border; as well as tolerating a broad range of growing conditions, the wide, flat-topped flowers also make stunning contrasts with both tall, upright spire shapes and mound-forming plants.

Right: Day lilies *(Hemerocallis)* are very collectable nowadays and available in a huge range of colors, including lovely pinks and deep red, besides the usual yellows and tawny orange shades. This is 'Red Damask'.

Above: Hellebores hybridize naturally when grown together in the garden. Try to leave seedlings until they flower and save the best. This is a hybrid, *H* x *ericsmithii*.

Below: Medium-tall, late-flowering *Phlox paniculata* is invaluable for keeping borders colorful after the main flush of flower is over. This plant will root easily from cuttings.

Contrasting shades

Color schemes are very much a matter of personal taste. Recently, relaxing pastel schemes of pink, mauve and purple have been popular, as have 'one-color' borders, in white, blue or yellow. But now stronger color schemes are making a comeback, and red, yellow and orange are reappearing in gardens. They are useful for brightening up an otherwise dark corner without looking garish. To make more of the display, team perennials with toning or contrasting foliage shrubs.

***Right:** Contrasting colors produce an attractive, unusual scheme, particularly when the flowers vary in shape. These are* Salvia farinacea *and the yellow* Rudbeckia *'Goldsturm'.*

***Below:** Frothy white 'filler' flowers, such as* Gypsophila paniculata, *placed between the bright colors of* Helenium *'Moerheim Beauty' prevent clashes.*

***Left:** Shades of pinks blend together to give an autumnal glow to a late border. Here,* Dendranthema *'Raquel' and* Sedum spectabile *'Brilliant' work extremely well together because of their very different flower shapes.*

PERENNIALS FOR CUTTING

Many kinds of perennials provide good flowers for cutting, between them offering a wide range of inspirational material for the creative floral artist. By cutting carefully from the back of a group, the decorative effect of a border should not be spoiled. Some perennials provide upright linear shapes, such as *Delphinium, Astilbe* and *Schizostylis.* Some have large striking individual blooms that form a good centerpiece to arrangements, such as peony, while other plants make good 'filler' material, such as *Gypsophila, Alchemilla* and *Aster ericoides.* Some plants have striking flower shapes, such as the flat-topped heads of *Achillea* and *Sedum spectabile,* or daisy shapes, such as *Pyrethrum.* Perennials such as *Physalis* (Chinese lantern) with dramatic seedpods that can be used fresh or dried are great fun. Sometimes material can be 'improved' by a spot of pruning - many arrangers, for instance, remove the leaves of Solomon's seal *(Polygonatum)* in spring to reveal the neat rows of dangling, white, bell-shaped flowers suspended from the graceful, arching stems. Consult the catalogs of specialist nurseries to find unusual shades and little-grown perennials to provide material for highly creative styles.

Above: *Alstroemeria ligtu* hybrids in a range of colors are hardy and thrive in well-drained soil and sun. They resent root disturbance.

Below: *Echinops ritro* has a profusion of gunmetal blue globe flowers. Immature blooms are well colored, too, so material can be cut from plants over a long period.

Below: Perennial penstemons thrive even in hot spots with dry soil. If you remove dead blooms or cut flowers for arranging, plants will flower from midsummer to fall.

Perennials suitable for cutting

Left: *Alchemilla mollis* and hostas are good dual-purpose perennials, with flowers and foliage that can both be used for cutting; in the garden, the two associate well together in shade or partial sun.

Above: Tall bearded irises like this 'Jane Phillips' are excellent for cutting, since the longer stems make them most generally useful. Cut as the buds begin to unfurl.

Above: Perennial rudbeckias, such as this 'Goldsturm', produce similar flowers to the annual kinds, but on much bigger plants - and they need not be replaced annually.

Above: *Sedum spectabile* has the dramatic shapes that flower arrangers love. It flowers in late summer and fall, when material can be scarce, though the immature flower heads can also be cut 'green' to use earlier in the season.

Perennials for drying

Some perennials produce colorful seedheads suitable for drying for winter arrangements. Perennial grasses, such as pampas grass, the seedpods of Physalis *and the huge heads of artichoke, cardoon and some species of centaurea, all make striking dried materials.*

Left: Physalis alkekengi *makes a smaller plant than the better known* P. a. franchetii, *but has similar lantern-like seed containers. The stems can be cut to use fresh in displays of live material or dried for later use.*

Creating a display

In a vase the same rule applies as in a garden border - a good range of contrasting sizes and shapes create the most impact, particularly when you are working with a limited color scheme. Remove any leaves that will be under water, otherwise they will rot.

VARIEGATED PERENNIALS

Variegated perennials combine colorful flowers with bright foliage. They bring welcome flashes of light to a border that can often look a bit dark by late summer, when all the plants have grown up to their maximum heights. Most variegated plants grow less vigorously than all-green versions, so take care that they do not become swamped by weeds or invasive neighbors. Give them good growing conditions, with generous mulching and feeding, and prevent the soil drying out in summer. Variegated plants tend to scorch easily, as white or cream parts of the leaf are susceptible to both sunburn and drought. A shortage of green pigment (chlorophyll) means that they will not grow happily in shade - a light situation protected from strong midday sun is ideal. Since variegation can be rather unstable, it is worth keeping a close watch on variegated plants and removing any stems that do not show the characteristic coloration, otherwise plain green leaves - which grow faster than variegated ones - can soon take over the plant. Similarly, if previously unvariegated plants suddenly produce a variegated stem, this is worth removing and rooting, to see if the pattern persists. If it remains, despite being propagated several times, the chances are it is stable and a new plant has developed.

Above: *Tovara virginiana* (painter's palette) has attractively blotched and marbled oval leaves. Plants grow to about 2ft(60cm) tall, forming ground-covering clumps. Needs moist (not waterlogged) soil and some shelter.

A selection of variegated perennials

Right: Variegated versions of many popular garden plants are available; indeed some people collect variegated plants, which can be used as the basis of stunning flower and foliage borders.

Left: *Pulmonaria* 'Roy Davidson' and *Hosta* 'Wogon' are ideal for moist, humus-rich soil in light shade. Put with dwarf spring bulbs.

Below: The striking variegation of *Polemonium* 'Brise D'Anjou' remains this good all season; here teamed with *Heliotropium* 'Marine'.

Above: *Lamium maculatum* 'White Nancy' is one of the best foliage forms of ornamental dead-nettle; the foliage almost appears to have been coated with powder.

Right: *Physostegia virginiana* 'Variegata' grows about 30in (75cm) high and looks striking grown among delphiniums and other upright shapes in a tall herbaceous border.

Variegated hostas

A surprisingly large range of different variegations are available within the hosta family. Team large-leaved kinds with small, variegated ones, and variegated hostas with plain green or gold-leaved types, and add a few other plants that enjoy similar conditions for contrast. Astilbe, Mimulus, *candelabra primulas and waterside plants such as* Iris laevigata *look good with hostas in moist soil in sun beside water. In shade, go for hardy ferns, ivies,* Alchemilla mollis *or woodland plants.*

***Above:** Closely planted groups of different hostas add variety and interest to shady borders. Here,* Hosta crispula, H. fortunei albopicta *and* H. ventricosa *provide a contrasting display.*

***Right:** The bold leaves of* Hosta montana *'Aurea Marginata' glow in the dappled sunlight beneath a rhododendron bush. Without chalk for their shells, slugs are rarely a problem on acid soils.*

***Left:** Like most hostas, 'Shade Fanfare', shown here, thrives in shade, but will also tolerate a fair amount of sun as long as the soil stays very moist. However, in shade, hostas are nearly immune to scorching, even if the soil is a bit drier.*

PERENNIAL GRASSES

With their linear shapes, waving airy seedheads and subtle coloration, grasses make fascinating contrasts with other plants. They associate particularly well with perennials, although they are also useful in mixed borders or with trees and shrubs. A collection of perennial grasses can make an attractive garden feature in a lawn or a 'cameo' within a perennial border. As a group, they encompass such an enormous number of species, each with their own distinctive characteristics, that it is not difficult to find grasses to use in virtually every situation around the garden. Sedges and similar grassy-looking plants are usually included with perennial grasses as they have similar requirements. They also make stunning plants for containers on a patio, or bordering water features. Grasses thrive in various soil types, as they include so many different species. However, as a general rule, aim to grow them in sun in fertile ground that receives reasonable moisture but is not poorly drained. Most grasses tolerate wind - they associate well with heathers and birches for this reason - though acid soil is not essential for grasses. When the wind blows through their stems, the resulting sound adds tranquillity and relaxation to the garden, while the movement creates interest.

Above: *Stipa gigantea* is a very architectural evergreen plant with tall oatlike seedheads in summer. It thrives in dryish conditions. The leaves have sharp edges, so beware when weeding nearby.

A selection of perennial grasses

Most popular perennial grasses are hardy, but some pennisetums are killed by frost. Pot them up and keep them in a greenhouse over winter. True species can be propagated by seed, but divide named cultivars in spring, as seeds do not come true.

Right: Carex are actually sedges rather than true grasses. However, they are usually included with grasses by nurseries as they contribute similar effects to the garden. This one is *Carex buchananii.*

Above: *Miscanthus* are robust, clump-forming grasses of various heights and spread depending on cultivar. This is *M. yakushimensis*. They prefer moist conditions.

Below: *Milium effusum* 'Aureum' is invaluable for moist soil in light shade. The warm lemon-and-lime striped foliage adds flashes of light to the shadows.

Below: Some grasses, such as *Pennisetum villosum,* have outstanding seedheads. It grows about 18in (45cm) tall, making it suitable even for a small garden. Grow it among low perennials with bright flowers.

Displaying grasses to best effect

Team together grasses with contrasting leaf size, seedhead shapes and coloring - both variegated and plain. Include a mixture of plant shapes and sizes, but avoid mixing the biggest and smallest, as the scale looks out of proportion. Grasses also look good distributed throughout a border, mixed with other perennial plants. Site Japanese blood grass (Imperata cylindrica) *where the sun is behind it, to light up the leaves with startling shafts of color.*

Left: *Bright steely blue is a very eye-catching color in grasses. For this reason,* Helictotrichon sempervirens *makes an ideal foliage contrast in traditional perennial plantings. The foliage is by far the best feature, though the seedheads are much the same color. This medium-sized, clump-forming grass does not spread excessively.*

Grasses in containers

THE SUMMER BORDER

Perennials that flower in and around midsummer are some of the most generally useful kinds. They follow on naturally after the main flush of spring flowers is out of the way, and finish before the late-season flowers begin; they are the floral hallmark of midsummer. The most striking way to use them is all together in a border of their own as a celebration of midsummer; at other times of year, flowering interest is taken over by different 'sets' of plants in other parts of the garden, thus creating a strong sense of the changing seasons. Base the summer border on strong, upright, spiky shapes of traditional favorites, such as lupins, delphiniums, *Campanula, Astilbe* and *Achillea.* Add some of the exciting new colors to be found in *Hemerocallis,* and place peonies where their good foliage will be an asset after the huge powder-puff blooms are over. Use oriental poppies carefully; their immense, brightly colored flowers make an enormous impact while they are out, but their flowering season is short and once they are over, the plants sprawl and need cutting back, which leaves a big gap in the border. (This is a good place to stand pots of lilies - the traditional accompaniment to summer perennials in a herbaceous border.) Use shorter, bushier shapes to fill in the front of the border; *Dianthus, Astrantia* and *Heuchera* team up well together, as they all have contrasting flower shapes.

Above: Poppies, lupins and alchemilla set the traditional summer scene for this border, where perennials are joined by the hardy annual poached egg plant, *Limnanthes douglasii* - a great encourager of beneficial insects.

Above: Day lilies are prized for their strong foliage shapes and trumpetlike blooms; each one only lasts a day, but each spike contains several buds. This is 'Cartwheels'.

Right: Pink *Dianthus* 'Hidcote' and lime green *Euphorbia* x *pseudovirgata* make an unusual and pleasing plant association. Both plants need sun and prefer soil that is low in humus, while happily tolerating drought conditions.

Left: The bold, single, golden, chalice-shaped blooms of *Paeonia mlokosewitschii* associate superbly with late daffodils and the first *Euphorbia wulfenii* of the spring.

Below: *Salvia superba* cultivars have compact foliage underlying masses of upright flower spikes topped with tiny bright flowers - a useful contrast with large blooms.

Right: Feathery heads of astilbe look wonderful with bold foliage and striking flower shapes. Team with rounded hostas and geometric iris blooms for great effects. Astilbes are found in a good range of colors; this one is *Astilbe* x *arendsii* 'Spinell'.

Maintaining a summer border

In early spring, weed the border well, apply a sprinkling of general-purpose fertilizer and mulch. Surround sprawling plants, such as oriental poppies, with plant supports, and stake delphiniums, lupins and other tall species as soon as young shoots emerge through the ground. Give plants an occasional liquid feed with tomato fertilizer during early summer and keep new growth regularly tied in to ensure straight flower stems. After the first flush of flower, deadhead plants that may produce further blooms. When all the flowers are over, remove dead flower stems but leave the foliage to complete its growth cycle; clear beds in the fall, weed and tidy up for winter.

Left: *Lupins do best on slightly acid soil, but the flowers are soon over. Unless secondary buds are forming higher up, it is worth cutting the flower stems close to ground level to encourage a second flush of flower.*

Above: *To ensure a good summer show of delphiniums, protect dormant crowns, growth buds and emerging shoots with slug pellets in early spring.*

Left: *To keep perennial borders looking their best, snip off dead flower heads before they turn brown. This also stops plants setting seed, so new buds may follow on shortly.*

LATE-SEASON BORDER

Towards the end of the season, many herbaceous borders are looking past their best as summer flowers come to an end. But there are plenty of species that flower in late season. By planting these among the summer-flowering kinds, the late bloomers provide foliage that acts as a foil to summer flowers, then take over the interest from them as the earlier flowers are deadheaded or cut down. (Some early summer flowers, such as delphiniums and lupins, give a second, later show if they are cut down almost to ground level as soon as the flowers are finished.) To make the most of late flowers, plant tall kinds behind shorter summer flowers and make sure that all plants are given sufficiently wide spacing, otherwise it is easy to find your late crop of flowers have been smothered by earlier plants. Short late flowers, such as *Liriope muscari,* and clumps of fall bulbs, such as colchicums, are useful for planting at the front of the border to mask seasonal gaps.

To make the most of a late display, make sure that you regularly deadhead the whole border and cut down early flowers to ground level when the foliage starts dying down, so that late flowers stand out against clean foliage. For much the same reasons, it is important not to get behind with routine chores, including weeding, feeding and slug control, if you want a good late show from your border. And have a few pots of late-sown annuals (sown thinly in pots in early summer and planted out in a clump) ready to tuck into any bare gaps for an instant show of color.

Above: This typical late-season border planting scheme features *Rudbeckia* 'Herbstone', *Phlox* 'Fujiyama' *Helenium* (sneezeweed) and *Solidago* (golden rod).

Below: Kaffir lily, *Schizostylis coccinea,* has coppery red spikes of mini gladiolus-like blooms that last for many weeks in the garden.

Above: *Kniphofia* 'Little Maid' is a compact plant with short, upright spikes of flower and sharp-edged spiky evergreen foliage.

Liatris spicata has 2ft (60cm)-high magenta-pink flower spikes; needs sun, humus and good drainage.

Penstemon 'Hidcote Pink' is very drought-proof, with a long flowering season.

Sanguisorba obtusa (bottlebrush, not to be confused with the exotic shrub with the same common name) likes sun and moist rich soil.

Aster x *frikartii* has large, single, 'Michaelmas daisy'-like flowers, but is less likely to suffer from mildew. A tough plant for most sunny spots.

Left: *Agapanthus* makes a superb show in a hot dry spot or container. Headbourne Hybrids are the most reliable strain for all but the warmest climates. Leave undisturbed until it becomes essential to divide overgrown clumps.

Right: Heleniums are amongst the brightest of late blooms, available in shades of deep red, gold and orange. This is *H. hoopesii* 'Moerheim Beauty'.

Below: *Aster amellus* 'King George', *Sedum* 'September Glow', *Dendranthema* 'White Gloss' and the pink Japanese anemone 'Prinz Heinrich'.

Winter interest

The average perennial border is nothing to look at in winter but a sea of dead leaves or fresh mulch. However, some plants classified as perennials have evergreen foliage or produce winter and/or early spring flowers. Use these to provide out-of-season interest in a large perennial border or plant them in a special bed of their own, combined with shrubs such as hamamelis to make a winter garden.

Right: Bergenia *has low clumps of large rounded leaves. Some varieties, such as* B. purpurascens, *take on colored tinges in cold weather. The plants flower in early spring, producing short pink spikes.*

Below: *The felty textured, silver leaves of* Stachys byzantina *remain in place all year round, and in winter have a frosted look.*

Above: Ophiopogon planiscapus *'Nigrescens' makes short dense clumps of black straplike leaves. It makes a good background to spring bulbs, compact summer and evergreen perennials.*

Below: Helleborus niger *flowers very early, before there is much else about. Team it with bergenia and snowdrops in light shade.*

CHOOSING PLANTS

A large border will contain a range of planting situations. Choose shade-tolerant perennials to put between larger plants, place sunlovers to the front of the border and select suitable plants for dry shade to grow under shrubs.

Perennials for cutting
Acanthus
Achillea
Agapanthus
Alchemilla mollis
Alstroemeria
Delphinium
Echinops
Gypsophila
Helenium
Heuchera
Hosta
Iris
Liatris
Paeonia
Penstemon
Phlox
Polygonatum
Rudbeckia
Scabiosa
Schizostylis
Solidago
Tanecetum
Thalictrum

Late-season flowers
Aconitum autumnale
Agapanthus (African lily)
Anemone japonica
Aster amellus, A. ericoides, A. novae-angliae (New England asters), *A. novi-belgii* (Michaelmas daisies)
Cimicifuga (bugbane)
Dendranthema (formerly *Chrysanthemum) rubellum*
Helianthus (perennial sunflower)
Heliopsis
Kniphofia Ligularia
Liriope muscari
Penstemon
Phlox
Phygelius
Physalis alkekengi franchetii
Rudbeckia fulgida
Schizostylis (kaffir lily)
Solidago (golden rod)
Tricyrtis (toad lily)

Perennials for moist, light or dappled shade
Ajuga
Alchemilla mollis
Anemone japonica
Aruncus dioicus (goats rue)
Astilbe
Bergenia
Brunnera
Caltha palustris
Cimicifuga
Dicentra
Filipendula
Geranium phaeum
Helleborus
Hosta
Meconopsis
Omphaloides
Polemonium
Polygonatum
Primula
Pulmonaria
Tiarella
Viola

Perennials for a hot, dry, sunny situation
Acanthus
Agapanthus
Alstroemeria
Anaphalis triplinervis
Artemisia
Bearded iris
Centranthus (red valerian)
Crambe cordifolia
Crocosmia
Dianthus
Echinops ritro
Eryngium
Euphorbia cyparissias, E. wulfenii
Incarvillea delavayii
Kniphofia
Limonium latifolium
Nepeta
Oenothera
Papaver orientale
Penstemon
Sedum spectabile
Sisyrinchium
Stachys
Verbascum

Perennials for dry shade
Ajuga
Alchemilla mollis
Bergenia
Brunnera
Euphorbia amygdaloides
E. a. robbiae
Iris foetidissima
Lamium

Perennials for wet or heavy clay soil that stays moist in summer
Caltha palustris (kingcup)
Darmera (was *Peltiphyllum) peltata*
Filipendula
Inula
Ligularia
Lysimachia
Lythrum
Primula
Rodgersia

Poisonous perennials
Aconitum
Aquilega
Euphorbia
Helleborus
Iris

Delphinium 'Black Knight'
Sanguisorba obtusa
Delphinium 'King Arthur'
Phlox maculata 'Natasha'
Penstemon 'Firebird'

PART EIGHT

ANNUALS AND BIENNIALS

Annuals and biennials are short-term occupants of a garden, bringing with them the opportunity to try out new color schemes, styles and planting associations. Use them to fill odd gaps in shrub borders, add instant splashes of color or to create novel seasonal displays. And, of course, they are a vital ingredient of containers.

Planting annuals

1 Prepare the ground and then mark out patterns on the soil with silver sand. Mix long, narrow shapes with blocky and 'teardrop' ones for a 'Persian carpet' effect.

2 Sprinkle seed by hand; do not overlap the edges. Adjacent patches should have contrasting colors and flower shapes. Put taller kinds to the back or center.

3 When the whole bed has been sown, rake it very gently. Barely disturbing the soil, work the seeds into the soil surface. The sandy lines should disappear, too.

4 Water the bed thoroughly, so that the seeds and soil are evenly damped. Use a fine rose to prevent the seed being washed away from their correct place.

Left: Informal grouping suits the cottage garden character of hardy annuals. These are *Agrostemma githago* 'Milas' (corncockle), *Coreopsis* (mixed) and *Godetia* 'Sybil Sherwood'.

Right: Cultivated Californian poppy (*Eschscholzia californica)* blooms continuously from early summer to fall, though individual flowers only last a few days. There is a huge range of colors.

HARDY ANNUALS

Hardy annuals are plants that complete their entire life cycle in one season. From seed sown in spring, rapid growth produces a mass of flower and then a harvest of seeds that secure the next generation, with plants exhausting themselves by the fall. Much of the seed will survive the winter, and offspring will appear the following year in the most unlikely places and with a spontaneity that is impossible to contrive. With their short lifespan, keeping a space for hardy annuals provides the opportunity for changing the effect every year.

Hardy annuals can be sown straight into the garden soil. This way, there is no need to buy pots, trays or seed-sowing mixture, so it is a far cheaper way to produce plants. Being tough and weather-resistant, hardy annuals such as cornflower, clarkia and godetia can be sown outdoors in early spring to start flowering in early summer. For direct sowing, it is essential to have good, well-prepared soil that is free of weed seeds, otherwise you will not be able to tell the flowers from the weeds - they all look similar as seedlings. Two methods are used for sowing seed straight into garden soil. One is to scatter the seed over well-dug and raked soil, where you want them to flower. Seed of several different kinds of flowers can be sown in adjacent groups, marked out in advance with a trickle of sand. The second method is to sow seeds thinly in rows in a spare patch of well-prepared soil (perhaps the vegetable garden), thin the seedlings to 1-2in(2.5-5cm) apart, and transplant them to the flower bed. Sown in rows, it is easier to hoe between flower seedlings. The second method is also useful for sowing hardy biennials, such as wallflowers, Canterbury bells and polyanthus, and herbaceous flowers (delphiniums, etc.) sown in early summer and transplanted in early fall.

Above: Mallow (annual lavatera) is like a short bushy version of the perennial tree mallow, with flowers in shades of pink and mauve.

Above: Blue is the traditional color of *Nigella damascena* (love-in-a-mist), though nowadays pink and white shades are also available.

Right: *Dianthus* 'Princess Scarlet' and *Gypsophila* 'Rosenschleier'. Although perennial varieties are better known, these are both hardy annuals raised from seed.

Pansies and violas

Sowing mixed annual seeds

Colorful, natural-look, random floral carpet effects are fashionable and easy to create, simply by mixing together a suitable 'palette' of seeds and broadcasting them over carefully prepared ground. Choose a good mixture of varieties with contrasting shapes and colors, but roughly similar heights. Use approximately equal quantities of each.

1 For an explosion of summer color, mix together the seeds of a collection of annuals for sowing in one place.

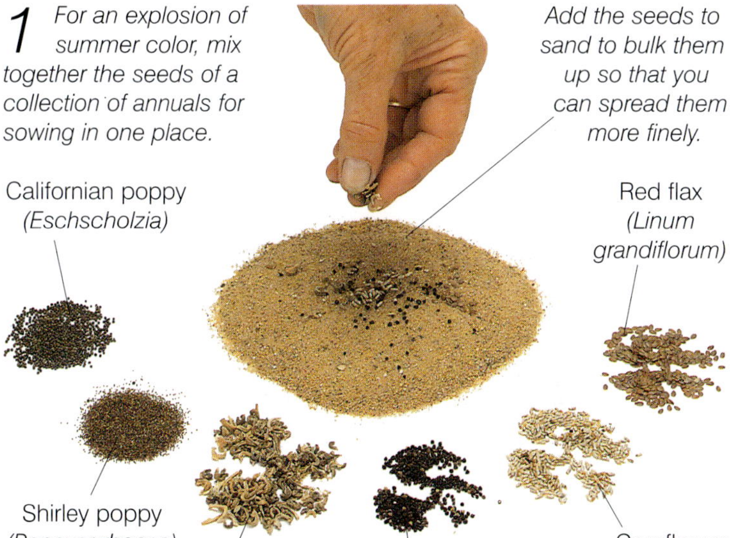

2 The sand marks where you have scattered the seed. To prolong the display, make two sowings four weeks apart.

Below: *Calendula, cornflower and nigella are all non-invasive, self-seeding hardy annuals and ideal for a cottage garden effect.*

HALF-HARDY ANNUALS

Half-hardy annuals are what gardeners know as bedding plants, for example petunia, salvia, ageratum, cosmos and China aster. These are planted out already in bloom after all risk of frost is past and continue to flower through to the first frost of fall, which kills the plants. What distinguishes half-hardy annuals from hardy annuals is that they will not stand very cold weather. For this reason, they cannot be sown straight into the garden, but have to be raised in a heated greenhouse early in spring. Since few gardeners have the facilities to grow their own bedding plants, nurseries sell a good range in trays at around planting out time. Take care not to buy too early; local gardeners will know the date you can expect the last frost in your area. If cold weather threatens, keep trays of bedding plants in a cold greenhouse, sunroom or enclosed porch for a few weeks more. If you buy bedding plants from a nursery that has kept them in a greenhouse rather than outdoors, harden them off by standing them outside during the day and bringing them back under cover at night for at least a week after buying. This acclimatizes them gradually to the cooler conditions and moving air outdoors. Water trays well, and give plants a last liquid feed the day before planting for a good start.

Above: *Tagetes* are compact, low-growing bedding plants, with a neat symmetrical shape that makes them ideal for edging formal beds. Their habit also makes them ideal for tubs.

Left: *Molucella laevis* has spikes of green bracts that flower arrangers love to use in their displays. This plant needs a warm sheltered site to do well. Grow it among bright flowers for a contrasting effect.

Left: Even without any deadheading, the flamboyant flowers of *Cosmos* keep flowering continuously through to the frosts. This is *C. bipinnatus.* Team it with spider flower *(Cleome spinosa)* for a sensational effect.

Below: *Helichrysum petiolare* is a half-hardy perennial often used with bedding plants, such as these petunias, for foliage contrast.

DEADHEADING

To keep bedding plants flowering all summer, regularly nip off the flowers just below the base of the head as soon as they are over.

Right: *Salpiglossis sinuata* grows about 2ft(60cm) high and has large heads of trumpet-shaped flowers, which are normally attractively striped or streaked. Plants can be used in containers or beds and as cut flowers.

Left: Heliotrope is one of the old-fashioned half-hardy perennials, now available as seed mixtures, that can be treated as half-hardy bedding plants. Few seed-raised heliotropes have the scent of the old kinds grown from cuttings.

Below: Musk *(Mimulus),* including the popular 'Malibu' Series shown here, are superb bedding plants for moist soil. Be sure to keep them well watered, since plants suffer badly if they dry out.

A vivid display for a sheltered spot

New Guinea hybrid Impatiens *and the creeping fig both thrive in a relatively warm, sheltered, humid environment. An indoor arrangement such as this will grow outdoors in summer in light shade; many indoor plants do better outdoors in summer than left neglected in the house.*

1 As this is a ready-lined container, add some gravel to provide drainage. Expanded clay pellets are also suitable.

2 Add a layer of peat-based, multipurpose potting mix. Give the plants a thorough soaking before planting them.

3 Plant the New Guinea hybrid Impatiens*, fitting the stems around the handle; allow some of them to overhang.*

4 Add creeping fig (Ficus pumila) *so that the trailing foliage looks as though it is growing out between the* Impatiens.

ANNUALS FOR CUTTING

A lot of annuals make good cut flowers. Since the plants are so cheap to raise - and prolific - they are a very economical source of flower arranging material throughout the summer. If only a few stems are needed, it is perfectly feasible to cut a few blooms from the back of a group of flowers in a border, with no risk of spoiling the garden display. However, if you are going to need large quantities, it is worth planting a few rows of flowers in the vegetable garden specially for cutting, or even creating a special 'cutting bed' well away from the house. Given rich soil, shelter, regular liquid feeding and generous watering, annual flowers will respond by producing more stems than ever. And with most annuals, the more they are cut, the more new flowers are produced, since cutting acts like early deadheading, preventing plants running to seed. This is particularly true of sweet peas, which if not cut regularly for vases, need frequent deadheading; otherwise, flowering comes to a complete stop. Cut flowers with only as much stem as is needed; cropping too close to the roots removes side shoots that would otherwise produce the next crop of flowers.

Right: To dry everlasting flowers, hang bunches upside down in a current of dry air. A few kinds may turn up towards the light, so keep them in the dark for best results.

Below: Squirrel tail grass *(Hordeum jubatum)* grows 18in (45cm) high, with graceful 3in (7.5cm)-long 'tails'. Use it fresh, or dry for winter arrangements.

A selection of annuals

Below: Daisylike blooms make brilliant cut flowers with a country garden character. *Rudbeckia* 'Rustic Dwarfs' and *R.* 'Marmalade', helichrysum and sunflowers, seen here, all last well in water.

Freshly cut annuals ready for display

FRESH FLOWERS FOR CUTTING

Amaranthus
Annual dahlias
Antirrhinum
Aster
Clarkia
Cosmos
Rudbeckia
Stocks
Sweet peas
Sunflower
Zinnia

Below: Sweet peas are the perfect cut flower for home growing. Picking has the same effect as deadheading, so the more you cut, the more flowers you get. Scented varieties are particularly delicious.

Left: Zinnias are one of the most striking of cut flowers, but need a warm summer to do well outdoors. This is 'Chippendale', one of the old-fashioned Mexican type.

Treating annuals before arranging them

All annuals need 'conditioning' for a couple of hours between cutting and arranging. A florist's tip is to clean out buckets and vases with bleach and rinse them clean between uses to keep bacteria counts low. This prevents the water going slimy and clogging stems.

Left: *China asters are some of the loveliest flowers for cutting. Avoid growing them in the same place twice, since a root disease can build up in the soil that kills plants off fast.*

1 When cutting, leave stems as long as possible. Cut when flowers are barely fully out. Unopen buds may never open; open flowers will not last long.

2 Strip the leaves from the bottom half of the stems, as they foul the water in vases. This clogs stems with bacteria, making flowers go over prematurely.

3 Take a bucket of water with you when cutting any flowers. After stripping the leaves, plunge stems straight into deep tepid water almost up to their necks. Annuals last longest if carefully treated from the moment they are cut.

The two-minute flower bed

1 To transform an empty patch of prepared ground into an instant flower bed, choose good-sized, flowering, pot-grown plants. Tip the plants out of their pots.

2 Fuchsias and busy Lizzie team well together and provide plenty of bright color; add a foliage plant for contrast, such as this silvery *Senecio maritimus.*

3 Keep adding more plants, making sure that neighboring plants bring sympathetic colors and a change of shape to the scheme. Any that clash can be separated by foliage.

4 To create a formal display, repeat a plant grouping like this regularly across a bed, with perhaps a few 'dot plants', such as standard fuchsia. Or use it for a tub or to fill a gap in a border.

GARDENING WITH ANNUALS

For instant color almost anywhere, annuals are the answer. They are the simple solution for the new homeowner who wants a garden in a hurry, or for making an existing garden look its best for a special occasion. They are good for filling odd gaps in a border, for planting up containers and perfect for a balcony, patio or pathway. Annuals can also be used creatively in traditional knot gardens - or for Victorian-style carpet bedding schemes now enjoying a revival. They are also good value for planting in beds of their own where you need a splash of color that will last all summer. Use annuals in informal 'random-look' cottage-style planting schemes, or in formal beds edged with straight rows of flowers and blocks of color broken up by occasional 'dot' plants - perhaps standard fuchsias. However, annual beds are a lot of work, so do not take on more than you can comfortably manage. Plants can be grown from seed on a warm windowsill indoors, or bought ready to plant from garden centers in early summer, just as they are coming into flower. Do not plant them out until after the last frost. Annuals need good soil and a sunny situation with reasonable shelter to do well. To keep plants flowering continuously they need frequent attention - watering, feeding and deadheading regularly. Since the plants do not survive freezing, pull them out in the fall and replace them with spring bulbs or winter and early spring bedding, to avoid leaving the beds empty.

Above: Traditionally, semi-formal borders were edged with a continuous strip of low flowers, such as these sweet alyssum. China asters add a color contrast.

Below: For an out-of-season display, winter-flowering pansies combine well with winter-flowering heather in a border or container.

Left: Annuals can be used to create entire gardens, like this small front garden display. Although more work than shrubs or a lawn, annuals provide a carpet of brilliant ongoing color for five months of the year.

Below: Alternatively, tuck groups of annuals between a permanent framework of shrubs and perennials. The effect is more muted and the other plants provide interest outside the main bedding season.

Right: Creating fine displays of spring bedding plants is a much-neglected art. Here *Erysimum (Cheiranthus)* 'Fire King' (wallflowers) combine with 'West Point' tulips to create a formal bed that is full of color.

A basket of bedding plants

Annuals are the classic plants for containers such as hanging baskets. The secret of success is to choose reliable varieties with a long flowering season (e.g. petunias, pelargoniums and fuchsias). Kept well fed and watered and regularly deadheaded, the same plants should flower from early summer almost up to the fall frosts.

1 Lodge the basket into the top of a bucket for stability and fill it almost to the rim with a peat-based potting mixture.

2 Before planting, cut the top from a plastic bottle and sink it into the basket. The 'funnel' makes watering easier.

3 Plant the taller plants in the middle of the basket around the funnel to hide it, and to give the display a definite center.

4 Add tumbling and trailing plants around the sides. Turn them round so that the stems cascade over the edges.

5 Water the basket, so that the potting mix holds as much moisture as it can. Fill the plastic funnel 'reservoir' and refill it every day.

Above: *Eccremocarpus scaber* is a self-clinging vine with masses of trumpetlike flowers all summer; flowers change color slightly as they mature, giving plants a two-tone appearance. In a mild area, plants die down to ground level and roots survive winter, allowing new stems to regrow the next year.

CLIMBING ANNUALS

There are some situations where color is called for but traditional annuals are not flexible enough. Here, climbers or trailers are often the answer. Their unique style of growth makes them invaluable for covering large, often inaccessible areas with flower quickly. Climbers such as black-eyed Susan *(Thunbergia alata)*, canary creeper *(Tropaeolum canariense)*, cathedral bells *(Cobaea scandens)* and Chilean glory vine *(Eccremocarpus scaber)*, are useful for cladding walls, fences or outbuildings; being annual, they grow quickly and flower prolifically, all in one year. Use them to give a new garden a mature look, or to provide a temporary flowering display while perennial climbers are getting established. (These often take several years to begin flowering well.) Annual climbers are handy for covering the bare stems at the base of perennial climbers, particularly climbing roses, where their flowers make a cheerful splash of color against the woody stems. Grow them up through large shrubs or perennial climbers on pergolas and arches to give them a second attraction. Unusual kinds, such as ornamental gourds and climbing dicentra *(Dicentra torulosa* or *D. scandens)*, look very striking grown in this way.

Far left: *Thunbergia alata* is very tender; keep it in a mild sheltered spot. Grow it up canes in a pot or in a hanging basket, where the twining stems both climb and trail.

Left: The flowers of *Mina lobata* (quamoclit) open red, change through orange to yellow then white. Needs warmth, shelter and an early start.

Right: *Tropaeolum peregrinum* is a rugged, hardy annual climber. It drops seeds in late summer from which a new crop of plants appear the following year. Does well in hanging baskets or on a wall trellis.

Right: *Cobaea scandens* is slow to start flowering and needs a warm sheltered spot. If possible, protect plants in winter, as they flower best the second year from seed.

Below: Dwarf varieties of hardy annual sweet peas will grow in containers or, with support, as low hedges. Use tall kinds for cladding walls or growing up canes.

Left: Trailing annuals, such as nasturtiums (here 'Alaska'), *Convolvulus* and *Mesembryanthemum* are good for raised beds, banks, the tops of low retaining walls and containers, where they can dangle down like a flowering curtain.

Training Ipomoea *around a hoop*

Annual climbers such as Ipomoea *(morning glory) make good plants for a container on the patio. If no wall space is available, you can train them around a framework; they actually flower better due to the degree of root restriction, plus the larger area of horizontal stems, which always flower best. Start by repotting the climber into a larger pot.*

1 Slide the 'legs' of the frame down the pot sides to brace them; the final plant will be heavy enough to pull the frame over.

2 Lead new shoots in the direction they naturally twine. Once started, the stems make their way up on their own.

3 Twine stems around the frame until a dense cover of foliage and stems is formed. Once roots fill the pot, flowers will appear. Although each one is shortlived, a plant trained in this way can bear a mass of blooms.

UNUSUAL ANNUALS

Most people know a dozen or so popular annuals, yet the seed catalogs contain hundreds of little-known kinds. Some of these have distinctive features that make them perfect to use wherever something special is needed. For scent, it is sometimes possible to find seed of old-fashioned sweet peas, such as 'Painted Lady' (pink and white) or 'Matucana' (deep purple). These are both hardy annuals (HA) with smaller flowers than modern varieties, but a far more powerful fragrance. In the early evening, the scent of the night phlox *(Zaluzianskya capensis,* HA) fills the air; in daytime, the tiny white flowers are insignificant. More unusual are two chocolate-scented annuals: *Gilia tricolor* (birds eyes) has masses of 0.5in(1.25cm)-wide, blue, gold and purple flowers, and *Berlandiera lyrata* (half-hardy annual/half-hardy perennial HHA/HHP), a daisy with 2in(5cm)-wide yellow flowers with maroon centers. Group them round the garden where their scent will not clash with others, or grow them in a chocaholic's corner with chocolate-scented cosmos. Some annuals grow their own self-defense system; plants of *Caiophora acuminata* and *Loasa triphylla* (both HHA) are protected by stinging hairs all over. Their buff-orange or white flowers look as if they are made of folded tissue paper. Odd shapes are eye-catching; *Calceolaria rugosa* (HHA) is a small plant, with flowers like bright red and orange pouches suspended on airy stems above the rosettes of leaves; it is specially striking in containers. Ornamental forms of sweetcorn *(Zea mays)* and quinoa (an ancient grain crop, *Chenopodium quinoa,* both HHA) look very striking in the middle of a border. Ornamental quinoa has tall spikes of millet-like sprays in red orange-green, and grows 5-6ft(1.5-1.8m) tall. An old favorite - 'love-lies-bleeding' (*Amaranthus caudatus,* HHA) - has spectacular trailing 'ropes' of red flowers on 24in(60cm) plants.

Above: *Amaranthus* (love-lies-bleeding), a half-hardy annual, produces 'ropes' of summer flower that trail down to the ground from the top of 24in(60cm)-high plants.

Left: *Reseda odorata* (mignonette), a superbly scented hardy annual. Grow in beds or sow in fall in pots in a porch or cold greenhouse.

Below: *Loasa triphylla* has papery flowers with minute stinging hairs on both leaves and petals, which react to the slightest touch.

Left: Castor-oil plant *(Ricinus communis)* is a very striking HHA, mainly grown for its large tropical-looking leaves (this is 'Impala'). It is a perfect foil for tall bright flowers, such as tithonia and cannas. All parts of the plant, including seed, are poisonous.

Above: *Gilia tricolor* 'Alba' (HA) produces a mass of tiny, chocolate-scented blooms. It is a white version of the plant commonly known as 'birds eyes', which has purple, blue and yellow flowers.

Left: As the petals drop from *Papaver somniferum,* the seedpod 'hen' develops a mass of 'chicks', hence the common name, 'hen-and-chickens daisy'.

Below: *Phacelia tanacetifolia* is an annual flower that organic gardeners, often sow to dig in as green manure. The flowers are much loved by bees and other insects.

Ornamental cabbages

Ornamental cabbages are available with pink, purple or cream foliage in a variety of shapes. Raise from seed like normal cabbage. Planted in early summer, the same plants last well into winter, but be prepared for caterpillar attacks in late summer. Grow in tubs for a fall display.

Right: *With orange calendula marigolds, purple cabbages look quite vibrant. The full color takes time to develop. For a more restrained display, team paler yellow marigolds with cream cabbages.*

Using ornamental cabbage

1 Prepare the ground well with organic matter and general fertilizer. Buy or grow plants in individual pots so that they can develop a symmetrical shape.

2 Plant out in early summer without breaking up the rootballs and bury so the top of the rootball is just below that of the surrounding soil. Firm in well.

3 For a winter display, in a sheltered spot with well-drained soil, team ornamental cabbages with primroses and wallflowers. The cabbages eventually start running to seed in spring, although even then the flowers look decorative.

HALF-HARDY PERENNIALS TREATED LIKE ANNUALS

Half-hardy perennials are longlived plants, such as fuchsias and pelargoniums, that do not survive frost. They are grown outdoors in summer in the same way as bedding plants, in containers and borders. Then - just before the first frost - they must be dug up or made into cuttings that spend the winter in a heated greenhouse or on a windowsill indoors. (Rooted cuttings are the best bet as they take up less room than mature plants, and young plants will flower better than old woody ones the following year.) Half-hardy perennials cannot be planted back outdoors until after the last risk of frost is over, in early summer, so 'storage' space is needed each winter. Nurseries now stock many newly fashionable half-hardy perennial flowers, such as *Felicia* (kingfisher daisy), marguerites, *Osteospermum*, *Laurentia* and *Gazania*. Like annual bedding plants, they are good value in the garden, as they flower continuously from planting time in early summer right through to fall, asking only to be kept well fed, watered and regularly deadheaded. A few plants commonly treated as annuals, such as petunias, are really half-hardy perennials. While it is possible to keep them from one year to the next, in practice it is not easy. Unless kept very warm in winter, they easily die from mildew, and in summer, aphids transmit virus diseases that weaken them.

RAISING HALF-HARDY PERENNIALS FROM SEED

In the past, it was always necessary to raise half-hardy perennials from cuttings, but now fast-maturing seed strains have been developed that make it possible to grow some half-hardy perennials from seed in much the same way as bedding plants. However, for this to be successful, you must sow the seed in late winter in a heated propagator, and then grow on the young plants in a well-heated greenhouse. This is the only way to be sure of having plants sufficiently well advanced to flower abundantly in their first year. You can take cuttings from seed-raised plants if you want to, which is a good way of propagating favorite colors from a mixed packet.

Right: Marguerites *(Chrysanthemum frutescens)* are popular plants for summer containers and will tolerate hot dry sites as long as they are kept well watered. This one is 'Mary Wooton', with attractive anemone-centered flowers.

A selection of half-hardy perennials

Above: Use bright half-hardy perennials such as these red pelargoniums, yellow and peach argyranthemums and white osteospermums to create striking color combinations that stand out well against stone on a patio.

Left: Standard fuchsias are a great way to pack more flower power into a small space; the plants are also surprisingly economical of greenhouse space in winter, as other plants can stand beneath them. Be sure to prepare them carefully for their winter storage.

Right: With its unusual fan-shaped flowers and horizontal sprawling habit, *Scaveola aemula* is a natural choice for container gardening. This variety is called 'Blue Wonder'. It strikes easily from cuttings; pinch tips out in spring to make the plants bushier.

Cutting back a standard fuchsia for the winter

The soft green shoots of a standard fuchsia are the ones most likely to be damaged by cold, encouraging fungal diseases to colonize the plant. Remove as many as possible, leaving a framework of dark woody stems from which healthy new shoots will emerge the following spring.

1 Use sharp secateurs to produce a good, woody, well-balanced shape. Try to cut above a division of branches.

Pruning back hard in winter means that plants take up less space in the greenhouse and there is less risk of rotting.

2 Ideally, the head should be no more than a third to half of its original size when you have finished and as symmetrical in shape as you can make it.

3 Remove all the leaves left on the wood, otherwise you may encounter problems with fungal infections, such as botrytis and damping-off.

4 Now there is a good framework for the new growth. There may be a little leakage of sap, but this will soon stop and does not harm the plant.

BIENNIALS

Biennials are hardy plants that have a two-year life cycle. They include old-fashioned favorites, such as wallflowers, Canterbury bells, sweet Williams, honesty and foxgloves. In their first year, biennials grow from seed, spending the winter as a leafy rosette, then flower in the second year. After the flowers are over, the seeds shed naturally during the summer give rise to self-sown seedlings that flower during the following year. By letting biennials naturalize themselves in this way, you get flowers every year. Biennials were important plants in old-fashioned cottage and country gardens; many, such as sweet Williams, were traditionally grown under roses to provide early color before the roses bloomed. They fell from favor for a while, since many gardeners found it more convenient to do all their seed sowing at the same time - in spring - and by summer had no room left. But now they are making a comeback, and plants are often sold in garden centers in summer and fall.

UNUSUAL BIENNIALS

Less well-known kinds are valuable for self-seeding through borders, where they give a natural effect. *Verbena bonariensis* is perfect with shrubs, where the purple flower heads appear to float among other plants without visible means of support. *Eryngium giganteum* (Miss Willmott's Ghost) is a huge sea holly with silver-blue foliage and bracts, and *Verbascum bombyciferum* starts as a cabbagey silver rosette and then throws up a huge, branching, candelabra-like spike of yellow flowers on silver-fluff clad stems.

Above: *Verbena bonariensis* has tall slender stems with small leaves topped off by purple flowers that attract butterflies.

Left: The giant *Verbascum bombyciferum* self-seeds gently about on well-drained soil. It tolerates hot dry sites.

Above: Dried seed heads of honesty are prized for winter arrangements; do not deadhead plants after flowering.

Above: Honesty *(Lunaria annua)* is happy in light or dappled shade under trees and shrubs, and the pink flowers associate well with them in late spring and early summer. Variegated honesty plants are plain green during their first year.

Left: Foxglove *(Digitalis purpurea)* is ideal for light woodland and large shrub or flower borders. Self-sown seedlings are far more tolerant of drought than transplanted seedlings, since they do not experience any root disturbance.

Right: Sweet William *(Dianthus barbatus)* is a traditional cottage garden favorite and a good cut flower. The blooms are long lived; if deadheaded when they go over, the same plants will keep growing for several years.

GROWING BIENNIALS FROM SEED

To grow biennials from packets of seed, you must sow the seeds outdoors around early midsummer to have plants big enough to flower the following year. Biennials are normally sown in a row in a vacant patch in the vegetable garden, thinned out and transplanted to their flowering positions in early fall. Alternatively, sow seed in trays outdoors and pot up singly.

1 Sprinkle seeds thinly into shallow drills made in rich, very fertile soil. On soil that dries out or forms a surface crust, cover the seed with vermiculite.

2 Rake very gently so that the seed is barely covered with soil. Water well, and do not allow soil to dry out; this could delay or prevent germination.

Right: Hollyhocks *(Alcea)* are another cottage favorite; since rust is a problem (orange dots on the foliage, which slowly turns leaves brown and gradually kills plants), burn old plants after flowering to prevent it spreading.

Left: Forget-me-nots *(Myosotis)* combine wonderfully with tulips, as they flower at the same time. Plants can be put out in fall, but to avoid winter damage, plant young plants from pots or trays in spring after the worst weather is over.

Planting wallflowers

Wallflowers make spicy scented, colorful carpets of spring flower. They also make good container plants. Plant these up in winter and move them to a cold greenhouse or porch for protection until flowering time. The plants will look perfect when they are put out on the patio in spring.

1 Separate out individual plants, trying not to break roots or take off more soil than necessary. They transplant best if you water them a day or two before removing them from their pots.

2 Lay plants out before planting. If you want clumps, make informal groups; when large areas need filling, plant randomly - avoid straight lines. This gives a softer, more natural effect.

3 Immediately after planting, water new plants in thoroughly. They will probably wilt slightly at first, but soon pick up. Keep watered during dry spells, which can happen even in winter.

Right: *Wallflowers bloom prolifically from mid-spring until early summer and may have to be pulled out while still in bloom to make room for the summer bedding plants that often follow them. Cut the heads and keep them in a vase.*

CHOOSING PLANTS

Annuals and biennials are the most temporary residents of the garden and as such allow you to change some aspect of the planting, such as container color schemes, from year to year, without great expense or major structural work.

A = Annual
HA = Hardy annual
HHA = Half-hardy annual
HP = Hardy perennial treated as an annual
HHP = Half-hardy perennial treated as an annual
B = Biennial

Cut, dried or craft flowers

Amaranthus caudatus (cut) HHA
Ammobium alatum (dried) HHA
Antirrhinum (cut) HHA
Aster (cut) HHA
Atriplex hortensis cupreata HA (fresh-cut seedheads)
Carthamnus tinctoria (fresh or dried) HA
Celosia (cut) HHA
Cosmos bipinnatus HHA
Craspedia globosa (dried) HHA
Gomphrena globosa, G. hybrida (dried) HHA
Gourds, ornamental (dried fruits) HHA
Gypsophila elegans (fresh or dried) HA
Helichrysum monstrosum (dried) HHA
Helipterum (dried) HHA
Lathyrus (sweet pea) (cut) HA
Limonium (fresh or dried) HHA
Molucella laevis HHA
Nigella damascena HA (dried seedheads)
Papaver somniferum (dried seedheads) HA
Stokesia laevis (cut) HP
Viola - pansy (pressed) HP
Xeranthemum (dried) HA
Zea mays A
Zinnia (cut) HHA

Scented annuals

Alyssum (some cultivars) HA
Berlandiera lyrata (hairgrass) HHP
Cleome spinosa HHP
Dianthus barbatus (Sweet Williams) B
Erysimum cheiri (wallflower) B
Heliotropium HHA, HHP
Hesperis matronalis B
Lathyrus (sweet pea) 'Antique Fantasy Mixed', 'Painted Lady', 'Matucana' B
Matthiola bicornis (night-scented stock) HA
M. incana - Brompton stocks B
Nicotiana alata 'Grandiflora' 'Fragrant Cloud' HHA
Zaluzianskya capensis HA

Annuals and biennials for a hot dry sunny site

Cerinthe major 'Purpurascens' HA
Dianthus (bedding types) HA
Gazania HHP
Mesembryanthemum HHA
Oenothera biennis B
Onopordum arabicum/nervosum B
Osteospermum HHP
Portulaca HHA
Verbascum bombyciferum B

Annual grasses

Aira elegantissima (hairgrass) HA
Briza maxima (quaking grass) HA
Briza minor (little quaking grass) HA
Echinochloa crus-gallii (hedgehog grass) HA
Hordeum jubatum (squirrel tail grass) HA
Lagurus ovatus (hare's tail grass) HA
Panicum violaceum HA
Setaria glauca (foxtail grass) HA

Annuals for light shade

Begonia semperflorens HHA
Impatiens HHA
Nicotiana HHA
(A useful tip is to plant these out when they are already in flower.)

Annuals for foliage effect

Amaranthus tricolor HHA
Coleus HHP
Euphorbia marginata 'Summer Icicle' HHA
Kochia trichophylla HHA
Ornamental cabbage HA
Ricinus communis (castor-oil plant) HHA

A palette of annuals

Annuals are available in a great diversity of flower shapes and sizes and a huge range of colors.

1 Alyssum
2 Violas
3 Pansies
4 Impatiens
5 Pansies
6 French marigolds
7 French marigolds
8 Begonias
9 Petunias
10 Verbena
11 French marigolds
12 French marigolds
13 French marigolds
14 Gazanias
15 Begonias
16 Pansies
17 Alyssum
18 Gazanias
19 Bedding dahlias
20 Pansies

PART NINE

BULBS

Rather than leaving containers empty in winter, after you have pulled out the summer bedding, why not plant bulbs? You can also use bulbs to bring color to your beds and borders throughout the year. From tiny snowdrops in spring to fragrant lilies in late summer, there are bulbs for every season and style of garden.

PLANTING BULBS

Bulbs and corms are rather like whole plants in suspended animation. They contain a stored food supply and embryo flowers and roots, all surrounded by a tough protective skin. This means that unlike any other plant, they are virtually guaranteed to flower, at least in the first year, unless harmed by poor growing conditions or pests. Correct planting helps to prevent most problems. Spring bulbs take root during winter, so a well-drained soil is vital. A sheltered spot ensures flowers will not be spoiled by poor weather, common in spring, and sun is vital for ripening the bulbs of all but a few species. (Snowdrops, *Anemone blanda* and narcissi are all tolerant of light shade such as you find in a border between shrubs.) On heavy soils, it is beneficial to dig in grit to improve aeration and drainage. In addition, some bulbs such as tulips and crown imperials, which are specially susceptible to rotting, should be planted on top of an inch of grit so water runs away fast. (See page 173 for planting a crown imperial.) All bulbs need phosphate and potash fertilizers rather than nitrogen, so apply bonemeal or a specially formulated feed for bulbs before planting, and fork well in. The correct planting depth is important; many bulbs are planted far too shallowly, and though they will flower the first year - since the embryo bud is already present - it may be several years before they flower again while bulbs 'winch' themselves down to the right depth using their contractile roots. As a general rule, plant bulbs so they have twice their own depth of soil above them - this means digging a hole three times the depth of the bulb.

PLANTING BULBS UNDER GRAVEL

Bulbs such as *Iris reticulata* (shown below) can be naturalized to add spring interest to any well-drained area that is fairly dry in summer, such as graveled areas in a patio. Use them to create small 'cameo' features next to a garden seat, ornament or a statue.

1 Scoop out a depression and scatter the bulbs at random. Press in and twist to ensure contact with the soil.

2 Cover with soil, ensuring the bulbs remain upright. These dwarf iris bulbs need 2in(5cm) of soil above their tips.

3 When the soil is level with the surrounding area, add a thin layer of stone chippings as a mulch and decorative finish.

4 Dwarf irises (*Iris reticulata*) flower in blue or purple with yellow or orange markings in early spring. Up to 6in(15cm) tall.

Choosing daffodil bulbs

Large single bulbs will have the biggest and best flowers.

'Double' bulbs are a good buy if both are equally large, but the small 'pup' here is too small to flower and will only have leaves next spring.

Above: Daffodil bulbs are the easiest to plant. Simply dig out a hole three times the depth of the bulb and place it at the bottom with the roots facing downwards.

Below: Narcissi (daffodil family) are one of the few bulbs that grow well in light shade, but do not plant too close to trees or hedges.

Planting anemones

1 For a natural effect, the easy way to plant bulbs is to scatter them over the selected area and then plant them where they fall.

2 With small bulbs, such as these anemones, which have no right way up, simply press them into the soil with your finger.

Below: *Anemone coronaria* 'De Caen' is a favorite spring-flowering bulb that grows about 8in(20cm) tall. Planting a few corms several weeks apart in the fall provides a succession of flowers the following spring. Cut and display the flowers.

Planting tulips

1 Choose healthy bulbs. Remove the dry brown outer skin of tulips - this helps the bulbs to start rooting.

2 A double row of tulips makes a good edging to a formal bed. Run two strings to ensure straight planting rows.

Above: Tulips need well-drained soil to prevent them rotting, so in heavy soil sit the bulbs on a 1in(2.5cm) layer of gritty sand.

Using a bulb planter

A bulb planter is useful for planting a few bulbs individually or for spacing them widely over a larger area. Still plant the bulbs at the correct depth for their type. Some bulb planters have depth markings to help - if not, use a permanent marker pen to show the required depth. You can also use bulb planters to plant individual bulbs in grass.

Right: *The elegant blooms of* Tulipa *'West Point' would grace any garden in late spring. It is one of the so-called 'lily-flowered' types.*

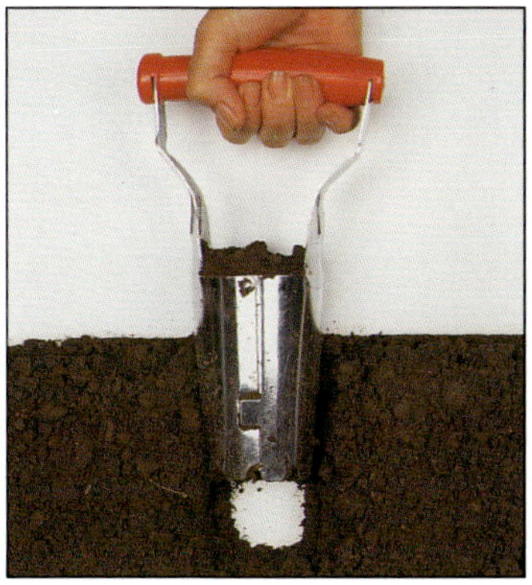

1 Scatter bulbs, then lift each one to make a hole. Press the planter into the ground and twist to remove a core of soil, which stays inside the planter.

2 Place a bulb in each hole. If possible, press it slightly into the soil to ensure it remains upright. If the hole is too narrow and deep, simply drop the bulb.

3 This view shows clearly that the soil above the bulb is twice the depth of the bulb itself. For clarity, no grit (good for tulips) has been added to the hole.

4 Reinsert the planter into the hole and squeeze the handle to drop the core of soil back into place over the bulb. Gently firm the soil down level.

Deadheading daffodils

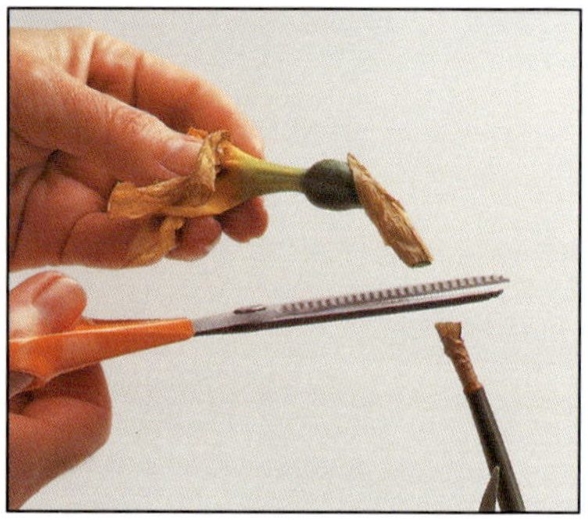

Above: As soon as the flowers are over, remove the deadheads to prevent bulbs wasting energy setting seed. Do this regularly every few days in spring.

Right: Use scissors or secateurs to snip just below the old flower head or simply pull deadheads off by hand. There is no need to remove the stems; these die back.

CULTIVATING BULBS

After planting, bulbs spend the winter forming roots; the foliage of most species does not appear until spring. During this time it is vital that underground shoots, and indeed the bulbs themselves are not damaged by careless hoeing, so mark clumps of bulbs with plant labels or scatter sand or grit on the soil above them after planting. Ground where bulbs are planted may be given a sprinkling of general fertilizer in early spring, and where they are grown under shrubs or roses, the spring feed you use for them will be fine for bulbs, too. However, to avoid scorching, wash off any fertilizer granules that become lodged in bulb foliage at once. After flowering is over, remove deadheads. Around this time, feed with a high phosphate bulb fertilizer or liquid tomato feed, either of which will help build up the size of the bulbs. Underfed bulbs actually shrink in size from one season to the next, and small bulbs do not have the capacity to produce flowers, hence the importance of feeding. Allow at least six weeks between the end of flowering and cutting down the foliage; this is when the leaves are manufacturing plant food which goes to recharge the bulbs and form next years embryo flower buds. Leave naturalized bulbs in the ground during summer, they will only need dividing when clumps get overcrowded several years after planting.

Above: Do not tie the foliage of daffodils into knots to tidy up the border. It will prevent the leaves sending nutrients down into the bulb to build it up for the following season.

Left: While the leaves of 'over' daffodils are dying down naturally, you can position other plants in front to mask them. A cranesbill *(Geranium)* would be ideal, as shown here.

Dividing snowdrops

1 Dig clumps up carefully when they become overcrowded (about every 3-5 years), complete with as much root as you can.

2 Wash of as much of the soil as possible to loosen the roots. Simply dunk each batch of bulbs into a pot of clean water.

3 Gently pull the clumps apart with your fingers, taking care not to damage the bulbs or tear off any roots. Run them under a cold tap every now and then to wash away more soil.

4 Divide the original clump first into several smaller clumps and then separate them further. Small bulbs are best left in small clusters of three or five, but separate good-sized bulbs individually.

5 Replant the snowdrop bulbs immediately, spaced out as shown here. Do not let them dry out in the process.

Planting a crown imperial bulb

Crown imperial (Fritillaria imperialis) *bulbs are notoriously susceptible to rotting. This is partly due to the hollow center left where the previous year's flower stem emerged from the bulb, which fills with water and cannot drain away. Free-draining soil is vital to grow this bulb.*

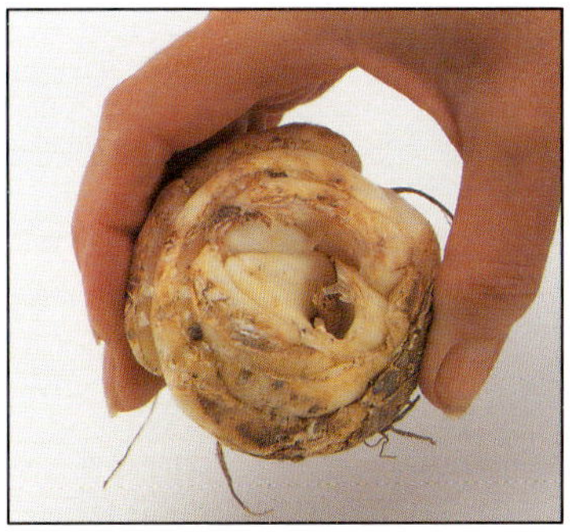

Above: *Plant the bulb on its side so water cannot lodge in the central hole; this will not affect the way the bulb develops.*

Above: *Always plant crown imperial bulbs on top of a layer of grit or gravel to improve drainage so the bulb does not lie in water.*

Left: *The flowers of crown imperials are as majestic as their name suggests. They grow about 5ft (1.5m) in height. If your soil is heavy, grow them in pots and stand in position for the summer.*

Pests and problems

Before planting, especially in new beds where soil pests such as wireworms may be a problem, treat the ground with a soil insecticide. Soil pests leave tunnels in the flesh that start to rot, and the whole bulb may have vanished before it has a chance to flower. Avoid planting bulbs that have cuts, bruises or slimy skins, as they are likely to rot in the soil - a common cause of bulbs that apparently 'disappear' after planting. Mice, squirrels, and even foxes and badgers may dig up and eat flower bulbs. Deter carnivores by not using bonemeal when planting bulbs; they are attracted by the smell. When planting, put plenty of prickly holly leaves into the planting hole above the bulbs to discourage digging, or for extra security, cover clumps of bulbs with strong small-mesh wire netting buried a few inches below the soil. Bulb leaves and flowers will make their way through this with no trouble, but it will put off predators. Bulbs that do not flower usually do so because they are not big enough; they must reach a certain size before their stored reserves are adequate to allow them to reproduce. Bulbs may also not flower when clumps spread so prolifically that individual bulbs are pressed tight together and so unable to reach their full size.

SPRING BULBS

Spring bulbs are highly versatile flowers, and useful for bold splashes of early color all round the garden. Naturalize them permanently in borders and lawns, on banks, and as colorful carpets under trees and shrubs, or use them as temporary spring bedding plants in containers or in formal borders. Some kinds of bulbs are better for one type of use than another. Tulips are best taken out of the ground and stored 'dry' for the summer, as they rot easily if left in the ground. This makes them particularly suitable for formal uses. Dig the bulbs up after the foliage has died down naturally, rub the soil off and keep them in a cool, dark, dry place till replanting time in the fall. Daffodils, *Anemone blanda* and many other popular bulbs prefer to be left undisturbed once planted, so they are better for naturalizing. Clumps of naturalized bulbs only need to be dug up and divided when they have become so overcrowded that they no longer flower well - in this case do so when the foliage dies down after flowering, or you may have difficulty finding them. In mixed borders, plant large leafy bulbs such as daffodils towards the middle of the border, with clump-forming summer herbaceous flowers as a 'screen' in front of them - these will be growing up as the daffodil foliage is dying down.

Above: Tulips and forget-me-nots *(Myosotis)* always look good grown together, and since they naturally flower at the same time, are guaranteed to form a successful plant association.

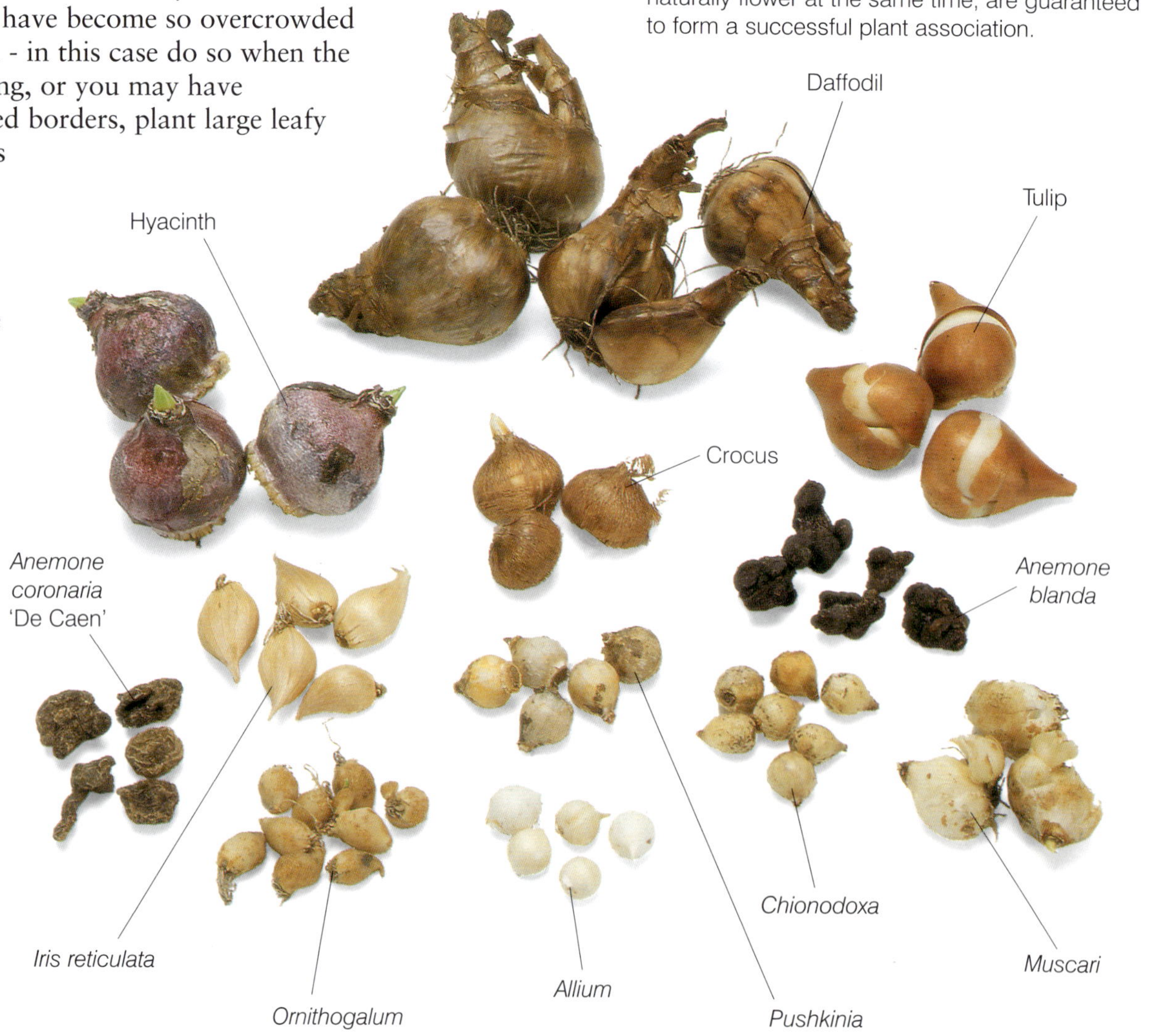

Above: *Chionodoxa* (glory-of-the-snow) are among the earliest spring flowers; normally blue like these 'Blue Giant', varieties are also available in pink or white.

Above: Spring bulbs do well under deciduous trees and shrubs, where they bloom before the canopy of leaves cut out the light. Here, narcissi, daffodils, hyacinths, dwarf irises, grape hyacinths and *Cyclamen coum* thrive beneath a birch tree.

Ideal planting depths

1 *Iris reticulata* 2in/5cm
2 *Anemone blanda* 2in/5cm
3 *A.* 'De Caen' 2in/5cm
4 *Crocus* 3in/7.5cm
5 *Pushkinia* 3in/7.5cm
6 *Ornithogalum* 3in/7.5cm
7 *Chionodoxa* 4in/10cm
8 *Allium* 4in/10cm
9 *Muscari* 4in/10cm
10 *Hyacinth* 4in/10cm
11 *Tulip* 4in/10cm
12 *Daffodil* 5in/13cm

Unusual and species bulbs

Bulb catalogs and garden centers often supply spring bulbs of unusual varieties that until recently were only grown by collectors. These include some very pretty bulbs that are not particularly difficult to grow so long as they are given specially well-drained conditions. Interesting kinds to look out for include Fritillaria *species (dwarf bulbs with mainly yellowish flowers marked with olive green, maroon or mahogany), species tulips (many with delicate flowers in terracotta pink, burnt orange and even greenish shades), the mourning widow,* Hermodactylus tuberosus, *(with bizarre black and green flowers, good for cutting) and* Ipheion, *which have large starlike flowers on compact clump-forming plants.*

Left: Ornithogalum umbellatum *(star of Bethlehem) is a European native plant of woodland clearings. Use it to cover ground under shrubs and trees. It has greenish striped white flowers in mid-spring, which open late morning and close late afternoon.*

Naturalizing

Naturalize these bulbs in raised beds filled with gritty soil, rock gardens or scree beds, or grow them in alpine sink gardens. Narcissus *species have delicate flowers and shorter, neater foliage than the giant hybrids; these are often naturalized in grass or on banks. Hardy cyclamen tubers are best planted so that their tops are just visible above soil level, in leafmold rich soil in light woodland, or in woodland clearings. The same conditions are ideal for dog's tooth violet* (Erythronium *species), which have some of the most beautiful late spring flowers of any bulb. Unlike hybrid bulbs, species can be left to set seed after the flowers are over, so that colonies slowly build up into carpets. Sow collected seed in trays of soil-based seed mix straight away, before it dries out, and leave outside. Germination may take up to a year, and seedlings may take up to seven years to flower.*

Above: Tulipa celsiana *is one group of species popularly known as water lily tulips, due to the shape of the open flowers. This is 'Chopin', one of the most popular varieties, which has attractive red-speckled foliage.*

SUMMER BULBS

If you mention bulbs, most people think of spring-flowering daffodils and tulips, but there are plenty of less well-known kinds that flower in summer. Some, such as *Gladiolus, Acidanthera* (now classified under *Gladiolus), Eucomis* (pineapple flower), tuberous begonia and *Tigridia*, are not hardy enough to leave in the ground through the winter, so plant them in spring. In the fall, when the flowers are over and the foliage dies down, dig them up, dry them off and store them in a frost-free place. Summer-flowering bulbs that can be planted permanently in a mild climate include summer hyacinths *(Galtonia)*, which bear large sprays of greenish white flowers similar to those of yucca, and *Crinum powellii*, the giant of the summer bulbs. Each one has a long thick neck that must remain above ground when it is planted. Give it rich soil. A hot, sunny, flower bed at the foot of a wall is the best place to grow *Nerine* and *Amaryllis hippeastrum* (not to be confused with the indoor plant *Hippeastrum*). Both like to be left undisturbed, with no other plants around them to prevent the bulbs ripening properly. The flowers appear in late summer or fall on bare stems, after the leaves have died down. All summer bulbs need a sunny sheltered spot and well-drained soil. Prepare the soil well, by forking in a handful of general fertilizer per square yard, and plenty of well-rotted organic matter - coir is ideal for summer bulbs, as it improves the soil structure without holding too much moisture.

Planting lily bulbs

Above: To plant lilies outdoors, lay the bulbs informally on the prepared soil, about 12in(30cm) apart. Dig a hole for each bulb.

Below: Plant them so that the tip of each bulb is covered by 6in(15cm) of soil. The soil should be moisture-retentive but well-drained.

Above: Gladioli such as this 'Perky' make superb cut flowers. For a supply from midsummer to fall, plant a few bulbs every two weeks from mid-spring to early summer.

Galtonia candicans (summer hyacinth)

Large-flowered gladiolus

Canna 'Lucifer'

Eucomis bicolor

Acidanthera bicolor 'Murieliae' *(Gladiolus callianthus* 'Murieliae')

Tigridia pavonia

Miniature *Gladiolus orchidiolus*

Below: *Lilium regale* is fragrant and a favorite for cottage-style borders - as here with *Lavatera* and *Selinum tenuifolium*.

Below: *Acidanthera b.* 'Murieliae' (*Gladiolus callianthus* 'Murieliae') grows to 2-3ft(60-90cm). Plant in late spring or grow in pots; harvest and store the corms in winter.

Left: *Tigridia pavonia* is called the peacock flower because of its bright iridescent colors. Plants bloom in late summer and need a warm sheltered spot. Store corms indoors during the winter.

Ideal planting depths

1 *Tigridia* 2in/5cm
2 *Canna* 2in/5cm
3 Miniature *Gladiolus* 3in/7.5cm
4 *Eucomis* 4in/10cm
5 Large *Gladiolus* 4in/10cm
6 *Acidanthera* 6in/15cm
7 *Galtonia* 6in/15cm

Planting a dahlia tuber

Dahlias are grown from tubers planted out in late spring, about two weeks before the last frost. Rooted cutting are occasionally available in spring, but do not plant these out until after the last frost. Dahlias need moist rich soil in a sunny spot and regular attention.

Right: *Dahlia flowers range from decoratives with large round flowers and broad petals to singles with daisylike blooms.*

1 Dig a hole in well-prepared soil about 8in(20cm) deep and wide enough to take the tuber with space to spare.

2 Place the tuber on a small mound of soil in the hole, and space the roots out so that they make contact with the soil.

3 Hammer in a strong stake just behind the tuber. Leave this till later and you risk damage to the tuber. Cover and fill.

4 The tip of the tuber should be 6in(15cm) below the ground. If a late frost threatens the first shoots, cover with peat.

Tuberous begonias

1 Loosely fill a 4 or 5in(10-13cm) pot with any good-quality potting mix to just below the rim.

Before planting, set the tuber on a saucer of seed mixture until pink buds appear. This avoids planting it upside down.

2 Press the corm into the mix, leaving the top just above the surface. Water and keep out of bright light at first.

Below: Increase the light when the corm is growing well. The end result should be a plant with perfect blooms the size of teacups that will make a stunning display.

GARDENING WITH BULBS

As an alternative to naturalizing bulbs (planting them permanently in borders or grass) they can be used temporarily in bedding schemes. Summer-flowering bulbs such as gladioli and eucomis are always bedded out, as most do not survive freezing winters; they have to be dug up after the flowers are over and the leaves have died down naturally. Store them in a frost-free place from mid-fall to late spring while they are naturally dormant, then replant each year. Spring-flowering bulbs like daffodils and tulips are planted from late summer to mid-fall, depending on type. They are traditionally planted in flower beds or containers after summer annuals have been removed, along with early spring bedding such as forget-me-nots, wallflowers, polyanthus, violas, double bellis daisies and colored primroses, which flower at the same time as the bulbs, creating a most impressive display. After the flowers are over, remove dead heads as usual, but when spring bulbs are used as bedding, it is not necessary to wait until their foliage has died down before digging them up. Dig up the clumps of bulbs as soon as the flowers are over but while the leaves are still green. Keep as much soil and root round the bulbs as possible. Transplant the clumps straight away, without letting them dry out or splitting them up, to a well-prepared area of vacant ground (perhaps in the vegetable garden). Keep them watered and feed with liquid tomato feed until the foliage turns brown, usually after about six to eight weeks. Then dig up and split the clumps, clean off the soil and leave them in the open air to dry. Once dry, store in labelled paper bags.

Below: *Allium giganteum* is one of the showiest and most spectacular summer-flowering bulbs; the huge spherical heads contrast strongly with other flowers in a country garden border.

Left: *Gladiolus tristis* is an early spring-flowering species with scented pale yellow flowers. Except in a warm climate, grow it in a pot in a frost-free greenhouse or conservatory. Plant bulbs in late summer.

Above: Tulips go well with spring bedding such as wallflowers and violas; here *Tulipa pax* is growing with *Erysimum* 'Scarlet Bedder' and *Viola* 'Princess Cream'.

Left: If the soil is too heavy or cold, grow bulbs in pots and plunge them to the rim or simply stand them in place when plants are well advanced for an instant display.

Below: Strong color combinations seem to work better in spring gardens, when we have been starved of color for months. Here tulips, hyacinths and pansies create a vivid color scheme.

Naturalizing bulbs in grass

One of the prettiest ways to grow spring bulbs is naturalized in grass. The most suitable types are those that are happy to be left undisturbed, such as narcissi and crocus, but many small bulbs are suitable, although hyacinths and tulips are not. Plant narcissi and crocus bulbs in natural 'drifts' (well-defined a. eas where bulbs are planted closely together) in an ornamental lawn to add spring interest.

1 Mark an area with a sharp spade and slide the blade beneath to avoid severing most of the roots. Roll back the turf.

2 Loosen the soil as deeply as possible. Add well-rotted and sieved organic matter to poor soil and grit to heavy soil.

3 Scatter the bulbs (crocus) and plant them where they fall. Scoop out enough soil to plant each bulb at the right depth.

4 Roll the turf back and firm it down lightly - the whole turf must touch the soil below. Water the area if the weather is dry.

***Left:** Crocuses make little foliage and do not 'swamp' the grass. Delay mowing until six weeks after the bulb foliage has died down. Avoid lawn feeds with weedkillers where bulbs are naturalized.*

INSTANT BULB DISPLAYS

The cheapest way to create a good display of flowering daffodils, hyacinths and tulips, etc. throughout spring is to plant dry, dormant bulbs in the fall. However, you can still have a superb, instant display by buying bulbs that are growing in pots. These are available from early spring until the plants are in flower. Team them with spring bedding, such as double daisies, polyanthus and violas, that are also sold in flower at this time, to transform tubs, windowboxes or entire garden beds. Although this is more expensive than buying dry bulbs, creating displays instantly from growing bulbs has much to recommend it. Since the bulbs are in bud when you buy them, it is possible to select plants at exactly the same stage so that they all open together - ideal for containers. And since it is possible to judge the color of the blooms, even from quite tight flower buds, you can choose bulb plants that will match with other spring bedding to create harmonious, color coordinated schemes. Best of all, each bloom will be in perfect condition since you will only buy the best. However, there are a few pitfalls to avoid. Bulb plants that are sold in bud or flower in spring will almost certainly have been grown in greenhouses during the winter, so harden them off for a week or more by standing them outside during the day and moving them under cover at night. Choose a sheltered spot and avoid planting during cold spells. Do not disturb the roots of growing bulbs; instead plunge the entire pot to the rim in soil.

1 Make sure that you choose a trough deep enough to take the potted bulbs without needing to break up their roots. Place a shallow layer of flower pot 'crocks' in the base to cover the drainage holes.

2 Add potting mixture until the trough is roughly half full; completely cover the crocks. Use either soil or peat-based potting mixture. There is no need to buy bulb fiber, which is for indoor use.

3 Bulbs need not be knocked out of their pots; simply plunge the complete pot to the rim inside the trough. You may need to compress the rootballs slightly to make them fit in; in this case gently tip the plants out of their pots first.

4 Pack in as many plants as possible to create a really full display. By choosing plants in flower, you ensure that they are all at the same stage and looking their best.

5 Use tall daffodils towards the center and back, and shorter, chunkier flowers such as hyacinths, to add 'weight' near the center of the group for a pleasing effect.

6 Buy short spring bedding plants, such as polyanthus, just as they are coming into flower. Tuck them at the front and sides of the trough for a graduated effect.

7 In a trough, a roughly symmetrical design looks best, so repeat the same flowers at both ends of the display, even if they are not the same color.

8 Trickle more potting mix into any spaces between the plants. Water well. The display could stand in a porch, on staging or a low wall. Lift out any plants that finish flowering early and replace them.

The foliage should hide the potting mix and the edge of the trough.

Variations on a theme

Test the effect of different plant partnerships by standing two or three groups of different kinds together, in their pots. For extra foliage, buy small ivy plants with long trailing stems. Consider teaming bulbs with small evergreen shrubs, such as dwarf conifers or euonymus, or using 'props', such as curls of birch bark, pine cones and unusual pots.

Right: *Containers of spring bulbs make a great display lined up on steps; here, 'Blue Delft' hyacinths and* Narcissus *'Tête-à-Tête' (a dwarf variety) steal the scene.*

A hanging basket with bulbs

Above: *This spring hanging basket includes* Narcissus *'Tête-à-Tête' and* Anemone blanda, *combined with a hardy hybrid primrose, heather* (Erica x darleyensis *'Molten Silver'), ivy* (Hedera helix *'Sagittifolia Variegata') and pink arabis.*

CHOOSING PLANTS

Bulbs have far wider uses than many people realize: grow them in beds, borders and containers and naturalize them in grass and under trees. Use them to add an extra tier of color - even to a garden that seems already full!

Above: You can dig up snowdrops - even in full bloom - and put them in a container for an instant display.

Bulbs for light shade under trees and shrubs
(Choose very early spring- or fall-flowering bulbs, as these can complete most of their growth cycle before trees and shrubs come into leaf and create shade. A few woodland species of bulbs are also suitable.)
Cardiocrinum giganteum 6-12ft (1.8-3.7m tall, woodland)
Chionodoxa (glory-of-the-snow)
Colchicum autumnale (autumn crocus)
Convallaria (lily-of-the-valley)
Cyclamen, hardy *Eranthis hyemalis* (winter aconites)
Erythronium (dog's-tooth violets)
Fritillaria meleagris (snake's-head fritillary)
Galanthus (snowdrops)
Hyacinthoides (bluebells - NB invasive)
Lilium hansonii, L. henryi, L. martagon, L. tigrinum
Narcissus, early-flowering ones, such as 'February Gold'
Scilla (squills)

Bulbs for hot dry sunny sites
(Small types are suitable for rock gardens and raised beds, tall kinds for the foot of a sunny wall)
Amaryllis belladonna
Brodiaea
Crinum powellii
Eremurus (foxtail lily)
Fritillaria - small species
Ipheion
Iris reticulata sp.
Nerine
Rhodohypoxis
Tulipa sp. and hybrids
Zephyranthes

Below: The daisylike flowers of *Anemone blanda* light up in partial shade at the base of a tree.

Above: *Narcissus* 'Tête à Tête, *Chionodoxa luciliae* and *Muscari armeniacum* (grape hyacinth) make a cheerful spring display in shiny metal pails. Deadhead the daffodils as they fade.

Good bulbs for bedding
(Plant in the fall, lift and store after foliage dies down ready to replant the following fall)
Grape hyacinths
Hyacinths
Tulip hybrids (not the species, which are more rockery plants)

Bulbs for naturalizing in grass
Fritillaria meleagris
Galanthus (snowdrops)
Hyacinthoides (bluebells)
Narcissi
Scilla

Bulbs for naturalizing in borders under shrubs
Anemone blanda
Cyclamen, hardy
Eranthis hyemalis (winter aconites)
Galanthus (snowdrops)

Bulbs for patio pots in summer
Begonia, tuberous
Dahlia, miniature
Eucomis
Lilium (lilies) especially 'Enchantment', oriental hybrids and *Lilium speciosum*
Nerine sarniensis (Guernsey lily)

Summer-flowering bulbs used outdoors that do not stand frost
(Lift and store these bulbs in frost-free conditions for the winter)
Begonia, tuberous
Canna
Dahlia
Eucomis
Gladiolus
Tigridia

Below: *Canna* flowers mid- to late summer. If kept well fed, the tuber will be larger the following year.

PART TEN

FRUIT AND VEGETABLES

Anyone who has grown their own fruit and vegetables will know the pleasure and satisfaction involved, especially when you eat them! Even in a relatively small garden, you can find space to grow a few choice varieties that will taste incomparably better than shop-bought ones and may well mature earlier, too.

BEANS • PEAS

With reasonable upkeep, climbing French and runner beans can start cropping in midsummer and continue until the first frosts. Treat both as half-hardy annuals and do not sow them outdoors until mid-spring, when the soil has warmed up and there is little risk of frost. If runner beans have difficulty in setting the beans, spray the flowers with water most evenings during flowering.

Dwarf French beans are usually sown before runner beans so that they mature ahead of them. There are two varieties: the traditional ones with fairly flat pods and the modern, stringless 'pencil-podded' kind that are good for freezing. Do not sow these fatter varieties until late spring or early summer, when temperatures are higher. Then sow them in succession. The older, flatter varieties, on the other hand, are hardier and more reliable in poor summers.

There are two main types of broad bean: those sown in late fall (Aquadulce type) and those best left until the late winter or early spring (Windsor and Longpod types). Dwarf varieties are particularly good for growing in small gardens or even in containers. Fall varieties crop a little earlier in summer and are less likely to be attacked by blackfly.

Broad beans

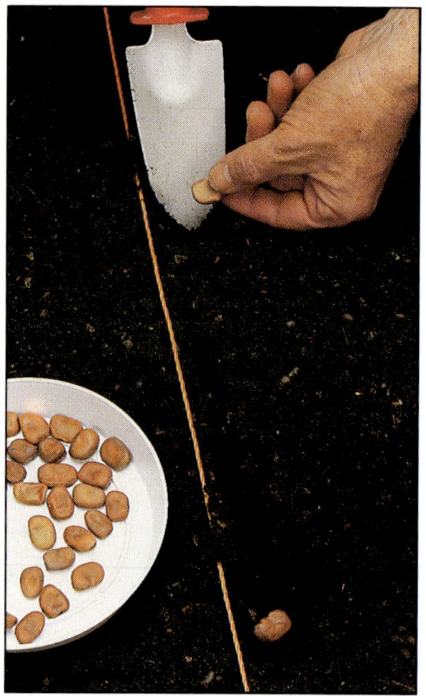

1 Sow seeds singly 1.5-2in (4-5cm) deep. Plant them in a straight line 9in(23cm) apart, with 18in(45cm) between the rows.

2 All broad beans need support once they are 12in(30cm) tall. Loop garden twine around canes, around the whole group of plants.

Climbing beans

1 Push four 8ft(2.5m) canes into the ground about 1ft(30cm) apart and tie them into a wigwam. Put one plant at the base and on the inside of each cane

2 If the garden does not lend itself to growing vegetables in rows, a block of four wigwams is a useful alternative strategy. Remember to keep the plants well watered.

Below: A crop of runner beans is one of the most valuable garden vegetables. Eat the beans at once or freeze them for winter use.

3 Once the lowest flowers on the stem have formed little beans, remove the stem tip to encourage bean formation.

4 The young pods are filling nicely. Do not allow the plants to run short of water and treat them against blackfly if necessary.

Above: A fine crop of small, tender beans for immediate use or for freezing. Do not let them become tough and black-eyed.

DWARF BEANS

1 Sow seeds outdoors in shallow drills or dibble holes 1.5-2in(4-5cm) deep and 2-4in(5-10cm) apart.

2 Give the plants plenty of water. When the beans are ready to harvest, cut them off if necessary, but do not pull them.

Left: 'The Prince', a traditional type of dwarf French bean, has flat, wide pods and is hardier than modern varieties, which allows for earlier sowing.

Growing peas

Although the true garden pea is the most widely grown, you can also obtain seed for several other types. The petit pois is small-seeded and extremely sweet; with mangetout, or edible-podded, varieties (snap and sugar snap peas), the pods are eaten whole. The 'asparagus', or 'winged', pea with its faint asparagus flavor, is also eaten whole.

1 Scatter the seeds about 2in(5cm) apart. This allows a good, thick stand of plants to develop without overcrowding.

2 Cover the seeds so that they are 2in(5cm) deep. Even coverage ensures that the seeds germinate more or less together.

3 Peas vary a great deal in height and even the shorter varieties are easier to manage if you provide them with some support to climb up. Sticks are a traditional choice, but plastic or wire netting is handier, longer lasting and easier to obtain.

Left: *Cook and eat the whole pod of sugar snap peas when the peas inside are almost full sized. They can also be used podded, like garden peas.*

Above: To grow onions from sets plant them 3in(7.5cm) apart, with just the tips showing, otherwise the birds will pull them up.

Above: A crop of good-sized 'Kelsae' onions. They thrive on firm, sandy ground and may even achieve a record-breaking size.

Left: When growing onions from seed, make sure that they have a firm, fine seedbed. Onions and related crops, such as leeks, have similar-looking seeds. Label rows straight after sowing to avoid confusion.

ONIONS • LEEKS

You can grow onions either from seed or from 'sets'. Sets are the least troublesome way of growing onions. They are the size of baby pickling onions and are planted in the garden normally in mid-spring, although some are suitable for fall planting. Once planted, these miniature onions will grow to the full size. You can sow onion seeds either in late winter in a heated greenhouse for planting out later on or, if you choose the right varieties, you may sow the seeds outdoors in the early fall or in mid-spring. They like a firm and fine seedbed. If you store them well, onions grown one year will keep until the spring of the following year. Dig them up when the tops have died down in the early fall, clean them, dry them off thoroughly and store them in a cold shed. If you keep them indoors, they will start growing and will be useless.

Shallots are very similar to onions but with a milder flavor. They are normally grown from offsets planted outside in late winter or early spring. Once the bulbs are planted, prevent the birds from pulling them out before they have formed roots by threading black cotton along the rows. Each shallot will split up into five or six new bulbs. Harvest these in summer when the tops have died down.

Onion varieties

There are many golden-skinned onions, including 'Hygro', 'Rijnsburger' and 'Sturon'.

Among shallots, 'Dutch Yellow' is excellent and 'Hative de Niort' has large, well-shaped bulbs.

Red varieties of onions include 'Red Baron' and 'Red Brunswick'.

SALAD ONIONS

Salad onions (green or spring onions) are easy to grow from both spring and fall sowings. Use them before there is much of a swelling at the base. If salad onions are not used young, they can be left to grow and will produce small bulbs that can be used for cooking later. A special over-wintering variety of 'White Lisbon' is available for fall sowing. The onions will be ready to use the following spring. Protect them under cloches in cold regions.

Left: Push the little shallot bulbs into the ground about 6in(15cm) apart. This will give the resulting cluster of bulbs enough room to develop. Shallots and onions enjoy the same growing conditions, so you can grow them in the same bed.

GARLIC

Divide a bulb of garlic into 'cloves'. Plant the largest ones in spring or late fall; fall-planted crops are biggest. You can use garlic from a store, but mail-order catalogs often list garlic specially for planting.

Growing leeks

Sow leeks either in a heated greenhouse in mid- to late winter or outside in early to mid-spring. In either event, plant the seedlings outside in their final position when they are about as thick as pencils.

1 Trim the seedling roots to 0.5in(1.25cm). Young leeks look very like salad onions and may be used as such.

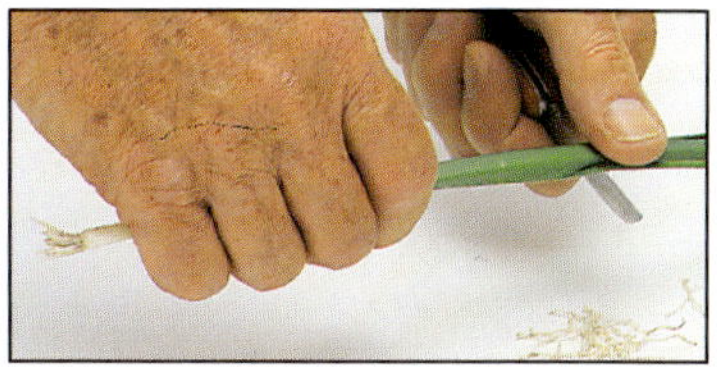

2 Trim the tops so that each transplant is 6-8in(15-20cm) long. This reduces water loss and speeds up establishment.

3 Make a hole for the roots and drop in each transplant so that a third to half is buried. Do not push the soil back into the hole. Pour water into each hole until it is full up.

Leeks planted further apart and left longer for more substantial stems.

Smaller leeks, planted closer together and lifted sooner.

LETTUCES

Lettuces can be raised in two ways, either by sowing seed directly into well-prepared ground in the place where they are to mature (in situ) or by raising them under protection for planting out when it is warmer. The latter method is mainly used for the hearting varieties - iceberg, butterhead and cos - whereas the leaf varieties, which include many of the exotics, are usually sown in situ. Once these are sufficiently well advanced, they can be thinned and singled to 10in(25cm) apart. All-year-round lettuces can be a complicated crop, but are quite easy to grow if you have the right conditions and varieties. When sowing lettuces in a greenhouse for planting out later, be sure to stop planting out in late spring and only sow lettuces in situ. If you do continue to plant them out, lettuces usually bolt (produce a flower head) because the check to their growth initiates flowering. Furthermore, seed germination is unreliable, or even stops, at temperatures above the mid-70s°F (mid-20s°C). It often pays to sow summer-maturing lettuces in semi-shade, where temperatures are likely to be lower.

ENJOYING LETTUCES ALL YEAR ROUND

Late spring to early summer:
Sow in heat mid- to late winter, plant outside mid- to late spring.
Early to midsummer:
Sow the seeds in succession outdoors in spring.
Midsummer to mid-fall:
Sow in succession outdoors late spring to late summer.
Early fall to early winter:
Sow outdoors in late summer.
Fall and winter:
Sow in cold frame in early and mid-fall, transplant seedlings to frost-free greenhouse.
Mid- and late spring:
Sow the seed outdoors in late summer and early fall.
Use recommended varieties for best results.

1 Before sowing, dampen the soil with a fine rose until water runs out of the holes in the base. This will aid germination.

2 Sprinkle the seeds evenly and thinly over the surface of the potting mix. If you sow too thickly, seedlings will be lanky and weak.

5 Cover the pot with a sheet of glass or plastic to maintain a damp atmosphere. Stand it in a warm, but not too sunny, spot.

6 Now the seedlings are ready for pricking out. Take a clump at a time and plant singly into a seed tray filled with potting mix.

Right: The cos is one of the heaviest lettuces. It also takes up a great deal of room; allow about 15in(38cm) between each plant and between rows. 'Lobjoits' is an excellent variety.

Left: Lettuces can be grown all the year round with protection. 'Kweik' is fine in an unheated greenhouse. Avoid excess watering after plants are half-grown to discourage mildew.

3 Cover the seeds with sifted potting mixture. Firm the surface lightly to ensure that the seeds are in contact with the mix.

4 If you prefer to water after sowing, stand the pot in a bowl of water until moisture soaks up to the surface of the potting mix.

7 Make a sufficiently large dibble hole, plant the seedling and firm in the sides so that each seedling is self-supporting.

8 Water the seedlings well with a fine-rosed watering can. Plant them out after about one month and start feeding them.

Above: This crisp 'Iceberg' lettuce is heavier and denser than the butterhead sort. There are many varieties of each to choose from.

Other types of lettuce

Little Gem: *An old variety dating from the turn of the century; one of the best-tasting lettuce ever.*
Lollo Rossa: *Pretty lettuces with very frilly leaves popular as garnishes. Outer leaves are red with tasty pale green hearts.*
Salad Bowl: *A 'cut-and-come-again' lettuce that never forms hearts; pick a few leaves as needed, leaving the rest of the plant to continue growing. Red and green varieties of 'Salad Bowl' are available.*

Above: *'Little Gem', a miniature cos lettuce, also called sugar cos.*

Above: *Clockwise from the top: 'Salad Bowl', 'Little Leprechaun', 'Carnival' and 'Red Salad Bowl'.*

Oak-leaved lettuce: *Several varieties, such as 'Cocarde', with unusual large, oak-shaped or saber-like leaves, in red or green. They make pretty additions to a mixed salad or use as a garnish.*
Cos, or Romaine: *This tall upright lettuce has oblong leaves with a thick midrib. Plants need tying round with raffia when half grown to encourage the formation of a good tender heart; protection from slugs is essential.*

Salad leaves

Baby spinach: *Sow seed thickly in rows and pick leaves 1in (2.5cm) across as soon as plants are a few inches high. No need to thin.*
Watercress: *Sow seed or root cuttings from shop-bought bunches into potting mixture and stand in a saucer of water. Pick often; do not let plants flower.*
Land cress: *Easier grown alternative with milder taste. Sow in rows in the garden and cut as suggested for baby spinach.*
Rocket: *An annual plant. Sow seed in short rows and snip leaves or cut clumps while plants are small. Keep well cut to prevent it going to seed. Sow new rows three or four times from spring to late summer.*

Lambs lettuce, or corn salad: *Annual plants that make small neat rosettes. Most useful grown under cover in winter when normal lettuce is difficult. Sow thickly in rows and cut or pull whole plants when 1in(2.5cm) or less. Delicious taste and texture; one of the best alternative salads.*

Below: *Land cress will thrive in shade and fertile soil. It will stay green during the winter months.*

Sowing tomatoes

1 Sow seeds in trays of seed or multipurpose potting mix. Put one seed in the center of each cell.

Tomato seeds vary in size with the variety. Sow them indoors or in a heated greenhouse.

2 Push the seed no more than 0.5in(1.25cm) into the potting mix with the flat end of a pencil.

3 Gently cover each seed with more potting mixture. This is a good way of raising a few plants.

4 Stand the tray in a basin of water until water soaks up to the surface. Drain for 10 seconds.

5 Cover the tray with plastic or glass and stand it in a warm place for the seeds to germinate.

TOMATOES • SWEETCORN

Both single stem and bush varieties of tomatoes will grow perfectly satisfactorily in the ground, either in a greenhouse or outside. First, dig the ground deeply and incorporate plenty of well-rotted garden compost or farmyard manure to provide an abundance of the organic matter that is essential for good results. Raise the plants in a greenhouse or indoors on a sunny windowsill. Once they are large enough, greenhouse tomatoes can be planted out at any time in spring, but do not plant outdoor varieties until the risk of frost is over. Plant bush varieties 20in(50cm) apart, disbudded varieties 2-3in(5-7.5cm) closer, and support the plants with a stout stick. Probably the greatest disadvantage of outdoor tomatoes is that the season is a good month (two weeks at each end) shorter than for greenhouse crops. You can partly compensate for this in the fall by covering the ground under the plants with straw, cutting the plants loose from the stake and laying them on the straw.

Then place large cloches or plastic tunnels over the plants to keep them warmer and drier, thus extending the season. When even this strategy ceases to work, cut off the fruit trusses and bring them indoors to finish ripening.

GROWING SWEETCORN

Sweetcorn needs a long growing season in an open, sunny, mild site and plenty of water. Plant the seedlings in soil well supplied with garden compost or manure and sufficient lime to correct strong acidity. Harvest modern varieties about four months after sowing.

1 Raise sweetcorn plants by sowing the seeds singly in cardboard tubes filled with seed or multipurpose potting mixture and supported in trays.

2 Place a seed in the top of each tube and press it about 1in(2.5cm) into the mix. Fill the hole with more mix and water carefully to avoid washing the seed down.

Tomatoes in the ground

1 When the first flowers open, plant out the tomato firmly, but gently. Water it in well and tie it to a cane with soft twine.

2 Unless it is a bush variety, remove any side shoots that appear as plants establish.

3 Remove the side shoot with a sharp tweak. Start from the top and work downwards.

3 Plant out seedlings (in tubes) a month after germinating when there is no risk of frost. Remove weeds by hoeing without damaging surface-feeding roots.

Position the young plants about 18in(45cm) apart, in blocks rather than rows; this helps pollination.

Tomato varieties

Gardeners Delight: *Enormously popular, flavorful, bite-sized mini-tomatoes for greenhouse or outdoors. Fruit held in large trusses. Like most 'cherry' tomatoes, fruit are faster to ripen and plants need less water than large-fruited tomatoes.*
Brandywine: *Large beefsteak-type tomato with superb flavor, but needs plenty of high-potash feeds for full flavor to develop. Plants are large and vigorous with 'potato' leaves. Greenhouse except in very mild climates.*
Sungold: *A yellow-fruited, early, prolific cherry tomato. Possibly the best flavor of any yellow tomato, greenhouse or outdoors.*
Moneymaker: *Well-known old favorite 'heirloom' variety, with small/medium-sized round red fruit, but flavor not outstanding compared to modern varieties. Greenhouse or outdoors.*
Sweet Million: *Exceptionally productive red 'cherry' tomato with huge trusses of fruit. Superb flavor, and excellent variety. Greenhouse or outdoors.*
Harbinger: *Turn of the century tomato with the true tomato taste. Medium-sized round red fruit. Grow in the greenhouse or outside in mild areas.*
Tigerella: *Unusual red/orange striped tomatoes with a tangy flavor. Grow in the greenhouse or outside in mild areas.*
F1 Hybrid tomatoes: *New varieties are bred for disease resistance, so if root diseases have been a problem in your soil, by growing these you can usually avoid the need to grow in growing bags or change the greenhouse soil. A choice of varieties is available each year. Consult seed catalogs.*

Sweetcorn varieties

Varieties available vary a great deal from year to year, but fall into several distinct groups - consult your seed catalogs for details.
Mini sweetcorn: *Each plant bears 4-6 'baby' cobs on full-sized plants. Pick cobs when they are about 3in(7.5cm) long before they start to swell out.*

Supersweet varieties: *These are bred to have an exceptionally sweet flavor. Grow supersweet varieties well away from 'normal' sweetcorn so that they do not cross pollinate, or the resulting cobs do not have the full flavor.*
Early varieties: *The most reliable in cold regions with a short growing season. Cobs form early and ripen fast, so that an edible crop is assured before fall.*
Popcorn varieties: *Specially for home popcorn production.*
Ornamental sweetcorn: *Decorative varieties, with red, orange, blue or multicolored cobs suitable for using in the same way as ornamental grasses in the flower garden. The dried cobs can be used with dried flowers in winter arrangements.*

SQUASHES • PUMPKINS

The cucurbit family, to which squashes and pumpkins belong, includes marrows, zucchini (courgettes), cucumbers, gourds and melons. While marrows and cucumbers are common enough in Europe, squashes and pumpkins are far more widely grown in America, though they are spreading fast. As far as gardeners are concerned, there are two distinct types of squashes: summer and winter. Marrows and courgettes are a form of summer squash; pumpkins of winter squash. Although their cultivation is similar, summer squashes are essentially used when they are ready, but winter squashes are sown later and stored, when ripe, for use in winter. Harvest summer squashes well before they are old and tough, but leave winter squashes to mature. Winter squashes need about four months from sowing to maturity; summer squashes, somewhat less. Both may be of either bush or trailing habit. Because of the longer summer required for winter squashes, they are more popular in America than Europe. Raise the plants in the same way as courgettes, from mid- to late spring sowings under cover, and plant them outside as soon as the risk of frost is over.

Squashes and pumpkins

Growing zucchini (courgettes) from seed

1 Raise courgettes in individual peat pots. Water well and put them in a plastic bag in a warm place to germinate. When they come through, put in full light.

2 Given warmth, young plants grow quickly and are ready for potting on or planting out when roots are growing out through the sides of the peat pot. Put two plants in a standard-sized growing bag. Leave the top of the rootball 0.5in(1.25cm) above the soil.

3 A good initial watering is vital for these plants. It also helps prevent red spider mites from becoming established; they dislike a damp atmosphere.

'Turk's Turban' has tough skin and the flesh is best boiled and mashed.

'Sweet Dumpling' squash has the same tasty flesh as 'Delicata'. The skins of both can be eaten.

'Golden Acorn' squash has a potato texture.

'Little Gem' squash is slightly watery. Inedible skin.

'Delicata' has sweet, chestnut-flavored golden flesh.

A selection of varieties

When growing marrows, pumpkins and squashes, it is important to consider the ultimate size of the plant. Some varieties have a trailing habit with long stems, while the 'bush' kinds are more compact. Make sure you buy the appropriate ones for your garden or greenhouse.

Zucchini (courgettes)

Ambassador: *Reliable and very productive plants with dark green courgettes; for outdoors. Good for early cropping in cold frame under cloches.*

Gold Rush: *Bright gold courgettes with slightly milder flavor than green. Not such a heavy cropper as the best green varieties.*

Clarita: *Lebanese zucchini with flask-shaped, pale green dappled fruit. This is the best variety for stuffing.*

Winter squashes

Vegetable Spaghetti: *Long trailing vines with medium-sized creamy colored fruit, baked or boiled when mature in the fall. The center is filled with delicious low-calorie strands that are used like spaghetti.*

Hubbard: *Large, red warty-skinned, teardrop-shaped squash. Excellent flavor. Good for roasting.*

Crown Prince: *Blue skin and orange flesh, the best-tasting squash for soup.*

Summer squashes

Use straight from the vine when young and cook like zucchini.

Patty pan types: *Flattened squashes with scalloped edges resembling pies. Varieties include 'Sunburst', 'Custard White', etc. Originally grown to 6in(15cm) diameter and baked with a stuffing in the seed cavity, but now often picked at 1in(2.5cm) and used as zucchini.*

Yellow Crooknecked: *Distinctive yellow fruit with bent neck like the handle of an umbrella.*

Rondo de Nice: *Small round squashes; pick when young.*

Pumpkins

Atlantic Giant: *One of the biggest, easily reaching over 100lbs(45kg) and perfect for Halloween and giant pumpkin competitions. Limit to one per plant for a real whopper.*

Jack be Little: *Lots of small tasty pumpkins for the pot.*

Cinderella: *Slow-growing to a large size. Rich edible flesh. Can be used for ornamental purposes.*

Below: *All squashes need to be grown in full sun, in rich, fertile, moist but well-drained soil. These summer squashes are 'Sunburst'.*

Above: Courgettes also grow well in the ground. Lay perforated black plastic around the plants to reduce mud splash and the risk of disease.

Right: With the right care and plenty of water, you can have courgettes throughout the summer. Always grow a proper courgette variety; a marrow will not do.

POTATOES • CARROTS

Maincrop potatoes are uneconomical in a small garden, but with the help of some cloches or a plastic tunnel, you could be lifting enough new potatoes for a meal when those in the shops are still very expensive. Plant two rows at the most and preferably just one. Even new potatoes take up a great deal of space; an earthed-up row will be at least 18in(45cm) wide. Even without covering the rows, you can still make the crop come earlier by 'chitting' the seed potatoes (causing them to sprout) in a warm room or greenhouse in late winter. Do not worry about keeping the potatoes in the light in the early stages, but once the shoots start to appear, put them in full light to prevent the shoots becoming drawn. When the soil has warmed up sufficiently (look for seedling weeds) in early to mid-spring, plant the tubers about 1in(2.5cm) below the surface and 12-15in(30-38cm) apart. As soon as the shoots appear, be ready to rake some earth over them if a night frost is likely. In any event, earth them up when the shoots are about 6in(15cm) tall so that all but the topmost leaves are buried. It is from the buried stems that the new potatoes grow. If the weather is reasonable, you should have a crop in about 16 weeks. You can also grow new potatoes - or specialist varieties that are hard to find in the shops - in large containers. You can produce early varieties even earlier by planting the tubers six weeks earlier than recommended and keeping the container in a frost-free greenhouse until after the last frost. Then move the container outdoors. The crop should be ready in early midsummer, leaving the tub free for flowers.

1 To 'chit' potatoes, stand them in a warm, dark place in small pots or on an egg tray, with the eyes (buds) pointing upwards.

2 Used soil-based potting mix or old growing bag mix is fine for potatoes. New potting mix can lead to rather too much top growth.

Chitted potatoes grow away much faster after planting out. Once the eyes have developed into shoots, do not damage them.

3 Fill the pot or tub with potting mix until it is one third to half full. Firm it down gently. This tub is about 18in(45cm) in diameter.

4 Lay in the chitted seed potatoes, 6-8in(15-20cm) apart. This will produce a good crop without overcrowding.

5 Cover the potatoes with about 1in(2.5cm) of potting mix and level the surface. There will be enough fertilizer left in the old mix.

6 Water the container well and stand it in a warm place. The tubers will take a few weeks to root and develop foliage.

Below: Use an early variety; they have the shortest growing season and are therefore ready the soonest. This one is 'Arran Pilot'.

REGULAR CARE

The main thing that you must remember when growing potatoes in a sunroom or greenhouse in this way is that the plants are dependent upon you for everything. Make sure that they have enough water and that they do not get too hot. You should not need to feed them, as there will be enough nutrients in the potting mix. If you like, you can move the tub outside, but not until you are sure that there is no risk of frost. The safest time to do this is usually early summer.

7 A fine display of foliage is the forerunner of a delicious crop. If you have the conditions and can obtain (or save) seed tubers, you can grow potatoes all year round.

Growing carrots

Carrots need deep, fertile, moisture-retentive soil. Never grow them on land that has just had compost or manure dug in, as they usually produce divided roots. For the earliest crops, broadcast the seed in rows in early spring and cover with plastic for about eight weeks.

1 Sow early carrot varieties broadcast in cold frames or under clear plastic. Sow thinly, rake the seed in and then water.

2 These maincrop seedlings are ready to be thinned and singled to 1in(2.5cm) apart. Thin them again when they touch.

***Above:** Protect carrots from carrot fly with a mesh barrier. Mesh allows the air to circulate freely around the carrots.*

***Right:** Early, frame-grown carrots are pulled at this stage. They are sweet and delicate, cooked or sliced into salads.*

***Left:** Juicy carrots make a good winter vegetable. Lift them, clean them and store them in net bags in a dark shed.*

APPLES • PEARS

The first thing to remember about planting an apple tree, or any other fruit tree, is that it should be with you for 20 years or more, so you must make sure that the site and soil are absolutely right for it before you start. The site for all fruit trees must be sheltered from the wind and yet open to the sun. This is because pollinating insects will only work during the blossom period if the site is warm and free from wind. Later in the year, sunshine will ensure that the fruit develops its full flavor, and shelter from the wind will enable it to remain on the trees until it is ready for picking. Having chosen the right place for the tree, you must prepare the soil. Allow about 1yd^2 (1m^2) for each tree. Dig the area and fork the base of the hole to improve the drainage and allow the roots to penetrate deeply. You must also dig in a good quantity of garden compost or manure to make the soil even better. Some people recommend adding bonemeal to the ground after it has been dug. This is fine if you are planting in the fall or winter, but in early spring it is far better to use a general fertilizer. Bonemeal only helps new roots to form; a general feed will nourish the whole tree, including the new roots.

Left: This pear, trained as a dwarf pyramid and pruned in summer, produces a heavy crop of fruit on branches of a restricted length.

Below: 'Comice' is probably the best flavored pear there is. Plant at least one other variety nearby to ensure good cross-pollination.

Planting an apple tree

1 Dig a hole for the root system and lay a cane across the top to show how deep to plant the tree. Drive in a stake now, so that you do not damage the roots later on.

2 Replace some of the soil in the planting hole and gently rock the tree about to shake the soil down amongst the roots. Tread it down firmly.

6 The result of these early stages of pruning is a well-shaped and balanced tree that will produce a strong framework of branches able to carry good crops.

7 By midsummer, the young tree has produced many more shoots. Prune them in winter to encourage more branches to form.

3 Nail the buckle end of the tree tie to the stake, pass the free end round the tree and back through the plastic ring. Push the end of the tie through the buckle.

4 Push the tie back through the plastic ring to stop it slipping. The tree should be held fairly firmly away from the stake. If plastic ties are stiff, dip them in warm water.

5 To shape a normal 'bush' tree, select and retain four or five suitable shoots as the future main branches. Shorten them by one third to half their length.

Right: 'Bramley's Seedling' is still probably the best cooking apple. It often keeps until early spring, but because it produces large fruits, it can also be used early in the season. This is a vigorous variety.

Left: 'Discovery' is one of the finest early eating apples. It has a good flavor if allowed to ripen, and regular heavy crops with brilliant red color. Do not keep the fruit too long after picking, as it will start to dry out and shrivel.

Storing fruit

Only apples and pears can be stored as they are; all other fruits must first be prepared and then frozen, bottled, etc. Late-ripening dessert apples destined for storing can be picked all at once. Pick dessert pears when they are still hard and allow them to ripen indoors. Cooking pears are picked and cooked or stored when hard. When dessert pears are ready for picking they part quite readily from the tree.

Above: *Place one apple in each cell of a 'concertina'. Fill the box with one variety of fruit; put a sheet of paper between layers.*

Above: *Once the box is full, lay a piece of card on top and put it in a cool, dark and airy place to store the apples.*

Left: *Another good way of storing apples is to wrap them individually in kitchen paper before placing them in a box. This prevents the spread of any storage rot that may appear.*

Storage trays

Storing apples and pears on racks is possibly the best way of keeping the fruit in good condition, but it also takes up the most room. Air can circulate and ripe or rotting fruit is easy to see. Remove deteriorating fruit, before any rot can pass from one fruit to another. Always put pears on racks, as they need air.

Right: *A homemade storage tray, with the added advantage of being mouseproof by virtue of wire netting back and front.*

STONE FRUITS

Plums, damsons, gages, nectarines, peaches and cherries make attractive and productive garden trees. They can be grown as standard trees or trained flat against a wall; the latter is the safer method in cold regions, since the trees need warmth to ripen the fruit and ensure proper pollination of the flowers. Given fertile, well-drained soil containing some lime (vital for stone formation), sun and shelter, they will give reasonable crops without needing much attention, although fan-trained trees need regular pruning and tying in.

Damsons and plums are the most trouble-free to grow; they were traditionally grown in mixed hedges around old cottage gardens, where they were left virtually untended. Plums are reliable performers, although some varieties tend to crop very heavily in alternate years with little or no fruit in the remaining years. This can be solved, at least partly, by thinning the fruit in heavy cropping years. It is also a good idea to prop up heavily laden branches to prevent them breaking. Cherries are attractive to birds and need covering with nets as the fruit forms. If they are grown against walls, it is easier to tack netting to a batten above the plants and roll it down until after the fruit has been picked.

PEACH LEAF CURL

When grown outdoors, peaches and nectarines are very prone to the fungal disease, peach leaf curl. Peach trees grown under glass seem to escape unharmed and produce earlier and heavier crops, but take up quite a bit of space, even when grown in large pots. (This technique allows you to stand plants outdoors after the fruit has been picked.) For this reason, many people now grow apricots as an alternative exotic fruit, since these are grown in the same way but are unaffected by leaf curl.

Above: Peach leaf curl causes first young leaves and then older ones to become blistered, swollen and bright red. Keeping the leaves dry can help to control the fungus.

Right: In early spring, hand-pollinate peach flowers by drawing a soft paintbrush over the open blooms. Given relatively warm weather, fertilization will follow and fruit will develop, as here.

Planting a peach tree

1 A young peach tree straight from the garden center. When planting, use the rootball to judge the size of hole you need to dig.

2 Once firmly planted, the tree should be very slightly deeper than it was in its original pot, so that new roots form from the stock.

3 Cut back the tree to leave two suitable shoots to form the first rays of the fan. This allows you to start training from the right basis.

4 Cut back these two shoots to two-thirds to three-quarters of their original length. Prune to a bud on the upper surface of the shoot to direct new growth upwards.

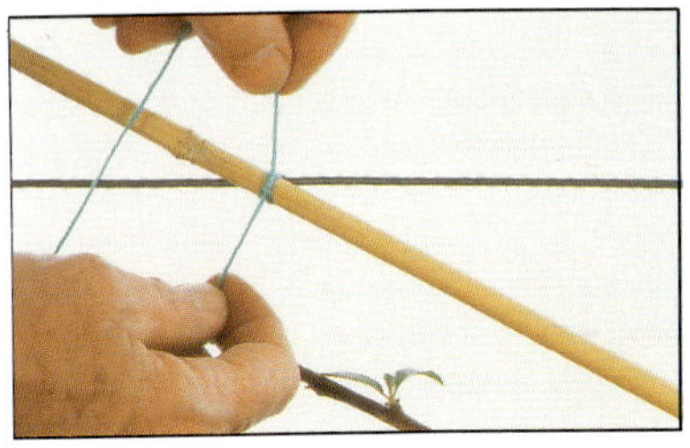

5 Tie two primary training canes to permanent wires, 9-12in (23-30cm) apart. Use plastic string or wire; bend in any sharp ends.

6 Tie the shoots to the canes with soft string. This avoids strangling the growing shoots, which can happen with plastic.

7 The peach tree is about to send out new shoots from the two that were trained in. If necessary, protect the tender growths from frost.

Left: Here is the tree in the following spring. It is best to leave all the buds to grow into side shoots before deciding on further pruning and training. A year later, the tree will bear enough flowers to produce the first real crop of succulent peaches.

Plums, damsons and gages

These are all descended from the wild Prunus domestica *and this close relationship means that their cultivation is very similar; tree forms, pests and diseases are common to all three. They are usually grown as free-standing 'bush' trees, but they can also be grown as cordons and fans, which take up very little room in small gardens. The worst pests are aphids, which infest the tips of the shoots in summer, and plum moth, whose maggot you often find in the ripe fruits.*

Plums: *Originally, plums were inferior in quality to gages and were destined for the kitchen and the pot. Many were of near-dessert quality. This led to the creation of dual-purpose varieties that were good all-rounders.*

Right: *The best-known plum in the world, 'Victoria' is a reliable and heavy cropper. Officially dual-purpose (meaning it can be eaten raw or cooked), but often thought of as a dessert plum, especially in gardens.*

Damsons: *Of the three 'plums', damsons are the nearest to the original. The name comes from their origin in Damascus. Several varieties exist today. They are essentially used for cooking and make excellent jams and jellies. Damsons are the smallest of the group and need little attention.*

Left: *Damsons are small cooking plums that often crop prolifically. 'Bradley's King' crops in early fall and is one of the largest and best-flavored damsons.*

Gages: *Originally regarded as the finest dessert 'plums', gages were of the highest quality and often yellow or golden in color, sweet and delicious. However, they were also the hardest to grow, being shy to crop and prone to pests and diseases. They have been replaced by dual-purpose, heavier croppers.*

Right: *'Merton' gage, a good-quality dessert variety raised in the 1920s, ripens in late summer and must be cross-pollinated.*

GOOSEBERRIES

Gooseberries need good soil conditions to give of their best. This is especially true of dessert varieties, which are grown to a larger size than cookers. Take care when tending bushes or picking fruit, as the thorns are long, pointed and very sharp. Unfortunately, there are no thornless gooseberry varieties worth growing, but one of the best ways of cultivating them is as cordons trained to a wall or fence or grow them in the open up canes. They are much easier to look after than bushes, the dessert varieties ripen better and you are less likely to be scratched. You can grow cordons with just one vertical shoot, or double or multiple cordons with two or more shoots. Single cordons are the quickest to reach the desired height but you need many more plants for a given length of fence. Another unusual shape is the standard, which, like a standard rose, is just a bush on top of a 3-4ft(90-120cm) stem.

For the biggest and best dessert gooseberries, prune both cordons and bushes in early summer. That is also the time to thin out the fruits to one per cluster, using the thinnings for cooking. Summer pruning simply involves cutting back new shoots (those you do not want for extension growth) to five leaves, about 5in(13cm). Summer pruning improves the berry size and color of dessert varieties and the crop weight of cookers. Early to midsummer is the normal and the most beneficial time to summer prune. Because you are removing the soft growth at the end of the shoots, which is the part most susceptible to mildew attack, summer pruning also plays a very valuable role in controlling this disease.

Above: The aptly named 'Early Sulphur' ripens early, is a heavy cropper and makes an upright bush. Do not be put off by the bristles on the fruits; this is a superb dessert variety.

Right: A row of well-trained and properly maintained U-cordons, cropping well after three or four years growth. Net the fruit to protect it from the attentions of birds.

Remove shoots closer than 5in(13cm) or so to the roots, and any buds among the roots.

Planting a gooseberry bush

1 Plant the bush firmly, leaving a clear leg of 5-6in(13-15cm) between the ground and the first branch. Nick out buds on the leg.

2 After planting, remove any weak shoots, cutting back misplaced ones and shortening the rest by roughly half their length.

3 Pruning stimulates side shoots; the original four or five 'branches' will give rise to eight to ten after the first growing season.

TAKING GOOSEBERRY CUTTINGS

Gooseberries are very easy to propagate. Simply take hardwood cuttings, retaining just the top three or four buds, and insert them into V-slits in the ground 6in(15cm) apart.

Right: Push the cuttings into the ground as near upright as possible so that the resulting bushes have a vertical 'leg'. Take cuttings in early winter when the leaves have fallen.

Left: 'Whitesmith' is a first-rate dessert gooseberry. It crops well and has an excellent flavor. The medium vigor of the bush makes it very suitable for growing as a cordon.

Below: 'Lancashire Lad' is a large-berried, coarsely bristled but popular dessert variety. It ripens in early to midseason and has a good flavor.

4 For a U-cordon (with two upright stems), prune back the bush to two strong shoots growing out opposite each other.

Pruning gooseberries

Gooseberries are pruned in either winter or summer. Winter pruning (shown below) is for shaping the plants and to improve their general vigor; summer pruning is largely to maximize the harvest of fruit.

1 A mature, unpruned gooseberry bush in winter has thorny shoots and branches growing in all directions.

2 Remove all shoots and branches growing too low or too far out, plus any branches that cross or crowd others.

3 Once the framework is tidy, shorten all branch leaders (young shoots on the end of each branch) to half their length.

4 Shorten side shoots on spurs or growing from main branches to 3in(7.5cm) to an up- or outward-pointing bud.

5 The tidily pruned bush is well equipped to carry heavy crops without collapsing under the strain. Upright training counteracts the gooseberry's natural weeping habit.

BLACKCURRANTS

Blackcurrants are an excellent soft fruit for making into jellies, for filling pies and for adding to summer fruit salads. They are also exceptionally rich in vitamin C and can be used for cordial or wine-making. Traditional bushes of most varieties are too large for many gardens, but by choosing a more compact variety and pruning it harder than normal, they become a more viable proposition. Nor is it possible to grow blackcurrants as cordons, because their best fruits and heaviest crops are produced on young shoots, which are removed when pruning cordons.

The aim of pruning is to keep the bushes young and compact. Choose the least vigorous variety, the relatively new 'Ben Sarek', with a recommended planting distance of 36in(90cm). Blackcurrants are usually pruned in early winter by cutting out branch systems when they reach four years old. To keep the bushes small, reduce this to three or even two years. Because the bushes will be smaller, also reduce the initial planting distance between them or the crop from a given length of row will be considerably lighter.

Cultivated not as conventional bushes but as cordons, both redcurrants and whitecurrants, take up little room and will grow either in the open garden trained to canes or against a wall or fence. U-cordons are more economical of plants than single vertical cordons, but the latter will cover the area more quickly. Prune back the new shoots to within 4in(10cm) of the main branches in early summer and, further, to 2in(5cm) in the winter.

Planting a redcurrant bush

1 Start with a strong, one-year-old bush. As it is best grown on a short 'leg', remove any shoots less than 5in(13cm) from the roots.

2 For the same reason, nick out any buds among the roots. If left in place, they would produce unwanted suckers later on.

Planting a blackcurrant bush

1 Dig a hole wide enough for the root system and deep enough for the bush to be planted 2in(5cm) deeper than it was before.

2 Cover with soil. Shake the bush so that each root is in contact with the earth and firm the soil to support the bush.

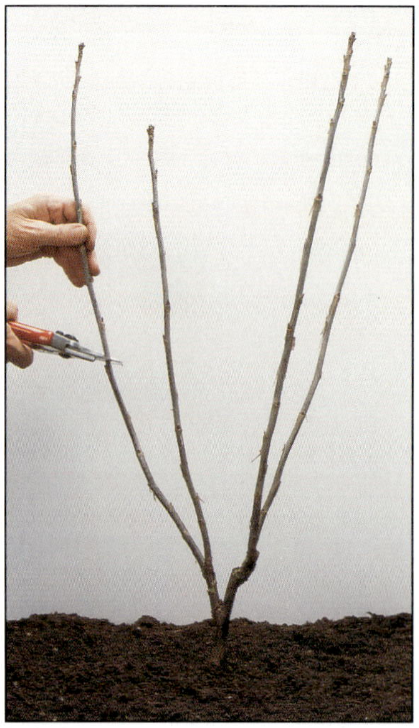

3 After planting, remove weak shoots. Cut back strong but badly placed shoots to 1in(2.5cm). Shorten remaining shoots by half.

4 Four branches pointing in the right direction form the basic shape. In a year's time there will be eight and this is often enough.

3 After planting at the correct depth, remove all the weak shoots and shorten the rest to two or three buds long.

4 This treatment encourages strong shoots to grow from the base and stimulates the root system to establish quickly.

Left: 'Ben Sarek' is a relative newcomer among blackcurrants. The bush is smaller than other varieties, yet heavy cropping.

Below: 'Jonkheer van Tets' is an early, high-quality, heavy-cropping redcurrant. The ripe fruit trusses are large, sweet and deep rich red.

Above: Whitecurrant crops are not as heavy, but the flavor is similar to redcurrants. They require the same method of cultivation.

Propagating blackcurrants

1 In midwinter, dig a slit in the ground 8-9in(20-23cm) deep. Cut the base of a 9-12in (23-30cm)-long shoot to a bud.

2 Carefully cut back thin tips to a strong bud. Always prepare cuttings from strong, straight, one-year-old shoots.

3 Push cuttings into the slit 6in(15cm) apart, leaving only the top buds visible. Shoots will come from below ground.

4 Push the soil down around the cuttings so that they are firmly in place for the winter. You need not water them in.

Propagating redcurrants

Propagating redcurrants and whitecurrants is largely the same as for blackcurrants. However, once you have taken the hard-wood cuttings in early winter, you need only retain the top four buds on each shoot. Improve the soil in the slit trench with organic matter or sprinkle in 1in(2.5cm) of coarse sand and the insert the cuttings 6in(15cm) apart, leaving 6in(15cm) between the lowest retained bud and the ground.

STRAWBERRIES

Strawberries are probably the most popular and easily grown fruit. Strawberry varieties are either of the summer-fruiting or perpetual-fruiting type. Summer-fruiting are the most popular and you can advance them under cloches or even in an unheated greenhouse. For later crops, use one of the perpetual varieties. These will start flowering and fruiting naturally at about the same time as the summer ones, but by removing the flowers as they appear until very early summer, you can induce them to fruit from late summer often until late fall, depending on the weather.

The worst disease is unquestionably botrytis (gray mold), which turns the fruits into gray puffballs of fungus. You can reduce the infection by putting down straw between the rows or using a proprietary alternative to keep mud off the fruit. In addition, spray fortnightly with a suitable fungicide once the first flowers are showing color. Strawberries nearly always need netting against birds. To keep summer-fruiting varieties for another year, cut off the leaves, old fruit stalks and unwanted runners after fruiting. This 'haircut' is not essential, but it cleans away many pests and diseases and helps to rejuvenate the plants. If you give them a high-potash feed at the same time, they will build up into strong plants for the winter and following year.

Planting strawberries

1 Buy strong, bare-rooted plants in late summer or early fall. Do not be tempted to choose larger but older plants that are growing in pots.

2 Use a garden line to mark the row and make a hole deep enough to take the whole root system without having to bend the roots to fit them in.

3 The base of the leaves must be at soil level. If the root tops are visible, they are not planted deep enough.

Protecting strawberries

1 Once the baby strawberries are about the size of a pea, cover the ground under the plants with straw or mats to prevent fungal infections affecting the fruit. Put a few slug pellets underneath the mats.

2 Open the mat and slip it carefully around the base of the plant. You can easily make your own protective mats from old carpet or underlay. Remove them once all the fruit has been picked.

This young plant in its first cropping year fits the proprietary mat well, but it may be too large for it next year. Buy a larger size mat then.

Above: As an alternative to mats, work plenty of clean straw under the plants so that the fruitlets are not splashed with rain and mud.

Below: Delicious strawberry crops are perfectly possible if you take care over them and grow modern varieties, such as this 'Elsanta'.

Using a runner for propagation

The simplest way to propagate strawberries is to peg down the plantlets (one per runner and leaving them attached) onto the soil surface near the parent. However, it can be inconvenient having the new plants dotted about all over the place, so a better plan is to peg them into 7-9in(18-23cm) pots of old potting mixture. Not only will they root more quickly, but you can also move the rooted plants after they have been parted from the parent a month later.

1 Leaving it attached to the parent plant, peg the plantlet down into the potting mix with a piece of looped wire.

2 After about a month, a good root system will have developed in the pot. Cut the new plant from the parent.

3 Remove the remains of the runner and dead leaves and flower stalks. If planted by early fall, expect a crop next summer.

4 Dig a hole large enough to hold the rootball and deep enough for the base of the leaves to sit at soil level after planting.

5 Push the soil back around the rootball and firm it in well to exclude any air pockets. This leads to quick rooting.

6 Water the plant in to settle it into its new position. It now has every chance of producing a heavy crop of fruit.

RASPBERRIES • BLACKBERRIES HYBRID CANE FRUITS

There are two types of raspberry: summer-fruiting and fall-fruiting. Apart from the obvious difference, the main one is that the fall varieties produce canes that fruit later in the same season, whereas the canes of summer varieties grow during the first year and fruit in the summer of the second year. Each cane carries just one crop of fruit and the pruning strategy is based on this. With summer varieties, cut down the fruited canes straight after fruiting and tie in the new ones to the wires in their place. All the canes of the fall varieties fruit together. Once they have fruited, leave them until new ones start to appear above ground the following spring. Then cut all the previous year's canes to the ground.

There are many ways of training blackberries, but with the exception of 'Loch Ness', all methods involve tying the canes to horizontal wires so that they can be tended and picked easily. One feature common to all systems is that the new canes are kept separate - and usually above - those that are about to fruit to reduce the likelihood of diseases being passed from old to new canes. With very few exceptions, hybrid cane fruits are all hybrids between blackberries and raspberries. Mostly, they have the long, supple canes of the blackberry but, except for the few thornless variants, their numerous small thorns are more like those of the raspberry.

Above: Raspberries early in the growing season. The fruiting canes are the first to show signs of life. If there has been any winter damage, cut back the tips to the top wire. Tie in new canes, bend them over if necessary and tie them down.

Planting raspberries

1 Plant the canes 15in (38cm) apart, so that all the roots and any buds are below ground. The buds will grow out to produce canes the following year.

2 Immediately after planting, cut back the canes, leaving them about 10in(25cm) long. This will allow just a few new shoots to grow from them in the following year.

3 It is important to have new shoots on the canes in the next growing season. They will keep the canes alive while more are being sent up from the buds on the roots.

Right: For a less vigorous hybrid, such as this loganberry, a fan system of training is ideal. Train the new canes up the gap in the center between next year's fruiting canes.

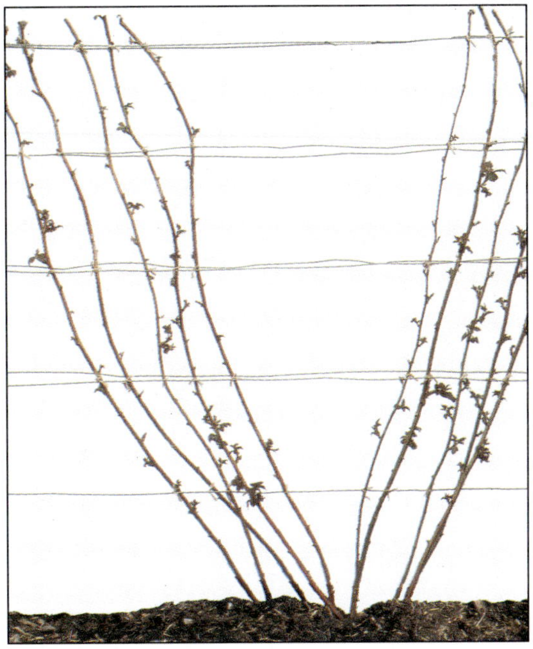

Below: The training method you choose depends on the kind of fruit you grow, as they vary in vigor and the stiffness of their canes. This thornless boysenberry has tall, supple canes so the two-way rope system is the best way to train it.

Left: 'Autumn Bliss' is a superb fall variety of raspberry and provides fresh fruit until the first frosts put a stop to cropping.

Blackberries and their hybrids

Hybrid cane fruits include the tasty loganberry, the tayberry, sunberry, marionberry, boysenberry and the recently introduced tummelberry. Like blackberries, prune the hybrid berries by cutting out the fruited canes soon after fruiting is over. Hybrids can suffer in a hard winter.

Left: *'Fantasia' is an immensely vigorous and thorny blackberry, but crops prodigiously and has an excellent flavor. Freezes well.*

Below: *One of many American hybrids, boysenberry has a blackberry flavor. Crops are lighter on the thornless form.*

Below: *The thornless loganberry came from California and was the first popular blackberry/raspberry hybrid. Excellent flavor, but not reliably hardy in cooler regions.*

Below: *Bred as a companion to tayberry, the sunberry is very vigorous and only suitable for large gardens. Good flavor.*

Below: *The first 'modern' hybrid, the tayberry is hardier than the loganberry and crops twice as heavily. No thornless form.*

Above: *A 'child' of the tayberry, the tummelberry is the hardiest hybrid. Excellent for freezing. Canes are semi-erect and thorny.*

A CODLING MOTH TRAP

One of the most troublesome pests of apples - and to a lesser extent of pears - is the codling moth. The adult moth lays its eggs on the surface of the fruitlets in late spring and early summer, and it is essential to destroy the caterpillars that hatch from these eggs before they have time to eat into the fruit. A convenient, non-chemical method involves attracting and trapping the male moths on a sort of fly-paper. There is also a trap for the red plum maggot (plum fruit moth), an equally serious pest. Both of these traps are 100 percent specific and only catch the one kind of moth.

Cut open a damaged apple and the core area will be black and revolting. You may find the offending pink maggot.

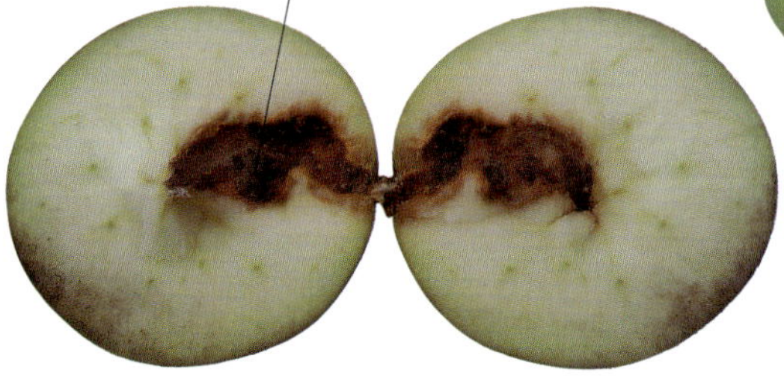

Above: A messy hole on the surface of the fruit signifies codling moth caterpillar attack.

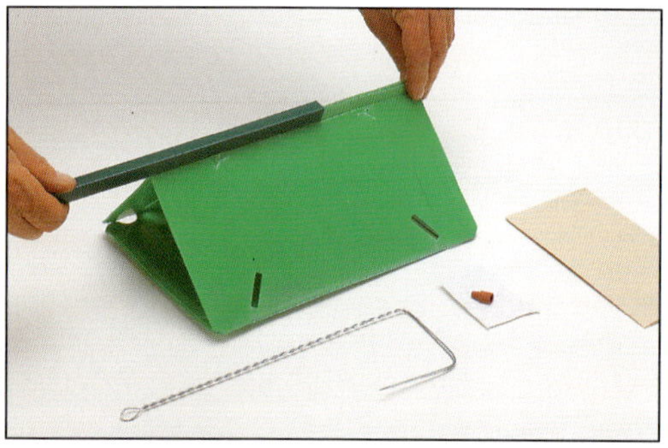

1 Begin to assemble the trap by forming a tent out of the main component. Hold the ridge together by sliding on the plastic clip provided.

2 Push the ends of the wire hanger through the two punched out holes. Bend the ends round so that the hanger also helps to hold the ridge together.

3 The 'flypaper' is folded with the sticky surface inside. Peel the card apart carefully. A piece of rubber impregnated with the female pheromone (scent attractant) is the bait. Place it in the center of the sticky card.

4 Slide the card with its bait carefully along the floor of the tent. Fold up the end edges of the floor and slot them into place. This stops the sticky card falling out when the trap is buffeted by the wind and rain.

Left: Bend the top of the wire hanger into a hook and hang the trap at head height in the apple or pear tree. One trap attracts male moths within a radius of about 30ft(9m).

Right: This catch of male moths indicates just how many there are to damage the crop. The bait will need renewing after about five weeks if it is still attracting moths.

PART ELEVEN

HERBS

Herbs are wonderfully versatile plants. The majority need little more than a sunny situation and free-draining soil, and many will thrive in pots and hanging baskets. You can grow herbs as a hedge, as an ornamental tree or as a scented lawn. Their scents pervade the garden and their leaves have a variety of culinary uses.

CREATING A HERB GARDEN

Half the fun of growing a herb collection is choosing and creating the garden or feature they are to make. If you just want a few culinary species within easy reach of the back door or have only very limited space, grow a selection of herbs in containers or in a bed with various easy-to-grow vegetables. Other people want to grow as many species as they can find, in a semi-organized profusion of scents and colors. The informal herb garden may look a bit wild, but in fact grows to quite a strict plan. This type of garden suits a large plot, but can be adapted to a small garden or even a single bed or border. If you prefer a formal style, bear in mind that many shrubby herbs, such as rosemary, thyme and lavender, can be clipped into formal shapes and hedges, and the wide variety of leaf shapes and sizes among herbs makes them ideal as contrasting clumps of color planted in an intricate knot design or formal pattern. The actual herbs you choose will be highly personal, too; you might treat them simply as ornamental and aromatic garden plants; select your favorite herbs for cooking; or perhaps make a selection of medicinal species or useful dye plants.

Below: An informal herb garden, where the scented patchwork of plants almost smothers a winding path and disguises the garden's underlying, rectangular shape.

Above: Formal herb gardens are usually based on geometric shapes; often square or circular, the interior is divided up into roughly equal-sized beds by neat paths traditionally edged with clipped evergreen herbs such as lavender or box.

Creating a herb garden feature

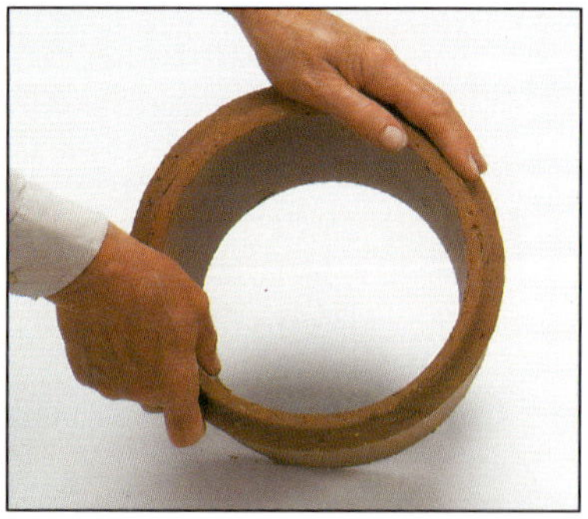

1 An open-ended flue liner lets plant roots grow into the earth beneath and is large enough to accommodate vigorous species.

2 Settle the base into the ground and fill it two-thirds full with good-quality garden soil. It is not a good idea to use potting mix.

3 Place the plant in the flue liner and water it. Top up the soil until it is 2in(5cm) below the rim of the liner to retain moisture.

SCENTED HERBS IN THE GARDEN

Lemon balm has a strong, pleasant, fresh fragrance. Since all herbs are naturally aromatic, growing them creates a scented garden automatically - heady with mingled scents on a sunny day as the heat of the sun releases the essential oils, and superb after a quick summer shower.

Dry sun

The leaves of creeping and bushy varieties of thyme provide a variety of textures and patterns, especially when covered with dew or frost. There are many varieties of lavender, with flowers that range from pale blue to deep purple, white to deep pink. Dry, sunny gardens are ideal for the gray-leaved curry plant, with its bright yellow flowers and curry-like aroma. Use to garnish soups and egg dishes. The pretty members of the hyssop family develop flowers from midsummer onwards, attracting bees and butterflies. Rock hyssop has rich, blue, upright flowers. Other varieties have pink, blue, purple or white flowers. The larger hyssops tend to bend with the weight of flowers and look beautiful on raised beds and banks. Do not forget the marjoram family, the purple, green and variegated sages, aromatic winter savory and rosemary - if you have space.

Right: *Golden feverfew* (Tanacetum parthenium *'Aureum') retains its bright gold leaf color in dappled shade.*

Dappled shade

The lemony acid leaves of French sorrel (Rumex acetosa) *and buckler sorrel* (R. scutatus) *will be more tender when grown in shade. Bugle* (Ajuga reptans) *is a good ground cover when edging a shady border. Many varieties have beautifully colored leaves and rich blue flowers. Golden feverfew produces a mass of bright green leaves and pretty white single or double flowers from spring to the fall. It has proved very helpful to migraine sufferers. Other herbs found at the edge of woodlands include primrose, wild strawberries, St. John's wort, foxgloves and valerian.*

Damp sun

Angelica needs damp soil to grow long, tender stalks for crystallizing. The leaves and stalks of this biennial are at their best in the first year. Coriander also thrives in sunny, damp locations. Because it bolts into flower, cut the leaves while young and pull out the plant when the 'carroty' leaves develop. The leaves of self-heal (Prunella vulgaris) *form a useful ground cover mat. It has deep blue, 4in(10cm)-tall flowers. Bergamot, with its red, white, pink or purple flowers, is good for flavoring tea. Mace* (Achillea declorans) *has white flower heads and leaves with a flavor reminiscent of the tropical spice of the same name.*

Damp shade

Curled and plain-leaved varieties of parsley are slow to bolt into flower in shade, but need rich, moist soil to thrive. Creeping and upright pennyroyal spreads into a carpet of scented leaves along paths and banks. Ginger mint, with its spicy green-and-gold leaf variegation, has pale blue flowers on upright stems from early summer until the fall. Other suitable herbs include flat-leaved golden marjoram, sweet and dog violets, celandine, centaury and hedge hyssop.

HERBS IN CONTAINERS

A trough or windowbox is the perfect way to grow a selection of culinary herbs in the minimum of space. The kitchen windowsill is an obvious site, providing the window opens conveniently enough for regular access to your mini-garden. Make sure that the windowbox is firmly secured; use strong brackets or ties and check these periodically for wear or weathering. The box might be home-made from new or old timber, painted to match window frames or shutters; or it might be lightweight plastic, antique stone or terracotta. If the windows provide too exposed a site, why not plant up an indoor windowbox, perfect for a few of the more tender species, such as basil? Regular cropping or trimming is important to ensure that the herbs remain small and leafy. Keep the box adequately watered and apply a liquid feed during the growing and cropping season to replace essential nutrients. A mulch of small pebbles helps to conserve moisture.

PLANTING UP A HERB HANGING BASKET

Herbs are good plants for hanging baskets, as they are naturally quite drought tolerant. This mixture includes colorful and sweetly scented golden marjoram, oregano and lemon thyme.

Planting up a terracotta trough

1 Choose a selection of herbs with a variety of foliage shapes and textures. Place a few crocks in the bottom of the trough.

2 Add a 2-6in(5-15cm) layer of washed gravel or pea shingle to make a well-draining layer at the bottom. Top up with planting mix.

3 Plant the herbs, maintaining a pleasing balance of appearance, height and habit. Tip them gently out of their pots and into your hand, supporting the rootball lightly between your fingers.

4 Top up with soil, making sure it settles between the plants without any air gaps. To allow for watering, do not fill to the top of the box

5 A sprinkling of gravel or small stones on top of the soil around the plants not only looks attractive, but also helps to slow down moisture loss.

The versatility of herbs in containers

Herbs look great in pots; you can group them in large containers or grow them in individual pots on walls, patios, decks, balconies or terraces. They are also ideal for small garden areas: not only are they edible, they also produce a prolonged, attractive display and scent the area, too. This in turn will attract butterflies and bees. Choosing the right blend of herbs for your containers can be great fun. Even taking into account soil compatibility and whether the plants need sun or shade, there is plenty of scope to create pleasing contrasts of color, from darkest green to fresh lime; of foliage, from broadleaved to spiky or fleshy; and of size, from tall to tiny trailing varieties.

A herb pot

Right: *Windowbox herb gardens are usually rather staid - just a selection of herbs standing neatly in a row. But this one is a really wonderful profusion of edible herbs and fruits, with an excellent variety of shape and color.*

MINT • CHIVES

Mint and chives are easy-to-grow perennial herbs that die down each winter, but reappear each spring. Many people are afraid to grow mint on account of its vigorous habit, but you can control it by growing it in a container, raised bed or in an old bottomless bucket or flowerpot sunk to its rim in the garden. Feed and water mints carefully. Most will enjoy some shade, and the creeping varieties make good carpet plants. Plant roots may need protecting with straw in cold areas in winter.

You can grow chives from seed or you can buy them from herb stockists. However, being a member of the onion family, perennial chives are usually propagated by dividing the bulbs and you should do this every three years in any case to regenerate the plants. Simply dig up a clump carefully and gently prize the bulbs apart before planting them out in small groups of four or five. The soil must be rich and damp, but chives are not too fussy about sun or shade. Sometimes the spiky, green, hollow leaves begin to look a little yellow and this means the soil has become too impoverished or possibly too dry. Enriching the soil with good-quality potting mixture or more conscientious watering is the answer, especially if the chives are growing in a tub or other type of container.

VARIETIES OF CHIVES

Above: All the alliums feature that mild onion flavor in the long hollow stems, so useful for adding to sauces and salads, although the larger types may have a coarser taste and texture.

Varieties of mint

Above: In spring, the deep purple flower buds of chives, such as this *Allium schoenoprasum,* open to a brighter purple and then fade to pale pink. Remove faded blooms.

Below: Growing a collection of mints in a variety of terracotta pots of different sizes is an ingenious way of displaying their range of color, shape and texture.

Cold herbal drinks

1 Pound 4oz(100gm) of herbs, such as mint, to a pulp with a pestle and mortar or food processor. Add 1oz(30gm) of finely ground sugar. Boil 2 pints (1 liter) of water with 2oz(60gm) of sugar for 5 minutes. Cool. Add juice of two lemons.

2 Add the pulped herbs to the cooled syrup mixture. The herbs will be darker in color; this is normal. Chill the mixture.

3 Transfer the drink to an attractive glass jug and decorate it with a sprig of mint or whichever herb is appropriate.

***Left:** A selection of refreshing drinks for summer might include an iced mint drink, a herb-infused white wine and a flowery cordial to be diluted with still or carbonated water.*

Hot herbal teas

Herbal tea is made in the same way as other types of tea; pour one pint of boiling water over ½oz(15gm) of dried herbs or about 1oz(30gm) of fresh herbs and leave the mixture to infuse for about 10 minutes before straining it, depending on how strong you like your tea. Some of the stronger flavors, such as chamomile and rosemary, need only the briefest dip.

Planting thyme along a path

1 To plant a creeping thyme beside a path, first hollow out a planting pocket in the soil the right size for the plant.

2 Press in the plant, leaving no gaps around the rootball. All the foliage should remain on the surface and not be half-buried.

Below: A creeping variety of thyme is perfect for growing between patio slabs or alongside a path. It spreads and softens the edges of the stones and survives being trodden on occasionally.

THYME • ROSEMARY BAY • SAGE

Thyme, rosemary, bay and sage are very useful culinary herbs that keep their leaves all year round. With its tiny leaves and dense habit, thyme creates a carpet, cushion or low hedge, according to variety. It thrives in any well-drained, sunny position and you should be able to crop it all year round, unless winter frosts are severe, in which case protect it with straw or soil.

Rosemary makes a deep green, upright shrub, glossy with essential oils. It will grow as tall as 6ft(1.8m) in a sunny, sheltered position in light, well-drained soil. The spiky leaves have a silvery hue and the stout stems become woody and gnarled with age. Trim it after flowering to keep it in shape.

Bay enjoys the same growing conditions as rosemary and both require indoor winter protection in cooler climates. Bay leaves are the main attraction of the plant, being large, shiny, deep green and aromatic. They can be picked and used at any time, but dry well, too, the flavor actually strengthening and becoming more mellow. The bay tree is an excellent subject for shaping into a variety of topiary shapes.

Sage is familiar as a pungent ingredient in sausages and stuffings, but it is also a valuable garden plant with many attractive varieties, including beautifully colored types that are useful for coordinating and contrasting in planned planting schemes. Provide well-drained, preferably limy, soil in a sunny spot and trim plants after flowering.

Varieties of sage

Garden sage (*Salvia officinalis*) makes a shrubby plant with soft gray-green leaves.

S. officinalis 'Tricolor' has attractive cream-bordered leaves washed with strawberry pink.

Red or purple sage (*S. officinalis* 'Purpurascens') has attractive dark foliage.

Golden sage has softly smudged green and yellow leaves.

Planting a bay tree in a terracotta pot

1 Cover the drainage hole with a crock and fill the pot with a light sterilized soil. Lower the bay gently into the new container.

2 Keeping the bay upright, continue filling the pot with more potting mixture. Try to avoid getting any soil on the foliage.

3 A layer of small stones or gravel on the surface of the soil not only helps to retain moisture and discourages weed growth, but also looks pleasing. Bay looks particularly attractive in a terracotta container.

Rosemary as edging

Right: Choose young plants of a similar size and the same variety. Plant them into a light, well-drained soil every 20in(50cm). Allow each plant to spread itself a little as it settles into position. A little bark mulch will keep down weeds. Water the plants in well.

Jellies and preserves

1 Chop 4lb(about 2kg) of tart apples, skin and all. Add a sprig of rosemary or other herb. Cover the fruit with water, bring it to the boil and simmer gently.

2 Leave the pan uncovered. Stir the mixture occasionally with a wooden spoon. When the apples have softened to a pulp, remove the pan from the heat.

3 Pour the pulp into a clean jelly bag or muslin square and leave it to drip overnight into a clean bowl. Do not squeeze the bag or the jelly will be cloudy.

4 Measure the juice carefully and for each pint (500ml) of juice, add 10oz (300gm) of sugar. Stir over a low heat until dissolved and then boil till set.

5 The jelly is ready when a teaspoon of juice dropped onto a cold plate forms a skin. Pour the jelly into sterilized jars.

6 Seal the jars and for an extra finishing touch, make a decorative fabric cover from printed cotton remnants.

PARSLEY • FENNEL

Parsley is probably one of the most used culinary herbs; a vital ingredient in stuffings, marinades and bouquet garnis, and invaluable as a garnish. However, it does not dry well, so it is worth growing it yourself to ensure a fresh supply. Parsley can be chopped and frozen for adding to soups, stews and marinades, but you can eat it fresh throughout the winter by sowing seeds indoors.

Cropping plants by the handful rather than the sprig can quickly outstrip supply if your garden is small. If space is limited, the answer might be multipocketed strawberry barrels, which suit parsley just as well and are perfect for backyards and patios. A partly shady spot is ideal for parsley and be sure to provide plenty of moisture. Parsley is a biennial and the leaves taste best in the first year, becoming bitter and rather coarse in the second, so try to sow a fresh supply each year in spring and late summer. The seeds can take at least six weeks to germinate, but you can speed this up by soaking them overnight in warm water and soaking a fine tilth seed bed with boiling water before planting. Cover the seeds thinly with fine soil and thin the seedlings to about 10in(25cm) apart. Parsley does not like being transplanted, so always sow thinly in rows where you want the plants to grow. Alternatively, sow a small pinch of seed in a pot of seed mixture and germinate it in a heated propagator or on a windowsill indoors (where it will come up much faster due to the warmth). Leave all the seedlings unthinned, so that the plant grows as a clump, and when the pot is full of roots plant the whole clump undisturbed out into the garden.

Growing fennel in the garden

Left: Fennel is a superb architectural plant, tall and elegantly feathery in the herb bed or herbaceous border. Dill and fennel cannot be grown near each other as they will cross fertilize, so unless your garden is a large one, you will have to choose between them.

TYPES OF PARSLEY

The most commonly seen parsley is the form with curly leaves, which makes a good garnish. The best parsley for cookery is the plain or flat-leaved kind, which has far superior flavor. Seeds of the various kinds are available from specialist seed firms, and plants from herb farms.

Planting up a parsley pot

1 Place a few crocks or broken pieces of china in the bottom of the pot so that the drainage holes do not become blocked.

2 Fill the pot with potting mixture to just below the level of the planting holes - in taller pots, these might appear at various heights.

3 You may need to squeeze the rootball slightly to make it fit through the holes in the parsley pot. Avoid damaging the roots.

4 Insert the plants through the planting holes, pressing them firmly into the potting mixture. Make sure that the rootball is covered and the plants are the right way up.

5 Place the final plant in the top of the container, making sure that it is planted at the correct height to grow right out of the top.

6 After firming with potting mixture, sprinkle a handful of small stones or gravel on the surface to reduce moisture loss.

Parsley seeds or seedlings are both suitable for planting.

7 The pot provides plenty of parsley for picking within a very small planted area. To maintain good growth, pinch off flower stalks as they appear.

Freezing individual fresh herbs

1 Gather the herbs and lightly wash the trimmed sprigs in clean water to remove any dirt or small insects concealed within.

2 Absorb any excess moisture by patting the sprigs gently with a piece of kitchen paper or a clean tea towel.

3 Package the herbs ready for freezing in individual plastic bags. Squeeze out as much air as possible, fasten and label clearly.

Drying herbs

1 Hang the bunches to dry freely in a warm, airy place away from direct sunlight. The quicker the herbs dry, the better.

2 When the herbs are dry, shred them off the stalks, taking care not to crumble them too much or they will lose flavor.

3 Store the dried herbs in clearly labelled glass or ceramic jars with tight-fitting lids. Keep them away from direct light. Replace dried herbs every twelve months.

BASIL • DILL MARJORAM • CHERVIL

Basil, dill, marjoram and chervil are all popular and useful culinary herbs. They do best in a rich, but well-drained soil in a warm, sheltered sunny spot. They are all shortlived annuals; sow them every six to eight weeks throughout the summer to maintain a continuous supply. This is because they come into flower fast and once this happens the leaves fade and lose their flavor and scent, even if you remove the flowers. Basil is particularly tender, so is most reliably grown on a windowsill indoors. Variously scented forms are available, but the most useful for culinary purposes is the large crinkly lettuce-leaved basil. Purple-leaved and ruffled forms of basil are very ornamental as well as good for cookery. Dill is a tall hardy annual sown outdoors in spring; pick a few leaves occasionally and use the flower heads in salads or to flavor vinegar. Chervil makes a feathery plant with a delicate aniseed scent; sow it thickly and cut it as required. The best kind of marjoram for culinary use is the annual sweet or knotted marjoram. Perennial marjorams, such as golden marjoram, are available, but are less well flavored and best used as decorative garden plants that also attract butterflies and bees. A very strongly aromatic form of perennial marjoram called oregano is used in Greek cookery - grow it in a hot, sunny spot.

Above: Members of the origanum family vary in flavor from sweet and mild to a biting, pungent warmth. This is *Origanum vulgare* 'Aureum'.

Left: A native of India, bush basil *(Ocimum basilicum)* is worth growing as an annual plant in cooler climates for its flavor. Dried, it has a completely different taste.

Varieties of basil

Above: Pinching out the top growth of basil is essential if you wish to create a compact, well-shaped, bushy plant. Pinch the stem sharply between the finger and thumb to remove the top set of leaves. The trimmed plant will grow strongly from the sides.

Using dill for cooking

Left: When the dill is 4-6in(10-15cm) tall, the foliage will be very soft and tender; trim off what you need with a pair of sharp scissors. The soft feathery leaves have a strong, pungent flavor; use them in salads and egg dishes and as an attractive garnish.

Above: At this size, the dill has become slightly coarser and more robust and is perfect for adding to or garnishing fish dishes, such as pickled or poached salmon.

The mature dill plant, with its sturdy stem and flowers not quite out of bud, is used in pickles and chutneys. Its spicy flavor counteracts the acidity of the vinegar.

Greek basil (*Ocimum basilicum minimum* 'Greek')

Dark opal basil (*Ocimum basilicum purpurascens*)

Bush basil (*Ocimum basilicum minimum*)

Making a herb oil with basil

1 Using a pestle and mortar, lightly bruise a handful of basil leaves. Put them in a clean glass jar or wide-mouthed bottle.

2 Cover the herbs with a good-quality, mild-tasting oil, such as sunflower or safflower or a mild olive oil.

3 Fasten a piece of clean muslin over the jar and place it on a sunny windowsill or similar warm place in the kitchen. Shake or stir the oil with a wooden spoon once a day for two weeks to help the flavor to develop.

The oil may absorb some of the color of the herb.

4 Strain the herb-flavored oil through muslin into a suitable container. You can use thyme, dill, tarragon or rosemary instead of basil in this recipe.

5 Press the herbs to extract oil and flavor. Repeat the entire process with fresh herbs for extra strength. Herbal oil is a great way to preserve the true herb flavor.

COMPANION PLANTING

If you are interested in gardening as organically as possible, you should explore the possibilities of companion planting: the pairing of herbs and wild plants with your hybridized flowers and vegetables, which will ultimately enrich the precious soil and not deplete it in the way that chemical control of pests and disease does. Companion planting is believed to work through the scent of certain plants acting as a deterrent - which is why so many useful plants are herbal ones - and through exudations of the roots, which alter the nutrient and bacterial make-up of the soil. For it to work effectively, you must introduce a system of mixed planting that does not have regular beds separated by paths.

Left: Nasturtiums among vegetables not only provide colorful ground cover, but also help to keep the vegetables free of unwelcome pests. They will attract aphids away from the vegetables and can repel ants and whitefly.

Below: The pretty blue flowers of borage help to improve crop yields of fruit and vegetables by attracting beneficial butterflies and bees.

HERBS AS COMPANION PLANTS

Herbs are not only beautiful - they are useful garden plants. Every plant affects the plants around it, such as large leaves offering shade and protection to more delicate plants. Some herbs deter pests and many attract beneficial insects that are valuable pollinators or act as predators of garden pests.

Right: The nectar-filled flowers of *Calendula* (pot marigold) will attract hoverflies that eat aphids.

Borage, thyme and hyssop	Attract bees which improve crop yield in strawberries and other fruit.
Chamomile	Has been found to repel insect attacks, thus improving crop yields.
Chives	Have a reputation for preventing black spot on leaves and deterring aphids.
Dill and fennel	Attract hoverflies, which then go to work on aphids.
Garlic	With its strong odor is thought to be beneficial to roses.
Mint	The pennyroyals *(Mentha pulegium)* in particular have been found to be good fly and midge repellents.
Rosemary and thyme	Mask the scent of carrots, which deters the carrot fly.
Sage	Repels the cabbage white butterfly.
Nasturtium	Has an excellent and interesting reputation as a companion plant. It keeps pests away from the vegetable garden, partly owing to the way it attracts aphids away from them. Nasturtium has also been found to repel ants and whitefly. It provides good ground cover and young leaves and flowers are delicious in salads.
Pot marigold	A good all-round and attractive companion plant in the vegetable garden. It grows freely, is self-seeding and deters nematodes in the soil.

PART TWELVE

PATIOS AND CONTAINERS

Whatever it is constructed of, the patio has become one of the most important features of the modern garden. At the same time, there has been a huge increase in the popularity of containers and plants to grow in them. Patios and containers go hand in hand and together they provide some unique gardening opportunities.

PLANTING IN PAVING

To add interest to a stretch of paving, you can remove some of the slabs and make beds, or plant low-growing plants into the cracks between slabs. You could even combine the two ideas for a bigger, more imaginative planting scheme. The best way to establish plants is to improve the soil and then plant or sow subjects that are suited to the conditions. If possible, improve the soil before you lay the slabs, otherwise you will need to prise up the slabs around the cracks to work on the soil. Remove any rubble and stones and if the soil is poor, replace some of it with good topsoil and a similar amount of well-rotted organic matter. Put any large plants in before replacing the slabs; lift the edges of the plants carefully out of the way to avoid damaging them when you replace the slabs. Alternatively, replace the slabs first and tuck smaller plants in between them. Use an old fork or spoon to make planting holes in confined spaces.

SOWING SEEDS BETWEEN SLABS

Sprinkle seeds of alpine flowers, alyssum or creeping thymes thinly in the cracks between paving slabs. Do this instead of using grown plants or to fill the gaps between existing plants or for a denser planting scheme.

Planting in a paved area

1 Prise the slab out - this one is easy as it is only loose-laid over soil, but you may need to use a crowbar or power hammer. Excavate the hole so there is room to put in plenty of good soil.

2 If the existing soil is fairly good, simply add some suitable organic matter to improve the texture and help moisture retention. Choose a selection of compact low-growing plants.

3 Put the largest plant in the center of the new bed. This potentilla is compact and bushy, with a long flowering season throughout the summer. The surrounding slabs keep the roots cool.

4 Plant all four corners for a neat look. Choose plants that contrast in color and shape, and that will spill out over the paving.

Planting in the cracks between paving

1 Make a hole the same size as the rootball and pop in the plant. Planting is easier if the gaps between slabs are wider than usual.

2 Plant up several adjacent corners. In time the plants will almost cover those slabs, so leave the main walking areas fairly clear.

3 Sprinkle pea-sized shingle over the cracks and under the necks of the plants. It aids drainage and helps prevent rotting.

4 Water plants and seeds in well and do not allow them to dry out during the first growing season. After that, they should be able to survive, except in unusually long, hot, dry spells.

Plants that thrive in paving cracks and beds

Because the surrounding paving slabs keep roots cool and prevent evaporation, the soil dries out much more slowly than potting mixture in containers. The plants have a bigger root run, too. The following plants will flourish in paving, many self-seeding once they become fully established: Acaena, Alchemilla mollis, Alyssum, Antirrhinum, Arabis, Calendula *marigolds,* Corydalis lutea, Cistus, Cymbalaria muralis, Dianthus, Diascia, *ericas,* Erinus alpinus, Frankenia, Helianthemum, *hollyhocks, junipers, nasturtiums, pansies, rosemary, sedums,* Sisyrinchium, *thymes, sages and wallflowers. The color range of suitable plants spans the spectrum and many will fill out into ground-covering mounds that effectively hide the margins of their own beds.*

Above: *This pretty* Phlox subulata *seems at home growing in a tiny space between paving slabs.*

Below: *The tall cream flower spikes of* Sisyrinchium striatum *add welcome height to a bed in a paved area. It will self seed freely.*

Below: *The billowing sprays of* Alchemilla mollis *soften the hard edges of slabs. Cut back in midsummer for fresh new growth.*

Right: *The bright orange-red blooms of* Helianthemum *'Henfield Brilliant' provide superb a vivid glow against the subtle tones of slabs. These lovely easy-care plants will form dense clumps.*

PLANTING IN GRAVEL

One way of having a garden that is quick and easy to look after, yet full of interest, is to create a gravel garden. Here, plants are grown in beds covered with a deep mulch of gravel, which suppresses weeds and helps retain moisture. However, unlike a conventional organic mulch that slowly rots, gravel lasts forever. To make the mulch totally effective against weeds - even persistent perennial ones - put gravel over a layer of perforated plastic or over special heavy-duty woven plastic landscape fabric. The most suitable plants for growing through a permanent mulch are trees, shrubs, roses, conifers, perennial herbs and shrubby rock plants, as these all have a definite main stem around which you can tuck the plastic. Bulbs and herbaceous plants are not very suitable for growing where plastic is used under gravel, because the clumps spread under the surrounding plastic mulch, which smothers out the new growth around the edge. They also need lifting and dividing every few years. Nor are annuals practical, as they need replacing every season. If you want to incorporate these plants, the answer is to set aside special areas where the plastic is excluded, leaving only gravel.

1 Cover the soil with perforated black plastic. Spread a 2in (5cm)-thick layer of washed pea gravel evenly over the plastic.

2 Scrape back an area of gravel to reveal the plastic. Leave the spare gravel nearby as it will be replaced after planting.

3 Make two diagonal cuts in the plastic in the middle of the planting site, each one about twice the diameter of the pot.

4 Peel back the corners of the plastic; place stones or gravel on the flaps to hold them back while you put in the plants.

5 Scoop out soil from the planting hole. If the soil was not first prepared for planting, dig a larger hole and add organic matter.

6 Make sure that the planting hole is large enough for the plant rootball. Sit it in position, with its best side to the front.

7 Fill in the space around the rootball with soil and firm down lightly. Water well and then push back the plastic flaps, so that they fit snugly around the plant. This will prevent any weeds from establishing.

8 Holding the plant over to one side, sweep the spare gravel back round the plant with your hand, so that all the plastic sheet is completely hidden. Now the plant looks as though it has grown up naturally through the gravel.

9 Group several warmth-loving and fairly drought-tolerant plants together. Make a separate planting hole for each one.

10 Choose plants with varying flower shapes and heights; plant the tallest at the center and the shortest to the sides and front.

Plants that thrive in gravel

You can grow all kinds of plants in gravel; heat-loving, drought-tolerant flowering plants that provide year-round interest are popular choices, but many smaller flowers, such as spreading rock plants, hardy annuals and even wallflowers, are also happy in gravel. Where gravel is placed over soil, they will often self-seed freely, creating natural effects.

Right: *Many herbs, such as this golden-leaved marjoram 'Thumble's Variety', look superb against a background of gravel. The sharp drainage also suits them well.*

Above: *Sprawling rock plants provide welcome mats of color in a graveled area. The main ones growing here are the compact shrub* Linum arboreum *(yellow) and* Erinus alpinus *(purple).*

Left: *A scree garden plays host to a pink-flowered diascia and the yellow-tipped spires of euphorbia, against a dark purple backdrop of sedum. These are all reliable plants that will thrive in a hot and sunny, free-draining site.*

Left: Team the character of the containers with the plants that are displayed in them. Mediterranean-style terracotta suits the sunny nature of pelargoniums, such as these scented leaf varieties.

CHOOSING CONTAINERS

Since patio gardening first became fashionable, the choice of containers available has never been greater than now. But before buying, consider the different kinds available. Decide which is to be the most important part of your display - the containers themselves or the plants in them. If it is the former, then it is worth paying more for beautiful glazed ceramic or handmade terracotta pots. However if plants are to be the most important consideration, then cheaper plastic pots will do just as well; in this type of display the plants will cover the container entirely. When choosing pots and tubs, decide if they are to be used only in summer, of if they will be used all year round - perhaps for evergreen shrubs, or a changing sequence of summer and winter/spring bedding. Cheap containers are adequate for summer displays as they can be put away for the winter, but where containers are in use outdoors all year round, then good-quality pots are essential. For this purpose, choose containers made of frost-resistant terracotta or ceramics, wood, fiberglass, polypropylene or very good quality plastic.

Pieris formosa var. *forrestii*

Wooden containers are available as tubs, troughs or half-barrels.

Fiber pot made from reconstituted paper slowly biodegrades as it absorbs water from the potting mix.

Mediterranean-style terracotta pot

Reconstituted stone and concrete tubs are long-lasting and quite frost-resistant. Scrub with a stiff brush to clean them.

Terracotta effect plastic pot. Good-quality plastic and other synthetic containers are long-lasting, resistant to cracking in winter and easy to wipe clean.

To prevent wooden containers rotting, treat them with timber preservative and line the inside with plastic.

Small terracotta pot cover with potted double primroses

Oriental-style glazed pots are good value - often far cheaper than similar terracotta pots. They are claimed to be frost-resistant, so should not crack if left outdoors in winter. Often come with a matching saucer.

Classic-style square terracotta pot. Being porous, terracotta pots dry out much faster in summer than glazed or non-porous ones. Normal clay pots can crack if left outdoors in winter. Look for frost-proof terracotta.

Plastic and clay pots

Below: Plastic pots are lighter than clay ones and the potting mix in them is slower to dry out as the sides are impervious to water

Below: Clay pots are more attractive, but being porous, the potting mix dries out quickly due to evaporation through the sides.

Plastic pots usually have a ring of small drainage holes round the base.

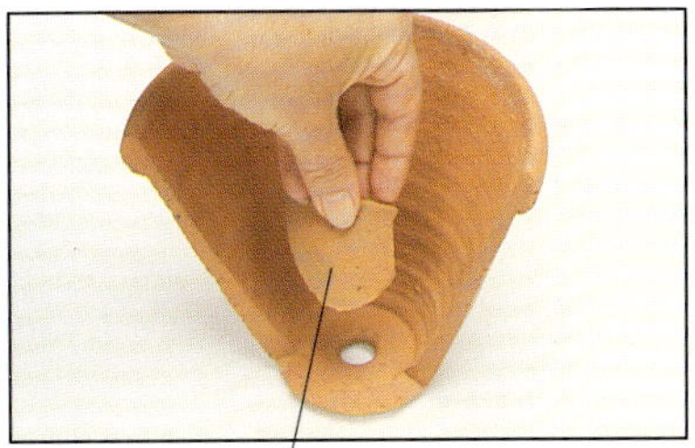

Cover the large holes in the base of clay pots with crocks to keep soil in and allow surplus water out.

Soils for containers

Use ericaceous mix for lime-hating plants, such as rhododendrons.

Special hanging basket formulas are lighter in weight than ordinary potting mixes.

Soil-based mix for plants that remain in the same tub for several years.

A peat-based multipurpose mix suits annuals and bulbs.

Coir is a 'green' alternative to peat mixes.

Watering and feeding

It is vital to check all planted containers at least once a day and water them whenever the potting mix feels dry. If necessary, use a water-retaining gel in the mix that soaks up surplus water for later release. To flower well over a long season, plants need a continuous supply of nutrients. If they go short, flowering soon suffers. If you forget to feed regularly, use slow-release fertilizer pills, granules or sachets.

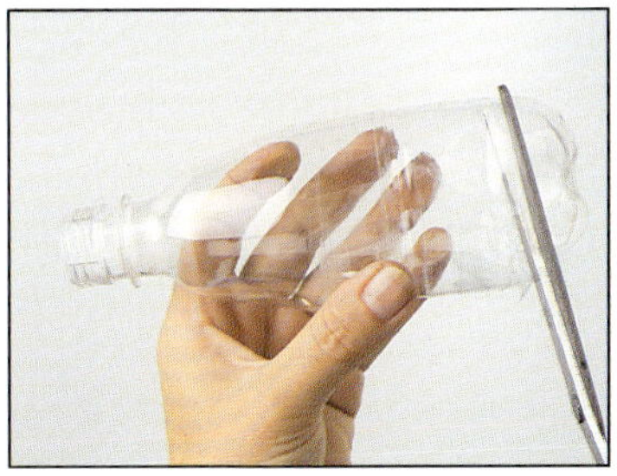

1 Cut a plastic bottle in half to make a watering funnel. Push the open neck into the soil so that the funnel is half-buried.

2 When the funnel is filled, the soil wedged in the neck prevents water running out too quickly. Ideal for hanging baskets.

Left: *Water seeps slowly out through the porous sides of a terracotta 'water well' so that the soil can absorb it gradually.*

Below: *This wall basket has a reservoir for water that drains from above. As the soil dries out, the wick draws up the moisture.*

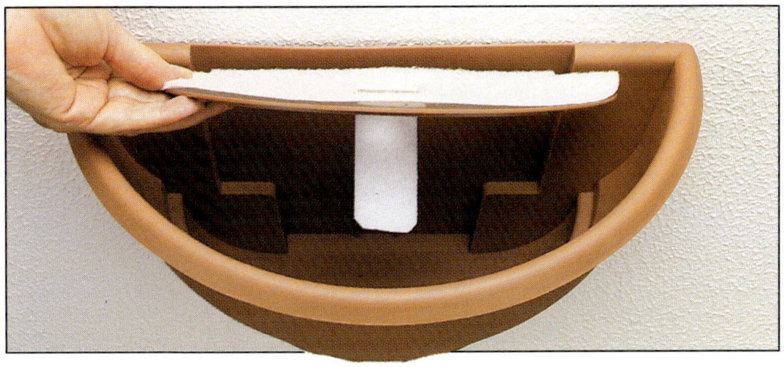

Left: *You can mix slow-release fertilizer granules with potting mix before planting up a container. To top up later in the season, sprinkle more granules over the soil. You can also buy fertilizer in the form of capsules.*

CONTAINER PLANTS

It is surprising how many garden plants thrive in containers. Naturally compact kinds look best and naturally drought-tolerant kinds survive best, although damp-loving plants thrive in containers if kept well watered. For long-lasting displays, choose really striking foliage plants and flowering plants with a long flowering season. Traditional container planting schemes made up with annual bedding plants are fine for bright spring and summer color, but nowadays people want container plantings that are a bit different. And now that everyone is busier, the trend is changing towards plants that can stay in the same containers all year round. It can create a more subtle effect, too. Choose a mixture of small trees, shrubs and ground covering plants, with herbaceous flowers for a complete potted garden where there is no flower bed. If you choose a plant that will grow big, give it a good-sized container or it will quickly become potbound. Here are a few ideas for suitable plants.

Large-flowered hybrid clematis are excellent in large containers, but give them a good support. This is 'Elsa Spath'.

Small trees with good foliage add height to a collection of permanent patio plants. Japanese maples, such as this *Acer palmatum* 'Ornatum', are very attractive.

Miniature and patio roses are fine for containers, although other roses do not do very well in them. This one is 'Anna Ford'.

Variegated evergreens are particularly valuable in all-year-round planting schemes. *Euonymus fortunei* varieties, such as this 'Emerald 'n' Gold', make neat compact shapes.

Containers are a good way of growing compact shrubs that might not otherwise thrive in your garden soil. This *Pieris japonica* 'Variegata' needs a slightly shaded, sheltered spot with lime-free soil.

UNSUITABLE PLANTS FOR CONTAINERS

Plants with short flowering seasons, a straggly growth habit, uninteresting foliage, tall gangly stems or only one feature of interest generally make unexciting subjects for containers. Some plants need putting in the ground soon after you buy them, as they quickly spoil if they dry out at the roots. Other plants are unsuitable for long-term growing in containers because they get too big or grow so vigorously that they soon exhaust the limited amount of potting mixture, even in a large container. This is particularly true of climbing roses, cane fruits and large climbers. Do not be put off using shade and moisture-loving plants - many of them make very good container plants, given the right conditions. All container plants need repotting every few years, so avoid species that do not respond well to this, such as hellebores and euphorbias. Large trees are unsuitable for containers unless you train them as bonsai specimens.

Houttuynia cordata 'Chameleon' is a first-class container plant. The shoots do not appear above ground until late spring.

Junipers tolerate the occasional dry spell. Dwarf varieties are the most suitable for containers; this 'Gold Cone' grows to 36in(90cm).

Lewisia cotyledon is a particularly drought-proof alpine. It makes a rosette of thick leaves, with salmon-pink flowers in early summer.

Pinks are free-flowering, compact and survive the occasional drying out. Every three years, take cuttings in midsummer to replace old plants.

Container plants for sun

Some container plants will tolerate hot, sunny and dry situations outdoors better than others. There are plenty of plants to choose from. As a general rule, look for plants with felty or woolly leaves, silver foliage, and waxy or very narrow or needlelike leaves. Suitable plants include many rock plants, tropical shrubs and climbers, succulents with fat leaves and even cacti.

Below: *The spiky leaves of* Agave americana *and the red blooms of* Vallota purpurea *dominate this collection of sunloving plants.*

A pot for a shady place

Good plants for shady containers include Alchemilla mollis, Ajuga, *cultivated celandines,* Brunnera, *camellias, hydrangeas, pieris,* Pulmonaria *and rhododendrons. This biodegradable pot made from recycled paper hosts a collection of shade plants in subtle colors.*

Primula denticulata (Drumstick primula)

Dryopteris filix-mas 'Crispa Cristata' (Hardy fern)

Primula vulgaris (Primrose)

Hedera helix (Ivy)

Viola labradorica

Planting up a strawberry pot

1 Cover the large drainage hole in the base of this pot with a small handful of crocks. These will help to keep the soil in the pot.

2 Fill the pot to 1in(2.5cm) below the bottom row of side planting pockets. A soil-based mix will keep the pot stable.

3 Plant the strawberries from inside the pot and firm potting mix around the roots. Put two or three plants in the top of the pot so that it is well filled. Use more potting mixture to fill any gaps. Water the plants very slowly but thoroughly.

'Serenata' has pink flowers and a useful crop of fruit.

4 Stand the planter in a sheltered, sunny spot and feed and water it regularly. Replace the potting mix and the plants every two or three years to keep the container productive.

TERRACOTTA CONTAINERS

Plain, neutral-colored, classic-style containers are probably the best value plant holders. You can bring them out year after year, planted up with a different set of plants to create a completely new look each time. In general, pots in a group should be of the same color and material - terracotta is ideal in this respect - and planted in a complementary color scheme. There is no limit to the displays that lend themselves to terracotta planters. You could choose a traditional plant arrangement, using bedding plants such as tuberous begonias and lobelia or a Mediterranean design based on vivid pelargoniums. Terracotta pots dry out more quickly than plastic ones, so herbs do well in them as they are fairly drought-resistant and would rather be slightly on the dry side than too wet. Not all terracotta pots are guaranteed frost-proof; give the larger ones some protection from frost by raising them on small clay feet.

Experiment with daring color schemes and bold plant shapes. You can never really tell how plants will look until you see them together, so buy enough for several containers and try out all the possible combinations before deciding which to plant together. You can easily come up with something quite sensational.

Planting up a winter tub

1 For a colorful formal display in a large container, choose a compact evergreen shrub, trailing ivies and winter-flowering annuals.

2 With a crock covering the hole in the base of the pot, fill the tub to just below the rim with any good soil-based potting mixture.

3 Put the largest plant in the center. Keep the rootball intact, as space will be short and there are other plants to put in.

4 A large trailing plant, such as ivy, softens the straight edges and helps the evergreen to blend in with the arrangement.

5 Fit in as many flowering plants as possible. Once in bloom, they do not grow any more, so the finished result provides the impact.

Variegated ivy

Young, pot-grown winter-flowering evergreens, such as *Skimmia japonica* 'Rubella', look good in containers.

Cultivated primrose hybrids *(Primula acaulis* hybrids)

6 Pull out strands of ivy for a wispy effect. Sit the arrangement in a prominent position. Water in well. Apply a weak feed during mild spells.

Grasses in terracotta

Container planting schemes need not consist solely of bedding plants. One of the most unusual ideas is to use grasses and their larger relatives, such as bamboos. A large terracotta container filled with a mixture of contrasting grasses looks particularly striking in a modern setting, where the dramatic shapes really stand out well. It could also be teamed with smaller containers of evergreens, conifers and heathers to make a fuller display. They all go together very well. Ornamental grasses range in height from several inches up to several feet. The real giants, such as the tall bamboos Arundo donax *and* Miscanthus, *are best grown in large tubs of their own once they have reached a good size. Medium-sized grasses suitable for growing on a long-term basis in containers include Bowles' golden grass* (Milium effusum *'Aureum'),* Carex comans *(an unusual bronze form of sedge which, although not a true grass, does looks like one),* Hakonechloa macra *'Alboaurea' and* Helictotrichon sempervirens. *Among the smaller grasses are many species of* Festuca, *which have vivid blue foliage.*

Mediterranean displays

Colorful pots of flowers evoke a Mediterranean atmosphere on the patio. Osteospermums, bay, basil, Helichrysum microphyllum *and* Celosia cristata *thrive in a sunny spot, as here. Livingstone daisies and red pelargoniums are popular and you could try potted climbers, such as bougainvillea, cacti and succulents.*

Lilies in a pot

Lilies in a terracotta pot make a striking focal point. They need care if they are to flourish, so water and feed them on a regular basis. Do not overwater them, but do not let them become dried out, especially by wind. If you have chosen really acid-loving varieties, plant them in an ericaceous mix. The Asiatic hybrids (right) are short, easy to grow and lime-tolerant. Buy your bulbs directly from growers.

PLASTIC CONTAINERS

Plastic containers are a bit different to work with than some materials. Plastic is not porous, so the potting mix in it dries out less quickly. This is a benefit on hot summer days, but can be a problem at the start of the season, as small, young plants do not use a great deal of water, especially when the weather is cool. It is easy to overwater them, especially if you use a peat-based potting mixture, which holds much more water than other types. Water with care for the first four to five weeks. Another difference lies in the drainage holes. Plastic pots usually have several holes spread around the base. Because the holes are quite small, there is no need to cover them with crocks, especially if you use a soilless potting mixture, which is more fibrous in texture and less likely to trickle out. Some people prefer plastic containers for plants that only last one season - typically spring or summer annuals. This is probably a throwback to the days when plastic containers were rather poor quality and often became brittle after a year or two out in the sunlight. A hard frost in winter was often enough to make them disintegrate entirely. But nowadays, good-quality plastics are available that last very much better and can be used outside all year round.

Planting up a plastic cauldron

1 This inexpensive plastic cauldron would look equally effective planted with a selection of colorful spring bulbs or summer annuals.

A TUB OF ANNUALS

Group a selection of plants to see how they will look together. This is a bright color scheme of red, yellow and orange.

1 A soilless potting mix is suitable for annuals. Fill the container to just below the rim and insert a cane in the middle to support the climbing plant.

2 Plant the centerpiece first - here a climbing black-eyed Susan *(Thunbergia alata)*. Tie it loosely to the cane and tie in new stems regularly as they develop.

3 A foliage plant makes a good 'foil' for groups of annuals. This coleus goes well with the color scheme of the tub. Pinch out flowers as they appear.

4 Water the well-filled tub well. As the plants grow, the effect will become even more abundant-looking. Water it once or twice a day once established.

2 Group plants with different shaped flowers next to each other. Plant the palest species towards the front to add depth to the finished arrangement.

3 Use a narrow trowel to tuck soil into the gaps between rootballs. When all the plants are in place, add 0.5in(1.25cm) of soil over the entire surface.

Planting up a plastic urn

A formal container such as an urn looks best with a formal planting style. Here, a tall foliage plant is surrounded by smaller flowering ones around the edge. You could leave the conifer in place and plant different annuals around it in successive springs and summers.

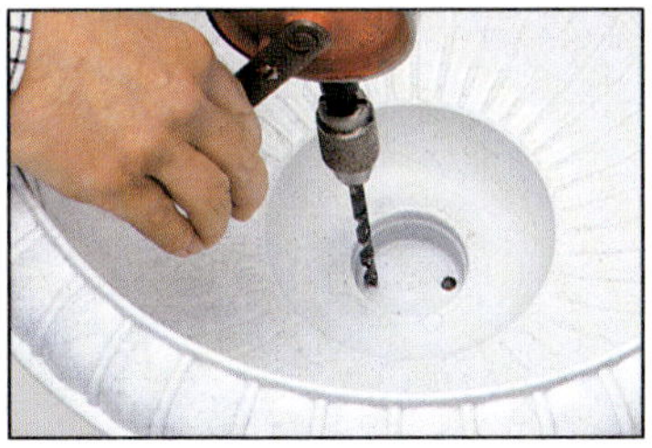

1 If there is no drainage hole, make one, following the positions marked; the plastic is thinner there and easier to drill.

2 Cover the drainage hole with a 'crock' to stop the potting mixture running out through the hole when you water.

3 Add a trowelful of gravel or potting grit for drainage and to prevent the soil being washed out under the crock.

4 Loosely fill the urn with a soilless potting mixture to within 2in(5cm) of the rim. It suits both the conifer and the annuals.

5 Plant the conifer first and then the annuals. Fill any gaps with more potting mix and water the plants in well.

Treating a wooden barrel

1 Drill a hole at least 0.5in (1.25cm) in diameter in the base of the barrel. Alternatively, make a group of smaller holes.

2 A drainage hole is essential, otherwise the potting mixture becomes waterlogged in wet weather.

3 Using a plant-friendly wood preservative, paint the barrel inside and out (including the base) and leave it to dry out completely for a few days.

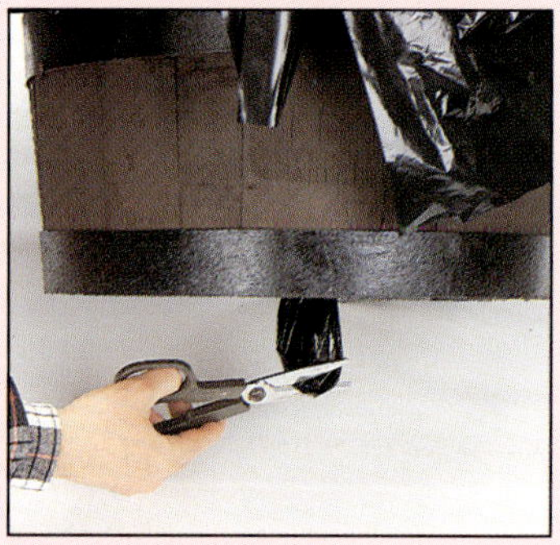

4 Place a large layer of plastic in the barrel. Push the center 2in(5cm) out through the base and cut off the tip protruding through the hole .

WOODEN BARRELS

Wooden half barrels are the favorite choice for permanently planting woodland shrubs, such as dwarf rhododendron, pieris or camellia, as they go so well together. You will need a large barrel, but do not choose one larger than you can comfortably move when it is full of soil. A 12in(30cm) container is the very smallest you should consider; 15-18in (38-45cm) is better and 24in(60cm) the ultimate. The larger the container, the larger the plant will be able to grow, as there will be more room for the roots. In a small pot the plant will be naturally dwarfed, but it will also dry out very quickly and need more frequent watering. To protect a wooden barrel from rot, paint it with a suitable preservative and line it with plastic as shown here.

The rhododendron featured here is a lime-hating plant that needs a lime-free potting mix and not the normal kind. Special lime-free (ericaceous) potting mixes are available, but these do not normally contain soil, being based on peat or coir instead. On their own, they are not ideal for plants that will be left in the same container for several years. You can make up your own mix, consisting of half ericaceous soil and half soil-based potting material. There is a little lime in this, but the mixture seems to suit ericaceous plants. Many heathers also need a lime-free potting mixture. Conifers and many evergreen shrubs will be happy in this, too, but some evergreen shrubs, such as box, prefer normal soil, so do not plant them in the same container. If you prefer to plant other shrubs, choose reasonably compact kinds and fill the container with normal soil-based potting mixture.

1 Allow the plastic sheet to hang over the sides of the barrel. This one is for a rhododendron, a lime-hating plant, so partly fill the barrel with a mixture of ericaceous and soil-based potting mix.

2 Knock the plant out of its pot and place it in the center of the barrel. If the pot is filled with roots, gently tease a few of them out first, otherwise they will not be able to grow out into the mix.

3 Fill round the roots with more potting mix, leaving the top of the rootball level with the surface. The plant should be no deeper in the barrel than it was in the original pot.

4 Cut away the surplus plastic, leaving 2in(5cm) or so around the rim. Press the sheet against the barrel edges for a reasonable fit.

5 Roll back the remaining plastic; tuck it inside the barrel edge to form a protective 'collar'.

6 Water the plant in well, so that the potting mix is thoroughly moist. Check it at least once a week and water again whenever the soil feels dry when you press a finger in it.

Planting up a mixed barrel

A miniature garden in a barrel makes an easy-care, year-round display. Suitable subjects include dwarf conifers, heathers and grassy plants. and even very compact shrubs, but check how big and how fast each plant grows so that the scheme does not become unbalanced.

Planting foliage shrubs

Naturally compact evergreen shrubs make ideal specimen plants. Box and bay can be clipped into shapes, while evergreens with colored or variegated foliage or green foliage plants with large leaves stand out well. They can grow in the same large tubs for many years, but repot them into fresh soil every two or three years in spring.

***Right:** Water evergreens, such as this lovely* Choisya ternata *'Sundance', every day in summer and once a week in winter. If the soil is waterlogged or bone-dry plants may shed their leaves.*

SINKS AND TROUGHS

Large shallow containers, such as sinks and troughs, are traditionally used for making plant displays resembling miniature gardens. Since the display will be permanently planted, include evergreens for winter interest, a selection of tiny flowering plants (as none will have a very long flowering season, you need plenty of different kinds to keep the display colorful) and some trailing plants to soften the edge of the container in places. Suitable subjects for a site that receives sun for at least half the day include rock plants and dwarf conifers. With their sculptured shapes and dense foliage, compact, slow-growing conifers make a good year-round backdrop for seasonal flowering rock plants, which enjoy the same growing conditions. In a shady spot, go for mossy saxifrages, small ferns, ivies and ramonda (something like an outdoor African violet).

A sink garden will need regular attention. Watering is the most frequent chore; you cannot assume that natural rainfall will be sufficient. Many dwarf conifers will turn brown if their roots dry out, but the juniper family are much more drought-resistant. Feed the plants every two weeks from spring to late summer or add a slow-release fertilizer to the potting mix before planting the container, and add a new supply each spring by making a few holes in the potting mix and putting the feed down them. After two or three years the potting mixture will be exhausted and must be replaced, and some of the plants will have become untidy or overgrown, so the sink garden is best dismantled and remade using fresh plants. You can then plant out the old ones onto a rock garden or raised bed.

1 Choose a mixture of plants that contrast well together in shape, texture and color, while providing year-round interest. You will also need a bag of soil-based potting mixture.

2 Put crocks over the drainage holes and add a 1in (2.5cm) gravel layer. Part fill the 'sink' with soil-based mix, leaving room to take the plants in their pots, plus a margin of 0.5in(1.25cm) between the pot and the rim of the sink.

3 First put in the largest plants; they will make the most impact. Knock the plants out of their pots and stand them in place; position a curving conifer so that it leans towards the center of the container.

4 Place the second conifer alongside and push both conifers as close to the back of the container as possible, since they will be the tallest plants and will form a background to the finished display.

5 Tuck rock plants into the gaps between the conifers and put in plants with a slightly trailing habit at the front of the container. They will cascade over the edge and soften the hard lines. Use plenty of plants.

6 Add a little extra potting mix to fill any gaps between rootballs. After watering in, this extra mix will probably sink slightly, so top up any depressions with extra mixture later.

Suitable plants for sinks and troughs

Conifers: Chamaecyparis obtusa *'Nana Gracilis'*, Cryptomeria *'Vilmoriniana'*, Juniperus *'Blue Star'*. ***Other evergreens:*** Saxifraga *(with silver-encrusted leaves)*, Sedum spathulifolium, Sempervivum. ***Rock plants:*** Arabis, *dwarf phlox* (douglasii and subulata*)*, Leontopodium, Lewisia cotyledon, Lithospermum, *saxifrages.* ***Trailers for edges:*** *Creeping thyme*, Mazus reptans, Raoulia, *prostrate rosemary.*

Left: *Sink gardens are not only for rock plants and alpines. Here a stunning display of blooms is provided by this superb* Convolvulus sabatius, *a trailing perennial that flowers during the summer and into early fall. Needs a sunny site.*

Year-round care

Spring: *Trim back dead stems and sprinkle fresh gravel around plants. Feed with half-strength, general-purpose liquid feed when plants begin growing well and remove dead flower heads.*
Summer: *Feed monthly as before and water the container well whenever the soil feels dry.*
Fall: *Remove any seedheads and sow seed straight away. Stop feeding; water only in dry spells.*
Winter: *Rock plants are at risk of rotting in winter, so ensure that containers are sheltered from excess rain and raised up on bricks, allowing surplus water to drain away quickly.*

Above: *The main attraction in this stone sink are the purple and pink blooms of* Cyclamen coum.

Below: *A classic alpine sink garden with* Lewisia, Saxifraga, Armeria *and* Viola *'Jackanapes'.*

A HYPERTUFA CONTAINER

As an alternative to old stone containers for growing alpines, you can now make your own containers from a cheap and versatile fake stone mixture called hypertufa. You can make free-style containers from scratch using the mixture to cover a foundation made of scrunched up small-mesh chicken wire, or you could try the cardboard box method, shown here, to make a 'stone' sink or trough. Hypertufa takes a long time to dry out, so make the container where you will not need to move it, or put it on top of a firm wooden base that you can lift without touching the sides of the container. Allow six weeks for a large sink or trough made by the cardboard box method to set before you remove the boxes. Do not worry if there are some imperfections, as they add character. Hypertufa continues to dry for a time after the mold is removed. When it is completely dry it turns a pale gray color similar to stone. If you used coarse-textured sand and peat in the mix, it will also have a craggy texture. The longer you leave hypertufa containers in the open air, the more weathered and stonelike they become. To speed up the aging process, spray the sides with diluted liquid houseplant feed. This encourages lichens and moss to colonize them, creating the look of a genuine aged stone container.

1 Select two strong boxes that fit inside each other, with a gap between them of 2in(5cm) all round. The outer box will be the depth of the finished container.

2 Cut a piece of board to fit exactly inside the base of the outer box. Nail in four wine corks; these will form the drainage holes in the base of the container.

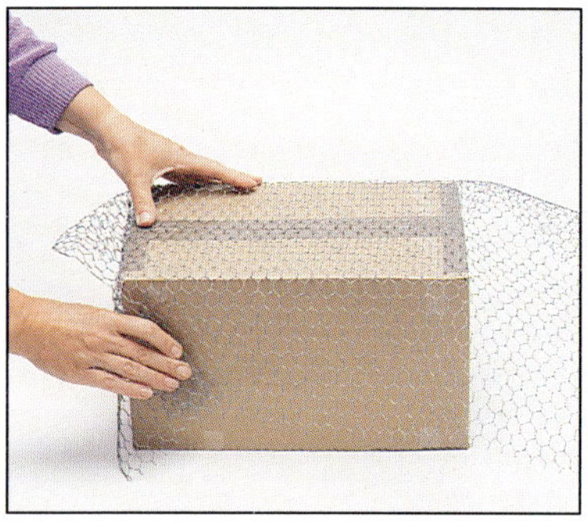

3 Cut a piece of small-mesh chicken wire to cover the inner box completely. Fold the corners to form a loose cage very slightly bigger than the inner box.

4 Slip the smaller box, with its reinforcing wire cover, into the larger box. If the wire sticks out at all, bend it down more firmly until it slips in easily.

5 To make hypertufa, mix equal parts by volume of cement, gritty sand and moss peat or peat substitute with enough water to mix to a sloppy paste.

6 Remove the inner box and wire netting, and trowel enough of the hypertufa mix over the base to come to the top of the corks. Do not cover them or you will prevent them becoming the drainage holes.

7 Fit the inner box and wire cover evenly into the outer box. Press down firmly, so the wire sinks into the hypertufa. Fill the gap between the boxes with hypertufa.

8 Ram the mixture well down between the two boxes on each side of the mesh, leaving no air pockets that would turn out as holes in the sides of the container.

9 Finish off by roughly rounding and smoothing the exposed surface of the hypertufa. If the walls of the outer box bow out slightly, it will improve the final shape.

10 After six weeks, remove the inner box by folding it inwards, then lifting out the base one end at a time. Take care, as force may damage the container.

11 To remove thin slivers of paper on the sides of the container, wet them and peel them off with a knife, or try wire-brushing. They will eventually disappear.

12 Gently turn the container over to prise the cardboard and the wooden board away from the base. The corks will be left behind in the hypertufa.

13 The container has good drainage holes for its size - something genuine old sinks never have. When it is in its final position, raise the container on two bricks to allow surplus water to drain away.

Planting up a hypertufa container

1 Place crocks over the drainage holes and put in a 1-2in(2.5-5cm) layer of coarse gravel to prevent the crocks from becoming clogged with soil.

2 For growing alpines in this container, add 1 part of coarse grit to 4 parts of soil-based potting mix. Bury a craggy chunk of tufa rock in the center.

3 This trough has a small hole where an air pocket was left in the mixture. It makes a good planting hole for a sedum, pushed through from outside.

4 Choose alpines that need the same soil and growing conditions. Aim for an interesting combination of flowers, hillocky shapes and colored foliage.

5 Topdress the surface with a coarse mulch, such as granite chippings. It improves surface drainage and prevents alpines rotting at the neck.

GLAZED POTTERY

Glazed pottery is one of the newer arrivals on the garden scene; surprisingly inexpensive, much of it is oriental in origin, attractively patterned, often available in sets of three of five containers in different sizes, and usually available with matching saucers and pot feet. The more expensive kinds are likely to be more reliably frostproof. Choose pots with striking oriental designs to team with plants on a similar theme; suitable 'plant partners' include bamboos, grasses, hostas, houttuynia, irises, Japanese maple, conifers or evergreens. For more colorful flowering plant displays based on annuals, etc., choose plain colors or very simple designs that do not distract. Or if teaming a flowering shrub with a patterned container, choose a flower whose coloring matches that of its pot. Alternatively decorate an interesting collection of various types of glazed pottery jars and pots on raised staging, planted with different green foliage plants chosen for their varied shapes and textures, to create a striking display in which the pottery is the focus of attention.

Bamboo in a glazed pot

1 Start by putting a 'crock' - a piece of broken clay flowerpot - over the drainage hole in the base of the pot to stop the potting mixture running out when you water the container later on.

2 Add 1in(2.5cm) of coarse grit or fine gravel to cover the crock. This provides valuable extra drainage, as well as preventing any soil from trickling out through the drainage hole.

PANSIES IN CERAMIC

1 Start in the usual way by using a small crock to cover the drainage hole in the bottom of this prettily patterned, frost-resistant glazed ceramic pot.

2 Pack in as many plants as possible for a good display. A small pot like this takes four. Loosely fill the pot with potting mix to within 1in(2.5cm) of the rim.

A soil-based potting mix is heavier than the soilless types and will help to keep the pot stable. It also 'lasts' longer so it is better for permanent pot planting.

3 Put a handful or two of potting mix in the pot, so that the bamboo roots do not stand directly on the grit. Knock the plant out of its pot by tapping the side of the pot firmly onto a hard surface.

3 Carefully remove each plant from its pot by pushing up through the hole in the base. Squeeze the rootballs gently to fit them all into the container.

4 Stand the pot on its saucer and water the pansies in. The pot will dry out quite quickly, so check it regularly, especially during hot weather.

4 Sit the plant in the middle of its pot. Check that the top of the rootball comes to about 1in (2.5cm) below the rim of the pot.

5 Fill the gap between the rootball and the sides of the container with more potting mix and firm it in lightly to make sure that the pot is completely filled.

Creating an oriental display

If aiming at an oriental effect, use a 'nest' of similar containers of different sizes - each planted with a single type of plant only - and position them so that they form a group, consisting of a flowering plant, a foliage plant and a shrub or small tree. Add an oriental wind chime for sound effects resembling a mountain stream, and for added authenticity, stand the pots on raked gravel or plain paving with a leafy foliage or architectural background.

Below: *Regular and shallow containers look good together and the deep blue glaze adds an extra dimension to this 'oriental' collection of trees and shrubs.*

Heathers in a glazed pot

A glazed container with planting pockets at various levels is ideal for displaying a range of heathers and other plants that provide interest in the fall and winter. The callunas in the pockets are 'Beoley Gold', 'Alexandra', 'Marleen', 'Glencoe', 'Schurig's Sensation' and 'Dark Beauty'. The top of the pot plays host to Leucothoe *'Carinella',* Gaultheria mucronata *(pink berries) and* Erica vagans *'Valerie Proudley'.*

UNUSUAL CONTAINERS

Any number of unusual and amusing bygones have been pressed into service as plant containers, from boots and buckets to saucepans and chimney pots of varying sizes. With chimney pots, the height will dictate the type of plants to grow in them; the tallest ones look better with plants that flow out and down, such as ivy or trailing pelargoniums. There are also plenty of tender perennials to choose from. Short, stubby pots look good with erect, bushy or trailing plants, such as *Phormium*, grasses, *Hosta* or *Helianthemum*.

Rough-textured log baskets and wicker baskets make excellent containers for exotic plants with big bold leaves or bright colorful flowers. Given a coat of yacht varnish, they will last for several years in the garden. Rough bark or coconut fiber containers are also very effective.

However enticing, any shape that curves in too acutely at the top, such as a kettle, makes a poor container. Not only is the hole too small to accept a decent-sized flowerpot, but it is also difficult to give the plant sufficient water once its roots have spread inside.

Planting up a wicker basket

1 Half fill the basket with moist potting mix or peat. A coat of yacht varnish protects the container from the damp mix. 'Plunge' the plants, in their pots, into the soil.

2 Choose a mixture of striking flowering and foliage plants. Spiky foliage and large or unusually shaped flowers make a good exotic combination.

PLANTING UP CHIMNEY POTS

Chimney pots in groups of varying styles and height make a striking display. Look at the chimney both ways up; tall ones are often a better shape upside-down. Do not fill it with soil, as it will become too dry and compacted; plant into a flowerpot lodged in the rim.

1 This chimney pot has been reversed. Lodge a flowerpot with a suitable diameter inside the rim, put in some crocks and add potting mix until it is two-thirds full.

2 Position the plants around the pot so that they lean outwards a little. Generously fill the spaces between them with potting mixture, firm down and water well.

3 Put the biggest or boldest plant into the middle of the group and arrange the others around it. Tuck extra potting mix under the small pots to bring them all up to just below the rim of the container. Pack in as many plants as possible. Groups of three or five plants look better than even numbers.

4 This arrangement has a maroon theme; each item has a small touch of the same color, which 'pulls together' plants that are otherwise very individualistic in appearance.

Converting household objects

Saucepans and buckets make good plant containers, as they have relatively straight sides. If you plant directly into them, drill drainage holes in the base, but it is easier to stand a plant pot on a layer of shingle inside. For an attractive matt black look, paint galvanized buckets with quick-drying blackboard paint. Here, a mop bucket makes an attractive container for a display of pink pelargoniums.

Above: *Apply the black paint evenly, retouching it where necessary after it has dried.*

Above: *Arrange the plants in their pots around the 'upper' half of the bucket. Water them well.*

Pansies in a metal bucket

1 Here, a bucket is used as a pot holder. A layer of shingle on the base of the bucket raises the pot and improves drainage.

2 Choose a flowerpot with a diameter that will fit inside the bucket and stand it at the right height on the shingle bed.

3 Plant up the flowerpot with a selection of suitable plants. An arrangement like this looks at home in a cottage-style garden.

THE PATIO YEAR

WINTER

Small evergreen shrubs with variegated, silver or aromatic foliage, such as *Euonymus*, *Santolina* and rosemary, together with ivies, make the backbone of most winter displays, in tubs, windowboxes and hanging baskets. Add long-lasting berries of *Skimmia* (also good for winter buds, depending on variety) and flowers of winter jasmine. Use young plants bought from garden centers, give them a season's use in containers before planting them out in the garden. For flowers, add winter heathers or - in mild spells - winter-flowering pansies. Polyanthus, wallflowers, double daisies and spring bulbs turn late winter into early spring, and lead on colorfully to the start of the summer bedding season.

SPRING

Even though it may be too cold to sit outside in spring, the patio is still visible from indoors and a colorful display of flowers is specially welcome at the end of a long winter. Good plants for spring displays include bulbs - daffodils, hyacinths, tulips, etc. - and flowers such as polyanthus, wallflowers, forget-me-nots, stocks and double bellis daisies. In mild areas, you can plant these out in the fall after removing the summer annuals. However, by waiting until spring, you may find a wider range of plants available and as they have not had to weather the winter outside, they will probably be in better shape than those planted out in the fall. Harden them off in a cold frame or start off by standing them outside during the day and bringing them in at night for a week or so before planting. Choose plants that are still in tight bud rather than those with wide open flowers, to give them a bit of time to adjust to the conditions before the flower opens. Add a few evergreens, such as ivies and small conifers, as temporary background plants to set off a container of flowers.

SUMMER

Summer is the patio season: bedding plants, summer-flowering bulbs, patio roses, dwarf shrubs, herbs and perennials all contribute to a riot of color. You can choose a traditional mixture of colors or, for a more sophisticated effect, a scheme based on one or two colors. Use color with care; decide whether you want to create a strongly contrasting effect or a gentle harmonizing one. Bright colors stand out best against a contrasting background. In containers you can achieve these effects by teaming bright flowers with colored foliage plants, such as coleus and purple-leaved basil. For a harmonious effect, use similar colored flowers and foliage together - blue, purple and mauve or shades of pink and red. Color can also create an atmosphere. A 'hot' scheme of red, yellow and orange looks tropical and busy, while cool green and white or blue and mauve are still and relaxing. Play with color to make a small patio look bigger. Bright red and yellow plants in the foreground give the impression that they are very close to you. Muted mauves and misty purples at the other end of the patio give the impression of distance. By grading colors from hot to cool across the patio, you can create the sensation of space. Heighten this effect by making the patio narrower at the far end.

Above: Two terracotta containers planted with a colorful mixture of cottage garden flowers capture the essence of summer on the patio.

FALL

Patios can easily lose their impetus in the fall as summer annuals come to an end; to keep the display going, why not raise or buy a late crop of annuals and plant them in midsummer? By late midsummer, they will be coming into flower nicely and be ready to replace any annuals that have flowered themselves out by then. Alternatively, winter-flowering pansies are available in garden centers, already in bloom, throughout the fall, so you can replant summer containers then for an instant display. Another plan is to cultivate containers of fall-flowering perennials, such as *Schizostylis*, *Phygelius* (Cape figwort) and miniature pompon dahlias, which team up perfectly for a late-season display.

Left: The vivid red berries of *Skimmia japonica reevesiana* add bright points of color to this winter patio display that also features conifers, grasses, heathers and winter-flowering pansies.

PART THIRTEEN

BASKETS & WINDOWBOXES

The wonderful thing about hanging baskets and windowboxes is that the display is only temporary. You can ring the changes from year to year and from season to season and experiment with different plants and color schemes. And once in place, the planted containers will transform bare bricks into luxuriant hanging gardens.

HANGING BASKETS

Practicality, safety, aesthetics and the needs of your plants are the points to bear in mind when hanging a basket. Do not hang it where people will knock their heads on it, or so close to the door that you must fight your way through trailing foliage to get in and out; remember that baskets can grow considerably bigger than when first planted. Baskets need almost daily attention - feeding, watering and deadheading - so hang them for easy access or fit pulleys for raising and lowering. Keep plants with similar requirements for light and moisture together, so that you can hang them where they will have the optimum conditions for growth.

The sooner you can plant up your summer baskets, the sooner they will start flowering. Baskets kept under glass until they are well established not only look better when hung outdoors, but also tend to be more resilient in unfavorable conditions. So, if you have a conservatory or frost-free greenhouse, you could start planting in early spring. However, in cold areas prone to late frosts, you may have to keep baskets under cover until early summer.

A classic white arrangement

1 Stand the basket on a bucket for stability. Cut a circle from an old potting mix bag and place it black side down in the basket. Fill the plastic circle with potting mix.

2 The plastic acts as a reservoir for the plants, trapping water and preventing soil from washing through. Tuck sphagnum moss under the edges for camouflage.

A SELF-WATERING BASKET

If regular watering presents problems, then a self-watering hanging basket is the perfect solution. Immediately after planting, water the basket in the normal way to ensure that the potting mixture is thoroughly wetted. Thereafter, water will be drawn up from the reservoir at the bottom of the basket, as and when the plants require it. If you use the tube to fill the reservoir, there is no danger of overwatering, as seep holes in the sides allow the excess to drain out.

1 Feed the wick through the base plate. It draws water up from the reservoir and keeps the capillary matting damp.

2 Push the watering tube through the hole in the base plate before adding potting mix. You will be able to camouflage it easily.

3 Completely cover the capillary matting with a layer of moist potting mix formulated for hanging baskets. Now plant up the basket.

4 Hang the basket in a lightly shaded, sheltered spot and water it via the tube. Remove individual blooms as they fade.

3 Cover the basket sides with the sweetly scented white alyssum, feeding the rootballs through the gaps so that they rest horizontally on the soil.

4 Pack moss around the necks of the plants to stop them drying out. Add a busy Lizzie, a pot of *Lotus berthelotii,* white petunias, ivy, and a white pelargonium.

5 Fill any remaining gaps with soil and water the basket copiously. Replace the chains and hang the basket in a sunny spot.

Liners for hanging baskets

Sphagnum moss is the traditional choice for lining wirework baskets, and is sold ready-bagged in garden centers. Always choose fresh, green live moss; if it has been allowed to turn brown, it will not green up again later. There are a number of other lining options to consider.

Flexible whalehide liner

This flexible 'whalehide' liner is made up of overlapping panels that adjust to different models of hanging basket of the same width. Where the panels overlap, you are left with small slits through which you put the plants. This makes it possible to create the 'ball of bloom' that is characteristic of a traditional moss-lined basket. The liner is more water-retentive than moss and dries out less quickly.

Recycled paper rigid liner

Fiber liners soak up water, which helps to keep the potting mix moist, and are far less porous than moss. Unless the basket is heavily overwatered, it won't drip much. The disadvantage of fiber liners is that you cannot plant through the sides and base.

Coir matting

Many of the liners available for hanging baskets are made of recycled or waste materials, such as this coir matting, a by-product of the coconut industry. Wool, foam and paper are also used. If you use a wool liner, lay a sheet of the material in the basket, press it into place and trim off the excess. Cut planting holes in the sides. Choose dark-colored liners, as they look more natural when the basket is planted up.

WALL BASKETS

Large expanses of wall look much more interesting when they are decorated with containers of colorful flowers, and as an alternative to normal hanging baskets, you can also buy wall baskets. These are like hanging baskets that have been sliced in half and mounted on a wall. Wire wall baskets will need lining and, once planted up, copious watering. Wall planters with solid sides are generally more practical, but still tend to dry out quite quickly. Due to the relatively small volume of soil they contain, all wall baskets also need frequent feeding to keep the plants looking good for the entire growing season. Wall baskets are useful where there is not enough room for normal hanging baskets, or where a container mounted flush against the wall looks better. They are also a useful way of adding interest to a fence or the side of a shed. You can also hang wall baskets from trellis with hooks, or mount them more permanently on a wall. A single wall basket can look rather lonely on a large wall, so group several together for a better display. Threes or fives always look better than even numbers, and a staggered row looks better than a straight line. A single wall basket tends to look best where there is less room, perhaps on a short piece of wall or filling a gap between climbers.

Hyacinths and primulas

1 Line a terracotta wall basket with black plastic and cut a hole in the base in line with the drainage hole.

2 Put a flat stone over the hole to prevent soil loss and add a shallow layer of gravel to provide good drainage for the plants.

3 Cover the gravel with moistened potting mix. Always use fresh potting mix and not garden soil or compost, which contains too many pests and diseases.

1 Line the back and base of the basket with black plastic to protect the wall and prevent soil loss when watering. Camouflage the plastic with a layer of sphagnum moss.

2 Continue to line the front of the basket with moss, leaving a gap near the top to allow for planting. Fill the base with a potting mixture recommended for hanging baskets.

3 Plant the sides using bedding impatiens with a small rootball, such as those sold in trays. Push the rootball through the gaps and rest it horizontally on potting mixture.

4 Surround the neck of the plants with moss to prevent soil leakage. Add more impatiens, and a variegated tradescantia in the top. Arrange the trails so that they cover the moss at the front.

4 Put the hyacinths at the back of the basket, leaving space for the primulas in the foreground. You may need to shake some of the potting mixture from around the roots to create more room.

Reddish pink hyacinths

Primula 'Wanda' hybrid

5 Winter and spring baskets do not grow as much as summer ones. Squeeze the rootballs to fit in as many plants as possible.

Tradescantia fluminensis 'Tricolor'

Impatiens 'Super Elfin Swirl' F1

5 Fill the basket with more tradescantias. Alternatively, plant extra impatiens at the back. Fill in any gaps with mix, and water well. Hang on a shady, sheltered wall.

Portulacas for hot spots

Vibrantly colored portulacas are the perfect choice for this little Mexican-style wall pot. These succulents thrive in a sun-baked position; in shade or if the sun goes in, they close up their flowers. Portulacas tend to be sold in midsummer as mature plants in flower, and pots often contain a blend of different shades, which gives a very rich effect. The flowers are grouped in tight clusters at the shoot tips and it is quite difficult to remove spent flowers individually without damaging the buds, so wait until the whole cluster has flowered and then cut the stem back to a side shoot. Take care not to overwater succulent plants such as these.

Wall pots, especially glazed ones, must have adequate drainage.

Portulaca grandiflora

Grasses and succulents

Here, sunloving succulents and the steely blue grass, Festuca glauca, *fit together perfectly in a simply decorated terracotta pot.*

Kalanchoe blossfeldiana (flaming Katy)

Festuca glauca (fescue)

Sempervivum 'Feldmaier' (houseleek)

WICKER BASKETS

Wicker baskets are available in all shapes and sizes. Most are unlined, but lining them is a very simple process. Just cut black plastic (perhaps an old potting mix bag turned inside out) to fit. Since wicker is best kept under cover to prevent weathering, a wicker basket makes an ideal container for winter bedding. Such plants relish the protection of an open or enclosed porch, unheated conservatory or sunroom, as they can suffer if the potting mixture freezes. Provided a basket is protected from the elements, it can be reused time and time again. Secondhand wicker baskets can be recycled to use in the garden. Paint them with yacht varnish to give them a more weatherproof finish. The displays shown here highlight the natural look of wicker and how well it combines with 'informal' flowers such as pansies, primroses and campanulas.

DAHLIAS IN A WICKER BASKET

This rustic basket features the charming annual climber *Thunbergia alata* (black-eyed Susan) with bedding dahlias and a purple-leaved *Ajuga*. This combination of muted colors creates a soft autumnal feel.

1 The basket has been lined with plastic and gravel added for drainage. Place the black-eyed Susan in the basket so that it will trail over the front.

2 Add the dahlia and then tuck the *Ajuga* underneath the dahlia's foliage, arranging the trails of bronze-purple leaves so they fall over the sides of the basket.

A cottage garden basket

1 Line the basket with black plastic to prevent drips if used indoors, and to protect the wicker from rotting. To make trimming the edge of the plastic easier, put some gravel in the base first to keep it in place.

2 Add more gravel or bits of broken styrofoam plant trays to create a drainage reservoir to prevent overwatering.

3 For seasonal arrangements, use a peat-based potting mix. For border perennials and alpines, add grit or use a soil-based mix.

4 Arrange the longest trails of ivy to create a rim of greenery that spills over the basket's dipped edge. Make the composition asymmetric for a natural look.

Variegated ivy (*Hedera helix* cultivar)

5 Fill the center of the basket with the campanulas. Try not to hide the handle, as this is very much part of the overall design. Fill any gaps with potting mix and firm in lightly.

3 Complete the basket with a purple-leaved euphorbia and more ajugas and fill in round the plants with potting mix. Hang it up out of extreme midday sun, which would bleach the flowers.

6 Water the basket and hang it in a cool, well-lit spot indoors, such as a conservatory or large glass porch. Pick off dead blooms regularly to prolong flowering.

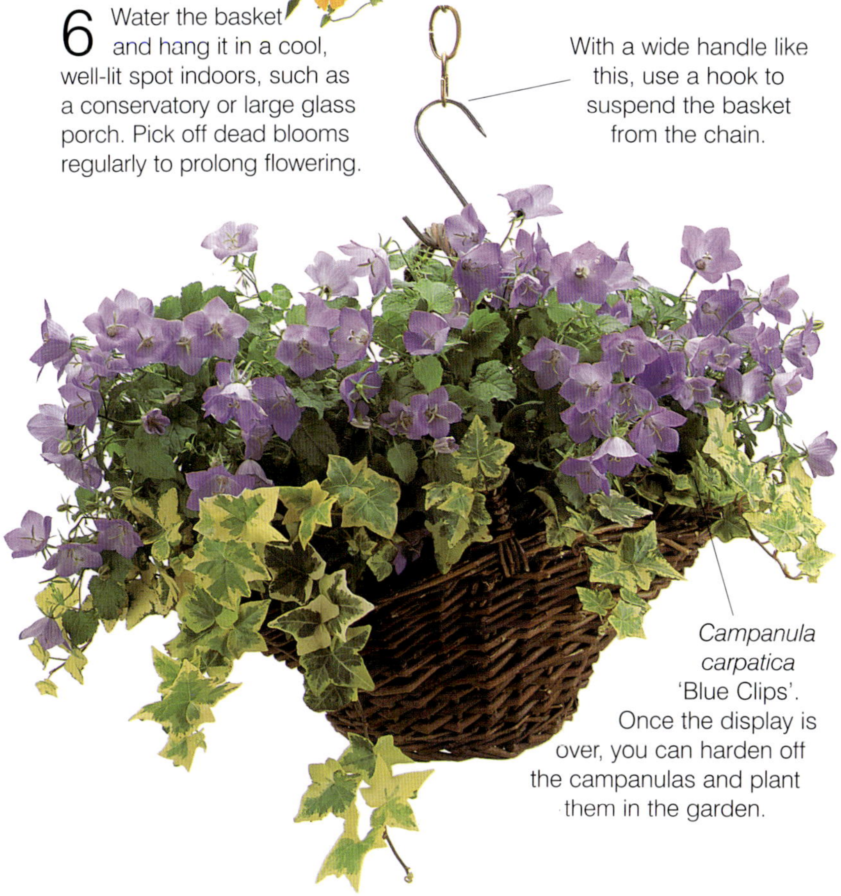

Variations on a theme

Even small wicker baskets make eye-catching displays. Planted up with bright flowers, they are ideal for temporary color in porches and sunrooms, especially in winter. During the summer, why not grow some hardy annuals from seed and plant them up when they are in flower?

Hardy primroses

The yellow flowers and gold chain echo the gilt detailing on this basket. Primroses are available through the winter, but do check that they are frost hardy. Buy compact plants in flower with plenty of buds.

Pansies

These sky blue pansies planted with variegated ivy put on a superb show in this lined rectangular basket. Pansies are available throughout the year. In the winter, protect the basket from frost.

Mini-baskets

Planted up, this tiny woven silver basket would make a lovely gift. Here, the lilac-blue blooms of the alpine bellflower (Campanula sp.) *make a fine show. The flowers and leaves are naturally compact, but growers can now produce temporarily miniaturized plants that flower at a small size.*

AN IVY CHICKEN BASKET

This unusual wire basket is actually an egg holder. The black plastic coating really makes it stand out and also prevents rusting. Baskets like this can be tricky to keep, especially in hot weather, as you must keep the moss moist. The easiest method is to soak the basket by sitting the base in a bowl of water, as well as watering the top.

1 Stuff the head with moist, tightly packed sphagnum moss. Line the 'body' with a thick layer of moss, leaving a hollow planting center.

2 Fill the center with a moisture-retentive, hanging basket potting mixture. Work it thoroughly into the interior space and firm it down gently.

3 Plant ivy trails evenly in the top of the basket. Cut a few lengths of florist's wire and bend them like hairpins. Cover the moss-filled body with ivy by pinning the trails at intervals.

4 Attach a handle of fine chain to the basket so that you can hang it up using a butcher's hook. Adjust the position so that it hangs level.

NOVELTY BASKETS

There is no need to limit yourself to what you can find at the garden center - any kind of container will do, provided you can devise some means of suspension. The chicken basket demonstrates a simple but very effective technique that you can apply to make other hanging shapes, including spheres, which are made by joining two ordinary wire hanging baskets together. You can either plant in the top of the basket and train foliage to cover the outside or, using small rooted cuttings, plant directly through the sides.

A wall pot decorated with a carved face adds a theatrical touch to the garden. Trailing ivy, evergreen grasses or grasslike plants such as *Carex*, would perfectly complement the ancient craggy features and untamed beard.

By painting plastic terracotta-effect pots with acrylic paint, you can transform them into unusual and dramatic garden containers. Pots and planters with a high relief, such as a face, are the most convincing when painted, as the dark and light shading emphasizes the contours.

1 Ivy is mostly used a foil for flowers, but this blend of variegated and plain *Hedera helix* becomes a feature in its own right.

2 Instead of drilling holes in the base of the container, fill the narrow space in the bottom section with gravel to provide drainage.

3 Cover the gravel with potting mixture, filling the wall pot but allowing space on top for the ivies. Try one of the plants for size.

BUCKETS FULL OF BULBS

Shiny metal pails make fun containers, especially for children's gardens, and are easily converted to hanging baskets with a length of chain. The mixed planting of bulbs is unusual, but the contrast of form and color works well. As an alternative, plant a whole group of buckets with individual polyanthus or hardy primrose hybrids.

4 Squeeze the rootballs into ovals so that you can plant as many different kinds of ivy in the top as possible to make a thick head of silvery-streaked hair.

5 Fill the gaps between the plants with more potting mix, and water the plants. Hang the pot on the wall in a sheltered, shady position to prevent damage by cold winds or scorching in strong sun.

Painting plastic containers

Using a variety of simple paint techniques, it is possible to invest plastic pots with a patina of age. Acrylic paint, mixed and thinned with water, is an ideal medium, as it remains wet and soluble for long enough to work on and correct mistakes, but dries to form a waterproof coating.

1 Mix a small amount of white, yellow and dark green acrylic paint with water until the mixture becomes quite runny. Tilt the pot and apply the first coat.

2 If the terracotta color does not start to show through soon, use a clean, wet brush and go over the raised portions of the face again, diluting the paint.

3 Using a pad of damp kitchen towel, dab off some of the paint from the raised parts of the face in irregular patches.

4 Once dry, apply a second coat. The paint runs down in streaks, much like weathering caused by damp conditions.

Paint pigments separate out, adding to the illusion of age.

5 When dry, mix up some dark green paint and water. Using a damp, natural sponge, dab over the surface and work paint into the crevices of the face.

BASKETS FOR SPRING AND SUMMER

From early spring, garden centers are stocked with potted bulbs and spring bedding - perfect for a splash of instant color. These are followed by a myriad of summer bedding varieties, including annuals and tender perennials. Certain fruit and vegetables also do well in baskets, so try mixing in cascading tomatoes or strawberries. And do not forget scent and aroma. Among the herbs, you will find many varieties with colorful foliage. For summer baskets a plant's ability to survive heat and drought is of prime importance and the pelargonium comes close to being the perfect candidate. Available in a wide range of vibrant shades, pelargoniums could be used in a basket all by themselves. In the simple arrangement (right) they are teamed them up with felicia, another excellent drought-resistant plant.

A PURPLE THEME FOR SUMMER

This basket contains an unusual mixture of plants in subtle shades of purple and silver-gray. The deep velvet-purple bedding viola makes a superb contrast with the colors of the osteospermum and nemesia, and all are offset by the shapes and textures of the foliage.

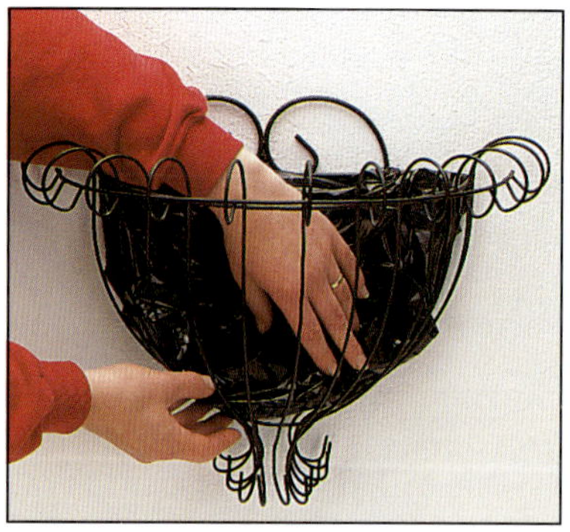

1 Line the back and base of the basket with plastic to prevent damp seeping into the wall behind. Trim off any excess at the top or tuck it behind the frame.

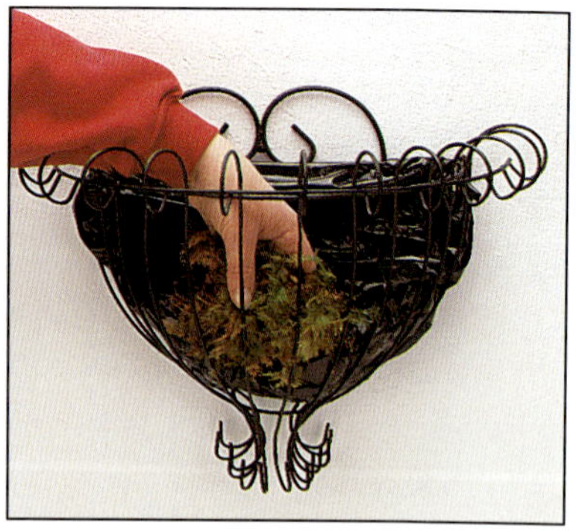

2 Using thick clumps of moist sphagnum moss, begin lining the front of the basket. Tuck some of the moss between the wire and the plastic for camouflage.

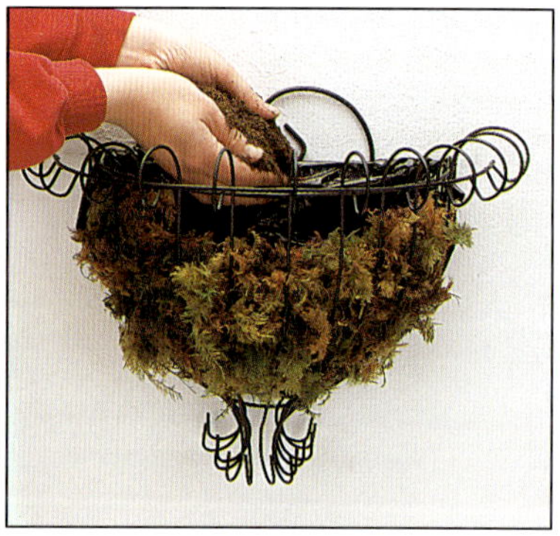

3 Firm down the moss. Add potting mix up to the point where you intend to plant through the front of the basket.

4 Rest the rootballs of the kingfisher daisies horizontally on the potting mix at varying heights. Tuck more moss around the plants.

5 Add the first of the ivy-leaved trailing pelargoniums, arranging the trailing stems so that they point out to the side. Finish planting the top of the basket, making a balanced arrangement that is wider at the top than at the base.

A FUCHSIA BASKET

Garden centers now sell seedlings and rooted cuttings in small pots or 'plugs'. Some of these are perforated, allowing the roots to grow through the sides and are designed to be planted pot-and-all to lessen the shock of transplanting. They are ideal for hanging baskets.

6 Fill in any gaps with potting mix, and water the arrangement well. Hang it up by hooking the frame over two screws fixed into a sunny wall. Deadhead fading blooms.

A spring wall basket

A large, manger-style basket can create an impressive wall feature to brighten up a bare expanse of brickwork. In this sparkling spring display, the polyanthus are the exact color of wild primroses and to take the wild theme a step further, the spaces between all the plants are filled with moss, giving the impression of a bank in the hedgerow filled with spring flowers. There are several other colorways that work well. For example, if you want a more vivid scheme, try scarlet red tulips, such as the dwarf 'Red Riding Hood', white daisies, deep blue polyanthus and blue-and-white violas.

A summer display

This scheme shows how easy it is to give the same container a new look, simply by choosing very different plants to fill it. Large containers such as these give you greater scope for combining plants creatively.

LATE-SEASON BASKETS

From fall to early winter, garden centers should stock all the ingredients you need to make up some imaginative baskets. Many young shrubs in small pots are available at this time; they may seem quite expensive for a seasonal basket, but you can of course plant them out in the garden once the display is over. You can find pots of ivy with long trails in the houseplant section of garden centers; outdoor ones are rarely so luxuriant. Gradually introduce the ivy to outdoor conditions and temperatures before planting it. Although more often associated with summer bedding displays, some plants, such as cineraria, are reasonably hardy and it is worth potting up a few plants towards the end of summer. Cut back long straggly shoots or flower stems to promote bushy new growth and keep them in a sunny spot for use later on. Conifer hedge clippings make a good substitute for moss in baskets. Their fresh green coloring is very welcome in winter and lasts for months without turning brown.

1 Cut a circle of plastic from an old potting mixture bag and use it black side down to line the base of a wire basket.

2 Add some potting mixture to act as a small reservoir that helps to prevent water from draining away too rapidly.

3 Build up the conifer lining inside the basket, tucking the foliage under the edge of the plastic circle. Weave the pieces into each other and through the bars.

Line the basket thickly to improve insulation and prevent the soil from freezing.

4 Add more potting mix until you reach the point where the first plant is to go in. Offer up the euonymus and adjust the soil level.

5 Continue to build up the conifer lining, adding more potting mix. Plant the silver cineraria followed by the primroses.

6 Add another euonymus and a trailing ivy, water in well and allow to drain. Water again when the surface of the potting mix starts to dry out.

A WINTER DISPLAY

The planting in this pale blue-green classical basket is designed to create a frosted effect. A deep pink and a much paler frilly-leaved cabbage are accompanied by the marble-like berries of *Gaultheria*, winter pansies and weather-resistant, winter-flowering heathers. A peat-based potting mixture will suit these ericaceous plants well.

A WINTER WALL BASKET WITH BERRIES

In a sheltered, frost-free spot, the festive-looking winter cherry is an ideal subject for a basket. Look for bushy plants with plenty of mostly unripe berries that will eventually turn orange. White cyclamen and white-variegated ivy provide a foil for the berries.

A late-season pastel display

Hypericums and hebes are two mainstays of the late summer and fall border and the compact varieties also make good temporary subjects for baskets. Caryopteris x clandonensis, Ceratostigma willmottianum, Abelia grandiflora, *fuchsias and bedding dahlias are all suitable for the back of the basket. At the front, try heathers* (Calluna *and* Erica *cultivars) dwarf Michaelmas daisies or* Ceratostigma plumbaginoides.

1 *Assemble this self-watering basket as instructed and cover the base with potting mix. Offer up the largest plant (here a hebe) to check the soil level.*

2 *Arrange the trailing sedum on one side and variegated hypericum opposite. Add white begonias to bridge the height gap between the front and rear.*

3 *The gentle plant colors complement the pale stone-colored basket. Hang it in a well-lit spot, sheltered from the midday sun.*

A WOODEN WINDOWBOX

This smart windowbox is made from tongue-and-grooved cladding, topcoated with high gloss burgundy-red paint. When using gloss, it is important to prepare surfaces well, sanding down as smoothly as possible and wiping off the dust. Prime the wood and then apply one or two coats of the recommended undercoat. With dark colors such as this, you will need at least two top coats. Coat the inside and base with anti-rot preservative and drill holes in the base to allow water to escape. A plastic liner raised slightly off the base keeps damp soil away from the wood, and a piece of fine-mesh plastic windbreak netting over the holes in the liner prevents potting mix leaking out with the drainage water.

Bulbs are especially useful for providing early seasonal color, and apart from dwarf daffodils, the following would also work well in this windowbox: deep blue hyacinths, grape hyacinths *(Muscari armeniacum* cultivars) or *Scilla siberica* and red early dwarf tulips, such as 'Red Riding Hood' or *Tulipa praestans* 'Fusilier'. Bulbs often perform best in their first year, so as soon as flowering has finished, either deadhead and lift the clumps, transferring them to the garden to finish ripening, or discard them. In the fall, select the largest grade of bulb and pot to grow in the greenhouse or cold frame over winter so that you have good, strong plants to insert in the spring. The problem with planting dry bulbs is that they do not always perform, leaving you with gaps in the container. A more expensive alternative is to buy pot-grown plants from the garden center.

1 Choose a plastic trough to act as a liner. Construct the decorative box so that you have room to grip the liner at each end and can remove it for replanting or replacement. The liner should be slightly raised off the base of the box.

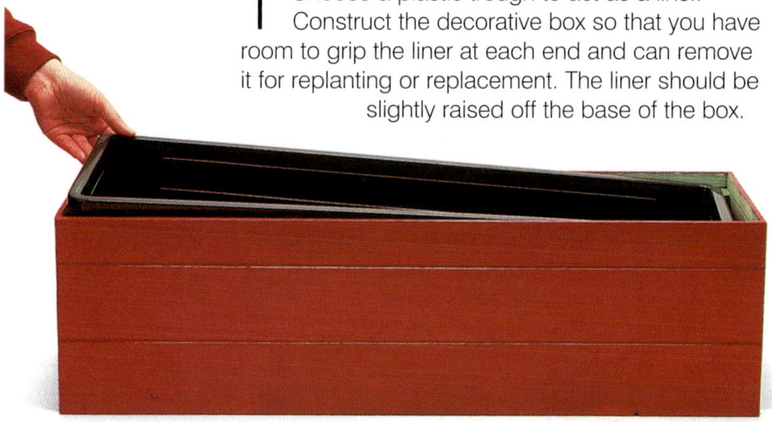

2 Add 1in(2.5cm) depth of gravel to provide drainage and prevent the plant roots from becoming too wet. You could also use styrofoam packaging chips.

3 Cover the gravel with a peat- or soil-based potting mixture. Peat-based mixtures are ideal for seasonal displays. They are lighter, but more prone to drying out.

4 Try the largest plant (here a *Heuchera)* to check the depth of the potting mix. Leave a gap between the soil surface and rim of the box for watering.

5 Use pot-grown ajugas to soften the front of the box with bronze-purple trails. The foliage separates the red of the box from the red impatiens.

6 Plant one large (or several smaller) red-flowered busy Lizzies on either side of the *Heuchera*. As an alternative, try red petunias (e.g. the Junior Strain), zonal pelargoniums, such as Century hybrid, dwarf dahlias or tuberous begonias.

7 All these plants thrive in full sun or light shade. Deadhead the busy Lizzie flowers and watch for aphids on the ajuga. *Heuchera* flowers are long-lasting and add height without spoiling the display.

PRESERVING WOOD

Wooden boxes last longer if you use a plastic liner and treat the insides and underneath of the box itself with a penetrating wood preservative. Always check first that the preservative is safe for plants once dry. Alternatively, use a water-proof sealant. Before applying a topcoat of paint, seal with an aluminum primer.

A spring windowbox

The predominantly red and yellow color scheme brightens up dull winter and spring days and demonstrates a useful labor-saving approach to windowboxes. This is to use a backbone planting of evergreens and swap over the small seasonal element - bulbs, bedding or flowering herbaceous perennials - as the display finishes.

1 Start by planting three equally spaced specimens of gold-variegated Euonymus japonicus *'Aureus'. They will make an excellent foil for the daffodils. Or try using small plants of spotted laurel* (Aucuba japonica *'Variegata').*

2 Plant two clumps of miniature daffodils between the shrubs. 'Tête à Tête' is a multiheaded type that flowers early in the season. Remove dead flowers to keep the display fresh.

3 This scheme will perform well in a sunny or moderately shady spot and needs just light trimming from time to time. Replace the daffodils once they fade.

STENCILLED WINDOWBOXES

The two windowboxes featured here have been decorated with stencils; the beauty of stencils is that you can use different motifs to emphasize whatever mood and visual style you have chosen for your house and garden. Heraldic lilies, otherwise known as fleur-de-lis, and medieval stars adorn the 'gothic' wooden windowbox. It would look well on an older facade, but to achieve the patina of age, roughly brush over the windowbox with artist's acrylic paint - here in a shade appropriately called Monestial Blue - and apply the antique gold paint unevenly to make it appear worn. The planting was also chosen to be reminiscent of olden days - roses, double primroses and ivy all have a long history as garden plants. You would not normally see roses flowering at the same time as primroses, but in spring the houseplant sections of garden centers often have miniature roses that have been forced into bloom early. These prefer a cool, airy situation and can be acclimatized to outdoor conditions quite quickly if given frost protection.

1 Protect wooden containers from rot caused by contact with damp soil by using a rigid plastic inner liner. You should be able to remove it easily.

2 Cover the holes in the liner with a piece of fine plastic mesh to prevent soil loss and stop leakage into the base of the wooden surround.

3 The decorative cover should be about 0.4in(1cm) higher than the liner. Ensure good drainage by pouring in a layer of gravel or styrofoam chips.

4 Fill the back of the windowbox with miniature roses. Feed with a suitable liquid fertilizer and remove dead heads regularly.

5 Plant a row of equally spaced double primroses along the front and fill the gaps with a small-leaved ivy. Trim back long trails.

A SEASIDE WINDOWBOX

This wooden box with sides reminiscent of weatherboarding has a strong seaside flavor. When gardening next to the sea, select varieties that are resistant to salt-laden winds. Shrubs, herbs and grasses with silver-gray foliage are worth looking out for because, being protected from moisture loss, they often perform well in this environment.

1 Before planting up the box, arrange the shrubs on the ground to work out the best combination. Put the *Brachyglottis* in the center; add the euonymus to soften the hard edge.

2 Plant the cotton lavender in the back corner. Avoid straight lines, as they do not look natural. Add the low-growing hebe and a lavender. Work the soil around the rootballs to avoid air pockets.

6 Regularly remove fading flower heads and yellowing leaves from the primroses. Use secateurs to deadhead the roses. Feed and water the box regularly and watch for aphids.

3 A gravel mulch protects and sets off the plants. Trim the lavender lightly after flowering. The hebe should not need attention. Prune other plants hard back if necessary in spring.

Stencilling a gold fleur-de-lis

Stencil designs, from shops or by mail order, are easy to use and very effective. You can buy special pots of stencil paint, but provided you use paint of a suitable consistency, you can just as easily use artist's acrylics or dilute matt emulsion - even one of the mini 'tester' pots.

1 Shake the pot to get a little paint onto the lid. Dip the brush lightly into the lid. Remove excess paint on a piece of paper.

2 For a stippled effect, lightly tap the paint onto the wood. Overlap the stencil as you work. Keep the brush perpendicular.

3 For a more solid coverage, keep the brush in light contact with the wood, making small circular movements.

4 A combination of stippled and solid paint application creates light and shade and an aged, three-dimensional look.

Painting and stencilling a seashell windowbox

Paint the wood with blue emulsion, diluted down to color the wood like a stain. Once stencilled, seal the paintwork using exterior-quality or yacht varnish (matt or silk/low sheen); the paintwork will darken slightly.

1 Attach a stencil with small pieces of low-tack masking tape. Use a stencil brush and dilute artist's acrylic paints.

2 You can also achieve a stippled look using a natural sponge. Dab excess paint onto newspaper before applying it.

PAINTED TERRACOTTA

Painting terracotta may seem rather unconventional, but an effect like this is very easy to achieve (see panel). As an alternative colorway, try a mint-green base coat sponged over lightly with white to give a mottled effect and fill the windowbox with soft apricot tuberous begonias, fuchsias and busy Lizzies in shades of pink, peach and white, all with a foil of white-variegated foliage. A rich powder-blue would suit the strong orange and lemon shades found in a pot marigold mix such as *Calendula* 'Fiesta Gitana', or mixed nasturtiums such as 'Alaska'. Alternatively, use a mid purple-blue as a base coat and add touches of crimson, blue and white paint diluted with water to the relief pattern. Plant with deep purple, velvet red and light lavender-blue flowers and silver foliage. For example, at the back you might use *Salvia farinacea* 'Victoria' and in the foreground crimson-red verbena and deep purple petunia, interplanted with silver cut-leaved cineraria and red trailing lobelia. Highly ornate terracotta windowboxes are perfect for a period setting, but if you plant with modern-looking bedding varieties, you could spoil the illusion of age. Look out for soft, subtle and muted shades of pansy, verbena and nicotiana. And do not forget the many herbs, small-flowered bedding violas, *Erigeron karvinskianus* 'Profusion', marguerites, heliotrope and scented-leaf pelargoniums.

1 Cover each drainage hole in the windowbox with a clay crock to prevent soil from being washed out during watering.

2 A layer of gravel for drainage is important if a terracotta container has been lined with plastic to prevent moisture loss.

3 Use a peat-based potting mix for summer bedding; a soil-based mix for shrubs, herbs and long-term planting and a soil-based seed/cuttings mix for nasturtiums.

SUCCULENTS IN PLAIN TERRACOTTA

Try experimenting with different combinations of succulents. The large rounded echeverias in this display came from the houseplant section of a garden center, but like most succulents, they prefer to be outdoors for the summer and grow much more quickly.

1 Position the purple-leaved sedum in one corner so the foliage drapes over the side. Plant the blue-gray echeveria.

2 Tuck the silvery sedum under the echeveria where it can fill out gradually. Add the second echeveria, again at the front.

3 Finally add one or two pots of variegated *Sedum lineare*. This grows more quickly; pinch it out regularly.

4 Pick a shade of *Impatiens* that tones with or complements the container. Here, a blush-pink busy Lizzie with a dark eye is teamed up with a deeper pink one. Interplant the front row with a white-variegated ivy.

5 This deep pink busy Lizzie picks up on the dark eye of the paler flower. Use it to fill in the gaps at the back, then work in more mix around each of the plants to cover the rootballs.

6 This pastel display is perfect for shady walls. Other summer interest plants include tuberous and fibrous-rooted begonias, bedding fuchsias, violas and *Lamium maculatum* 'White Nancy'.

Painting a terracotta windowbox

Terracotta can look raw and orange when new. You can 'age' the surface quickly using a dilute color wash of artist's acrylic. As the water is absorbed into the terracotta, an uneven and natural-looking covering of white pigment remains. This is how the pink finish was applied.

1 Using diluted white artist's acrylic paint, roughly apply a wash to the surface of the dry terracotta container. The uneven coverage or drips are all part of the distressed look. Blot off the excess paint.

2 Mix your colors together, here crimson and ultramarine, with some more white paint. Apply in downward strokes to create darker and lighter 'weathered' streaks. Apply darker colors cautiously.

A color variation in tones of yellow

Above: *This pastel display is set off perfectly by the yellow paintwork of the terracotta trough. It demonstrates how simple it is to make a perfect match between container and plants.*

PAINTED WINDOWBOXES

Another way to add a note of distinction to windowboxes is to use decorative wood moldings. Once firmly secured and painted, the effect is of carved wood or cast metal. You could be fooled into thinking that the white windowbox featured on this page was an example of Victorian cast-ironwork, but the effect has been achieved with molding. If you have a formal garden, then symmetry and architectural form will feature strongly. In this case, a traditional topiary shape has been used as the central focus. Clipped geometric shapes, such as cones, spirals, pyramids and ball-headed standards, would also work well, but the sphere is the easiest shape to clip if you are new to the art of topiary. Dwarf box *(Buxus sempervirens* 'Suffruticosa') is ideal, as the foliage is fine and densely packed and specimens can be kept small enough to remain in the windowbox permanently. Another plant that produces a symmetrical outline and also does well in containers is the cabbage palm, *Cordyline australis,* with its airy fountain-shaped spray of foliage. Three flame-shaped dwarf or slow-growing conifers spaced equally along the box, such as *Chamaecyparis lawsoniana* 'Elwoodii' or 'Ellwood's Gold', would also produce a formal structure or effective backbone planting.

1 To protect the wooden cover and for maintenance, use a rigid plastic trough as a liner. Cover the drainage holes with fine-mesh netting to prevent soil escaping.

2 Add 1in(2.5cm) of gravel as a drainage layer, to keep the soil in place and prevent clogging of the drainage holes. Sharp drainage is vital for drought-tolerant plants.

3 Cover the gravel with potting mix and then try the box in the trough for size. Adjust the level accordingly. Leave a gap between the soil surface and rim of the liner so that water has a chance to soak in. Plant the box.

4 Arrange the marguerites to fill the two empty halves. Add small pots of *Plecostachys serpyllifolia* (also sold as *Helichrysum microphyllum)* to soften the edge of the box, and white-variegated ivy at either end of the box.

5 Deadhead and trim back the marguerites; do not allow them to swamp the box sphere. Trim the *Plecostachys* occasionally.

A NARROW WINDOWBOX WITH ZINNIAS

This box was made from sawn-down fencing planks. The wood was given a hint of color by painting it with a mixture of rich blue and black artist's acrylic paint. This makes the perfect foil for the sun-loving zinnias and brightly variegated kingfisher daisies. For a similar effect, use dwarf dahlias or daisy-flowered arctotis.

1 Put a drip-tray in the base of the box to protect the wood from the long-term effects of damp. Then line the whole windowbox with black plastic.

2 Trim off the excess plastic with a pair of sharp scissors. Next, add a layer of drainage material and cover that with a layer of potting mixture.

3 Arrange a row of variegated felicias along the front, tilting the plants slightly to cover the rim. Next, add the row of zinnias and fill the spaces in between with more potting mixture.

4 Zinnias will continue to flower on side shoots produced once the terminal bloom has been removed. Deadhead regularly to sustain flowering.

Applying decorations

You can apply a range of decorative moldings, including carved beading, to smooth-sided windowboxes using waterproof wood glue. Novelty magnets and mini wall hangings could be used to similar effect. For an oriental look, try split bamboo canes, stained and finished with yacht varnish. Ceramic tiles are available in a wide range of patterns and styles and can be applied with waterproof cement.

1 Measure and mark the position of the molding. Glue it in place and weight it down. When dry, thoroughly seal it with wood or universal primer.

2 Depending on coverage, apply two or more coats of high gloss paint, sanding lightly between coats. Paint moldings on the flat to prevent dripping.

Choosing the right scheme

Color-scheming makes all the difference to the success of a container. Here, a soft mint-green paint was chosen to act as a foil for the silver and green foliage and to contrast with the light purple osteospermum. Dark highlights in the form of verbena flowers provide a contrast that lifts the planting. The paint was roughly applied over a base coat of primer to produce a more rustic effect.

SUMMER FLOWERS AND HERBS IN A TROUGH

Most herbs are drought tolerant and make excellent subjects for containers, especially if you forget to water regularly. There are many attractive foliage forms with colored or variegated leaves, as well as plants with attractive flowers, and most combine easily with flowering bedding plants and tender perennials. In this windowbox, an interesting mix of textures has been created by blending the rounded shapes of the pelargonium and pansy with the feathery upright shoots of rosemary and low mounds of golden oregano. Other shrubby herbs that would provide an attractive foil for flowers include lavender, hyssop, curry plant (*Helichrysum italicum* - its leaves smell strongly of curry!), cotton lavender (*Santolina chamaecyparissus*), several of the silver-leaved artemisias and sage, especially the highly ornamental *Salvia officinalis* 'Icterina', which has gold variegation, and the purple sage (*S. o.* 'Purpurascens'). Low-growing alternatives to oregano for the front of the box might include double-flowered chamomile (*Chamaemelum nobile* var. 'Flore Pleno'), with creamy pompon flowers and feathery foliage that smells sweet and fruity when disturbed, or the golden, creeping lemon thyme (*Thymus* x *citriodorus* 'Aureus') which, as its name suggests, has the aroma of lemons.

1 To avoid overwatering, drill small holes in the trough sides just above the perforated plate that separates plants from the reservoir.

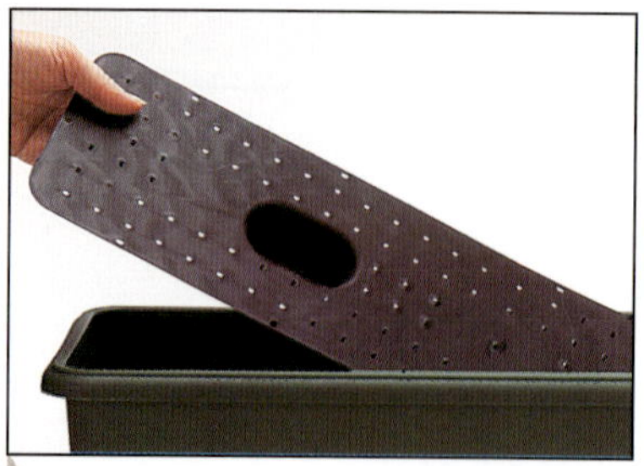

2 Cover the base plate with a layer of soil-based potting mixture. For drought-resistant plants and herbs, add extra grit.

3 Plant pelargoniums at the back and interplant with rosemary; if its growth is thin, trim shoot tips to encourage bushiness.

DIASCIAS IN A CLASSIC-STYLE TROUGH

The plants in this box complement the pale stone-colored trough with its classical swag detailing. You could choose a darker or more vivid selection of flowers; adding cream or white flowers and silver foliage would provide a visual link to tie the plants in with the container. Flowers and foliage are often more effective than flowers alone.

1 Plastic containers usually have the drainage holes marked on the base. Drill them out with a large screwdriver.

2 Add a layer of styrofoam chips or gravel for drainage, cover with potting mix and plant the diascias in a row along the back.

3 Silver foliage plants make the perfect foil for the salmon-pink diascias, which will flower over a long period. Keep the planting proportions in scale by trimming the foliage occasionally with scissors.

4 To soften the front edge, plant five equally spaced oreganos. Gently squeeze the rootball into an oval to allow more room for the pansies.

Rootballs must be thoroughly moist before planting.

5 Add sparkle to the display with some cream-colored blooms. Fill the gaps between the plants, both at the front and back of the box, with as many pansies as possible. Instead of pansies, you could use variegated sage or double chamomile.

Pansy F1 hybrid

Pelargonium Century Series Orchid F1

Rosmarinus officinalis 'Miss Jessopp's Upright'

Origanum *vulgare* 'Aureum'

6 Choose a brightly lit situation for this planting. Feed and water it regularly, but do not let the soil become too wet. Remove dead heads and flower stems and pinch back rosemary shoot tips to keep the growth compact.

Using houseplants outdoors

Several houseplants perform well outdoors in summer. For example, the trailing forms of tradescantia, including white-, pink- and purple-variegated, as well as the delicate plain-leaved kinds that produce clouds of starry white flowers. Outdoors grow them in sun or moderate shade, but avoid deep shade as variegated forms may revert to green. Tradescantias are easy to root in water, but you can buy them as 'tots' in garden centers.

Above: *The feathery asparagus fern is at home outdoors in summer, but avoid a hot, dry position. The long trails are useful for hanging baskets.*

Left: Solenostemon, *or coleus, is available in a range of vibrant colors. You can usually find one to match the scheme you have in mind.*

Below: *White flowers and variegated foliage combine to create a cool, sophisticated, yet inexpensive scheme that looks well against the dark green plastic trough.*

Hedera helix cultivar

Nicotiana F1 hybrid

Chlorophytum comosum 'Variegatum'

Impatiens F1 hybrid

RESCUING A DRIED OUT HANGING BASKET

As long as the plants in a basket are not completely dead, they can usually be revived. Unless you used water-retaining gel crystals in the soil before planting, you will find that dried out potting mix is very difficult to rewet; if you pour water into the top of the container, it simply runs around the sides without wetting the center. To combat this, try adding a tiny drop of liquid detergent to the water as a wetting agent. The simplest solution is to stand the container in a deep bowl of water to have a really good soak.

1 The soil in this basket is dry, the moss is yellow and the flowers need attention.

2 Start by snipping off the dead flower heads - this makes the basket look better straightaway. Remove any dead, damaged or browning leaves at the same time.

3 Where there are no buds on the same shoot to follow on, cut complete stems back close to the base to encourage a new crop of shoots and buds.

4 Plants with trailing stems often become tangled and droop down around the basket. Tease them apart and see which pieces are worth keeping.

5 Cut old, yellowing shoots with no new buds back to where they branch from a healthy shoot. The plant will quickly make new growth to fill out the display.

6 Tie back healthy green shoots using loose twist ties or thin string. Trailing and climbing plants look best growing up the chains or trained round the sides.

7 As you tidy the basket, you will remove a lot of material. The basket will look better for it, however, and it is quicker than trying to revive dead pieces.

8 Stand the basket in a deep bowl of tepid water for at least an hour and spray more water over the plants. This makes it easier for the potting mix to take up water.

9 Support the chains with a cane while the basket is soaking.Top up with water until the basket is saturated. Do not feed dry plants for a few days.

PART FOURTEEN

WATER GARDENING

A water feature in the garden is an instant focal point; the gleam of a pool, the sparkle of a fountain and the shapes and colors of lush water plants are irresistible. Once correctly installed, a water feature is easy to maintain, attracts a range of wildlife to the garden and is a constant source of interest and pleasure for you.

INSTALLING A POOL

Before you install a pool, consider the lining options, as this is likely to be your greatest expense. The easiest type of liners to buy are the preformed pools, available in a choice of sizes and in both formal and informal styles. Most incorporate a marginal shelf for plants. Rigid pools are also available in much thicker plastic, and even stronger, but more expensive, are the preformed GRP (glass reinforced plastic) shapes. You can also buy flexible liners that stretch to fit every contour of the excavation. These range from inexpensive forms of PVC (polyvinyl chloride) and polyethylene (polythene) to a butyl rubber liner, a highly durable material available in various thicknesses.

Mark out the shape of your proposed pool on the ground and when you are satisfied, dig out the subsoil to your required depth - a minimum of 24in(60cm) and usually no more than about 48in(120cm). Incorporate a shelf for marginal plants about 10in(25cm) below the final water level. Check the level of the excavations by knocking a 48in(120cm) post into the center of your pool area. Use this to balance one end of a straightedge extended from a series of small 12in(30cm) pegs or posts sited around the edge of the bank. Place a spirit level along the top to show where any adjustments need to be made. Make sure there are no major bumps or hollows, and remove any sharp stones.

1 To protect the liner against damage from sharp stones, etc. use a custom-made pond cushioning material or use a layer of sand, old carpet, sacking or loft insulation material, as shown here.

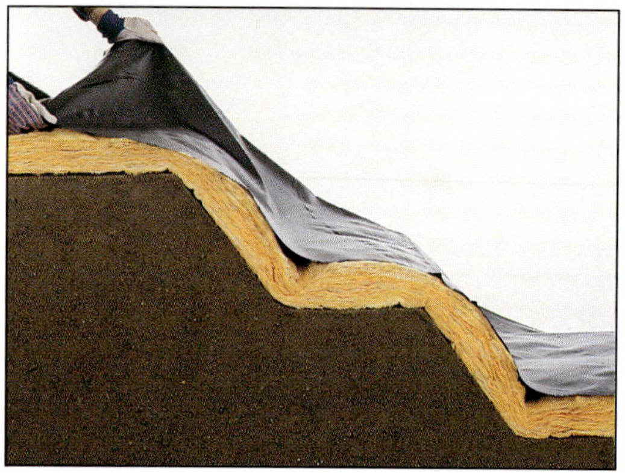

2 Lay the pool liner over the excavated hole, taking care that there is an equal amount of excess around the outside. For large pools, you will need help moving the liner.

HOW MUCH LINER?

Pools vary in size; to calculate the amount of liner you will need, add twice the maximum depth of the pool to both the overall length and width. Thus, a 10ftx6ftx2ft(3x1.8x0.6m) deep pool needs a liner 14x10ft(4.2x3m). Liner is flexible and stretches to fit with the weight of the water, so there is no need to allow for the gentle contouring of an informal pool or the extra few inches of a marginal shelf.

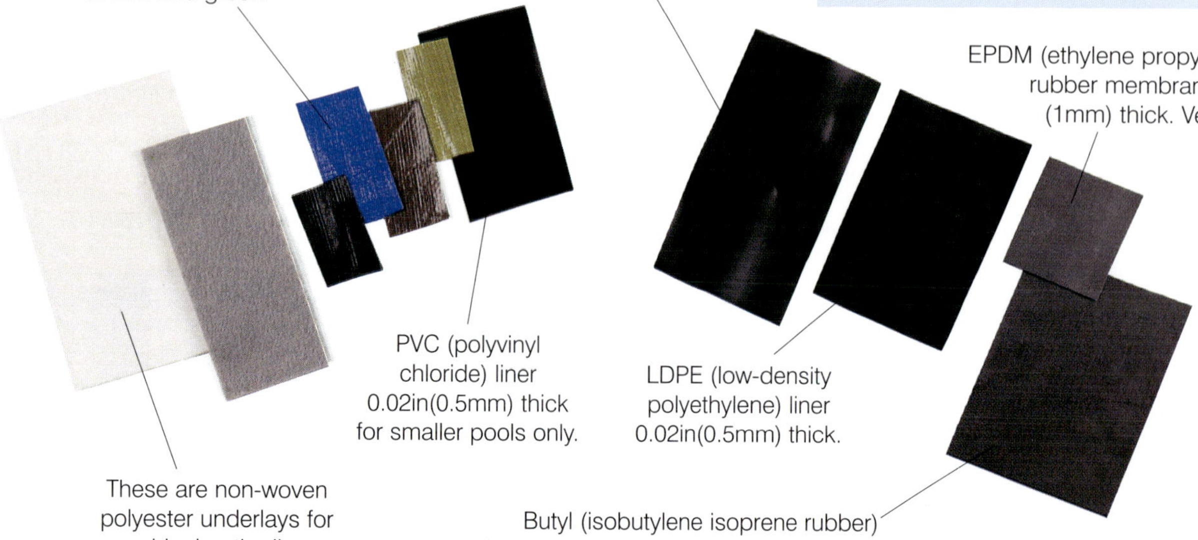

Inexpensive polyethylene material in black, blue, brown and green.

PVC blend with a high plasticizer content to improve flexibility and durability. Also 0.02in(0.5mm) thick.

EPDM (ethylene propylene diene rubber membrane) 0.04in (1mm) thick. Very durable.

PVC (polyvinyl chloride) liner 0.02in(0.5mm) thick for smaller pools only.

LDPE (low-density polyethylene) liner 0.02in(0.5mm) thick.

These are non-woven polyester underlays for cushioning the liner.

Butyl (isobutylene isoprene rubber) 0.03in(0.75mm) thick. Very strong and long lasting.

Below: This rigid plastic shell is typical of a wide range of preformed shapes that enable you to create an 'instant' pond.

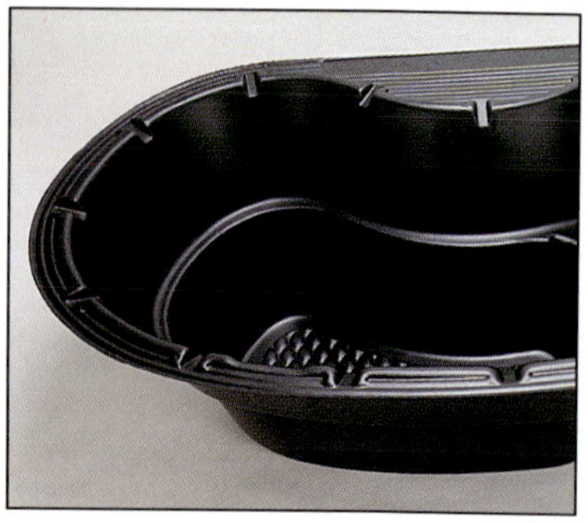

3 Anchor the edges of the liner with smooth slabs, boulders or bricks. You can move these around as the pool fills with water to help the liner settle into place.

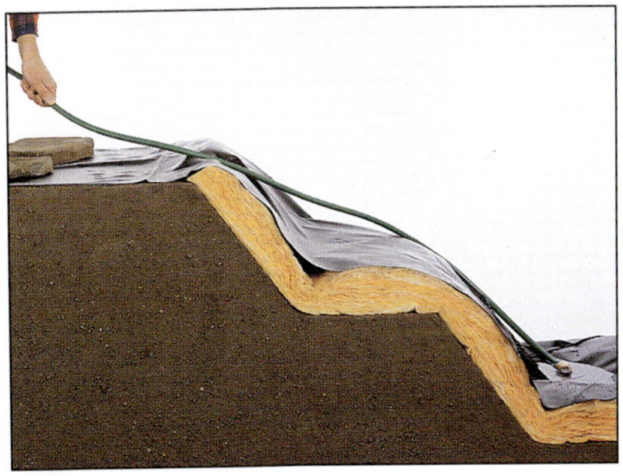

4 Now fill the pool slowly using a hosepipe to produce a steady trickle of water. The weight of the water will pull the liner into place.

5 When the pool has filled to its level, cut away any excess liner, leaving about 12in(30cm) to be anchored and hidden by your choice of edging.

6 This profile represents a small liner pool filled for the first time. It is used to show edging options and how to install pumps.

Pool edging ideas

There are several ways of edging a garden pool. The aim is to provide access to the water and to soften and disguise the junction of the pool liner and the surrounding garden. Here are a few options.

Above: *Turf edging produces a natural look and is easy to lay. The pool liner can be anchored beneath the soil and turves.*

Left: *Grass, with stone slabs set on sand at intervals around the edge and slightly overlapping the water, hide and anchor the liner.*

Right: *Brick edging that slightly overlaps the pool needs good foundations: a 6in(15cm) layer of hardcore, 1in(2.5cm) of sand and 1in (2.5cm) of cement.*

Right: *Paving slabs have a larger surface area to spread the weight of the people walking on them. Lay a 3in(7.5cm) layer of hardcore to give substance to a damp or crumbly soil base.*

Left: *Unless you want to create a natural sloping beach running into the pool, contain an edging of pebbles with wooden battens to prevent the stones spilling into the water.*

SETTING UP A WATER PUMP

If you have sufficient depth of water, a submersible pump is a neat way to run a water feature, such as a fountain or waterfall. Submersibles are easier to maintain and more economical to run than surface-mounted pumps. Be sure to calculate accurately the size of pump you need or the results may be disappointing, especially if you hope to run more than one feature from the same pump. As the head of water increases, so the output will decrease; the length of pipe, its bore and the number of bends also affect performance. It is better not to run a pump at full capacity all the time, so buy a model slightly larger than your needs. Installing the pump is simple enough if it is close to an outdoor electrical point. This should be installed by a qualified electrician.

SETTING UP A PUMP FOR A FOUNTAIN

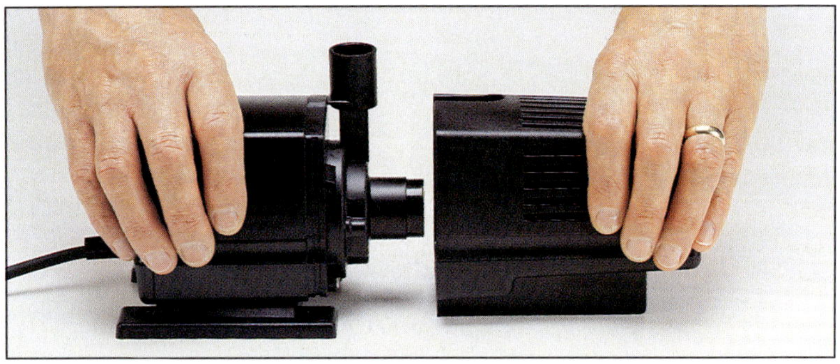

1 If you want to use the built-in filter, which contains a block of plastic filter foam, simply push it over the inlet pipe of the pump until it clicks into place. It is easy to remove for cleaning.

2 If you plan to run a fountain and perhaps a waterfall as well, push the T-piece adapter onto the outlet pipe of the pump. Make sure the two pieces fit firmly together so that they do not come apart once the pump is below water.

SETTING UP A PUMP FOR FOUNTAIN AND WATERFALL

1 Remove the blanking cap. Push on plastic tubing to supply the waterfall. This tube has a 1in(25mm) bore. Use an adapter for different diameters.

2 Use the adjuster to control the flow of water. Fully screwed in, all the water will go to the waterfall; fully out will split the flow both ways.

3 Set up like this, the pump is ready to have a fountain head fitted on top of the outlet pipe. The built-in foam pad will filter the water as it is sucked through the vents in the casing.

Here, the tubing has been left exposed to show where it runs. You can hide the tubing so that the water appears to spring from the stones.

The maximum size of the fountain depends on the height of the waterfall and the length of tubing involved.

DIFFERENT TYPES OF FOUNTAIN

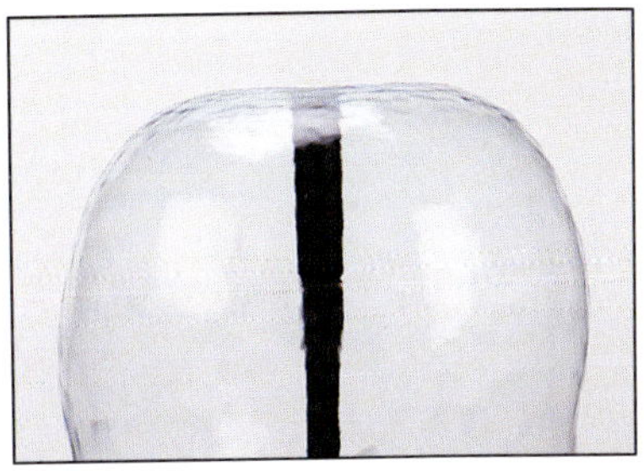

Above: Correctly adjusted, a bell fountain head produces a smooth and symmetrical dome of water.

Right: Change the bell shape by pushing in the plastic cone at the top of the head. Start with a reduced water flow and slowly increase it.

Above: A fountain head with two circles of holes produces a tall two-tier pattern of water droplets.

Right: A geyser fountain head produces a strong jet of aerated water. For the best effect, operate the pump at its most powerful setting.

Setting up a water filter

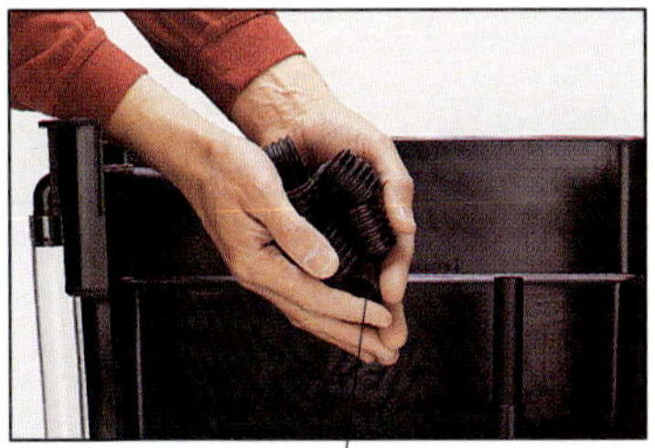

These provide a large surface area for beneficial bacteria to colonize.

1 Fill the base of the tank with a biological filter medium, here plastic corrugated pipe sections. These are inert and do not affect the water chemistry.

2 Two layers of plastic foam cover the filter medium. These strain out any debris in the water flowing from the pond.

The top layer of foam is a coarser grade than the lower one.

Below: *Here a submersible pump powers a spray fountain and a biological filter at the side of the pond. Place the filter above the pond water level so that the cleaned water flows back freely under gravity.*

OXYGENATING AND FLOATING PLANTS

A selection of oxygenating plants is essential for the good health of your pool, especially if the pond is new. These are mostly submerged, or occasionally floating, species of water plants that use up waste nutrients in the water by means of their underwater foliage. This, and the fact that such plants grow prolifically, will quickly deprive bothersome algae of nutrients and minerals, and thus help to keep the water clean. They not only prevent green water and blanketweed, but also provide useful cover for pond insects and small fish. For the average pool, you will need about one oxygenating plant for every $2ft^2$(five clumps per m^2) of surface area. Larger pools, over $150ft^2$ ($14m^2$), can reduce that requirement to nearer one plant per $3ft^2$(three bunches per m^2). Different species flourish at different times of year, so a selection of at least two or three species is the most successful way to beat murky water.

Floating plants are all those that are unrooted - that is, they float on, or just below, the water surface. Most require a water depth of 12-36in(30-90cm) and are generally very easy to install, simply by resting the plant gently on the water surface and allowing it to find its own level. They grow quickly and you may need to take them out of the water and cut them back if they become too rampant.

Left: *Eleocharis acicularis,* or hairgrass, is an evergreen sedge that spreads prolifically by means of rhizomes to produce a dense mat of narrow green leaf spikes.

Ceratophyllum demersum grows best in cool water; it spreads to make a submerged mat of tiny dark green leaves.

PLANTING OXYGENATORS

1 Fill a perforated container with aquatic soil almost to the rim. Make a series of planting holes with your fingers or a dibber and position the plants evenly around the container

2 When all the plants are firmed in, top up the container with a layer of washed gravel or small stones to anchor the potting mix and to prevent fish from rooting out the plants.

Below: *Hottonia palustris* makes a clump of feathery, light green leaves, with tall spikes of pale lilac or white flowers in summer.

Ranunculus aquatilis has bright green feathery foliage that can become invasive if not kept in check.

The tiny, semi-evergreen leaves of *Lagarosiphon major* (also known as *Elodea crispa)* are clustered along each stem.

Fontinalis antipyretica thrives in sun or semi-shade and prefers running water, such as a stream.

Floating plants

It is not generally recommended that you put prolific floating plants into very large ponds unless you can devise some means of removing them, as they could soon dominate the feature.

Annual *Trapa natans* is grown for its attractive leaves, white summer flowers and edible nuts.

Right: Pistia stratiotes, *a tender perennial, needs tropical or subtropical conditions.*

Below: Eichhornia crassipes *is a glossy evergreen or semi-evergreen with attractive leaves.*

In sunny, limestone waters, *Stratiotes aloides* produces tiny white flowers in summer.

Left: *Planting a water soldier,* Stratiotes aloides, *is simply a matter of placing it in the water. It remains mostly submerged but rises to the surface in summer.*

MARGINAL PLANTS

The plants that grow along the banks and shallows of ponds and streams are among the most dramatic and beautiful species you could wish to feature in your garden. As a group, they include a wonderful variety of size, shape and color within the range of their foliage alone, while some have spectacular flowers, too, at certain times of the year. These plants are usually positioned on the marginal shelf, specially built just below the surface of the water, so that these mud-loving plants can keep their roots waterlogged. You can plant them directly onto the shelf in soil enriched with humus or pot them up into specially perforated plastic baskets for easy maintenance. It is not a good idea to plant marginals all the way around the pool, as this would totally obscure the pool itself and deny you access to the water's edge. It is more usual to plant up about one-third of the circumference as a kind of backdrop and gradually add more plants where you feel they might be needed. In the right position, marginal plants not only provide visual interest but also give some shelter from prevailing winds and can shade part of the water from midday sunshine. Minute forms of pondlife also enjoy the habitat created by the stems and roots submerged in the mud just below the water surface.

SOILS AND POTS

PLANTING A MARGINAL

1 Fill the basket with moist aquatic potting mixture and plant two or three plants in it. Backfill and firm in. Add a layer of gravel.

2 Holding the container firmly by the handles on both sides, lower it gently onto the marginal shelf without disturbing the water too much.

Iris laevigata 'Variegata'. Violet-blue flowers appear from early to midsummer.

Iris ensata (I. kaempferi) 'Variegata'

Ranunculus flammula

Cotula coronopifolia 'Brass Buttons'

Propagating aquatic plants by cuttings

Take cuttings in spring, so that new plants have the growing season ahead of them to establish. Grow them on in nursery beds or waterlogged soil. Introduce marginal species to deeper water as they grow.

1 This plant has started to produce roots from nodes along the stem, so it is an ideal subject for taking cuttings.

2 If you pinch sharply between finger and thumb, the required section of stem should come away in your hand.

3 Pinching off the top of the stem will give you another plant to propagate, even though there is no evidence yet of roots.

4 Make sure your cuttings are not damaged, diseased or affected by pests. These two, prepared from a single small section of stem, are ready for potting up. Do not leave them out of the soil for too long.

5 Gently insert the cuttings into small pots of damp potting mixture and firm in. Keep well watered until good leaf and root growth are under way and then transfer them to the water garden.

MAKING A BOG GARDEN

The beauty of creating a bog or marsh area in the garden is that it offers you the chance to grow a wider range of exciting marginal plants. Or you may welcome the chance to establish a rewarding water feature without the need for expensive excavation work. Ideally, the site should be sheltered from prevailing winds with a little, but not too much, shade. The most natural position is adjoining the banks of an informal pond or pool, but if you are planning an individual bog garden, then any slight depression or poorly drained area will be ideal. It is important to keep the area poorly drained and to make allowances for fluctuations in the water level according to the differing levels of rainfall throughout the year. Avoid positioning the bog garden too near any tree roots, as they tend to drain moisture from the soil. If your garden is small or unsuitable, you can still enjoy a miniature bog garden created in a stone sink or barrel.

1 Excavate the area to a depth of about 14in(35cm), level the base and spread out a large sheet of pond lining material. Anchor it with a few large, smooth boulders.

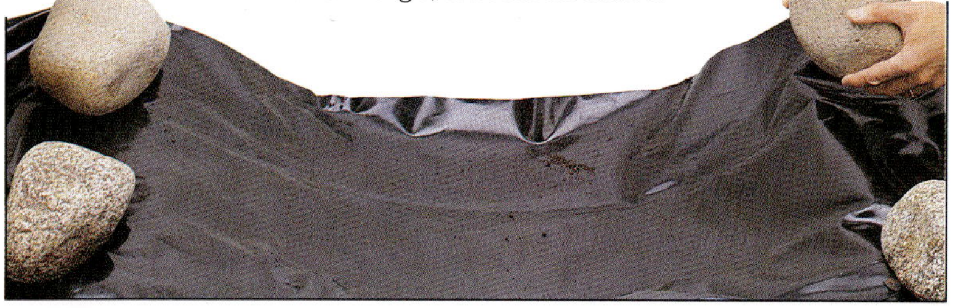

2 Puncture the bottom of the liner a couple of times with a garden fork, so that some water can escape later on. Add a layer of washed gravel.

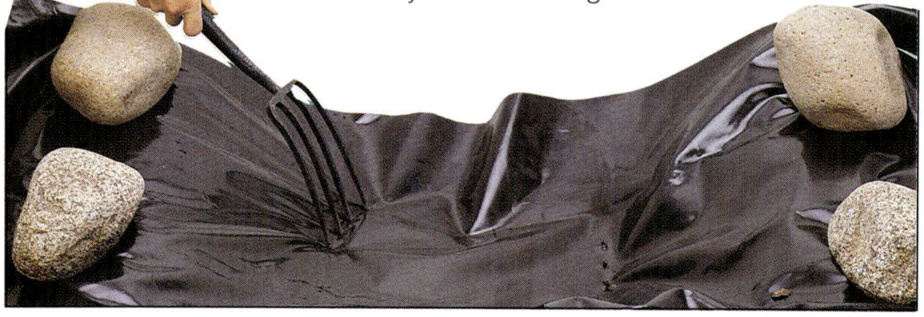

3 Lay a section of pipe, perforated at 12in(30cm) intervals, on the gravel. Allow the end to extend beyond the bog garden area and conceal it in the undergrowth.

4 In dry spells, trickle water into the pipe as needed. Fill the area to the original ground level with rich, moisture-retaining, aquatic planting mixture.

5 Soak the ground thoroughly, so that a layer of water about 3in(7.5cm) deep remains standing on the top of the soil before you start putting in any plants.

6 Position the plants so that they are at the same depth as they were in their pots. Firm them in. Hostas such as this have great shape and color possibilities.

7 Arrange more delicate plants, such as primulas, in clumps. Aim for a variety of shape, size and color for year-round plant interest.

Moisture-loving plants

There are many interesting plants that flourish in moist but well-drained soil and they look perfect when planted near, or leading away from, the pond edge. Some are marginal plants that tolerate damp but not totally waterlogged conditions, others are simply hardy garden perennials that you may already be familiar with from your herbaceous borders, and that prefer a moist, rich location.

Above: *Astilbes make an excellent display of feathery plumes along pond margins.*

WATER LILIES

For many pond owners, the large lily pad leaves and beautiful lotuslike blooms of the water lily are the epitome of a water garden. There is such a wonderful variety of types, offering different colors, forms and even scent. However, it is important to choose varieties with care, as the large vigorous types are totally unsuitable for smaller pools.

It is easy to be tempted by too many different types, and lilies will not grow well if they are crowded. Alternatively, they will swamp the water surface. It can be difficult to calculate exactly how many plants you should allow yourself, as size and vigor vary considerably. Your water lily stockist should be able to estimate the final size of your chosen plant. As a general guideline, you can cover about 40 to 50 percent of the water surface, assuming that about 10 to 30 percent will be covered with other floating plants.

Whatever the size of the pool, bear in mind that water lilies serve a practical purpose as well as a decorative one; the spread of their leaves shades a large part of the water surface, offering shade and shelter for fish and depriving algae of sunlight. Without light and heat, the algae cannot reproduce too rapidly and give you problems with green water. And do not forget that there is as much variety in the foliage of water lilies as in the blooms, with many different shapes, colors and markings.

Above: The base of the central petals of *Nymphaea* 'Attraction' are a deep wine color, fading to almost white at the tips of the outer petals.

Left: *N. caroliniana* 'Nivea' produces beautiful white, scented, semi-double flowers and attractive pale green deciduous leaves.

Below: The center of each pink bloom of *N.* 'Firecrest' blazes with a cluster of golden stamens streaked with orange and red.

CHOOSING THE RIGHT SIZE WATER LILY

It is vital to choose a water lily that will suit the size of your pond. This table is a guide to the eventual spread of different sizes of water lilies and the recommended planting depths.

	Spread	Planting depth
Miniature	1ft^2(0.09m^2)	4 9in(10 23cm)
Small	3ft^2(0.3m^2)	6-15in(15-38cm)
Moderate	6-12ft^2(0.6-1.1m^2)	6-18in(15-45cm)
Medium	12-15ft^2(1.1-1.3m^2)	6-24in(15-60cm)
Large	15-25ft^2(1.3-2.3m^2)	9-48in(23-120cm)

Left: The pale pink, cup-shaped blooms of *N.* 'Formosa' are stippled with darker pink and grow to 3.75in(9.5cm) across. They are also faintly scented.

Below: *N. tuberosa* 'Richardsonii' has large, white, globular blooms with prominent green sepals and apple green leaves. It only suits larger pools.

Right: Vigorous *Nymphaea* 'Colonel A.J. Welch' is excellent for deep water. It has large, star-shaped, canary yellow blooms with narrow pointed petals. The flowers are not plentiful, but they stay open later in the afternoons.

Planting a water lily

Water lilies are greedy feeders, especially the more vigorous types, so provide the largest container possible and a soil depth of at least 6in(15cm). Containers include perforated baskets and wide, solid-sided bowls. Transplant lilies in spring so they can establish themselves before the dormant season.

1 Lay the lily onto the potting mixture and top up the basket with more mixture, firming in the plant as you proceed.

2 Cover the surface with gravel or small stones to keep the soil in place once the basket is lowered into the water.

3 Place bricks in the pool to bring the basket to the right level below the water surface. See label for planting depth.

4 Lower the container into the water so that it rests on the bricks. Do not drop it in; you may damage the plant and pond liner.

5 If it has been correctly planted, the lily leaves will eventually float up to rest on the water surface. Place young plants in shallow water at first.

CHOOSING PLANTS

Ponds and water gardens offer a unique opportunity to grow plants that need to be grown in, on or by water. Make the most of their fascinating personalities and enjoy the new range of wildlife they attract to the garden.

Above: Primulas need soil that never dries out, and sun or slight shade, depending on the species.

MOISTURE-LOVING PLANTS

Anemone rivularis
Aruncus dioicus 'Glasnevin'
Arundo donax 'Versicolor'
Astilbe
Cardamine pratensis
Cornus alba 'Sibirica'
Filipendula ulmaria
Geum rivale
Gunnera manicata
Hosta
Iris ensata (I. kaempferi) 'Alba'
'Variegata'
I. hoogiana 'Hula Doll'
I. innominata 'Irish Doll'
'Jack o' Hearts'
I. sibirica 'Sparkling Rose'
Ligularia dentata 'Desdemona'
L. przewalskii 'The Rocket'
Lobelia cardinalis
'Queen Victoria'
Lythrum salicaria
Osmunda regalis
Parnassia palustris
Peltiphyllum peltatum
Petasites japonicus
Phalaris arundinacea 'Picta'
Primula denticulata, P. japonica, P. pulverulenta, P. veris, P. vulgaris
Rheum alexandrae, R. palmatum
Rodgersia pinnata 'Superba'
Scrophularia auriculata 'Variegata'
Trollius x cultorum 'Canary Bird'
T. chinensis 'Golden Queen'

Below: A water feature in a tub lined with a pond liner makes an excellent focal point for a drab corner of the garden or patio. Providing they are all scaled down, you can include water lilies, marginal plants in plastic mesh baskets - even a tiny fountain.

MARGINAL PLANTS

Acorus calamus 'Variegatus'
Calla palustris
Caltha palustris 'Flore Pleno'
Carex elata 'Aurea', *C. pendula*
Cyperus longus
Eupatorium cannabinum, E. purpureum
Glyceria maxima 'Variegata'
G. spectabilis 'Variegata'
Houttuynia cordata 'Chameleon'
'Flore Pleno'
Iris ensata (I. kaempferi)
I. laevigata
I. pseudacorus 'Variegata'
I. versicolor 'Blue Light'
Juncus effusus
J.e. spiralis
Lysichiton americanus
Lysimachia nummularia 'Aurea'
Mentha aquatica
Mimulus guttatus
M. luteus 'Nana'
Myosotis scorpioides, M. palustris
Myriophyllum verticillatum
Orontium aquaticum
Pontederia cordata
Sagittaria sagittifolia 'Flore Pleno'
Scirpus albescens, S. zebrinus
Typha latifolia 'Variegata'
T. minima
Zantedeschia aethiopica

FLOATING PLANTS

Azolla filiculoides
Eichhornia crassipes
Hydrocharis morsus-ranae
Lemna triscula
Pistia stratiotes
Utricularia vulgaris

OXYGENATING PLANTS

Callitriche hermaphroditica (C. autumnalis)
C. palustris, C. verna
Ceratophyllum demersum
Eleocharis acicularis, E. palustris
Elodea canadensis, E. crispa
Lagarosiphon major (Elodea crispa)
Potamogeton crispus
Ranunculus aquatilis
Stratiotes aloides

DEEP WATER PLANTS

Aponogeton distachyos
Nymphaea (Water lilies)

Below: *Aponogeton distachyos*, the water hawthorn, produces fragrant white flowers all through the summer.

PART FIFTEEN

GREENHOUSE GARDENING

No other part of the garden offers the sheer flexibility of a greenhouse. Use it to extend the gardening season all the year round, to grow edible out-of-season luxuries, create your own plant nursery, cultivate colorful tender plants to perfection or even set up a specialist collection, all with complete control over the conditions.

Above: Automatic openers consist of a cylinder of paraffin wax that expands and contracts as the temperature changes, moving a piston that raises or lowers the ventilator in the roof.

THE BASIC GREENHOUSE

A basic greenhouse consists of a glass roof and walls, with one or two ventilators that need to be opened and closed by hand. This is quite sufficient to grow tomatoes and similar crops in the soil. But if the greenhouse is to be used to the full, then a few extra facilities will prove invaluable. There is no need to buy everything at once - the 'extras' needed vary according to how the house is to be used. One of the first improvements is to add paving. The most versatile layout is to have a central path dividing the house, leaving one soil border for tall crops, and the other border paved over or covered in a layer of gravel to take staging. Another useful improvement is to replace the manual ventilator handles with automatic openers; these do not need an electricity supply. As an added refinement, it is useful to have louvered vents in the sides of the house. These allow cool air to enter the greenhouse to replace the warm air that constantly rises out through the roof, thus improving the ventilation still further.

General view of a basic greenhouse

Two tier permanent staging makes the best use of space; the top tier gets most light and is a good place for creating long-lasting displays of greenhouse pot plants that need maximum light. The bottom tier is useful for storage, and being well shaded, is ideal for growing shade-loving plants, such as streptocarpus, impatiens and ferns, and for trays of seedlings in summer when the sun is strong.

A high shelf is useful for trailing plants, such as these pendulous begonia and ivy-leaved pelargoniums, and is ideal in early spring for trays of seedlings when light levels are low - close to the glass the light is much brighter.

Temporary shelves and staging allows soil borders to be used for summer crops, but provides extra shelf space in the spring propagation season for trays of seedlings. Easy to take down.

Gravel is a cheap, low-maintenance surface that smothers annual weeds and can be damped down on hot days to create much-needed humidity. A good place for standing large pots.

Paving slabs are best for permanent greenhouse paths, and individual slabs can be used under the legs of staging to prevent them sinking into the ground.

A louvered ventilator allows cool air to enter near the base, rise as it warms up, and escape through the roof ventilators, thus encouraging a constant flow.

Soil borders are useful for edible crops or cut flowers. If the same crops are grown repeatedly, dig the soil out and change it to avoid soil diseases building up.

GREENHOUSE STAGING

Staging is essential for raising potgrown plants and trays of seedlings up to a convenient working height. Solid-topped staging is the best for small pots and trays that will need to stand on capillary water matting (a fibrous 'cloth' that helps to keep plants evenly moist) as it provides a rigid base. Metal trays are more versatile, allowing plants to be stood either on capillary matting or 'plunged' into a bed of gravel. Slatted staging is best for larger plants in pots, especially those that need good air circulation (such as orchids), as the gaps allow air to flow up through the foliage.

Left: Self-assembly staging is flexible; the tops can be set up as a flat surface or as trays for gravel or capillary matting.

Below: Temporary staging like this provides useful extra space at the right height for seasonal jobs such as potting up plants.

Left: A louvered ventilator consists of a series of glass panels operated by a side handle, which opens them to allow air in. Although they are available for louvered vents, automatic openers are not really necessary, as it is usually convenient to leave these vents open all summer.

Regulating the temperature

Greenhouses suffer from excess heat in summer and cold in winter. Most greenhouse plants grow best at between 40°F/5°C (winter minimum) and 86°F/30°C (summer maximum). An electric fan heater used for warmth in winter can often double as a cooling fan in summer simply by turning down the thermostat so the fan keeps running without the heating element cutting in. However, special shading and insulation products are available to assist temperature control throughout the year.

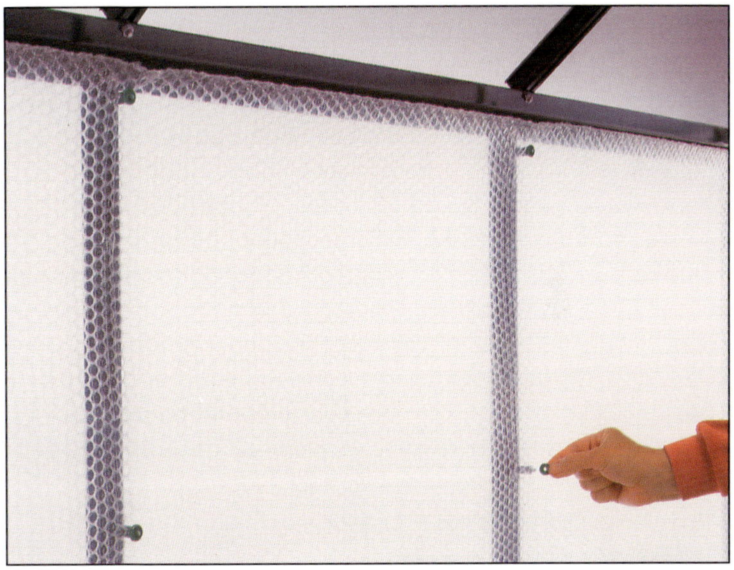

Above: *Plastic bubble wrap insulation is sold in sheets that can be cut to fit the inside of the greenhouse. Insulate the roof alone, or both the roof and walls.*

Right: *Woven plastic shading fabric dilutes the strong rays of the sun, thus reducing the temperature in summer. It is easily taken down in winter.*

Left: *Alternatively, apply greenhouse shading paint (or watered down white emulsion paint) to the outside of the greenhouse in early summer. Be sure to wash it off carefully in the fall, so that plants do not go short of light during winter.*

ROUTINE TECHNIQUES

The secret of a successful greenhouse is constant attention to detail. Make it a habit to visit the house every day and see what needs to be done. Regular attention to routine chores is vital, as plants soon suffer from neglect. Feeding and watering, pest and disease control and ventilation are vital all-year-round, though the need for each varies with the rate of plant growth. As a general rule, water in the morning during dull weather and in winter to avoid leaving the air humid at night, which encourages fungal disease. During hot spells, water in the evening so that plants can take up water slowly overnight before strong sun causes it to evaporate. In summer, stand plants on damp capillary matting to help keep the air humid and the roots moist, but remove it in the fall to permit drier conditions throughout winter. Plants should almost dry out between waterings then. Feed weekly or more when plants are making vigorous growth in summer, but less in spring and fall when growth is slow, and not at all in winter. Check plants once a week, and treat for pests or disease as soon as an outbreak is seen.

Repotting plants

1 Spring is the best time for repotting plants, since the fresh potting mixture supplies them with a high level of nutrients, ideal for the start of the growing season.

2 Knock the plant out of its original pot. If the roots form a solid pot-shape or are growing out through the drainage holes, the plant needs repotting.

Watering greenhouse plants

Above: Cover the top of solid staging with capillary matting that runs down into guttering fixed along the edge of the staging. Fill this with water and the plants virtually take care of themselves.

Left: A microbore drip system helps keep the potting mix evenly moist. Such systems can be connected to an outdoor tap via a water computer, which turns the supply on and off for a preset time every day.

Right: Combine water-retaining gel crystals with potting mix before potting greenhouse plants, particularly those such as impatiens and primulas that suffer badly if allowed to dry out.

3 Replant in a pot one size larger, with some fresh potting mix in the base. If the rootball is solid, gently loosen a few roots.

4 Firm in gently. Fill the sides with more mix and water well. When excess water has drained away, replace plant on the staging.

Feeding greenhouse plants

Right: When plants are watered by capillary matting or drip irrigation, it is easy to overlook feeding. In these cases, slow-release fertilizers added to the potting mix before planting in spring are useful.

Below: Slow-release fertilizers are also available as tablets and pellets. Insert them in the potting mix as directed.

Above: Liquid feeds, including soluble feeds that are first diluted, allow you to feed more often when plants are growing faster. Tomato feed (shown here) is useful for all fruiting and flowering plants.

The greenhouse year

Spring: *Repot long-term greenhouse plants into larger pots. If you do not want to give them bigger pots, scrape away the top 0.5in(1.25cm) of potting mix and replace with fresh mix . This is the time to take cuttings of most greenhouse plants and to divide large clump-forming types. Avoid overwatering.*

Above: *Remove dead flower heads regularly to encourage the production of new buds.*

Summer: *As the summer period progresses, there will be more room as bedding plants and vegetable seedlings are planted outside after the last frost. Increase watering and feeding as greenhouse plants start growing faster, and provide more ventilation to stop the house becoming too hot in sunny weather. Pests start to become a problem and will need tackling, either with pesticides, with biological control insects or by physical means, such as sticky traps. In midsummer, extra shading may be needed to stop plants being scorched by strong sun and high temperatures; liquid shading can be painted onto the outside of the house, or you can use fitted blinds. Crops growing in the soil, such as tomatoes, will need frequent attention to keep them healthy and productive. By the end of summer, growth will be visibly slowing down, and watering and feeding should be reduced.*

Below: *Leave tomatoes to ripen fully on the plants before picking, so they develop their full flavor.*

Fall: *Clear everything out of the greenhouse and wash the glass inside and out. Remove and store capillary matting and hose down staging. Pull out remaining summer crops. Replace those plants that will be kept through the winter. Set up the heater and use a thermometer to check that the required temperature is maintained in the greenhouse.*

Below: *Sticky traps are specially valuable in fall, winter and spring, when there are few beneficial insects about. In summer, they would trap beneficial insects and also biological control insects - avoid using the two together.*

THE GREENHOUSE AS A PLANT FACTORY

Propagating your own plants is a particularly satisfying achievement, and a greenhouse can act as a plant nursery, producing young plants for use all round the garden and in useful quantities that can save you money. Without any special facilities, the greenhouse can be used for propagating plants that simply need the constant care and controlled conditions of a greenhouse environment. These include summer cuttings (of fuchsias, pelargoniums and other half-hardy perennials, and many easily rooted outdoor shrubs) and seeds that are sown in summer, such as hardy perennials and biennials, including winter and spring bedding plants. Seeds of houseplants and conservatory plants can also be sown in summer to take advantage of the natural heat in the greenhouse. However, bedding plants, tomato and cucumber plants, etc., need an early start, coupled with steady high temperatures. To raise these successfully, you will need a thermostatically controlled, electrically heated propagator. Without a propagator, the best plan would be to buy seedlings of these plants (available in garden centers as 'plugs' ready for pricking out) a month or so after the normal sowing time, in mid- to late spring, and grow them in a moderately heated greenhouse.

Sowing seeds

1 Fill a clean pot with seed sowing mix, tap the pot down lightly and sprinkle a thin layer of horticultural vermiculite over the top.

2 Scatter seed thinly; do not tip the packet out over the pot. If the seeds are very fine, mix them with fine sand before sowing.

3 Just cover the seeds with a very thin layer of vermiculite. Do not cover very fine seeds at all; they will fall between the granules.

4 Label and date the pot and water carefully. Place it in a propagator or on the second tier of staging if no extra heat is needed.

Raising plants in the greenhouse

Staging space in spring is normally occupied by seedlings newly removed from the propagator waiting to be pricked out, and older seedlings growing on in their trays.

A heated propagator is essential if you plan to raise bedding plants and summer greenhouse crops like tomatoes and peppers from seed.

The bottom tier of the staging is useful in spring to house newly pricked out seedlings, which need protection from direct sunlight until well established.

A high shelf gets good light in winter and early spring, making it a useful place to put young plants of vegetables, bedding plants and perennials, plus rooted cuttings.

Temporary staging provides useful extra space to use as a potting bench in spring, when seedlings and rooted cuttings all need potting at the same time.

Under temporary staging makes a good place for dormant bulbs and tubers needing protection from frost, as well as providing storage space.

Pricking out seedlings

1 Prick out seedlings when they have two true leaves. Loosely fill a clean tray with fresh seed mix, remove any lumps and firm gently.

2 Using a clean watering can, water the seed mix well to make it soft. Make holes in the new seed mix about 1.5in(3.75cm) apart.

3 Lift out individual seedlings by loosening the roots free with a dibber. Hold them by one of their seed leaves (the first to develop).

4 Plant each seedling so that the seed leaves are just above the level of the mix. Firm the roots in gently with the tip of the dibber.

5 When the tray is full of seedlings, cover it with a clear plastic lid to trap humidity and stand it on the lower tier of the greenhouse staging or in a similar spot in good light, but out of direct sun.

MAKING A GROWING TENT

Seeds that do not need extra heat to germinate and newly pricked-out seedlings both need constant humidity, a steady temperature and protection from direct sunlight and drafts. An easy way to provide these conditions is in a growing tent. Surround the bottom tier of two-tier staging with plastic, or make a light frame from garden canes, drape it with plastic and stand it in a shady spot. Make a few holes near the top of the plastic for ventilation and put damp capillary matting in the bottom for watering and humidity.

Potting up seedlings and cuttings

Seedlings and rooted cuttings of many plants are potted into individual pots, rather than pricked out into trays as is done for 'bulk' crops like bedding plants and vegetables for transplanting outdoors. Individual pots allow plants to grow on with more space and no root disturbance.

1 Remove the rooted plants from their pots, keeping the old mix that falls from the roots separate from the fresh mix.

2 Tease the young plants carefully apart. Shake off any loose mix, but do not try to remove any that is full of roots.

3 Part fill a pot with new mix. Lower the young plant into the center, with the lower leaves just above the top of the pot.

4 Add potting mix until the pot is almost full. Firm gently, water well and allow to drain. Stand the pot on the staging.

Planting up plugs from garden centers

Plantlets in multi-compartmental containers, halfway between individual seedlings and young plants, are available as 'plugs' (below). Push each plantlet out of its plug and pot up singly as for rooted cuttings.

A RADIANT GREENHOUSE

Colorful greenhouse displays are often based on plants that would grow just as well outdoors, such as pelargoniums. Instead, choose varieties with large, fragile blooms and showy flowers; under glass, where their petals are protected from the weather, they can be seen at their best. Add flowering potplants, such as *Streptocarpus* and *Clivia*, and seasonal annuals, such as *Exacum*, to vary the display. And use foliage plants, such as coleus, or frilly, purple-leaved basil or perilla, to contrast with bright flowers, which stand out best against a leafy background. As some plants have rather specialized growing requirements, it can be difficult to cater for their needs. It is a good idea to use colored labels to pick out plants that need special watering, etc. Some growers set up a greenhouse specially to cater for 'hobby' plants, such as cacti and succulents, orchids, bulbs or carnivorous plants. Bear in mind that a special-interest collection may need special facilities or higher temperatures than normal greenhouse potplants. If you are starting to collect hobby plants, build up expertise on commoner kinds first, since rare plants are often difficult and expensive.

Cacti in the greenhouse

A greenhouse to grow cacti or bulbs, which need as much light and air as they can get, needs little more than plain staging, plus a heater for winter. Extra ventilators in the roof and a louvered ventilator in the back wall of the house are useful optional extras.

Plants in the greenhouse

Use the high shelf for floppy plants, like this trailing fuchsia, or plants that do not fit in well with the main display. The begonias are short and look lost on the staging.

Use the staging top to display popular flowering plants for summer color. Regal pelargoniums and fuchsias are set off here by the foliage of coleus and zonal pelargoniums.

In summer, the lower staging is ideal for plants that benefit from protection from direct sun, such as gloxinia, impatiens, streptocarpus and bromeliads.

You can adjust temporary staging to accommodate taller or shorter plants. This adds variety to the display, while making maximum use of all the available space.

When the staging is high enough, the space underneath can be used to extend the display using taller plants such as this arum lily, which needs protection from strong direct sun.

Standing space on the floor can be used to take tall plants, such as this pelargonium, or perhaps a standard plant like the *Anisodontea capensis* on the opposite side.

Exotic plants in the greenhouse

Tiered staging and shelving provide a versatile display area that is superb for more exotic plants. All these need a minimum winter temperature of 45°F(7°C).

Top: Abutilon makes a good greenhouse pot plant, and will flower most of the year.

Middle: Clivia, an evergreen bulb that flowers in spring. The large daisylike blooms of gerbera. Cymbidium, one of the easiest orchids to keep in a mixed plant collection.

Bottom: Streptocarpus bear single or double flowers in a wide range of colors during the summer and fall. Easy to propagate.

Displaying your plants

1 Stand a few taller plants on upturned pots to add height to a level display. If capillary matting is used for watering, hand water any plants raised in this way.

2 Use another plant to hide the upturned pot. Where possible, use tiered staging, shelving and hanging baskets to create a varied display on several levels.

Orchids in the greenhouse

Orchids need plenty of shading, high humidity, more heat than the average greenhouse plant, and very good air circulation. In fact, a well-organized orchid house often has sophisticated heating and ventilation systems, lath shading - which can be adjusted daily - and a fan running continuously to keep the air moving.

Above: *There is no limit to the orchid varieties you can grow in a greenhouse. Stand plants at the back of the staging on upturned pots to make it easier to see them. Do not overcrowd them.*

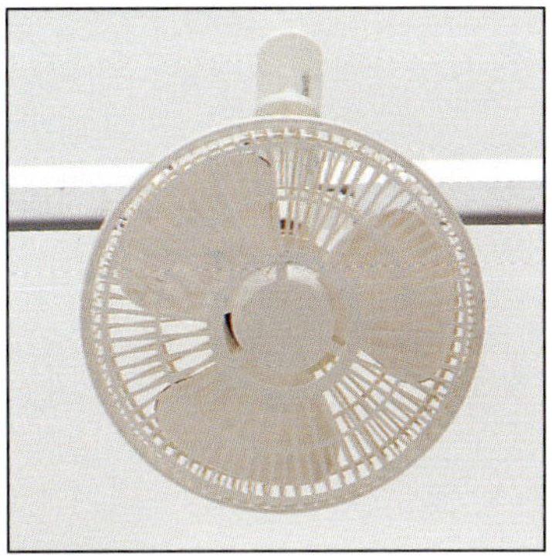

Right: *In a small greenhouse, a fan to circulate air is a most useful piece of equipment. Position it at staging level to move air through the plants.*

Left: *Provide staging for the orchids with a moisture stage underneath. This purpose-built slatted staging allows the moisture from a water-soaked gravel bed to rise around the plants creating vital humidity.*

TENDER CLIMBERS AND TRAILING PLANTS

Climbing and trailing plants make full use of all three dimensions, ensuring that every bit of greenhouse space is used to the full. The house only needs heating enough to keep it frost-free in winter to be able to grow a large range of interesting perennial climbers. Train vigorous kinds, such as passion flower, bougainvillea and plumbago, up the greenhouse walls supported by wires or trellis to give a conservatory-like effect. Prune lightly to tidy them in late fall and then cut back to within a few inches of the main framework of stems in early spring. If space is short, train flexible climbers, such as passion flower, round a hoop; the same technique can be used for compact varieties of passion flower. Trailing or scrambling plants, such as *Hoya carnosa* and *Ceropegia woodii,* can be grown in hanging baskets suspended from hooks on the glazing bars in the roof. In a slightly shady greenhouse, use large hanging baskets to grow epiphyllums - exotic relatives of cacti, with long ribbonlike leaves and orchidlike flowers. But modest trailers, such as trailing fuchsias, ivy-leaved pelargoniums, *Hoya bella,* and false strawberry *(Duchesnea indica)* can also be fitted into a mixed ornamental plant collection simply by growing them along the edge of the staging.

Displaying plants in the greenhouse

Variegated *Hoya carnosa* looks pretty all year.

The lipstick vine *(Aeschynanthus)* will thrive in a bright place.

Trailing fuchsias have a much longer growing season under glass.

Keep climbing plants compact by training them on supports; shown here are plumbago, bougainvillea and stephanotis.

Above: Climbers and trailers fit well in a mixed collection, or use them alone to make an impact, as here. Hanging baskets suspended from the roof are ideal for trailers.

Training passion flower round a hoop

1 To train climbers such as passion flower around a framework, unravel tangled stems and insert the frame into the pot.

2 Secure stems to the frame with plant ties or wire clips. Clips reopen easily, so you can add extra stems as you work.

3 As the plant grows, fix new stems into place until the framework is thickly covered with foliage. As the pot fills up with roots (around midsummer) the plant will begin to flower.

Below: During the summer, the developing pink buds of *Passiflora x caeruleoracemosa* produce these fabulous flowers.

CLIMBING AND TRAILING ANNUALS

Climbers can cover the greenhouse walls with color. Warmth-loving, large-flowered annuals, which do far better under glass than in even the most sheltered spot outdoors, are good for this situation. Growing individual plants in pots up canes adds high spots to a level staging display. To add yet another dimension, use trailing plants in hanging baskets. Since the plants are growing in pots, they can be rearranged or replaced for a new look.

Above: Ipomoea flowers only last for one day, but produce a rich succession of buds to keep them blooming most of the summer.

Right: The deep throat and tubular shape of mandevilla flowers is very appealing. This is 'Alice du Pont', an attractive, reliable, evergreen climber that grows to 10ft (3m). Unfortunately, it is not scented.

Supports for training plants

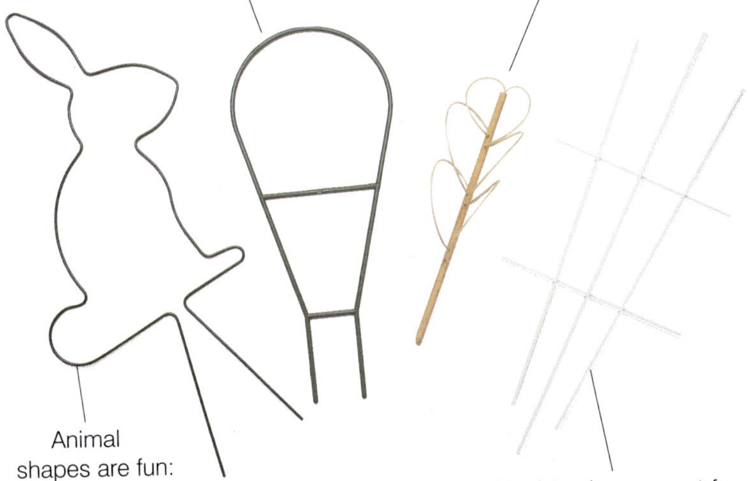

Propagating bougainvillea

Bougainvilleas are ideal climbers for a greenhouse, as they enjoy plenty of heat in summer (and, in fact, tolerate dry air and even occasional dry soil if neglected, without harm) but must have a cool spell at 45-50°F (7-10°C) in winter to allow flower buds to be initiated for the following year. Prune young stems to within 1in(2.5cm) of the main framework of stems in early spring to keep plants tidy. Use prunings for propagation.

1 Select healthy, semi-ripe, non-flowering shoots. Cut them into pieces, each with about seven leaves, just below a leaf joint. Remove a few lower leaves.

2 Removing leaves reduces water loss while the cutting is forming roots. If there are any large leaves on the cutting, you can slice or cut them in half.

3 Dip each cutting in water, then into hormone rooting powder. Insert the cuttings into peat pots of well-drained potting mixture and firm them in.

4 Keep the cuttings in a heated propagator set at 60-70°F(15-21°C). After about six weeks, roots should start to grow through the walls of the peat pot.

Right: *These cuttings were taken from a compact-growing cultivar,* Bougainvillea *'Raspberry Ice', which has bright red bracts and variegated foliage.*

THE GREENHOUSE IN WINTER

A greenhouse need not be left empty in winter. Even if there is no heating, you can raise a good range of winter salads in the soil border, plus spinach, early spring carrots, peas and spring onions from a sowing in the fall. On the staging, rock plants, hardy cyclamen, early spring bulbs and winter bedding, such as winter-flowering pansies or colored primroses, make a good display and flower much earlier. What is more, the flowers remain in perfect condition and are more easily enjoyed raised up on staging. Christmas rose *(Helleborus niger)* and camellias also make good temporary potplants for a cold greenhouse, brought in a few months before flowering for protection. For early spring flowers, sow hardy annuals, such as compact nasturtiums and calendula, in pots in the fall to decorate the staging. And in the soil border, sow taller hardy annuals, such as larkspur and cornflower, in rows for cutting in spring - long before outdoor flowers are ready. All will be cleared by late spring, leaving the greenhouse free for planting summer crops.

Left: Remove dead and diseased leaves from pelargoniums and cut the stems back to a few inches above the top of the pot in late fall to prepare plants for overwintering.

Below: Cyclamen flower in winter and spring, and need frost-free conditions during that time. Pots are best stood in a cool shady place outdoors during summer.

This is how a cyclamen looks just after it has finished flowering.

Remove the dead leaves and allow the potting mix to dry out slowly.

When flowers are over the leaves start to die back naturally.

General view of the winter greenhouse

Evergreen herbs for culinary purposes will keep in much better condition under cover than outdoors. Given some protection, the parsley will stay in leaf throughout the winter.

A late winter/early spring display of seasonal pot plants; these are fine for a greenhouse heated just enough to stay above freezing (in mild areas, no heating may be necessary).

These summer-flowering plants need a 'rest' during the winter when they are dormant; low temperatures and dryish potting mix are essential during this time and will encourage flowering during the following year.

Like bush fuchsias, standard fuchsias need a winter dormant period - cut the 'head' back to within a few inches of the main stem in mid-fall, and keep the mix dryish during the winter.

Early-flowering alpines flower weeks earlier than outdoors, and the protection of frost-free greenhouse keeps the flowers in perfect condition. Grown on staging, these tiny plants are easy to enjoy.

The border soil can be left uncovered and used to grow winter and early spring edible crops. If covered by staging, use the space for a heater, or to store mixes and pots for the spring jobs.

Above: Indoor azaleas prefer cool conditions, and thrive in a frost-free greenhouse in winter. Also use the greenhouse to keep plants that have bloomed in the house, after they finish flowering. Remove dead flower heads, and repot them in spring into a clay pot barely bigger than the previous one, using ericaceous potting mixture.

Below: Prune bush fuchsias hard in the fall when they finish flowering and leaves drop naturally. Water very occasionally in winter, to prevent complete desiccation.

Plants to overwinter in an unheated greenhouse

Alpine plants in the greenhouse

Rock plants appreciate cool, evenly moist conditions at the roots. In a 'plunge bed', where you water the sand not the pots, plants take up moisture naturally from below, with no risk of the crowns rotting.

1 Fill a deep tray with moist, washed horticultural sand. Stand the pots in shallow water to moisten the potting mix, then sink them into the sand.

2 As well as providing ideal growing conditions, the sand sets off the plants by making each one stand out individually. Water the sand just enough to keep it just moist.

Above: *In late spring, plant out these attractive flowering and evergreen alpines on a rock garden or repot them and plunge them outdoors in summer to reuse the following winter.*

A standard grape vine

1 Choose a young vine from a nursery with a single stem trained up a cane and as few side shoots as possible

2 Nip out the growing tip of the plant by gripping it firmly between thumb and forefinger.

3 Remove lower side shoots by twisting them out from the main stem, but leave the top four or five side shoots and nip out the growing tip of each. This will encourage branching, and begins forming the head of the plant.

Below: In temperate climates, you can use your greenhouse to grow dessert grapes that need warmth to mature and ripen properly.

GREENHOUSE FRUIT

One of the most fascinating uses for a greenhouse is to produce exotic fruit. Grapes are the first choice for most people. A single vine can be trained out along wires to cover one entire wall and roof of a greenhouse, and will produce a huge crop. However, the amount of shade it creates would prevent much else from growing in the same greenhouse. A much better way is to grow a vine in a pot and train it as a standard, which will give four to six bunches of fruit. Alternatively, you could train a double cordon vine against one end of the house, which would give a dozen bunches. Both methods still leave plenty of room for other plants.

Figs are very productive when grown under glass; choose true greenhouse varieties from a specialist nursery instead of simply growing outdoor kinds. Grow a fig in a pot to restrict the roots, train it as a standard or bush shape and each shoot will be crowned with ripening figs from late midsummer until fall. (To create a standard plant, nip out the shoots as shown here, but carry out more major pruning to reduce or reshape mature and overgrown plants during the dormant winter period.) Both greenhouse grapes and figs need little more than frost-free conditions in winter, when the leaves drop and the plants become dormant.

GROWING FIGS

Choose a greenhouse variety from a specialist nursery, and grow it in a large pot, tub or half-barrel about 18in(45cm) across and filled with a rich soil-based mix. From spring to midsummer when plants are making strong growth, feed weekly with half-strength tomato feed, and keep them well watered. In fall, the leaves drop and so reduce watering until the soil is nearly dry during the winter. Keep the winter temperature at 40-50°F (5-10°C); the higher it is, the more figs the tree will produce the following year. If the plants are kept warm in winter, three successive crops are possible in one year. A standard-trained tree kept at 40°F(5°C) during the winter can bear 50 fruit.

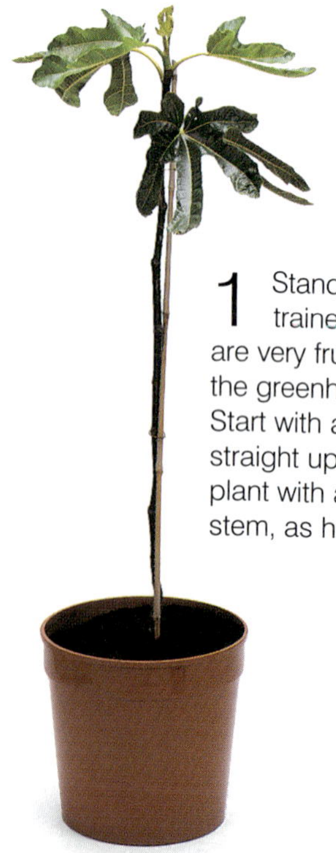

1 Standard trained figs are very fruitful in the greenhouse. Start with a good straight upright plant with a single stem, as here.

Strawberries in the greenhouse

Above: Bring potted strawberry plants into the greenhouse in late winter, after they have experienced a cold spell outdoors. Put in very good light; feed and water sparingly until flower buds appear.

Right: Strawberries fruiting in clay pots look good and are less vulnerable to pests and diseases.

2 Nip out the very end of the growing tip to encourage branching from the top of the plant.

3 After 'finger pruning', rub soil onto the cut to stop 'bleeding' that could weaken the plant.

4 Stop the side shoots when they reach about 3-4in (7.5-10cm) to form a neat head.

5 Fruits appear as little green swellings. Pick them when they change color and feel soft.

Citrus fruits in the greenhouse

Citrus fruits are evergreen and all but a few (notably kumquat and Meyer's lemon, which are happy at 45°F/7°C) need higher winter temperatures than grapes and figs. A huge range of different citrus plants is available, including pink grapefruit, variegated lemons (with both variegated leaves and fruit), tangerines and Jaffa-type oranges; for all these a minimum winter temperature of 50-55°F(10-13°C) is essential. If you cannot heat the greenhouse this much, keep the plants inside a plastic 'tent' with its own heater, so that only a small area within the greenhouse is kept so warm. Otherwise, move plants indoors in winter, and grow them in the greenhouse in summer only.

1 Citrus plants grown in containers do not need to be repotted every year, as they grow best when the pot is just about full of roots. Instead, topdress in spring; first, scrape away the top surface of the mix to a depth of about 1in(2.5cm).

2 If the exposed potting mix looks compacted, loosen up the next inch or so with the points of a dinner fork, taking care not to break any roots. Then replace with fresh potting mix to just below the rim of the pot. This will keep the plant growing well.

3 A standard kumquat makes a decorative evergreen tree for a greenhouse heated enough to keep the frost out; the fruit can be candied, or used to decorate summer food and drinks.

Below: *Meyer's lemon is the most reliable citrus fruit for growing in a frost-free greenhouse. Stand it outdoors on the patio in summer.*

GREENHOUSE VEGETABLES

A well-stocked greenhouse can provide year-round supplies of out-of-season salads and fresh vegetables, as well as hot-house crops that would not ripen reliably outside in the vegetable garden. Tomatoes are the single most popular greenhouse crop; six plants should be sufficient for the average family. Peppers and eggplants (aubergines) need similar growing conditions and routine care, and can conveniently be grown in the same house - a couple of each should be sufficient. Cucumbers and melons need warmer, more humid conditions than tomatoes, so are best grown furthest from the greenhouse door, away from drafts. Grow summer crops in the soil border, or in big tubs of potting mixture or growing bags. During the summer, they all need frequent watering, heavy feeding (liquid tomato feed is good for them all, though cucumbers and melons will appreciate a high-nitrogen liquid feed if available), and regular pruning, tying-up and training. If neglected, plants soon become overgrown and pests are hard to get at.

Growing cucumbers in a greenhouse

1 Support cucumber plants by twisting strings round the stems; avoid breaking leaves or bruising stems, since wounds are rapidly colonized by fungus.

2 Nip out side shoots where leaves join the main stems. Do not remove the tiny cucumbers that develop from the same place after plants are 18in(45cm) high.

Growing tomatoes in a greenhouse

1 Tomatoes make tall straggling plants that need support. Put young plants into their planting holes on top of the end of string supports.

2 Twist the string round the plant, threading it carefully between the leaves to avoid breaking them.

3 Twist the strings round the plants every week to support them as they grow taller. Twist in the same direction each time or the plants will 'unwind' themselves.

4 Regularly remove any side shoots growing between a leaf and the stem. Nip them out while they are small, and do not remove flower trusses by mistake.

3 Cucumbers need warmth and high humidity; overwatering can cause stems to rot, so keep young plants fairly dry until they are 3ft(90cm) tall. Feed little and often.

4 Modern all-female varieties of cucumbers are heavy yielding; they produce a succession of cucumbers all the way up the main stem. To encourage new fruit, pick as soon as the pointed end fills out.

5 Plants in growing bags dry out quickly, so water daily to keep the mix evenly moist (this avoids black patches at the blossom end of the fruit later) and feed often.

Below: Ghost spot is a form of gray mold (botrytis) that affects tomatoes. Avoid it by keeping the greenhouse well ventilated to prevent high temperatures and humidity. You can use a systemic fungicide spray, but this will not remove spots from affected fruits.

Below: Towards the end of the summer, reduce watering to encourage the tomatoes to ripen.

Vegetables all year round

Spring: *In early spring, sow fast-maturing crops, such as lettuce, spinach, early beetroot and baby turnips. The first of these will be cleared in time for planting tomatoes, with space becoming available for later peppers, etc.*

In early spring, start climbing beans or early potatoes in pots or growing bags. In mid-spring, start a few zucchini (courgette) plants. Move all these outside in early summer to provide early crops, weeks before those outdoors are ready.

Fall: *Tomatoes, cucumbers, etc. come to an end as the weather gets cold in mid-fall; this is the time to remove plants, clear away debris and fork over the soil. Sow or plant new crops for winter and early spring, such as lambs lettuce, some varieties of spinach suitable for fall sowing, over-wintering spring onions, many oriental leaf crops, such as pak choi, spring cabbage and cauliflower varieties that are suitable for growing under cover through winter.*

Eggplants (aubergines) in a growing bag

Eggplants (aubergines) and peppers in pots

Right: *Eggplants (aubergines) and peppers, including the hot chilli varieties, all grow well in pots of soil-based mix. They make bushy plants; support with short canes and feed and water as for tomatoes. Pick the fruit as soon as they are big enough to use. Green peppers and chilies will ripen to red if left on the plants longer.*

PEST CONTROL

The greenhouse environment not only suits plants, it also provides an ideal habitat for a wide variety of insect pests that enjoy the comfortable conditions and use the ready food supply to breed rapidly. Greenhouse gardeners need to be permanently alert, and take action before pests reach plague proportions. This need not mean using chemical sprays; nowadays, a wide variety of alternatives is available. Biological control uses live beneficial insects; they are supplied as dormant eggs or other immature stages, and must be ordered when needed and used on delivery - do not store them. Most biological controls should be used in early spring before pests are too numerous; extra heating may be needed since they need warmth to work. Pests to watch out for include red spider mite, barely visible pests that cause bronzing or yellowing of leaves. In heavy infestations, tiny webs are visible in the tops of plants; deter by keeping humidity high. Whitefly resemble minute white moths and are common on fuchsias and tomatoes; deter by spacing plants out. Aphids are found all year; these slow-moving green, cream, pink or brownish non-flying insects mass near the tips of shoots and under young leaves; take care not to introduce them on new plants. Scale insects, tiny, buff, limpetlike scales under leaves and on stems, are common on lemons, orchids and bay; use a systemic insecticide.

Biological control for whitefly

Left: Whitefly resemble tiny white moths that congregate on the backs of young leaves and only fly if the plants are disturbed. The young whitefly are 'scales' stuck tight under leaves, which rarely respond to chemical sprays, so biological control is the best way of dealing with them.

Right: The biological control used against whitefly is a tiny parasitic wasp, *Encarsia formosa*, which lays its eggs inside whitefly scales. The wasp larvae feed on the developing whitefly and affected scales turn black. *Encarsia* is supplied as eggs on cards which you hang onto the affected plants.

Biological control for red spider mite

Right: The biological control for red spider mite is an even tinier predatory mite called *Phytoseiulus persimilis* that eats them. Live predators come in small pots; open and hang these on the affected plants so emerging mites are close to their 'food'.

Left: Using a lens, you can see small red spider mites on the underside of the leaf. They pierce the leaves and suck out the contents of the cells, causing telltale discoloration.

Using nematode worms for vine weevil

Vine weevils are the fat white C-shaped grubs that eat entire root systems from cyclamen, primulas and other greenhouse plants. There is no effective chemical control; biological control using a special kind of microscopic nematode worm is the best solution.

1 Nematodes come as a freeze-dried 'powder'; mix with water as directed. Mid-spring and late summer are the best times to tackle vine weevil.

2 Stir the cloudy liquid into a watering can with a coarse rose and spray a steady film of nematode 'soup' over the soil in borders, gravel beds and pots.

Biological control for aphids

Left: The biological control agent used against aphids is *Aphidoletes*, a gall midge that lays its eggs near aphids and the small orange larvae that emerge feed on them.

Affected aphids turn into brown 'shells'.

Right: Midge pupae are delivered in small tubs; empty the contents in a pile on damp paper covered by pots close to affected plants.

Biological control for caterpillars

Above: Greenhouse plants may be attacked by caterpillars; if seen, use a bacterial biological control. This is based on a caterpillar disease caused by *Bacillus thuringiensis*. The sachets can be stored in a refrigerator before use.

Left: Mix the contents with water as instructed, and spray onto the plants where the caterpillars are feeding. This can also be used in the garden, such as for tackling caterpillars on cabbages.

Conventional pest and disease control

Many chemical remedies are available to tackle greenhouse pests and diseases. As yet, fungal diseases have no biological control, so using a fungicide spray is the best option. Always read and follow the instructions; check that the product is suitable for the affected plants (some say 'Do not use on ...'), avoid spraying open flowers, and with edible crops, allow sufficient time between spraying and picking.

Right: *One of the most widely seen diseases under glass in late summer and fall is powdery mildew, a mold that affects cucumbers (as here) and melons; tomatoes and pot plants can also be attacked. Spray with a systemic fungicide.*

Using a fungicidal spray

1 Dilute the fungicide with water as directed, using the bottle cap as a measure. Avoid getting the solution onto your hands and do not mix products.

2 Spray the plants thoroughly until droplets run off the leaves. Always mix fresh spray each time; do not store diluted chemicals as they deteriorate.

Using ready-mixed sprays

Left: *Some products are sold ready-mixed in 'trigger' operated containers that form their own spray gun. These are particularly convenient as no mixing is needed and you do not need to buy a sprayer.*

SITING A GREENHOUSE

In a small garden, there may not be much choice of site for a greenhouse, but selecting the situation with care can avoid practical problems later. A sunny site is essential for most greenhouse plants and a sheltered spot reduces the risk of glass breakage and reduces heating costs in winter. Avoid siting the greenhouse close to trees and large shrubs with branches that whip against glass and cause breakages on windy nights. A power supply close to the house lowers the cost of installing electricity if it is needed later on for heating, fans or a propagator. Avoid placing a greenhouse alongside a wall or fence so that you have good all-round access for repairs, timber treatment of wooden houses, etc. Ideally, make gravel or paved paths around the house.

Below: Metal-framed greenhouses are maintenance-free, but special fittings are needed to slot into glazing bars in order to install insulation, crop support wires, etc.

Right: A lean-to greenhouse on a house wall is cheaper to heat as it traps heat from the house, but the wall will cast some shade in the greenhouse for part of the day.

Below: Wooden houses are more expensive, but marginally warmer, look more natural and it is easier to fix shading or insulation materials to them. However, they need regular treatment with preservative to avoid wood rotting.

PART SIXTEEN

PRUNING AND TRAINING

Correct pruning and training will certainly improve the performance of any tree or bush. To prune effectively, you must have the right tools and know how and when to use them. Never prune simply for the sake of it; know why you are doing it and act with a purpose. This way, pruning will soon become second nature.

Bypass secateurs

Above: The two blades must be in contact throughout their length. Make sure the cutting blade is on the side facing the plant, so that any bruising is on the piece you are cutting off.

Anvil secateurs

Above: The anvil is wide so that any bruising will be on both sides of the cut. Keep the blade sharp and hold it at right angles to the shoot. If you hold it crookedly and apply pressure (right), you will crush the bark.

Using ratchet secateurs

1 Push the secateurs onto the branch as far as you can and squeeze the handles until they stop. The blade starts cutting. The click you hear as you release the handles is the ratchet moving up a notch.

2 Squeezing the handles again moves the blade further into the branch. Each time you squeeze and release the handles, the secateurs click and the blade slides easily through the branch.

PRUNING TOOLS

Secateurs are the basic and principal pruning tool. They are used for cutting shoots and small branches up to about 1in (2.5cm) across. With anvil secateurs, a single cutting blade presses against a plastic or alloy pad, or anvil. With bypass secateurs, a single cutting blade passes down the side of another blade in a scissor action. The non-cutting blade has a machined edge against which the cutting blade presses, producing a cleaner and more accurate cut with less bruising of the bark. Ratchet secateurs are similar to anvil secateurs and very useful for gardeners who do not have a very strong grip. They are very easy to use and make short work of cutting through small branches. Loppers are ideal for cutting shoots and branches that are too thick for secateurs. Long-arm pruners are invaluable for pruning tall trees or anything that you cannot reach from the ground. In fact, they are almost essential for that purpose, as the only other way to prune the tops is by using a ladder.

Saws should be used for pruning a lot more than they are. A good pruning saw will always have the teeth set so that it cuts best when pulled towards you. This produces good results and is also much safer when you are pruning up a ladder, as the pulling action draws you towards the ladder. Knives with a curved blade are useful for pruning thin shoots, while those with a straight blade are good for grafting. Keep knives sharp so that they cut smoothly.

Below: Choose the type of secateurs that suit you best and keep them in good condition. For some jobs, you will need to wear strong gloves, especially when dealing with prickly plants.

Loppers

Left: Loppers are really secateurs with long handles to give more leverage. They are ideal for pruning the thick stems of mature plants where access is difficult and a saw cannot be used easily, such as at the base of this *Berberis thunbergii atropurpurea*.

Long-arm pruners

Right: Long-arm pruners with a metal rod linking the handle and blade provide a precise cutting action. Here, the pruner is hooked around the branch and the cutting blade is halfway through the branch. If the hooked guide will not fit over the branch, then the branch is too big for the pruner to cut.

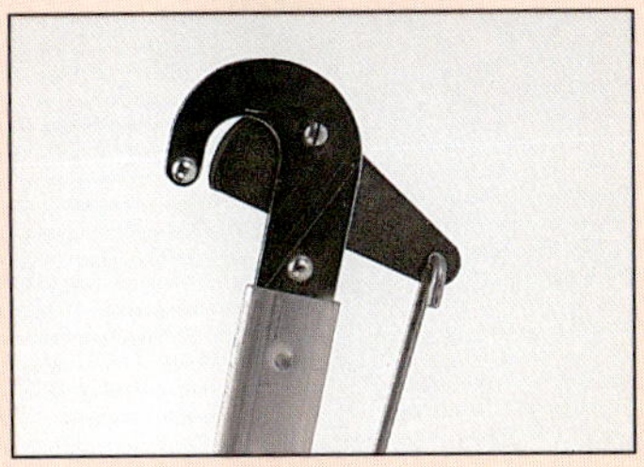

Above: With the handle pushed forward, the blade is ready to use. It may not be easy to hook a branch at an awkward angle or if there are branches in the way.

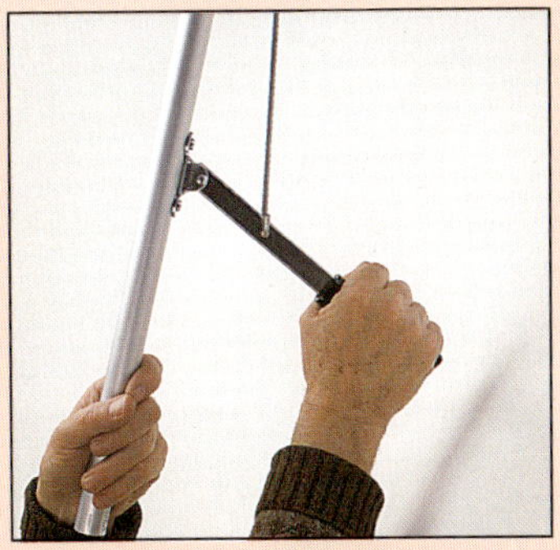

Above: Pulling the handle back closes the blade. If the branch is still attached after pulling the handle back, place the guide on the branch more closely.

Using a pruning saw

As a guide, it is best to use a saw on any branch more than about 1.25in(3cm) in diameter. You can cut straight through branches of this size at the appropriate place, taking the weight of the branch in your free hand just before it goes. Saw downwards without undue force from the top of the branch, using the weight of the branch to keep the cut open, but still controlling the branch with your free hand.

1 *When removing a branch that is too big for you to control fully with your free hand, start by making an upward cut from below at the point where the branch is to be severed.*

2 *Make a second cut above the first so that, as near as possible, they are opposite each other. Just before the two cuts meet, the branch is apt to fall suddenly, so be ready for it.*

3 *By first cutting the branch from below, you stop it tearing away that tongue of wood and bark that almost always occurs when a heavy branch is cut straight from above.*

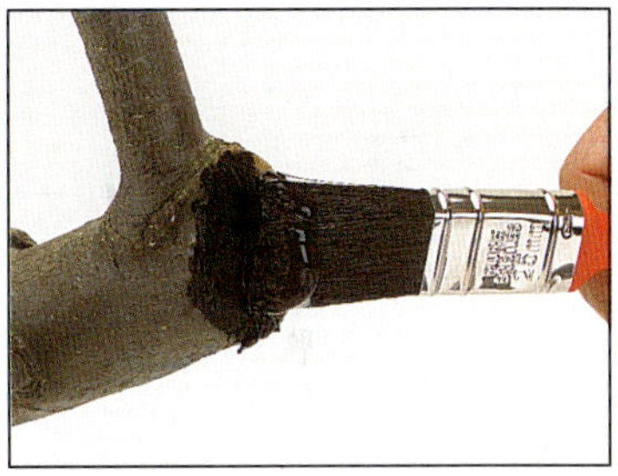

4 *Fruit trees (as here) tend to be more susceptible than many ornamentals to infection through large wounds; paint all saw cuts with a fungicidal paint as a precaution.*

Using a pruning knife

Left: *If you use a pruning saw with offset teeth, it leaves a rough finish. Pare away the outer edge, where the bark is, with a sharp knife. Paint the whole area with fungicidal paint. The smoothed edge will start the healing process quicker.*

PRINCIPLES OF PRUNING

Before you prune almost any plant, you should ask yourself two questions: 'How will a plant react if I do such-and-such to it?' and 'What should I do to make it do so-and-so?' In most cases, if a branch breaks or is cut off, a forest of shoots takes its place. This is fine if you want them, as you would with, say, buddleia, but what if you do not? In this case, you must decide whether it is a good idea to remove the branch at all. Shortening it may be more prudent. In other words, every cut that you make must have a purpose. Aimless snipping usually does more harm than good. On the other hand, if you do not cut out a certain branch, then a tree or shrub may become congested and flowering can be reduced because of a lack of young wood. Most flowering woody plants perform best when there is a good supply of new shoots, so removing old branch systems is often beneficial. The answer to the question of how to make a tree or shrub do what you want is not always so simple. However, there are ways of encouraging one bud to grow out and discouraging others. These techniques are described here and on page 313.

Left: Always prune close to a bud or another shoot so that no snag is left to die back. When using 'scissor' action secateurs, have the blade nearest to the bud and the pad on the outside.

Cutting to a bud

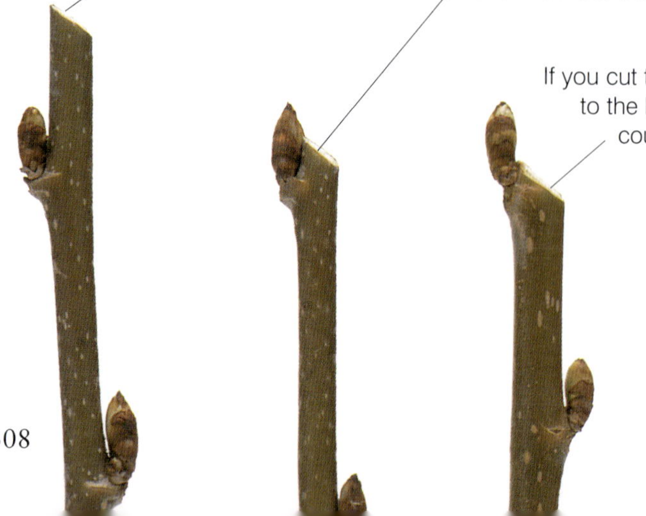

Shoots with alternate buds

Above: When you cut off the tip of a shoot, you remove the dominant effect of the former leading bud. This immediately causes the new top two or three buds to break into growth and form side shoots.

Shoots with opposite buds

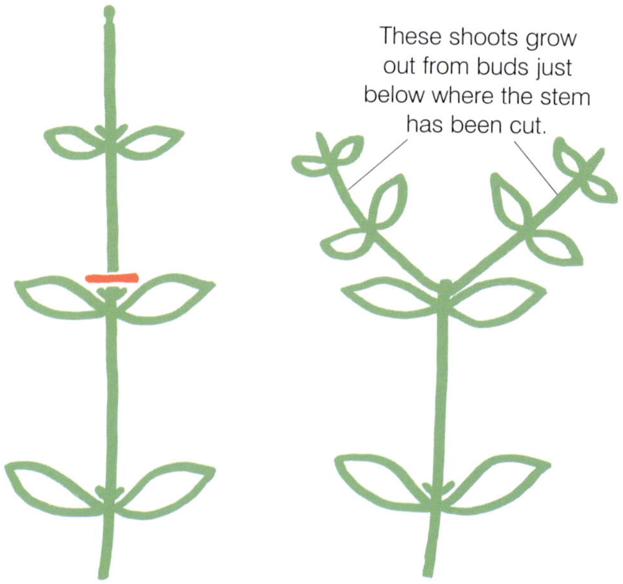

Above: A shoot with leaves set in pairs behaves in the same way. When its tip is removed, the pair of buds now at the top break into growth. Basically, any shoot reacts like this when its growing point is removed.

Pruning to affect branching

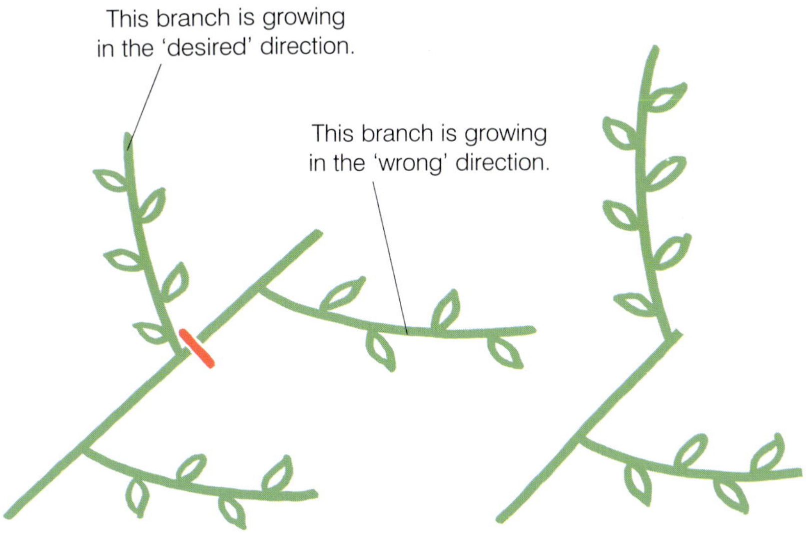

Above: This is a two-year-old shoot with side shoots. You can alter its direction of growth to any other direction by cutting it back to a side shoot that is already growing in the desired direction.

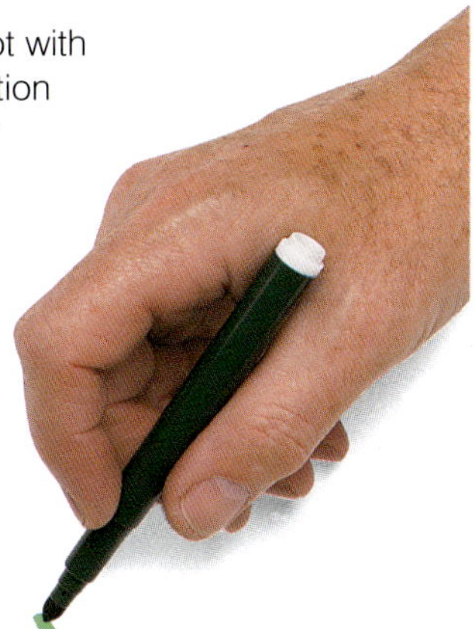

Pruning to change the shape

Above: Most young woody trees or shrubs can be made bushier by cutting back the central stem to a side shoot. This makes the new 'leader' (topmost shoot) more upright and encourages it and the lower shoots to grow strongly.

Maintenance pruning

Routine maintenance pruning is vital to keep many trees and shrubs in efficient 'working order' and looking good. Without it, they deteriorate. Do it correctly or the result could be worse than the original problem.

Right: *Prune back the tips of shoots affected by frost damage to good healthy growth in late spring after all frosts are over. This shoot is on a choisya.*

Below: *Remove seedheads from most ornamental plants. If left on, the plant has no need to produce more flowers and seeds and the flowering display will be cut short.*

Below: *Any vigorous, all-green shoots will soon dominate a variegated plant, such as on this* Sambucus. *Remove these all-green (or all-gold) shoots at once.*

Dealing with suckers

Above: *Most roses are budded onto seedling rootstocks. These suckers, with thin leaves and pale shoots, come from the rootstock.*

Below: *Remove rose suckers by pulling so that they bring some of the parent root with them. Do not cut them off or they will sprout.*

WHEN TO PRUNE

Understanding the two principles of pruning explained on page 308 will help you to decide when to prune your trees and shrubs. But another important point to bear in mind is that pruning is not always needed; it isn't compulsory. You should prune a tree, shrub or fruit plant only if pruning will improve its performance and not merely to satisfy a whim. If you do not prune a tree or shrub, no actual harm is going to come to it; it will merely operate less efficiently. This could mean fewer flowers and/or fruit, poorer flowers, less and/or weaker growth, poorer foliage and general untidiness. If you prune something in the wrong way or at the wrong time or, perish the thought, both, you will do infinitely more damage. On these pages you will find advice on when to prune ornamental trees and shrubs, and fruit.

EARLY-FLOWERING SHRUBS
There is no rigid line between early- and late-flowering, but early-flowering shrubs tend to produce their best and/or the most flowers on the previous year's growth. Prune these plants after flowering so that they have the most time in which to produce new shoots for flowering the following year.

ROSES
When you prune roses largely depends on when they flower. Tidy bedding varieties (hybrid teas and floribundas) and climbers in the fall and prune them in spring. Prune ramblers soon after their midsummer flowering. Treat shrub roses like other shrubs. Earlies are pruned after flowering and the lates in mid-spring. Prune roses with ornamental hips in spring.

HEATHERS
'Clipping' time is governed by when they flower. Prune spring-flowering ericas (heath) in early summer; summer- and fall-flowering ericas in late spring, and winter-flowering ericas and calluna (ling) in mid-spring. They are not really pruned in the classic sense, but clipped with shears or clippers to keep the beds or clumps compact and flowering well.

FRUIT
Apples and pears are usually pruned in winter, but prune trained trees in summer to encourage the formation of fruiting spurs. It is best to prune plums and other 'stone' fruit after fruit picking to reduce the incidence of 'silver leaf' disease. Most cane fruits are also pruned after fruiting. Bush fruits are usually pruned in early winter but prune cordons in summer.

TREES AND SHRUBS WITH FRUITS OR BERRIES
Most are early-flowering to allow time for the berries (botanically fruits) to develop before winter. Pruning after flowering would remove the embryo fruitlets. If needed, prune them in the winter or early spring. The emphasis must be on leaving as much flowering wood as you can; the flowers, after all, develop into the fruits.

LATE-FLOWERING SHRUBS

Shrubs flowering after about midsummer flower best on the current season's shoots. Prune them, if necessary, in the spring when growth is starting. This gives them several months in which to produce new shoots to flower later the same year. Do not prune them after flowering, because they would start growing again from the buds at the base of the pruned shoots. These would not mature and harden before the winter months and many would be killed by the frost and cold conditions.

CONIFERS

Conifers have their own individual shape and any pruning tends to interfere with this and spoil the plant. The main exception to this is conifer hedges. Clip them in spring, but fast-growing ones may need it in summer and early fall as well. If a conifer is damaged, administer first aid immediately (such as tying up) and any serious remedial work in the spring.

ORNAMENTAL SHOOTS

The beauty of these plants, such as *Cornus* (the dogwoods) and *Salix* (willows), lies in their juvenile growth, so prune them to produce as many shoots as possible. Mainly, it is the winter shoots that are the attraction, providing welcome color on dull days, so prune them hard in early or mid-spring. This encourages plenty of new shoots for the following winter.

The pruning year

This summary reflects the main pruning and training tasks through the seasons, but bear in mind that trees and shrubs will not always need pruning; the aim is to improve the plant's performance and appearance.

SPRING

Prune any fruit trees (though not plums) and bushes that were not pruned in winter, and also fall raspberries. Prune shrubs that have flowered since about midsummer, including winter and early spring-flowering ones, such as winter jasmine (Jasminum nudiflorum) *and* Forsythia. *Prune climbing and bush roses, plus any evergreens and conifers. This will include cutting back hard into old wood for rejuvenation. Clip or prune evergreen and conifer hedges. Prune* Salix *and* Cornus *being grown for their colorful stems.*

Above: *To prune potentillas after their first flush of flowers, simply grab a handful of shoots and cut them back as far as you can.*

SUMMER

After flowering, prune almost all shrubs that flowered in the spring and early summer. Prune cordon bushes of red and white currants and gooseberries in midsummer, and cordon, fan and espalier apples and pears in late summer. Prune plums after fruiting. Cut down the fruited canes of early raspberries when finished. Clip hedges. Deadhead roses, except those with hips, and other flowered shrubs. Summer prune wisteria. Prune rambler roses and tie in new shoots.

Above: *Once they are over, cut escallonia flowers off in summer to leave just growth shoots.*

FALL

Summer-prune trained fruit trees that were not mature earlier, along with later fruiting plums. Prune hybrid cane fruits and blackberries after fruiting and tie in the new canes. Cut down fruited canes of any summer raspberries not yet done. Cut off the dead heads of flowered shrubs. Lightly prune bush and climbing roses and tie in the shoots of the climbers. Tie in all trained fruit trees and climbers.

WINTER

This is the big pruning season for fruit trees (except plums) and bushes. It is best to wait until leaf-fall so that you can see better what you are doing. Prune trained fruit trees that were not summer-pruned. Spur back summer-pruned wisteria shoots. Prune most kinds of ornamental trees, except those that flower during winter and spring.

Using string to tie plants

1 Wind a length of string once round the support and then round the stem. String will only last about a year, so it is less likely to strangle a plant.

2 Tie the ends securely with a reef knot. Some thicker grades of string are very soft and will not chafe soft plant stems.

3 Snip off the ends of the string fairly close to the knot for tidiness. This brown string has been tarred to make it last longer.

TRAINING TECHNIQUES

Training is not always easy to separate from pruning because, very often, pruning forms a part of training, as in young trees and shrubs. In the main, though, pruning is connected more with the efficient working of a plant, whereas training is definitely a shaping operation. Now shaping may, of course, go hand-in-glove with 'production', as it does with cordon and espalier fruit trees. With ornamental trees and shrubs, there are other aspects to consider. Essentially, training involves making a tree or shrub grow in a way that it would not normally do. This can be done to a degree by pruning away the shoots and branches that are out of place but, sooner or later, you will have to secure shoots and branches in the positions that you want them to be. In its simplest form, this can mean tying one branch loosely to another but, with more formal types of training, you will need to erect some kind of support, such as a trellis or wires, to which you can tie the plant. There are many to choose from and you have to consider carefully the most appropriate kind for your plants.

A selection of plant ties

Inexpensive plastic-covered wire ties are useful for general tying work. Buy them ready cut or on a roll in a dispenser. Check them regularly.

Aluminum wire split rings are ideal for supple shoots; they expand as the shoots thicken.

Plastic split rings work on the same principle as aluminum ones and are just as convenient to use.

These plastic ties are an adjustable alternative to string for looping young shoots to canes and trellises.

String is cheap, versatile, can be treated with a preservative, and is available in a range of thicknesses and strengths.

These plastic clip ties are stronger than split ring ties. When assembled, they form a figure-of-eight shape.

Plastic clip ties

1 This plastic tie prevents the stem rubbing against its support by having a loop for each. First pass the tie around the cane.

2 Squeeze the tie to form a loop around the plant stem. Join the two ends by pressing the lug into the hole. It can be reused.

Fixing wires to a wall

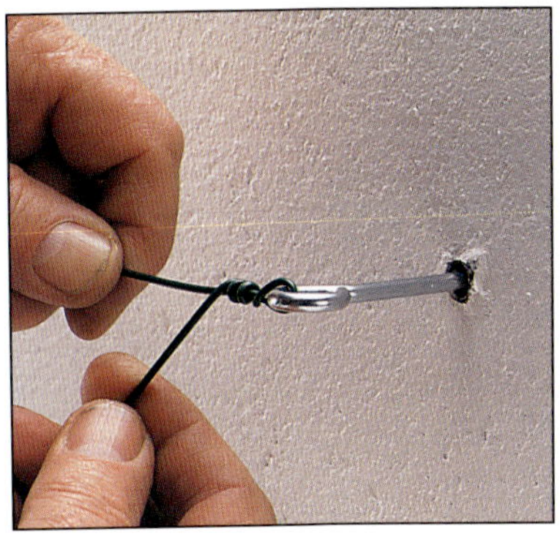

Above: Use screw eyes at each end of a run of wire to keep it away from the wall and allow room for tying in plant shoots. Twist one end of the wire through the first eye.

Above: To stop the wire sagging or coming away, drive in vine eyes every 6ft(1.8m). Thread the wire though all the vine eyes before attaching it to the final screw eye.

Plant supports

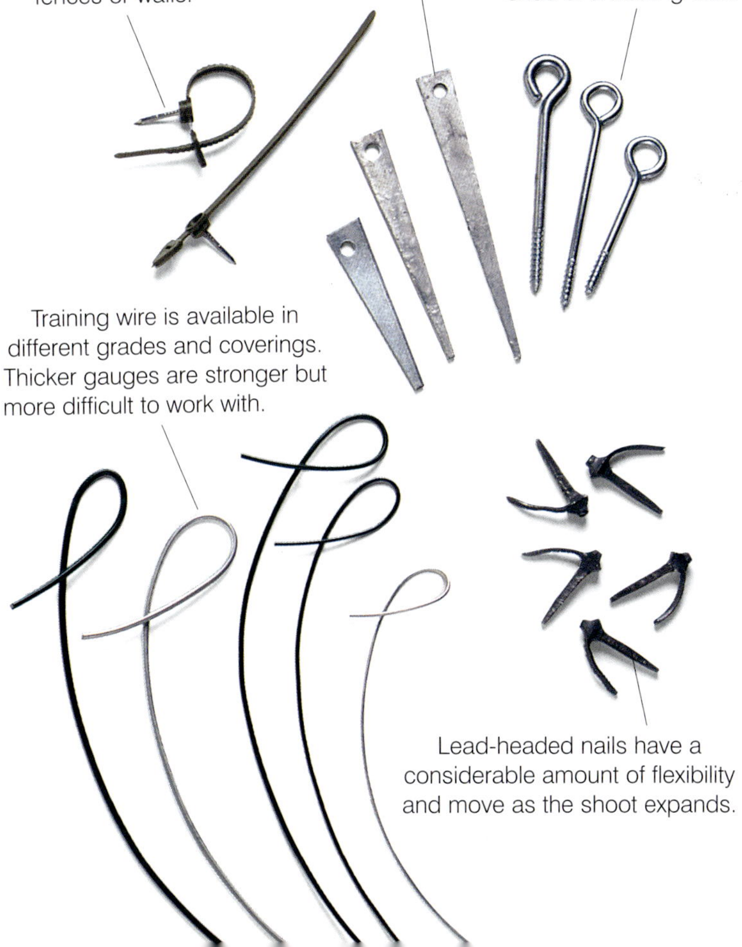

Notching and nicking

A growth bud will not normally grow out until buds above it are removed, but you can influence the development of a bud by cutting a small section out of the bark either above it (notching) or below (nicking). The effects of these techniques are shown here. It is important that the cut goes right through the bark but only just into the wood underneath.

Above: *Cut the notch 0.4in(1cm) above the bud. This has the maximum effect. Do this in winter.*

Above: *The completed notch. You can expect to see results soon after growth starts in spring.*

Sap flow in a stem

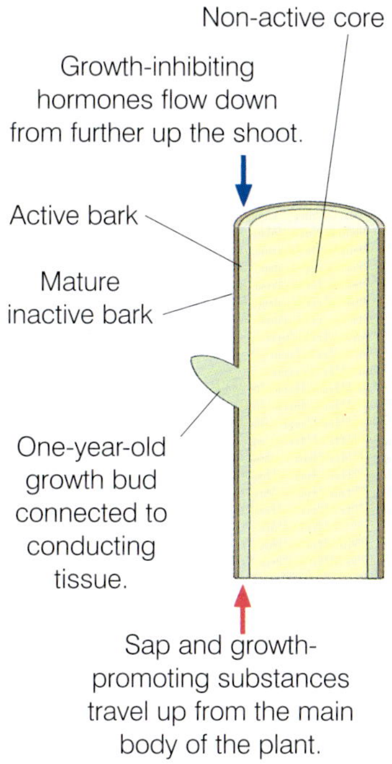

Notching

Cutting above a bud

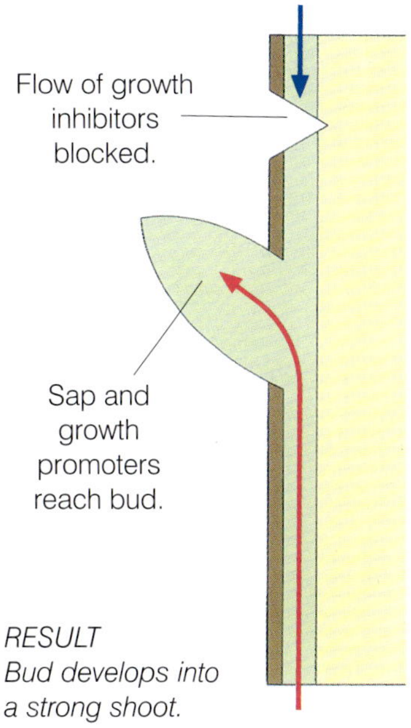

Nicking

Cutting below a bud

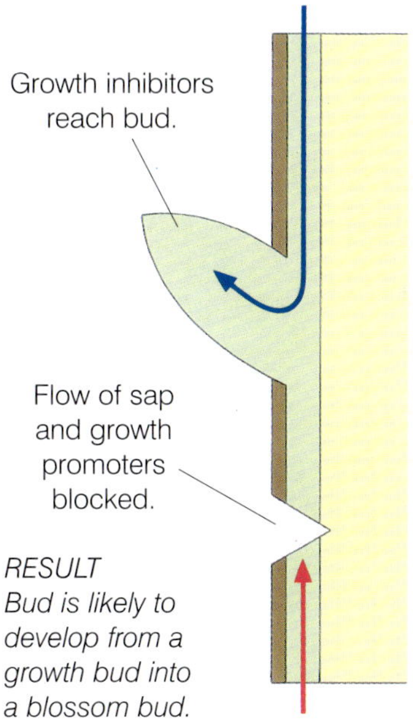

EARLY-FLOWERING SHRUBS

For the purpose of pruning, 'early-flowering' shrubs are those that flower before about midsummer. The correct and only way to find out which group a shrub belongs to is to look at the shoots with the best flowers. If these are the shoots that grew in the previous year (e.g. *Forsythia)*, then the shrub is described as 'early-flowering'. If the best flowers are on shoots that grew earlier in the same growing season (e.g *Buddleia)*, then it is 'late-flowering'. Shrubs that flower best on the previous year's shoots should be pruned straight after flowering to give the plant the longest possible time in which to produce long, vigorous shoots for flowering in the following year. Thus, a forsythia flowering in mid-spring will have the whole of the growing season until late fall to produce the following year's best flowering shoots. Remember, though, it is only the best flowers that will be produced on the new shoots; there will still be plenty of flowers on older shoots but they will not be of the same high quality. Pruning consists of cutting back or completely removing the oldest branch systems in the shrub each spring after flowering. This opens up the shrub and encourages the formation of new shoots and, at the same time, gets rid of some of the oldest and poorest flowering shoots. Pruning this group in the winter is entirely wrong, as it simply takes away flowering wood; leave it until after flowering.

Spiraea

Left: Cut straggly growth from the base with secateurs. Then cut below each spent flower head to just above a young, shoot lower down the stem. Trim long side shoots to restore the shape.

Right: Lovely spring-flowering *Spiraea* x *arguta* (bridal wreath), makes a medium-sized shrub with graceful arching branches. It is inclined to be untidy; if necessary, prune it after flowering to improve the shape.

Heather

Left: While heathers are young and recently planted, grasp each plant by the spent flower heads and clip them with secateurs. Clip established plants with shears.

Forsythia

Left: After flowering, remove the ends of stems that carried the current year's flowers. Cut just above an unflowered side shoot.

Above: Every branch of a well-grown *Forsythia* has the potential to be covered with vivid flowers.

Winter stems

Some of the shrubs with the most attractive winter stems are found among the dogwoods *(Cornus)* and willows *(Salix)*. Prune hard in spring.

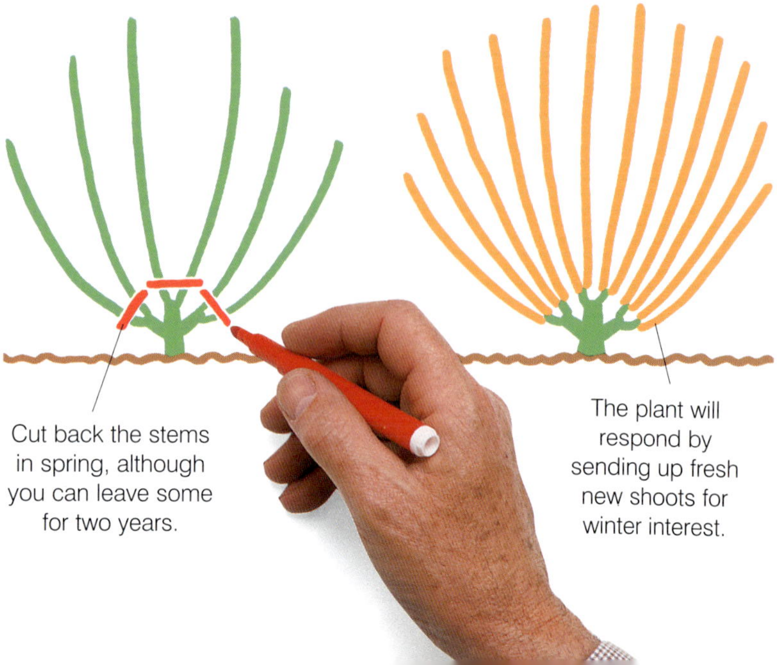

Hamamelis - dealing with suckers

1 Shrubs that bear two types of flower on one plant or a mass of non-flowering twigs (as on this hamamelis) may have developed suckers from the rootstock.

2 Trace non-flowering shoots or those with the wrong color flowers back to ground level and cut them out. If left, they would take over from the named variety.

Winter jasmine

1 The flowers are only produced on the previous year's shoots. Immediately after flowering, cut out all the weak, dead or dying shoots, regardless of whether they have flowered or not.

2 Cut back all the strong shoots that have flowered to about 1in(2.5cm) long, just leaving those that you want to keep to increase the size of the plant.

3 When a shoot of winter jasmine reaches the desired length, treat it just like any other shoot that has flowered and cut it back to a pair of strong buds.

Early-flowering shrubs

These shrubs are generally pruned in spring, after they have flowered on shoots that grew in the previous year. This keeps the plants young, and shapely and encourages healthy new growth.

Berberis: *Cut out old branches in late winter to keep the bushes open and young. Do this after flowering or in mid-spring for evergreen varieties.*
Buddleia globosa: *Remove twiggy growth in early spring to leave mainly strong shoots for flowering. If hard pruning is required, do it after flowering.*
Camellia: *No regular pruning needed. Remove or cut back over-vigorous shoots that spoil the shape of the bush as appropriate in mid-spring.*
Ceanothus: *Cut back wayward shoots on spring-flowering bushes. On trained plants, cut back all outward-growing shoots shortly after flowering.*
Chaenomeles japonica: *Thin crowded branches in bushes. With trained specimens, cut side shoots hard back after flowering. Trim hedges when blooms fade.*
Choisya: *If old bushes become leggy, cut them back quite hard after flowering and shorten long side shoots on wall specimens.*
Cornus: *For winter shoots, prune hard back to 2-3in(5-7.5cm) as growth starts in spring.*
Cytisus (some): *After flowering, snip back the young shoots that carried the flowers to keep them compact. Never cut into older wood, which seldom sprouts.*
Forsythia: *Cut out one or two old branches from* F. x intermedia *every year after flowering. With* F. suspensa, *cut back surplus long shoots at the same time.*
Hamamelis: *Only prune this shrub when necessary by shortening extra-long new shoots that threaten to spoil the shape and symmetry of the bush.*
Helianthemum: *Cut back or completely remove long, straggly shoots after flowering, along with the dead flowers.*
Kerria: *After flowering, cut back a high proportion of flowered shoots to the ground. Shorten remaining ones by a third to a half to keep them within bounds.*
Magnolia: *Prune deciduous species only if they really need it and then in summer, as wounds are slow to heal.* M. grandiflora *tolerates harder pruning .*
Mahonia: *Cut back the tall and showy species after flowering to prevent legginess. Low-growing* M. aquifolium *benefits from annual clipping in mid-spring.*
Philadelphus: *After flowering, cut back as many of the flowered shoots as possible, together with one or two older branches.*
Potentilla: *This shrub starts flowering in early summer on last year's shoots. Cut these back once the flowers have faded to encourage a second flush later in the summer. Then remove some old branches in the fall.*
Prunus (ornamental): *Little pruning is needed except shortening vigorous shoots to retain a good shape.*
Rhododendron (inc. azaleas): *No regular pruning but when leggy, cut back hard in mid-spring. Deadhead after flowering, taking care of the emerging shoots behind the flower head.*
Ribes: *Keep the bushes young and compact by cutting out some older branches every year after flowering, together with any that are spreading out too far.*
Rosa: *Specie and shrub roses flower from mid-spring onwards. Many are grown for their hips as much as for their flowers. Prune them all in early spring.*
Spiraea: *Keep early-flowering varieties, such as* S. x arguta, *young by removing old branches and cutting back others to younger shoots after flowering.*

LATE-FLOWERING SHRUBS

Late-flowering shrubs usually produce their best flowers on shoots that have grown during the current growing season. Prune these shrubs, if necessary, in the spring shortly before, or as, growth starts. This gives them the maximum length of time, i.e. several months, in which to produce and ripen the new shoots before flowering halts their growth. If you pruned shrubs of this sort straight after flowering, almost all the tender new shoots that grew out after the hard pruning would be killed during the winter. This is worse for the plant than if it had been left alone, because there will be far fewer strong buds left to grow out. You can carry out a secondary pruning (as with bush roses), in early winter to remove dead flower heads and any breakages. This only applies to plants that look untidy or are liable to wind rock.

Pruning hydrangea

Unlike most late-flowering shrubs, the mid- to late summer-flowering *Hydrangea macrophylla* Hortensia and Lacecap varieties produce their best flowers on strong shoots that grew the year before. Prune in spring, after winter frosts are over. Leave old flower heads of Hortensia varieties on until spring pruning to protect the terminal buds that produce the summer flowers. Deadhead Lacecap varieties after flowering.

1 When pruning the Hortensia hydrangeas, leave as many terminal buds (those on the ends of the shoots) as you can. They will produce the summer flowers. The old flowers protect the plant in winter.

2 Cut back dead flower heads to a strong growth bud. Cut back as far as 6in(15cm), or more, if necessary, to find a strong bud or to shorten a long, untidy shoot.

3 With nearly all the old flowers gone, reduce any congestion inside the bush. Overcrowding leads to weak and spindly shoots that are less likely to flower.

4 Shorten or remove any outer branches that are spoiling the overall shape of the bush. The final result is a well-balanced, shapely bush that should flower profusely.

PRUNING LAVENDER

Lavender needs regular pruning after flowering to stop it becoming sparse and leggy. You can snip off dead flower heads individually and dry them to use in lavender bags. Lavender is not a particularly long-lived plant, so replace it when it starts to deteriorate.

Left: Once flowers start to fade, trim the plants with secateurs or shears, removing the old heads and the tips of the young leafy shoots below them. Never cut back into old brown wood or you could kill the plant.

Right: Pruning lavender every year keeps the plant tidy and rejuvenated. This is *Lavandula spicata*, the old English lavender.

Pruning a newly planted buddleia

1 Establish a sturdy framework for a new plant by cutting back the main shoots to a suitable length in spring. This will determine the future shape of the bush.

2 Repeat the whole process with each stem until the plant is only a few inches tall. By the fall, several new, tall, flowering shoots will have developed.

Left: When pruned correctly, buddleia grows about 10ft(3m) tall and 6ft(1.8m) across. *Buddleia davidii* produces superb tall, arching shoots of scented flowers in white and lilac shades, much loved by butterflies.

Pruning hardy fuchsia

Left: When new growth reaches 2-3in(5-7.5cm) remove old wood that has been killed by frost. Make clean cuts with sharp secateurs.

Above: In areas without frosts, fuchsias still need partial pruning to ensure a good show. This is 'Dorothy', a fine hardy fuchsia.

Late-flowering shrubs

On the whole, late-flowering shrubs flower from midsummer onwards on shoots that have grown during the current growing season. It is fairly safe to assume that all ornamental shrubs in this category not mentioned below are pruned just before or as growth starts in spring.

Buddleia davidii: *In mid-spring, cut the flowered shoots back hard to about 4in(10cm) to encourage strong new ones.*
Ceanothus: *Late-flowering ones, such as 'Gloire de Versailles', thrive on hard pruning. In early to mid-spring, remove weak shoots and shorten the remaining side shoots to 6-12in(15-30cm).*
Cistus: *Older specimens need little pruning and, indeed, object to it most strongly. It is usually better to replace old bushes, as they seldom rejuvenate.*

Below: Cistus purpureus, *an excellent form with large pink blooms and deep green foliage.*

Deutzia: *In summer, as flowers fade, remove flowered branches with no young side shoots, and the occasional old branch.*
Escallonia: *Lightly cut back bushes after flowering or in the spring. Cut back side shoots on trained plants after flowering.*
Fuchsia: *If the top growth is killed in winter, cut shoots back to ground level as soon as new growth appears in the spring.*
Genista: *Late-flowering brooms, e.g.* G. hispanica, *need little pruning. Remove or cut back long shoots in early spring.*
Hebe: *Deadhead after the flowers fade. If hard pruning is required, do this in mid-spring.*
Hibiscus: *In spring, shorten the odd young shoot of* H. syriacus *to encourage branching.*
Hydrangea: *Leave the dead flower heads of the 'hortensia' (mophead) kinds until the spring to protect the flower buds. Cut out weak and twiggy shoots after flowering.*
Hypericum (shrubby): *During early and mid-spring, shorten the previous year's strong shoots by a quarter or more. Otherwise, just aim to keep the bushes tidy and compact.*
Lavandula: *Cut off the old flower stalks and trim the bushes in late summer after flowering. If any hard pruning is needed to correct legginess, do it in spring.*
Lonicera: *To keep shrubby winter honeysuckle young and relatively compact, shorten over-vigorous flowered shoots in the spring.*
Viburnum (some): *No regular pruning is needed. Remove out-of-place shoots and cut back over-vigorous ones. Do this in mid-spring for fall- and winter-flowering kinds and evergreens.*

Below: *The compact* Viburnum tinus *'Eve Price' has pink buds and white flowers in the fall.*

PRUNING ROSES

With the exception of rambler roses, which are pruned after they have finished flowering in summer, most roses, including hybrid teas and floribundas, are best lightly pruned in early winter and properly pruned in mid-spring. Lightly pruned bushes can rest in winter and will not rock about in stormy conditions. If a hole were to develop in the soil around the neck of the bush, it could fill with water and start a rot in the bark. There is one important exception to this general rule; roses that are grown as much for their ornamental hips as for their flowers, e.g *Rosa rugosa* and *R. moyesii* 'Geranium', are pruned in spring to allow their hips to develop fully and stay on the bushes as long as possible. After a mild winter, growth can start in early spring and you cannot bank on the early growth surviving. That is why it is best to delay the second pruning until the worst of the winter is over. Hybrid teas and floribundas are pruned in almost exactly the same way. The only real difference is the severity. The floribundas are not pruned as hard as the teas because the aim is a good display of many flowers, whereas the teas should have fewer but larger blooms. The length to which you cut back the individual shoots in spring will depend on their vigor. Cut back strong hybrid tea bushes to about 12in(30cm) high. Cutting them almost to the ground is going too far, unless they are being grown specifically for show. The extra hard pruning makes them produce later but larger flowers. For ordinary garden flowering, it is better to have the flowers earlier and more of them.

Bush roses - fall pruning

It is important to prune rose bushes lightly in the fall. Do not prune them any harder than necessary. Remove flowers, buds and hips, and cut back long shoots by about a third of their length (those taller than 24in/60cm). Remove broken and out-of-place shoots. This is not a proper pruning, just an opportunity to make the bushes smaller and tidier.

1 A hybrid tea rose bush in early winter. Remove the long shoot to leave it about 24in(60cm) long.

2 Cut out branches with hips, as they take energy from the plant. Remove them before winter.

Bush roses - spring pruning

In spring, first tackle any shoots that are clearly in the wrong place or causing overcrowding. Add to these any that are too weak and feeble to carry decent flowers. Cut both kinds right out or shorten them to a strong bud pointing in the appropriate direction. Cut back the strong shoots on floribundas to about 18in(45cm) long.

1 Cut dead branches back to their point of origin. Use a saw or loppers on thick branches.

2 Remove any dead stems or branches left over after the plant's light pruning in the fall.

3 Cut back this tall branch by about half its length to a bud pointing in the desired direction.

4 Hybrid tea roses need this treatment to perform well. Prune floribundas more lightly.

Climbing roses

The strategies for pruning climbing and rambler roses are very different. Climbers are normally vigorous growers and often sports (mutations) of hybrid teas or floribundas. In the early years, they are pruned to encourage them to grow quickly and cover the area allotted to them. Later, the aim is to create a good balance between growth and flowering. Much of the framework of branches stays, because the best flowers are found on the vigorous shoots growing from them.

1 Naturally weak climbers do not produce many new shoots each year. Shorten and keep some of the older ones for another year. Cut out spindly old growth and over-long new shoots. Cut flowered side shoots hard back.

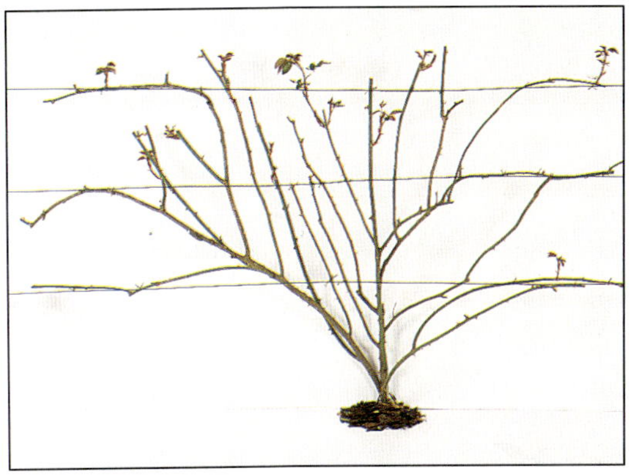

2 Spread out the pruned stems and tie them back to the supporting wires with soft string. Creating stress on the branches by bending them in an arched fashion persuades climbing plants to produce maximum flower and shoot from the base.

Rambler roses

In rambler roses, the long vigorous shoots grow one year and flower the next, after which they are pruned fairly radically. After flowering, towards the end of summer, untie them from their supports and spread them out on the ground. Identify the long shoots that have flowered and either cut them out completely or shorten them to a vigorous shoot of the current year's growth arising from near their base.

Right: A neat, tidy plant in winter and a blaze of summer color is the reward for correct and timely pruning and training. Ramblers have just one flush of flowers, but this can last for several weeks and is often spectacular.

Shrub roses

The term 'shrub rose' is a fairly loose one, and refers to specie roses, all the old-fashioned varieties, the moss roses and English roses. They are called 'shrub roses' because they are grown like - and look more like - shrubs than conventional rose bushes. Like other flowering shrubs, the shrub roses are largely pruned according to when they flower: early ones after flowering, later ones in the spring as growth starts. As with many flowering shrubs, the aim of pruning is to keep bushes young and flowering strongly by removing old and worn out branch systems and by shortening back any over-vigorous young shoots. Try to maintain a full, but not overcrowded, young plant. Deadhead those plants that you are not saving for their hips.

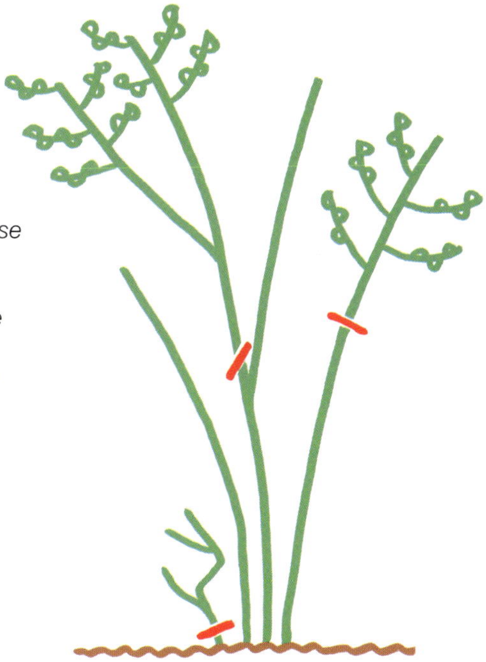

***Above:** Cut back weak basal growths. Prune older branches to young growth, and sections of flowered stems to a strong bud.*

Standard roses

A standard rose is a bush rose, propagated like any other rose but onto a stem that gives it height. Similarly, a shrub standard is a shrub rose on a stem and a weeper is a rambler on a tall stem. The same pruning principles apply to a standard variety as to the normal form, but bearing in mind the eventual shape of a standard in full flower, you may decide to keep a branch that you would have cut from a bush.

1 Start by thinning out the plant, removing all the twiggy growth, including any broken or strained branches. Always cut back to within about 0.25in(6mm) above a bud.

2 Cut the plant back by two-thirds to threequarters of its original size. Cut the long central branches to achieve the desired flat top. If any more weak growth comes to light, prune it out.

Pruning clematis

Pruning clematis is based on when they flower. Those flowering in spring or early summer do so on the previous year's shoots. If needed, prune them after flowering. Prune hybrids, and others that flower after about midsummer, in spring as growth starts. They flower best on the current season's growth, so cut them to within 1-2ft(30-60cm) of the ground. If not pruned, the flowers appear higher up the plant each year.

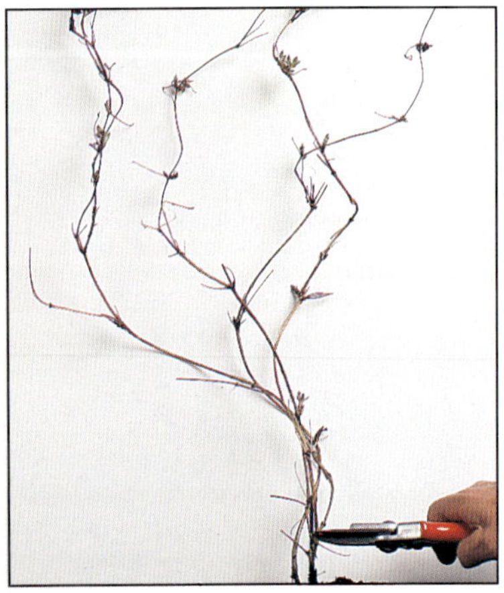

1 Clematis that bloom from midsummer onwards flower on shoots that grew earlier in the same season. Prune them in early spring after the first signs of growth.

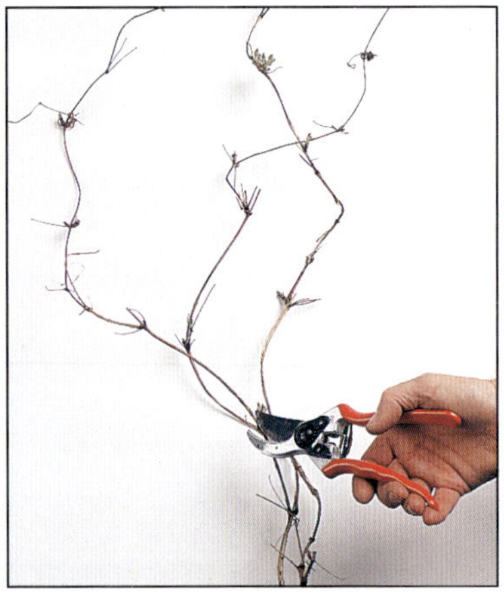

2 You need not prune every shoot every year; any left will carry on growing before they flower. This could result in flowers 10ft(3m) or more above ground level.

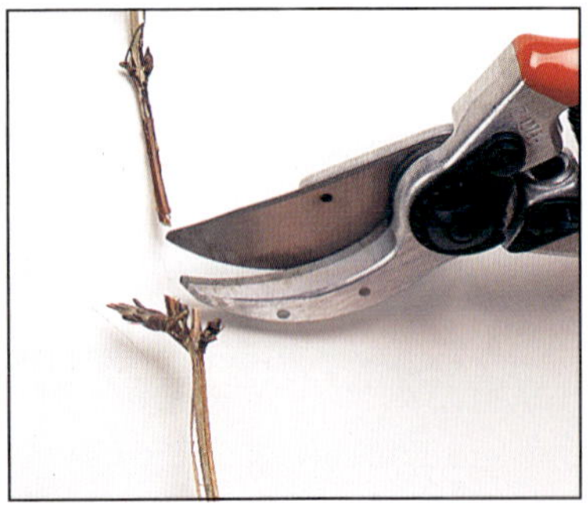

3 Always cut back to a live bud to avoid leaving snags that may become infected by fungal diseases. The direction in which the bud is facing is of no importance.

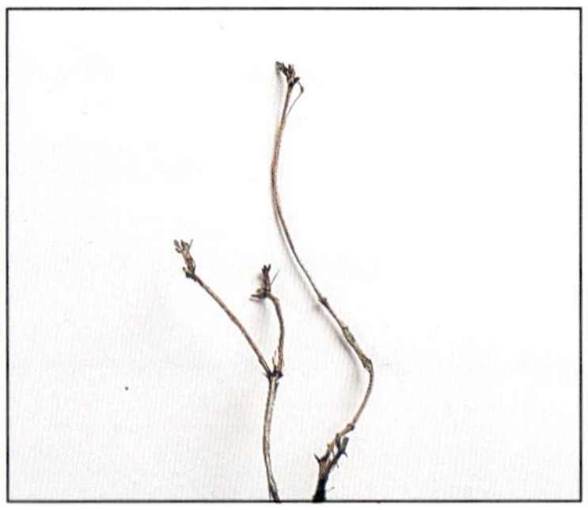

4 Many gardeners pruning late-flowering clematis for the first time are anxious that the severe treatment will kill the plant, but this is how it should look in the end.

Left: Pruned in spring as shown above, *Clematis* 'Nelly Moser', a very popular, large-flowered hybrid, will provide a reliable show of flowers.

WALL SHRUBS AND CLIMBING PLANTS

There are two definitions of a wall shrub. It is either any shrub that is not a climber but which is planted against a wall for support, or it is a shrub on the borderline of hardiness that is grown against a wall for protection from the weather. Because plants in the first category are perfectly hardy, a wooden fence would serve as well as a wall. However, true wall shrubs form quite a large group of plants that actually need the extra warmth or shelter from cold winds that a wall provides. By training them to a warm wall, you are showing them off better, as well as giving them more favorable growing conditions. Because there are many different kinds, shapes and sizes of wall shrubs, there is no one training system that does for all.

In contrast to wall shrubs, climbers have the means to hang on to a support with little or no help. They might twine around other plants, as honeysuckle does, hang on with tendrils, like clematis, or have aerial roots or 'suckers', like ivy. Climbing and rambler roses and the blackberry family climb by using their thorns. Without anything to climb up, all these plants would collapse. In gardens, most climbers need a little help at first; once started off, they carry on by themselves. There are also what might be called 'scramblers', such as winter jasmine and periwinkle. These will clamber up a support, but will run along the ground if not trained and secured. How you prune and train climbers depends on the plant in question.

Below: *Clematis orientalis* needs little pruning. If necessary, prune quite hard in spring; you may lose a year's flowers by doing this.

Above: Only prune *Clematis montana* when it has outgrown its position. Then, in spring, pull it down, cut back dead and young shoots and retrain the older wood. New shoots will soon grow.

WISTERIA

Both *Wisteria sinensis* (Chinese wisteria) and *W. floribunda* (Japanese wisteria) are vigorous climbers that can reach up to 100ft(30m), possibly damaging roof tiles and masonry. Once established, cut back new growth to 6in(15cm) in midsummer and, further, to 2in(5cm) in winter. This encourages flowering spurs instead of just new shoots.

Honeysuckle

1 Tie the shoots to the support rather than twine them back and forth through the trellis; this can easily strip buds off the shoots.

2 A fairly hard first pruning enables the plant to build up a strong framework with plenty of radial shoots. Prune to a live bud.

3 A young honeysuckle that was pruned back quite hard after planting grows away well and soon covers the area allocated to it.

Left: There has been much hybridization of honeysuckles. This *Lonicera* x *tellmanniana* is a hybrid between an American and a Chinese species. It bears attractive, but unscented, apricot yellow flowers.

Using trellis panels for climbing plants

Above: *A wooden trellis panel with the horizontal battens fixed directly to the wall may restrict plant growth due to the lack of space behind the cross pieces.*

Above: *Turn the panel round and the cross pieces are held away from the wall by the vertical battens. This might give climbers their best chance to develop.*

Forsythia

Although you would not normally grow Forsythia x intermedia *against a wall, it makes an excellent subject, flowers earlier and represents many shrubs that can be similarly treated.*

1 Using plastic-covered wire or string, loosely tie in the main shoots (here there are four), so that they cover a wide area of the frame. Cut out any weak, out-of-place shoots, plus any branches that are not needed.

2 Cut away any shoots that are growing straight out from the plant, as they will not be suitable for bending back towards the support later on. Always use sharp secateurs.

3 Lightly trim the remaining branches to encourage side shoots. With spring-flowering shrubs, you need plenty of new growth to produce abundant flowers the following year.

PRUNING TREE FRUITS

It goes without saying that we grow fruit trees and bushes to produce fruit. However, it is the earlier stage - flowering - that is influenced by pruning. The first thing to remember is that a fruit tree or bush will fruit tolerably well if it is not pruned at all. After all, this is what happens in the wild. Any pruning that we do, therefore, must be aimed at improving flowering and hence, fruiting. This may sound simple, but you need to know what you are doing before you can judge its effect. The next point is that, certainly with tree fruits, a vertical branch tends to grow at the expense of fruiting. If you cut back the tall shoots at the top of large fruit trees, they immediately grow more strongly and rigidly. However, if you allow them to fruit, the weight of the crop will bend them over and growth is dramatically reduced. On the other hand, a horizontal branch fruits at the expense of growth. This is clear to see in espalier-trained apple and pear trees, where the cropping branches are in horizontal pairs on either side of a vertical central stem. In fact, for their first year or two, the young branches are trained more upright, as they would take too long to grow out horizontally. The final point is that there must be a reason for every pruning cut you make. No snipping about in complete ignorance; it can do more harm than good. Always use the most appropriate tools for the job. It is vitally important to cut shoots and branches cleanly and effectively; ragged and bruised pruning cuts are among the main entry points for fungal diseases. Bear these thoughts in mind and you are halfway towards understanding pruning.

Apples

As we have seen, correct pruning improves both a plant's efficiency and its appearance. Although apple trees are available in many shapes and sizes, the reasons for pruning them are largely the same as for any other plant: first, to form and shape the tree and, later, to create and maintain the correct balance between growth and fruitfulness. If an apple tree is growing furiously, it will seldom fruit well.

Left: This is a blossom/fruit bud that developed from a growth bud during the tree's second growing season.

This new shoot grew from what was a one-year-old shoot (lower down). The wrinkles are the changeover point. Both are now a year older.

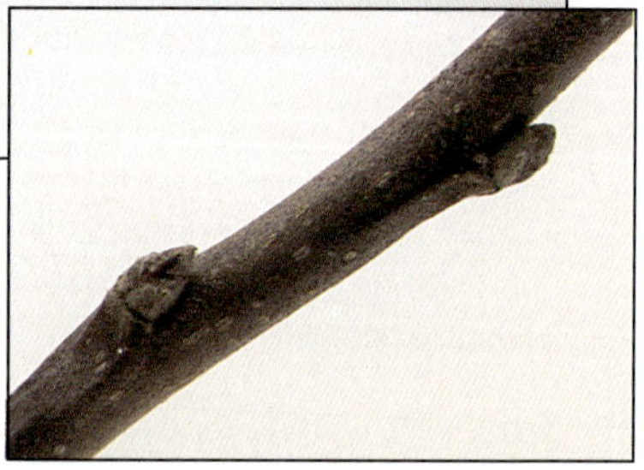

Right: A one-year-old apple shoot in its first winter. The two buds could grow into shoots next year or stay dormant or fatten into blossom buds.

Below: A few apple varieties carry much of their fruit on the end of small shoots, as here. These are known as tip-bearing varieties.

Above: Some apple varieties bear most of their fruit on spurs, as here. Each of the 'spur' systems, or 'fruiting spurs', develops from a single fruit bud that carried fruit. Reduce the size of overcrowded spurs to improve fruit quality.

Pears

In general, ordinary garden pear trees (not the trained sort) are pruned more lightly than their apple cousins. They fruit better when left wisely alone. Only prune them when they really need it by virtue of their size and/or shape. As a species, they also form fruiting spurs more readily than do apples, so they are ideally suited to training as cordons and espaliers.

Right: One of the most successful garden varieties is 'Conference'. It tastes pleasant and crops reliably. While it does not thrive on neglect, it needs no intricate pruning.

Peaches and nectarines

In temperate climates, grow peaches and nectarines against a warm and sunny wall for best results. This is most easily done by training them fan-shaped to canes that are themselves tied to wires. Remember that peaches and nectarines only fruit on shoots that grew the previous year.

Right: Thinning the fruitlets of peaches and nectarines will allow the remaining ones to develop into full-sized and well-colored fruits.

Below: This young peach tree is being fan-trained on horizontal wires against a wall. Train the outer branches first because they grow more slowly than the more upright ones in the center of the tree.

Plums and damsons

Growing fan-trained plum trees against a sunny wall is feasible, but the trees may be difficult to restrain where space is limited. Even using the less vigorous 'Pixy' rootstock, you will need 10-12ft (3-3.7m) of space on a 6ft(1.8m)-high wall. 'Festooning' is a good way of growing plums.

Right: To grow a tree in a festoon shape, start with a one-year-old tree. Without shortening any side shoots, bend them all downwards and tie them to the main stem. Repeat this in subsequent years at the end of each growing season.

Cordons, espaliers and step-overs

Above: *Oblique cordons are probably the most efficient way of growing several apple and pear trees in a small space. Most will readily form fruiting spurs.*

Above: *Criss-cross cordons have two stems instead of the usual one. Plant them 1yd(1m) apart with the stems trained at 45° so that they cross over.*

Left: *The step-over, or horizontal cordon, is another attractive and space-saving way of growing apples. Grow it beside a path to make it easy to tend. Summer pruning will improve the fruits' size and color.*

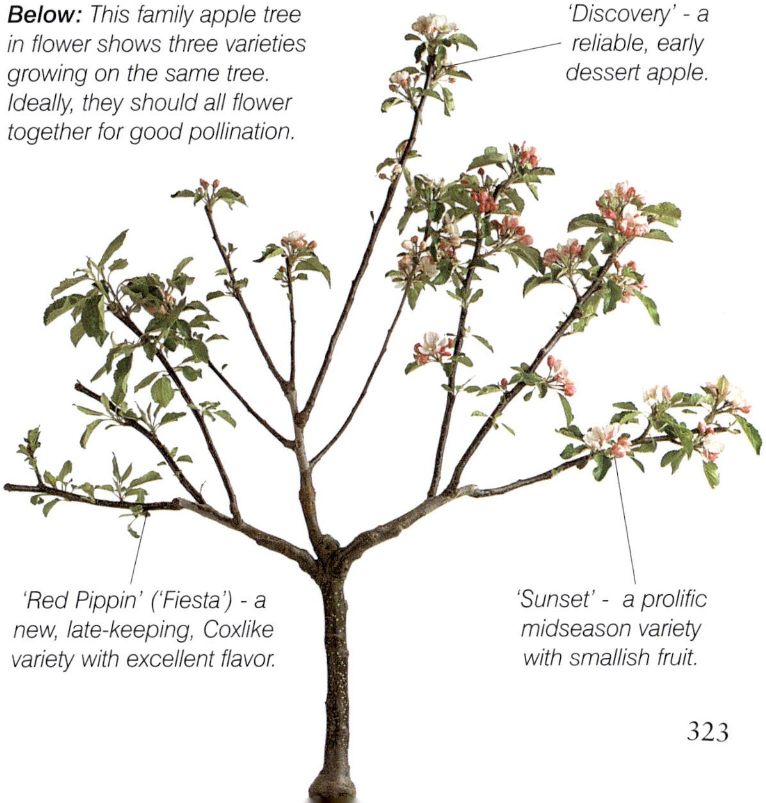

Below: *This family apple tree in flower shows three varieties growing on the same tree. Ideally, they should all flower together for good pollination.*

PRUNING SOFT FRUITS

It is important to prune bush and cane fruits to ensure that they remain healthy and carry heavy crops. In the early years, the aim is to build up the bush. After that, you must establish and keep a good balance between growth and fruiting. Bush fruits, such as blackcurrants, redcurrants and gooseberries, are not necessarily pruned in the same way. Blackcurrants produce their best fruit on the young shoots, whereas the others do so on spurs that are encouraged to develop on more or less permanent branches. These different managements are achieved almost entirely by appropriate pruning. Blackcurrants cannot be grown as cordons, fans and standards, but redcurrants and whitecurrants and gooseberries can. Blackcurrants should not be summer pruned; the others can be and definitely benefit from it.

Cane fruits include raspberries, blackberries and hybrids, such as the tayberry. Summer raspberries are pruned straight after fruiting whereas fall-fruiting varieties are cut back in the spring. Raspberries, along with some blackberries and the hybrids, usually have the fruited canes cut right out after fruiting. Some types, though, produce fewer new canes and the fruited canes are partially retained.

Gooseberries, redcurrants and whitecurrants

These bush fruits carry their best fruit on the older wood, so pruning with this in mind is essential. If a bush becomes cluttered with old branches, then cut these right out at their point of origin; it is simply not worth trying to make them smaller; just get rid of them.

Training summer-fruiting raspberries

It pays to prune and train summer-fruiting raspberries properly because, if these tasks are not carried out correctly and at the right time, results will be poor.

Below: If, after tying in, the tops of the new canes reach well above the top wire, bend them over and tie them down to prevent damage.

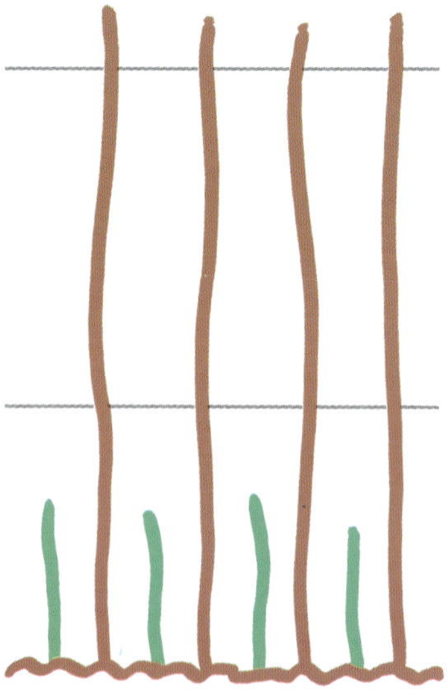

1 During the growing season, the one-year-old canes tied to the wires will develop fruit. At the same time, new canes are growing that will fruit the following year.

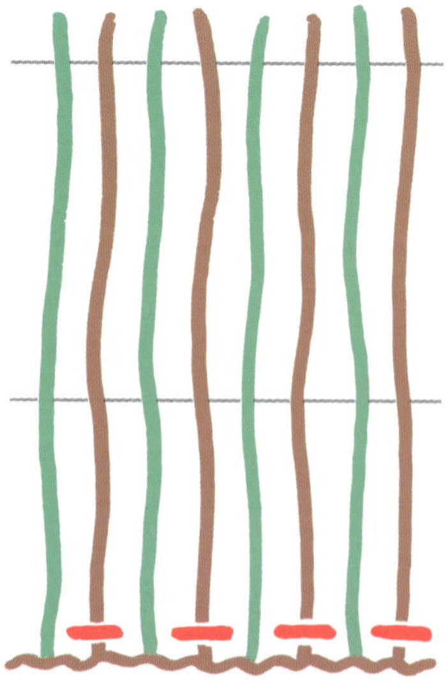

2 At the end of the season, the new canes will be as tall as those that fruited. Cut down the fruited canes to leave room for the new ones to mature and ripen.

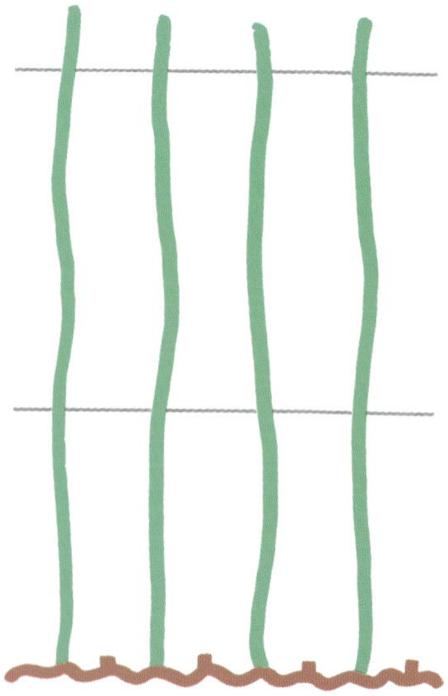

3 With the old canes out of the way, tie in the strongest and healthiest of the new canes 4in (10cm) apart on the top wire. Cut out any weak or diseased canes.

Blackcurrants

Blackcurrants are usually pruned in early winter by cutting out branch systems at three years old. Establish the age of a branch by counting backwards from the young shoot at the tip; each year's growth is darker.

Left: A one-year-old shoot. The fruit buds will carry fruit the following summer. Do not remove a shoot like this.

1 Even a well-tended bush can seem daunting when you come to prune it. In fact, you need only follow a few simple rules.

2 Cut out all branches that are more than three years old and any growing too close to the ground or across the bush.

3 Tidy the bush by cutting back any growth that extends beyond the space you want the plant to occupy.

4 Cut long shoots right out. Shortening a young shoot encourages growth and branching, which makes it even larger.

Right: The variety 'Ben Sarek' is a newcomer among blackcurrants. The bush is significantly smaller than other varieties, yet it is heavy cropping.

Blackberries and hybrid cane fruits

Of all the soft fruits, these are the ones that most need pruning and training. If neglected, they become completely unmanageable. You will need good secateurs, probably loppers as well and thick gloves.

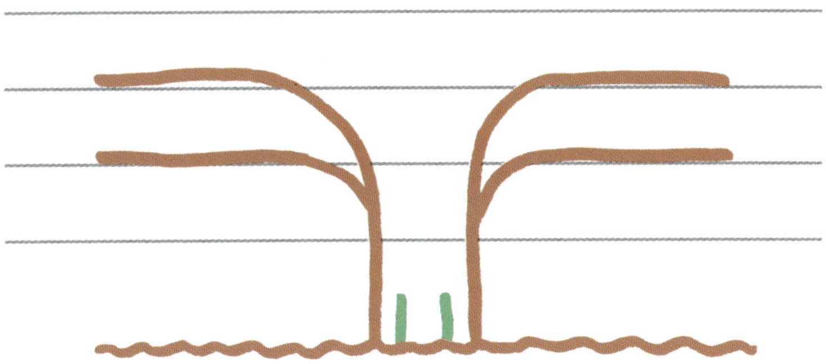

1 Make provision for the new canes to grow up the middle of the plant to lessen the risk of disease infecting them from the older canes.

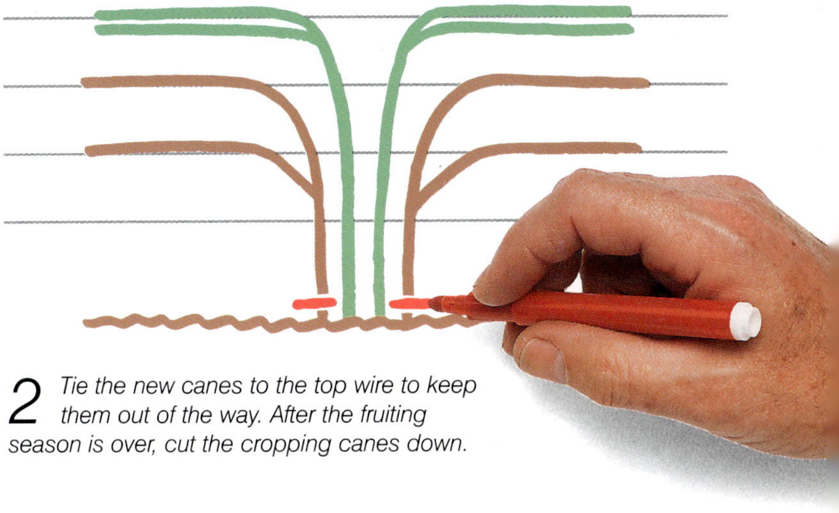

2 Tie the new canes to the top wire to keep them out of the way. After the fruiting season is over, cut the cropping canes down.

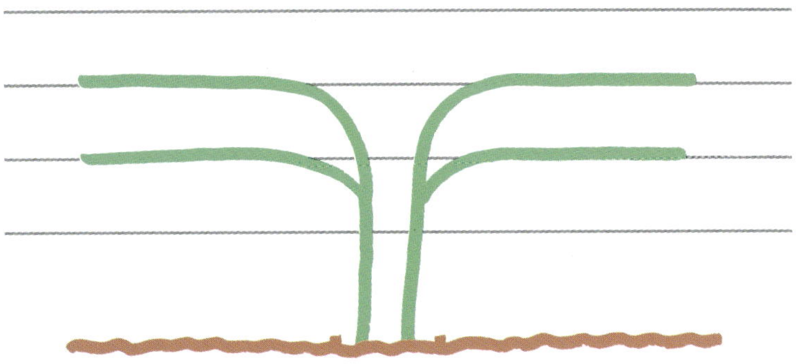

3 Bring the new canes down from the top wire and tie them in to replace the previous fruiting canes. Picking the fruit will be easier here.

SHAPING A BOX TREE

Box, *Buxus sempervirens,* is a popular and easily managed traditional topiary subject. To shape existing box bushes in the garden or fair-sized bushy plants from the garden center, the best technique is to choose a plant that already suggests a simple bun or sphere shape and simply exaggerate that by regular light clipping. To create more complicated shapes, start with a very small plant or, better still, rooted cuttings.

1 Start with a strong, rooted box cutting. Neatly nip off the growing tips of the shoots, using forefinger and thumbnail in a pincer movement. Repeat the process when the side shoots are 1in(2.5cm) long.

2 Trim the tips of the next crop of side shoots, so that each time new growth reaches 2in(5cm) long it is shortened. Roughly form the outline of the required shape.

3 Regular pruning makes the plant bushier. At this stage the result may not look precise, but there are plenty of side shoots growing out in all directions.

4 As the first pot becomes filled with roots, move the plant to a larger pot with fresh potting mix to keep it growing well. Continue regular clipping with small shears.

5 By now it should be possible to see a distinct shape. Frequent clipping ensures that side shoots are regularly 'stopped' to keep the growth bushy and dense.

6 When the plant reaches the required size, clip it back to the previous outline each time. By then, clipping three or four times a year should be enough.

7 Once large enough to clip, trim the tips of young shoots back just enough to encourage branching, which gives a dense leafy shape while allowing the shape to grow.

8 Using this method, it is possible to create a good box ball, about 9in(23cm) across, in three years. Clip two or three times a year to retain the shape and size thereafter.

PART SEVENTEEN

RAISING NEW PLANTS

Once bitten by the gardening bug, it won't be long before you want to raise new plants for yourself. With a little practice and help, you will be taking cuttings and splitting up existing plants, both from your own and friends' gardens, as though it is second nature. This is the point at which gardening becomes real fun.

SAVING YOUR OWN SEEDS

Saving seeds from your own plants is fine but it does have its limitations, because not all seeds are worth saving. Some, in fact, should not be saved. These are mainly the modern hybrid varieties; especially the F1 hybrids. These never come true from saved seed because they are the first generation of a cross between two distinct and selected parents. When saving seed, choose individual plants that are better than their neighbors or have characteristics that you like. Allow the plants to die naturally and, when ripe, collect the seedpods in a paper bag and hang them up to dry in a warm room or greenhouse. Once dry, shake the bag to release the seeds and keep them until the spring. The best way to store them is dry and cold; they will stay viable for some years like this. Saving flower seeds is great fun and, eventually, can lead to your own strain of a particular variety. Those of most vegetables, however, are hardly worth the trouble. The vast majority are hybrids and the progeny is usually inferior to the parent. On the other hand, beans, such as runner (stick), broad and dwarf French, are worthwhile because you can save seed from the best plants in a batch and, over the years, improve the strain.

Poppies - from bud to seedpod

SOLANUM

You can collect your own seed simply by splitting open a ripe berry in the spring and sowing the seeds at once. These fresh seeds have far better germination than dried ones. They are just like tomato seeds.

Aquilegia

Left: Because aquilegias usually grow in a mixture of colors, they are perfect plants for seed saving. It is best to save seed from several pods so that the mixture is complete for a brilliant display.

Right: Hang the seedpods in a paper bag in a warm room to ripen and then shake out the dry seeds. Store them in a small bottle or tub until the spring.

Below: Follow the same procedure with the opium poppy except that, if you want the seed from just one type and/or color of flower, save it only from the appropriate plant.

Foxgloves

Left: Foxgloves appear in mixed colors or shades of pink. Seed sets readily and is produced freely from pods that split when ripe.

Below: There is no need to wait until all the seedpods are ripe; shaking out the first two or three will produce ample seed.

Stocks

Right: Seed is only produced by single flowered stocks; fully double flowers are sterile. The seed from single flowers will produce both single and double-flowered plants.

Left: The seedpods of stocks (and wallflowers) need teasing open when ripe, so you can safely hang the plants upside-down to dry.

Below: Twist the seedpod when it is ripe and dry and it will split into two halves lengthways. Be sure to collect the seed from both halves.

Apples and tomatoes

Apples and tomatoes are two extremes in the seed-saving business. Do not bother with apples, unless you have endless patience; seedling fruit trees seldom have worthwhile fruit and may take ten years to produce any. Tomatoes, on the other hand, are well worth trying, even if the progeny is not exactly the same as the parent plants.

Apples

The seeds or pips from tree and bush fruits are hardly worth sowing. The plants are hybrids, so even the seeds from one fruit will give rise to a vast range of progeny. All will probably be inferior to the original.

Tomatoes

If you taste a variety of tomato and want to try growing it at home, it is well worth saving the seeds and planting them. You will probably be able to grow a similar kind to the one you liked.

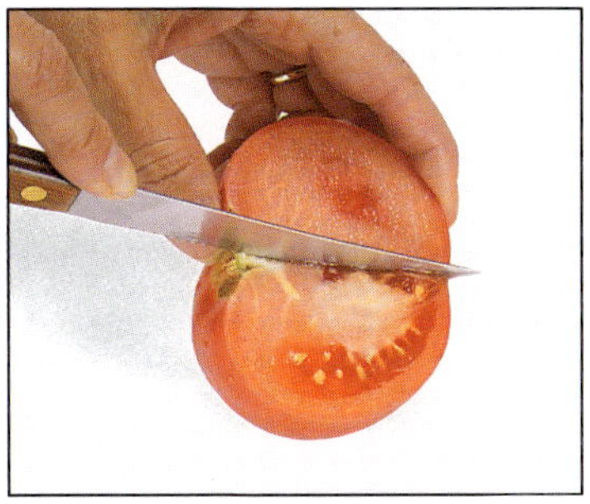

1 Cut open the tomato across the fruit to expose all the seed compartments inside.

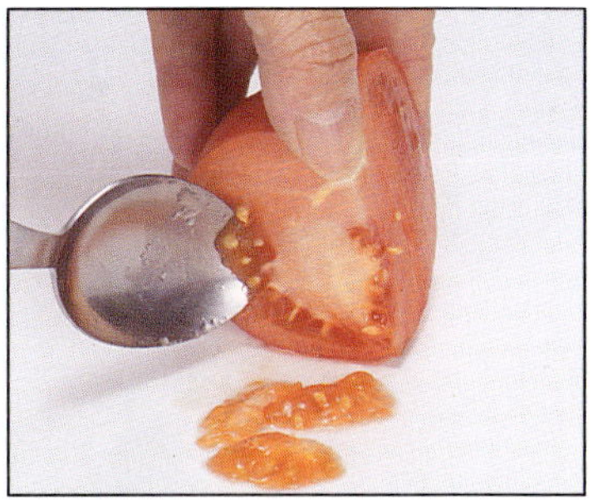

2 Use a spoon to scrape out the seeds, or as many as you want, complete with the jelly.

3 Put the seeds in a sieve under a running cold tap and carefully wash away the jelly.

4 Dry the seeds out on a piece of paper towel and plant them in a pot or seed tray.

Raising seed in trays

1 Slightly overfill the tray with loose seed-sowing mix and remove the excess by leveling the surface with a flat piece of wood.

2 Lightly firm the surface with the base of a clean flowerpot, leaving it level and about 0.25in (6mm) below the rim of the tray.

3 Tip the seeds into a piece of folded paper and tap it gently over the mixture so that the seed is sown thinly and evenly distributed.

4 Cover the seeds to their own depth with more seed mix. Sieve the seed mix to ensure an even covering of fine material.

5 Label the tray and water it by standing it in a dish of tepid water. When the surface of the seed mix turns a darker color, you know that it is wet right through.

6 Remove the tray from the water and cover it with a transparent lid or slip it into a large, clear plastic bag with short sticks inside to lift the bag into a tent. Or you can cover the tray with a sheet of glass or stiff plastic.

SOWING SEEDS

Although garden centers offer quite a good selection of flowers in bloom and ready to plant, it is much more satisfying to grow your own right from the start. Mail-order seed catalogs offer a far larger range of flower varieties to grow at home, including unusual ones that you may not be able to buy as plants. And, particularly if you want many plants of the same kind, raising your own can be far cheaper. Some kinds of flowers can be sown straight into the garden, but half-hardy annuals must be sown early on in reasonable warmth if they are to be in flower by the start of summer. Sow these in pots or seed trays under controlled conditions. If you intend raising many plants, it is best to use an electrically heated propagator inside a frost-free greenhouse. This way you not only have the means of maintaining the right temperature for germination (60-75°F /15-24°C depending on the type), but you will also have room to grow them on when the seedlings are pricked out. If you only need a few plants, then use warm windowsills. Choose shady sills for pots of seed that are germinating, as direct sun can harm them. Then when the seedlings are pricked out, move them to a brighter spot after a few days so that they do not become drawn up and spindly. If space is short and you only need a few plants of each kind, do not prick the seedlings out into trays; just plant them into small pots and these are likely to fit better onto a windowsill.

Sowing seeds in the ground

Hardy annual, biennial and perennial flower seeds, along with hardy vegetable seeds, are best sown either where they are to mature or in nursery rows in the ground. They make much better plants if not cosseted.

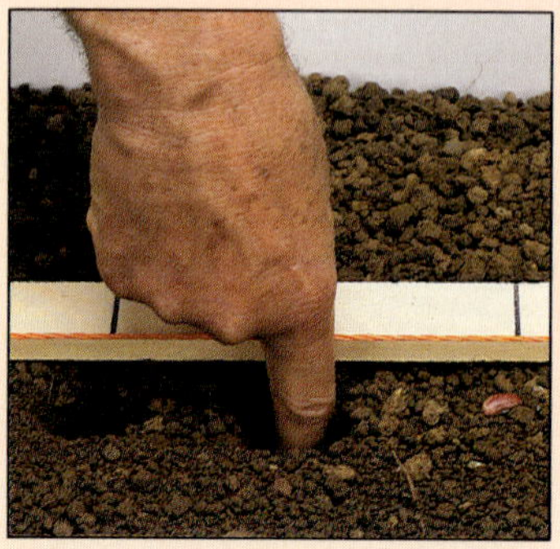

Above: Sow small seeds evenly and thinly in a shallow drill. Thin the seedlings in position or transplant when large enough.

Left: Sow large seeds, such as beans, singly or in twos where they are to stay. On heavy soil, use a stick to make the hole.

Raising seed in pots

1 Fill clean 3.5in(9cm) pots with seed-sowing mixture. Tip the seeds into a fold of paper and scatter them thinly over the surface.

2 If the seeds are very fine, sprinkle a thin layer of vermiculite over the surface of the pot before sowing them.

3 Tip the fine seed into a fold of paper and sow it thinly and evenly. Seeds fall between the granules; do not cover them.

4 Cover larger seeds to their own depth with sieved seed mix. Use a clean pot with small holes if you do not have a sieve.

5 Label the pots with the plant name and date of sowing. Stand them in a dish containing a few inches of tepid water and leave them until the surface of the soil turns dark, showing that it is wet right through.

6 Put the pots into individual clear plastic bags to create a humid atmosphere and secure them with rubber bands. Place on a warm windowsill (about 70°F/21°C) in good light but out of direct sunlight.

Sowing larger seeds in pots and cells

If you are sowing medium to large flower seeds, you can avoid the job of pricking out seedlings by sowing directly into small individual containers, such as 2in(5cm) pots or 'cells'. Since only about 50% of flower seedlings germinate, sow two medium-sized or one large seed per small container. As the volume of seed-sowing mixture is so small in these tiny cells, they dry out very quickly, so regular watering is vital.

Left: *Fill the cells smoothly and evenly with seed-sowing mix and make a shallow depression in each one. Drop in two seeds. Sow only as many of one variety as you need plants, plus a few spares.*

Right: *You can sow large seeds, such as nasturtium, singly into small pots. Fill each pot with seed-sowing mix and press one seed into the middle. Young plants are ready for planting out when the pots are full of roots.*

Removing seedlings

1 Prick out seedlings while they are tiny to give them more space to develop. Water the pot well the day beforehand.

2 Hold the seedlings by a leaf and transfer them to a clean tray of fresh seed mix. Use a dibber to make holes in the mix.

3 When the whole tray has been filled with seedlings, water them in using a fine rose on a watering can. Water them again when necessary; keep the soil moist but take care not to overwater the tiny plants.

TAKING CUTTINGS

Cuttings provide the most successful and productive way of propagating many plants vegetatively. Hardwood cuttings taken in the early winter are the least troublesome, but only certain plants, notably the currant family and some roses, are suitable. Soft cuttings taken in spring are probably the most difficult to root because they are the most fussy. If they are too wet or too dry, too hot or too cold, rooting will be delayed and they may die. In the right conditions, however, they will root very quickly. Fuchsias are a good example. Semi-ripe cuttings of many trees and shrubs will root fairly easily in the late summer. A propagator in a heated greenhouse is the surest way of rooting these and soft cuttings. Treating the base of the cuttings with a rooting compound is frequently a good idea but it does not make up for poor growing conditions. Semi-ripe and hardwood cuttings rooted outdoors are best left for a year before being moved.

Taking semi-ripe cuttings of buddleia

1 Select a stocky shoot; these will grow on the sunniest side of the shrub. Cut it off as close as possible to the older wood.

2 Pull or cut off the lowest leaves, leaving 1in(2.5cm) of clear stem at the base. This will be the part under the rooting mixture.

3 Trim off the very bottom of the cutting immediately below a leaf scar. Roots will form most readily from these 'leaf joints'.

4 Dip the base of the cutting in rooting powder and tap off any excess. Make a hole in the mix to accommodate the cutting.

5 With the cutting in place, gently firm in around the base of the shoot so that there are no large air spaces and to ensure that the cutting is held firmly in the rooting mixture.

6 When all the cuttings are in place and have been given a good watering, put the pot in a suitably sized plastic bag and tie up the top to keep the air inside moist to encourage rooting.

Taking cuttings of hydrangea and lavender

Hydrangea and lavender have virtually nothing in common and look totally different, but both are propagated from semi-ripe cuttings taken at more or less the same time of year and given the same conditions.

Below: Take lavender cuttings in late summer and prepare them as for buddleia. Use stocky 'growth' shoots without old flower stalks at the top. The rooting medium is a 50/50 mix of moss peat and coarse grit.

Above: Take hydrangea cuttings in midsummer, when the base of the shoot is mature but not woody. Cut below a leaf joint. If leaves are large, cleanly cut off the top half.

Stem and leaf bud cuttings

1 *Cotoneaster horizontalis* shoots are small, but root well. In late summer, remove pieces of the current year's growth.

2 Next, take off the bottom leaves and trim the base of the cutting to just below a leaf joint. It is now ready to pot up.

3 Although stem cuttings root perfectly well, you can raise more plants by cutting up the stem into short lengths each with one leaf and its accompanying bud. Shown here with ivy.

4 Push each 'leaf-bud' ivy cutting into the potting mix so that the bud is just visible but the base of the leaf is fractionally beneath the surface. The roots will form just below the leaf.

5 The cotoneaster and ivy cuttings can be rooted in the same propagator. Water them thoroughly with a fine rose.

6 To help the single good watering last until the cuttings have rooted, cover the propagator with a transparent lid.

Pelargonium cuttings

Although many bedding pelargoniums are now grown from seed each year, the only way to propagate a favorite old variety true to type is to take tip cuttings from the plants in early fall. It is seldom necessary to use rooting powder for pelargoniums and, indeed, too much powder can delay rooting. Insert these in a peat-and-grit or similar rooting mixture and overwinter them, preferably in a cold but frost-free greenhouse. During that time, only give them enough water to stop wilting.

1 Use a sharp knife to remove the lower leaves from a 3-4in (7.5-10cm) strong, young stem. Keep the blade away from your thumb. Otherwise cut on a board.

2 Remove any developing buds and flowers in the same way. Now the cutting will have two or three leaves at the top and a length of clean stem.

3 Make a clean cut across the base of the stem just below a node, or leaf joint. This is where new roots will emerge. Any ragged tissue left here will rot.

4 Push individual cuttings into a 2in(5cm) pot of seed-sowing mix, or put a few cuttings 1.5in(3.75cm) apart around the edge of a 4in(10cm) pot. Water in.

Potting up the cuttings

Once the cuttings have rooted and are growing away, normally after about six to eight weeks, tip them out and pot them up separately. Use 3.5in(9cm) pots and fresh general-purpose mixture for this first potting. A week later, when they have settled in and you can see that they are growing again, remove the tip of the main stem to encourage a stocky and bushy plant to develop. At the same time, remove any flowers that may have grown to allow more strength to go into the young plant.

DIVIDING PLANTS

The easiest way of increasing the number of herbaceous plants in your garden is likely to be by dividing them. This involves splitting up clump-forming plants into several separate pieces and replanting these. The only qualification is that you need to start with this particular kind of plant to make it possible. Herbaceous phlox and Michaelmas daisies are typical plants suitable for division. They are plants that spread each year by putting out short underground shoots around the perimeter that increase the size of the clumps. By splitting up the clump, retaining the younger portions on the outside and throwing away the older part in the middle, you rejuvenate the plant and, at the same time, create many more. If you want to divide a plant that is growing in a pot into many new plants, just knock it out of its container and tease it apart into as many pieces as you can make. Remember that each new piece must have at least one, and preferably more, growing shoots to make it viable. You might do this if you want to make the most of a plant you have just bought. You would also divide a clump of Michaelmas daisies if they are cramped and crowded in the border, and the flower quality is deteriorating.

DIVIDING HOSTAS

Sometimes, you may wish to divide a plant that you have just bought in order to make the most of it. Very often, you will find that a new acquisition is potbound and actually needs dividing.

1 This is the way to deal with a relatively small plant that either needs dividing or that you want to multiply. Tease the rootball apart so that it divides easily, but without damaging it.

2 Normally, you will only be able to divide a potted plant into two pieces. However, if the two bits are large enough to split up further, you can do so. These ones are probably not.

Dividing an iris

1 Propagate irises in the fall or spring, or after flowering. Cut behind the one-year-old rhizome so that each new 'plant' has one or, better still, two tufts of leaves.

2 Pull off the piece you have just severed, making sure that there are no old and 'blind' rhizomes left attached to it. These will not produce new shoots.

3 When splitting a plant after flowering, reduce the amount of transpiration from the leaves by cutting them back into a small fan. This will not harm the plant.

4 Replace the plant in the border, with the top of the rhizome above the ground, but the base of the fan in the soil. The new roots will grow from this part.

Dividing chives

1 Chives and similar bulbous plants can be easily divided in the spring soon after growth has started. First dig up the clumps.

2 Divide the plant, using a fork if necessary, and loosen the soil around the roots. Divide and transplant chives every three years.

3 Use your hands to tease the chives apart. They will divide naturally into small groups of bulbils that are easy to replant into a group or row.

DIVIDING A HERBACEOUS PERENNIAL

When dividing a large clump of a mound-forming herbaceous perennial, dig the plant up and split it into several pieces using two forks. Drive these into the middle of the plant back to back and then pull the handles apart. This will create enough leverage to split the clump into several sections, no matter how solid it is. Keep the young outside pieces for replanting. These will grow into vigorous new plants. Discard the old and woody center of the original. Prepare the soil well before replanting divisions; dig in lots of well-rotted organic matter and a dressing of fertilizer. Water in; mulch with 1-2in (2.5-5cm) of organic matter to conserve moisture and help the new plant get established.

Below: Herbaceous plants, such as this *Kniphofia,* are often divided in fall. However, most are safer divided in early spring, just before the new growing season starts.

Dividing daffodils

After two or three years, you may notice that the flowers are not as profuse as usual. This indicates that the bulbs are overcrowded and need digging up and replanting. There will be a lot of undersized bulbs, but replant these along with the larger ones. Even if they are small now, they will reach flowering size in a year or two.

1 Daffodils are best dealt with in the summer when the foliage has died down. Dig up the bulbs or turn them out of their pots and start to separate them.

2 Shake the bulbs loose. If the tops have completely died and dried, store them until the fall. If any of the bulbs are not dormant, spread them out to dry.

Dividing tulips

Only the largest tulip bulbs will flower the following year. Small ones may take one or more years to flower. If you want to keep them, plant them in nursery rows and grow them on to flowering size.

1 When they have died down completely, dig up the tulips and shake off all the soil. This will reveal bulbils of varying sizes.

2 Pull the clump apart and keep just the bulbils. Throw away the old root, dried flower stalk and the smallest bulbils.

3 The largest of this group of bulbs might just be big enough to flower, but the others are probably too small. In fact, it is not worth relying on even the biggest to flower; much safer to buy fresh ones.

LAYERING PLANTS

If division is the easiest method of propagating certain herbaceous plants vegetatively (as opposed to sowing seed), then layering must be the easiest and most successful method for shrubs and climbers. It involves bending down a shoot or small branch of the plant you want to propagate and burying a short section of it so that roots form on the buried part. A year or so later, you can sever the layered portion, complete with its roots, from the parent plant, dig it up and plant it out. It is also a very useful method for propagating plants that are difficult to root in other ways. In theory, you can layer at any time of the year but, because it is an advantage to have new roots growing on the buried portion as soon as possible, midspring to late summer is the preferred time. This quick rooting ensures that any wound made on the stem before burying it heals quickly.

Shoots of either the current or previous season's growth root the quickest. Older wood will take much longer to form roots and may never do so. It is worthwhile taking the trouble to find a suitable shoot that you can bend down to layer. Look all round the shrub until you find a good one.

PLANTS WITH RUNNERS

Although the strawberry is the obvious example, some other plants, including *Iris japonica* (right), also produce runners above or below the ground with plantlets on the end. Root these to produce new plants.

1 Push the plantlet at the end of a strawberry runner into a pot of used seed or potting mix. It will root quickly and you can move the pot later.

2 Hold the plantlet in place with a small wire loop, so that it is reasonably firm. Any cutting or plantlet must be held still while it is forming roots.

Layering clematis

1 Select a strong, disease-free shoot and tease it away from the mass of stems. The leaf joint must have strong buds showing, as these will form the new plant.

2 Remove the leaves, making a clean cut as close as possible to the main stem. Take care not to damage the buds lying in the joints where the stem and leaves meet.

3 Using a trowel, make a hole about 1in(2.5cm) deep in which to place the shoot. It is worth sprinkling a little silver sand into the planting hole to aid drainage and prevent rotting.

4 Place the layer onto the surface of the soil with the buds over the hole you have made. Bend pieces of garden wire about 3in(7.5cm) long into a U-shape and insert them in the soil on either side of the buds to prevent the layer from moving.

5 Make sure that you press the wires in firmly so that the leaf joint is directly in contact with the soil. This should prevent it from drying out during the summer months. It will be three or four months before any new shoots emerge.

Tip-layering blackberry

1 In midsummer, scrape out a 3-4in(7.5-10cm)-deep sloping hole. Mix in peat and grit to improve the rooting area.

2 Lay in the tip of one of the current year's new shoots, with the end pointing upwards. Secure it with a wire loop.

3 Holding the shoot in place, cover the layer with soil. Firm the soil down well so that it makes contact with the shoot.

4 Push in a cane by the shoot and tie the two together. This marks the layer and also holds it in position.

6 As an extra security measure, place some stones on either side of the layer to anchor it firmly. These will also act as a marker later on. At this stage, one of the greatest dangers is disturbing the layer while you are hoeing.

7 Cover the buds with soil or potting mix so that the surface is level. Firm down gently. Water lightly if the soil is on the dry side.

8 Until the shoots emerge, ensure that the soil does not dry out and protect with slug pellets during the summer months.

Layering winter jasmine

You need only look around the base of a winter jasmine plant in the fall to see that layering is Nature's way of propagating this plant. You can use the same principal, but improve on it if you require several new plants. And you need not leave the shoot attached to the plant.

1 Fill the base of a propagator with a 50/50 mix of peat and sharp sand or grit. Choose a shoot with several young shoots growing from it and cut it to fit into the seed tray.

2 Push the shoot into the mix so that the 'parent' is about 0.5in(1cm) under the mix, with the side shoots pointing upwards.

3 Water the tray well, not only to provide moisture to keep the shoot alive, but also to settle the mixture around the shoot.

4 Put the lid on the propagator and stand the whole thing either on a windowsill or in the greenhouse. Once roots measuring 1in(2.5cm) have formed, cut up the original shoot to give you several plants, each with a shoot and roots.

Hybridizing a new rose

1 Holding the bottom of the rose, remove the petals to reveal the stamens - the male, pollen-bearing parts of the flower.

2 Remove the stamens and keep them in a dry dish for later use. This flower is now the female partner in the hybridization.

3 After removing the petals and stamens, wait for 24 hours to allow time for the female stigma to become receptive to fertilization.

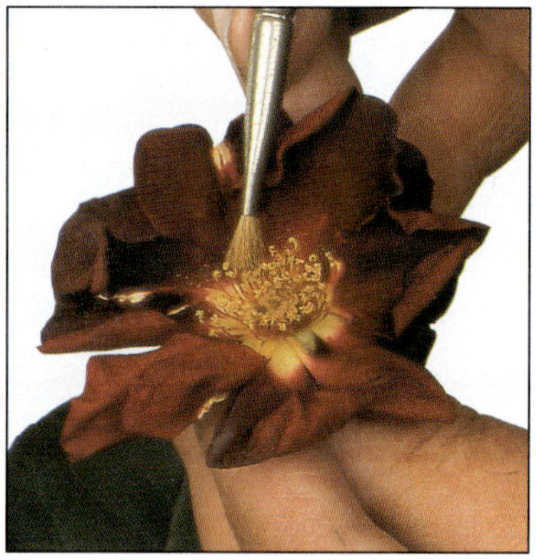

4 Use a fine brush to pick up pollen from the ripe stamens of the flower chosen to be the male partner in the cross.

5 Gently transfer the pollen onto the stigma of the female flower. One application is enough. Sterilize the brush before reusing it.

6 Allow the fertilized flower to ripen in a dry atmosphere for four to five months. Label each hip and record all the relevant details.

HYBRIDIZING PLANTS

In just the same way that it is an interesting exercise to save the seed from various plants in your garden, it is even more exciting to do some real plant breeding yourself. This can be as simple or as complicated as you like, but start off by hybridizing something simple that is almost bound to give good results. Roses are always a good subject for this because you are seldom likely to produce a complete flop.

Whatever plant you use for breeding, remember that both prospective parents should have strong characteristics that you like. Choose the parent plants with care and, if possible, begin with some idea of what you want to end up with. For example, if you want to produce a red rose, it would be sensible to start off with two red roses. The other important point is that, because every seedling resulting from the cross will be different, you should sow and raise every seed, otherwise you may have thrown out the one seedling that would have turned out to be what you were aiming at! Which flower or plant you use as which parent (male or female) is of little importance. All the genes and chromosomes that appear in the progeny are a mixture of those from both parents.

To pollinate a flower you must have access to the essential parts of the plant when the petals are well formed. Removing petals too early will damage the plant, too late, and the pollen will ripen and be released.

Sowing the seeds

Remove the hips in late fall and store them in damp peat or vermiculite for about three months to induce germination. Extract the seeds in late winter and sow them in pots or a seed tray in a good-quality seed mixture.

Some hips will contain just one seed, others a great many. Some will be empty.

Above: Cover the seedlings with a layer of coarse sand 0.5in(1.25cm)-thick. Rose seed takes a long time to germinate; the sand discourages lichen.

Breeding a new pelargonium

The pelargonium has been subjected to crossbreeding for many years, yet new varieties still appear. There is such a lot of variety in the progeny, not just in the flower colors, but also in the leaves.

Above: This pelargonium has a good red color and is to be the 'female'. The stigma is visible in the middle of this flower.

Below: The 'male' is a soft pink, with an attractive leaf. Both the male stamens and female stigma are visible here.

1 Remove all the flowers except the strongest. At the same time, remove all the stamens to avoid unintentional pollination.

2 Wipe a soft paint brush across the stamens of the male flower so that the pollen grains stick to the brush.

3 Wipe the brush across the stigma of the mother flower to leave a good helping of the yellowish pollen sticking to it.

4 Cover the pollinated flower head carefully with a paper bag to ensure that no other pollen at all lands on the stigma.

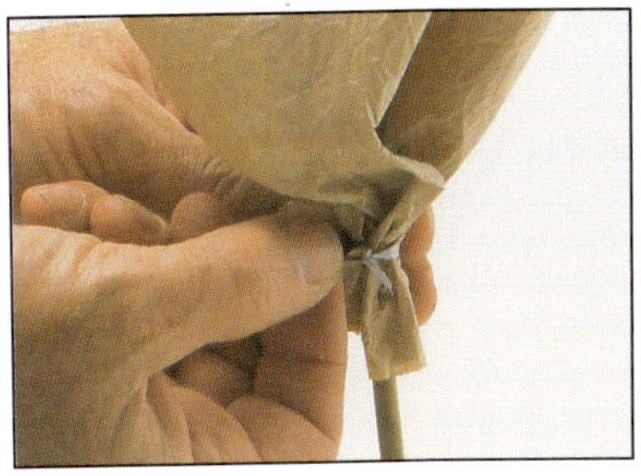

5 Tie the neck of the bag loosely to keep out any stray bees, etc. Look inside occasionally and once you see that seeds have formed, you can snip the flower stem and hang the bag up the right way up so that the seeds dry.

Creating a hybrid clematis

The clematis has also attracted plant breeders for ages. The result is hundreds of hybrids. Most of the good ones have been selected from carefully chosen parents but the odd 'cuckoo' can also turn out to be a star. The crossing procedure is exactly the same as for roses and pelargoniums, from choosing two suitable parents right through to protecting the seedhead and planting out the seeds.

1 This flower has been selected as the female. Carefully remove the stamens with tweezers, leaving the female parts that will form the seed.

2 To transfer the pollen from the male to the female flower, simply brush the two together. Do this around midday, when the pollen is most viable.

3 After pollination, remove the sepals to prevent them rotting and allowing disease to set in. Take great care not to damage the embryo seeds.

4 Cover the flower head with a paper bag and tie it at the base to prevent insects gaining entry and depositing stray pollen from another variety.

Clematis seedheads

The seedhead of a successfully pollinated hybrid clematis.

The seedhead of a successfully pollinated species clematis.

Only a few seeds have set and may not be viable.

Discard a sterile and unfertilized seedhead like this.

INDEX

Page numbers in **bold** indicate major text references and main features. Page numbers in *italics* indicate annotations and captions to photographs. Other text entries are shown in normal type.

Q

R

U

V

W

X

Y

Z

Picture credits

The majority of the photographs featured in this book have been taken by Neil Sutherland and are © Quadrillion Publishing Ltd. The publishers wish to thank the following photographers for providing additional photographs, credited here by page number and position on the page, i.e. (B)Bottom, (T)Top, (C)Center, (BL)Bottom left, etc.

Gillian Beckett: 163(CL)
Peter Blackburne-Maze: 205(BL), 207(CL, BL, TC), 208(TC, TR)
Pat Brindley: 206(TR)
Eric Crichton: 25(BL), 27, 28(BR), 29(TR,BR), 30(BL, BR), 31(BR), 33(TL, CL), 34(C, BL), 35(TR, BR), 37(TL, TR, BR), 38(BL), 39(TL, CL), 40(TR), 41(BR), 42(BL), 43(C), 45(TL, CR, BR), 47(TR), 49, 55(BL), 74(TR, CR), 77(TR), 78(BR), 79(TCL), 80(TR), 82(TC, TR), 83(CL, BL), 84(TC, TR, BC, BR), 85(CL, C, CB), 87(TL, CR), 89(C), 90(TR), 91(BL), 92(CR), 93(C, CR, BR), 97, 98(BL), 101(BL), 104(TR), 105(CL), 106(TC), 107(C), 108(TR, BL), 109(TC, BC), 110(TR), 111(TC, TR,), 112(CR), 113(TL, TR, BL), 115, 116(BL, CR), 117(CL, C), 119(C, CB), 120(BC, BR), 121(BL), 122(CR), 123(BL, BC), 126(BL), 128(BR), 129(TR), 130(TR), 131(TL, BL), 133, 134(TR), 135(CL, TR, BL, CR, BR), 138(CR), 139(CL, CR,CB), 140(TR, BL), 141(TL, TR), 143(TR, CR, BR, BL), 145(TL, C, TR), 146(L), 147(CL), 151, 154(T, BL), 155(CL, BL), 157(TR, BL), 158(BC), 159(TL), 160(TL), 162(C, BL), 163(TR), 166(TR, C, BL, BR), 167(CL), 175(TR), 176(CR), 179(CL), 186(TC), 189(TR, CR, BR), 193(BR), 197(BL), 198(CR), 199(CR, BR), 200(CR), 207(TR, C, BC), 210(TR), 215(TL), 221(T, C) 225(TCR, TR, CR, BR), 239(TR, BR), 247, 281(TR), 282(BR), 304(TR, BR), 310(T), 311(TL), 314(CR), 316(BR), 317(CL), 320(BL), 322(BR), 329(TL), 335(BL).
(Eric Crichton would like to acknowledge the following garden owners and designers: Peter Aldington, Mrs. Brockwell, Una Carr, Daphne Foulsham, Mrs. G. Francis, Rupert Golby, Mrs D. Hughes, Mrs. Kenison, Angela Kirby, Ester Merton, Mr. & Mrs. M. Metianu, Mrs. M.E. Pedder, Penny Pollitt, Penny Sinclair, Mrs. B. Sterndale-Bennett, Julie Toll, J.R. Tucker, Faith & Geoff Whiten. Also the gardeners who open under the National Gardens Scheme.)
John Feltwell/Garden Matters: 163(BL)
John Glover: 13, 22(CR), 30(BC), 31(TL), 32(TR), 33(TR, BR), 35(C), 36(BL), 39(TR, BR), 40(CR), 41(TR), 44(BR), 47(BR), 79(TR, CR, BR), 80(BR), 81(TC), 82(C), 84(BL), 88(TL, C), 89(CL, BL), 90(TC), 91(CR), 93(TL, TC), 95(TL), 112(TC), 118(TC, CR), 125(CR), 126(TL), 127(TL), 128(TR, BL), 129(BL), 130(CR), 141(CL, C), 143(TL, TC), 145(CL), 147(CR, BL), 148(BC), 152(BL), 153(CL, BR), 156(TC, TR), 159(CL), 165(CL, BL), 166(TC), 167(BL), 171(TC), 174(BL), 177(CL, TC), 178(BR), 181(TR), 199(TR), 211(CR), 213(BR), 216(TC), 222(BL), 228(TL), 239(CR), 271, 299(C), 310(C, BL, BC), 311(CL, BL), 317(BR), 329(CL)
S & O Mathews: Title page, 28(BL), 29(TL), 34(BR), 43(BR), 76(BL), 79(TL, TCR), 81(BL, CL), 83(BR), 84(CR), 87(TR), 91(CL), 92(TR), 94(CL), 95(CL), 110(TC), 111(TL), 116(TR), 117(TC, BL), 118(BL), 120(TL), 122(BC), 123(TL), 124(BL), 125(TC, TL), 126(BR), 135(C), 138(TR, BL), 142(T), 143(CL), 144(L), 145(BL), 147(TC, TL), 152(BR), 153(TL), 155(TL), 157(BC), 161(CL, BL), 166(BC), 170(CR), 171(TR), 173(CR), 174(T), 175(BR), 178(BL), 179(TL), 196(BC), 197(CL), 207(CR, BR), 223, 227(TR, BR), 299(BR), 303(C), 305, 310(CL), 314(BL) 317(CL), 319(BL), 320(BL), 321(BL)
Clive Nichols: 44(BL, Old School House, Essex), 73, 78(BL) 78(TC, Sir Harold Hillier Garden & Arboretum, Hants.), 79(CL, Wollerton Old Hall, Shrops.), 90(BL), 94(BR, Chiffchaffs Garden, Dorset), 95(BL, Valley Gardens, Berks.), 103(TL, Chiffchaffs Garden, Dorset), 106(C) 106(BR, Copton Ash, Kent), 119(TL), 122(BL), 129(TL, Lower House Farm, Gwent, Wales), 135(TL, Waterperry Gardens, Oxford), 138(TC, The RHS Garden, Wisley, Surrey) 138(BR, Crathes Castle Garden, Scotland), 139(TR, Waterperry Gardens, Oxfordshire) 139(BR, The RHS Garden, Wisley, Surrey), 139(TL, BL), 140(TC), 141(BL), 146(T, Greenhurst Garden, Sussex), 147(TR, Greenhurst Garden, Sussex), 148(T, The Old Rectory, Berks.) 148(BL), 149(TL, Hadspen Gardens, Somerset), 149(TR, Chenies Manor House, Bucks.) 149(CR, Lower Severalls Garden, Somerset), 149(CL, C, BL, BR), 153(TC, Sleightholme Dale Lodge, North Yorks.) 154(BC), 156(BL Photographer Graham Strong), 159(BL, The Lygon Arms, Glos.), 161(TL), 162(T, The Priory, Kemerton, Hereford & Worcs.), 164(T, Beech Park, Rep. of Ireland), 165(TL, Designer Nigel Colborn), 167(BR), 169, 170(BR, Ripley Castle, Yorks.), 177(TL), 179(BL, BR), 209(Cerney House Garden Glos.), 227(CR, Copton Ash, Kent), 231(TR, Beth Chatto's Garden), 298(BL, RHS Garden, Wisley Surrey), 304(BL, 28 Hillgrove Crescent, Kidderminster, Designers Mr. & Mrs. D. Terry), 328(C)
Geoffrey Rogers: 23(C, CR), 134(C), 329(TR, C, CR, BCR, BR)
Stapeley Water Gardens: 282(C), 283(CL, BL)
Thompson & Morgan UK Ltd.: 162(BR)
Unwins Seeds Ltd.: 163(TL)

Acknowledgments

The publishers would like to thank the following people and organizations for their help during the preparation of this book:

The National Institute of Agricultural Botany, Cambridge; Neil Allen; Clive Bowes; Blooms of Bressingham, Diss, Norfolk; J. Bradshaw and Son, Busheyfield Nursery, Kent; Bridgemere Garden World, Nantwich, Cheshire; Brinsbury College - The West Sussex College of Agriculture and Horticulture; Burnham Nurseries, Newton Abbott, Devon; Burton McCall Ltd. for Felco saws and secateurs; Cadmore Lodge Hotel, Tenbury Wells, Worcestershire; Shelley and Jonathan Choat; John Nash and Sally Cave at Costrong Farm, West Sussex; Cherry Burton and Sue Davey at Country Gardens at Chichester, West Sussex; Country Gardens at Alfold, Cranleigh, Surrey; Court Lane Nursery, Hadlow College, Kent; Darlac Products for Ratchet 2000 heavy duty secateurs; Peter Dench; The Flower Auction Holland, Naaldwijk; Forest Fencing Ltd., Stanford Bridge, Worcestershire; Garboldisham Garden Center; Glass Art Pools; Kath and Alan Goode; Grosvenor Garden Center, Belgrave, Cheshire; Harkness New Roses, Hitchin, Hertfordshire; Hillhout Bergenco bv, Zwolle, Holland; Hilliers Nurseries (Winchester) Ltd., Romsey, Hampshire; The Hillier Plant Center, Braishfield, Hampshire; The Sir Harold Hillier Gardens and Arboretum, Braishfield, Hampshire; The Royal Horticultural Society Garden at Wisley, Surrey; Hozelock Ltd., Haddenham, Buckinghamshire; Iden Croft Herbs, Staplehurst, Kent; Little Brook Fuchsias, Ash Green, Hampshire; Long Man Gardens, East Sussex; Midland Butyl Liners; Millbrook Garden Center, Northfleet, Kent; Gill Page and colleagues at Murrells Nursery, Pulborough, West Sussex; Natures Friends (natural pest control), Zeneca/Miracle; Ness Gardens, Liverpool; John O'Dell at Oast House Nursery, Ash, Kent; Reads Nursery, Norfolk; Mike Hannigan at Robinsons Greenhouses Ltd., Southampton, Hampshire; The Royal National Rose Society, St. Albans, Hertfordshire; Russell's Garden Center, Chichester, West Sussex; Lyn Hutton at Secrets Farm Shop, Surrey; Sharpe and Fisher Building Supplies, Pulborough, West Sussex; Philip Sonneville nv, Lochristi, Belgium; Stapeley Water Gardens, Nantwich, Cheshire; Fred Godfrey of Sussex Plants Ltd., East Sussex; Thakeham Tiles Ltd.; Timber World, Horsham; Town and Country Turf, Kingsfold, Horsham; Travis Perkins Trading Company Ltd., Crawley; Treasures of Tenbury Ltd., Burford, Worcestershire; Trehane Nursery, Wimborne, Dorset; Mike Warner-Horne; T. H. Waters, Gravesend, Kent.